Studies in Cultural Hi

1

EXPLORATIONS IN CULTURAL HISTORY:
ESSAYS FOR PETER GABRIEL McCAFFERY

STUDIES IN CULTURAL HISTORY

ISSN 2045-7650

1. *Explorations in Cultural History:*
    Essays for Peter Gabriel McCaffery
    edited by David F. Smith & Hushang Philsooph
    (2010. xiv+323 pp. ISBN 978-0-9567059-0-7)

Explorations in Cultural History:

Essays for Peter Gabriel McCaffery

edited by

DAVID F. SMITH

&

HUSHANG PHILSOOPH

THE CENTRE FOR CULTURAL HISTORY
UNIVERSITY OF ABERDEEN

Studies in Cultural History
ISSN 2045-7650

Explorations in Cultural History:
Essays for Peter Gabriel McCaffery

First published 2010
by The Centre for Cultural History,
University of Aberdeen

ISBN: 978-0-9567059-0-7
Printed in the E.U. on acid-free paper

Typeset by Nancy R. McGuire
Printed by The University of Aberdeen

Contents

Section Three: History and Sociology of Medicine, and Global Citizenship

Introduction

Peter McCaffery's arduous, but quiet, and long-continued service in the cause of cultural history in Aberdeen certainly deserves recognition and celebration, and so when David Dumville suggested a *Festschrift* for Peter in Spring 2010, I was all for the project. We agreed a deadline and I approached a number of past and present colleagues and students. All were excited about the idea of honouring Peter, and, had the deadline been less tight, we could have easily ended up with a multi-volume work. No doubt some readers will feel that I should have approached them too, and, if so, I apologise. Anyway, as it is, we have a book of impressive thickness. One of the prospective contributors whom I approached, Hushang Philsooph, volunteered to be co-editor, and I have been very grateful for his help.

With this volume we have launched the Centre for Cultural History's publication series, *Studies in Cultural History*, which in future will be used, for example, for publishing the proceedings of the Centre's workshops. The Centre has been organising such events, as well as a seminar series, since it was established following the conference in 2007 that celebrated twenty-one years of the Cultural History MA programme. At the suggestion of Peter McCaffery we commandeered the title of one of Peter Burke's books, 'Varieties of Cultural History', for the conference theme. We greatly regret the subsequent abolition of the Cultural History MA programme, from which the final students will graduate in 2011, but are very pleased that the 'Varieties' conference spawned the International Society for Cultural History, in which some Aberdonian colleagues are heavily involved. Nevertheless, we do now have a taught MLitt in Cultural History in Aberdeen, which is beginning to attract students.

At this critical time for cultural history at Aberdeen, this publication project has naturally encouraged reflection on the past of the MA programme. Norman Stockman's sociological account of the history of the Sociology Department, to which Peter McCaffery was originally appointed, also provides thoughts upon how universities as a whole, and Aberdeen in particular, have changed. Nigel Dower's essay on Peter's career includes much about Peter's experience of the Cultural History programme, while Nick Fisher's and Marius Kwint's personal accounts add to the existing literature on the degree: Joan Pittock Wesson, 'Interdisciplinary Studies at the University of Aberdeen', *Northern Scotland*, 21 (2001), 121–8, and William Scott, 'Cultural history at the crossroads', *Tidskrift för Kultur Studier*, 1 (1995), 56–96. Finally, Joan Pittock Wesson's poem, written in memory of a young colleague who committed suicide, highlights the harsh conditions in which the programme was born. By all accounts we are now entering a period of similar challenges during which, it is to be hoped, there will not be a repeat of such tragedies. Let us wish that, instead, in these conditions further creative inter-disciplinary engagements will be possible, of the kind that gave birth to the MA in Cultural History.

We have gathered the essays on Peter and the University of Aberdeen in the first section of the book, and have again re-cycled 'Varieties of Cultural History' as the title of the second section. Here we are fortunate to be able to print an essay by Peter Burke on the 'Polymath', a very apt theme for a book in honour of Peter McCaffery. The other papers, some by pioneer members of the Cultural History group, some by colleagues who became members of staff more recently, and some by former and current students, illustrate the rich and varied nature of cultural history in Aberdeen, and the continuing legacy of the teaching programme. The final section includes papers related to Peter's interests in the history and sociology of medicine, and international relations.

In conclusion, I would like to thank all those involved in the production of this book for their efforts. Thanks are due especially to Peter McCaffery for inspiring the project, to David Dumville for suggesting it, and to all the authors for their enthusiasm and support.

David Smith
16 November 2010

Notes on contributors

Alastair Bain acquired an MA from the University of Edinburgh in 1963 and then spent 30 years in NHS management in the Grampian region. In 1996, following early retirement, he began a degree in cultural history at the University of Aberdeen and graduated first class in 1999. He subsequently conducted postgraduate research under the supervision of Elizabeth Hallam, gaining a PhD in 2009 with a thesis entitled *A Cultural History of Silence in England, 1500–1800*. He is currently an independent researcher and lives in rural Aberdeenshire. He considers that his interest in the history of religion in Europe after 1500 originated in his undergraduate years in Peter McCaffery's lectures and tutorials. Although that subject remains his principal research interest, he is also pursuing some aspects of the social and cultural history of the county of East Lothian. E-mail: al@sunnybraecottage.com

Peter Burke is Emeritus Professor of Cultural History, University of Cambridge, and Life Fellow of Emmanuel College. He taught in the School of European Studies, University of Sussex, becoming Reader in Intellectual History before moving to Cambridge in 1979. He was one of the early external examiners of Aberdeen's Cultural History MA programme and attended several of the conferences of Aberdeen's Cultural History group. He was a keynote speaker at the 2007 'Varieties of Cultural History' conference in Aberdeen, which commandeered the title of one of his books, published in 1997. He has published over 20 books including *The Italian Renaissance* (1972), *Popular Culture in Early Modern Europe* (1978), *The Fabrication of Louis XIV* (1992), *The Art of Conversation* (1993), *A Social History of Knowledge* (2000), *Eyewitnessing* (2000), *What is Cultural History?* (2004) and *Languages and Communities in Early Modern Europe* (2004). He is married to a Brazilian historian, Maria Lúcia García Pallares-Burke, with whom he wrote *Social Theory in the Tropics: Gilberto Freyre* (2008). E-mail: upb1000@.cam.ac.uk

Nigel Dower is Honorary Senior Lecturer in Philosophy at the University of Aberdeen, where he taught for most of the period 1967–2004. He has also been a visiting professor a number of times in America and Iceland. He now acts as an academic consultant on 'Cosmopolitan agendas – ethics in a globalized world'. He was President of the International Development Ethics Association from 2002 to 2006. His research interests in the last twenty years have focussed on various issues in global ethics, including development, the environment, human rights, war & peace, and global citizenship. His publications include *World Ethics – the New Agenda* (1998; 2nd edition, 2007), *Introduction to Global Citizenship* (2003) and *The Ethics of War and Peace* (2009). He was associated with the Cultural History Programme in the University of Aberdeen from 1987 until 2002, contributing to the 'Approaches to Culture, II' Honours course and to the second year course on environmental issues. E-mail: n.dower@abdn.ac.uk

Paul Dukes is Emeritus Professor of History at the University of Aberdeen. He was a founder member of the Cultural History Group and learned much from colleagues and from students. He edited two books arising from the early cultural history conferences: *Culture and Revolution* (with John Dunkley, 1990), and *Frontiers of European Culture* (1996). He was elected FRSE in 1999, and was presented with a *Festschrift* entitled *Russia and the Wider World in Historical Perspective*, edited by Cathryn Brennan and Murray Frame, in 2000. His forthcoming publication, *Minutes to Midnight: History and the Anthropocene Era from 1763* (Anthem Press), reflects the Group's interdisciplinary approach. E-mail: p.dukes@abdn.ac.uk

David Dumville is Sixth-century Professor in History, Palaeography & Celtic at the University of Aberdeen, where he is also Director of the Centre for Anglo-Saxon Studies and the Centre for Celtic Studies, as well as Associate Director of the AHRC Research Centre for Irish and Scottish Studies. He is a Life Fellow of Girton College, Cambridge, where until 2004 he was University Professor of Palaeography & Cultural History. 2009 was very much his Irish year: in March he was elected Honorary Member of the Royal Irish Academy, and in August he became Honorary Professor in the Institute of Irish Studies, University of Liverpool.

Nick Fisher started studying chemistry, but found more fulfilment in the history of chemistry, and the history of science more generally. After a PhD from the University of Wisconsin in 1970, he taught history of science at the University of Glasgow before coming to Aberdeen in 1976. From 1976 to 1981 he edited *The British Journal for the History of Science* which he steered in a cultural historical direction. A founder member of the Cultural History Group in 1986, he very much enjoyed studying the breadth of new topics required by the undergraduate teaching, which have in turn stimulated his research interests in Victorian culture. He was Director of the Cultural History programme from 1995 to 1998. E-mail: n.fisher@abdn.ac.uk

Anders Ingram graduated from Durham University in 2010 with an Arts and Humanities Research Council (AHRC) funded thesis entitled 'English Literature on the Ottoman Turks in the Sixteenth and Seventeenth Centuries'. In 2004 he completed an MLitt in English Literature at the University of Aberdeen, having won an Andrew Mellon studentship attached to the Sawyer Seminar Series. More recently he has been working on a number of articles developed from his PhD thesis and taught at the University of Durham. His research interests include early modern English writing on the Ottoman Turks and Islam, travel writing, historical and geographical literature, and the history of the book. He is also interested in the impact of computerisation on humanities research and teaching practice. He first encountered Peter McCaffery's thoughtful and encouraging teaching as a student on the Cultural History MA at Aberdeen University, where he won the degree prize in 2002. E-mail: anders.ingram@durham.ac.uk

Marius Kwint is Senior Lecturer in Visual Culture at the University of Portsmouth and a member of the International Society for Cultural History. Between 1999 and 2008 he served as Departmental Lecturer in History of Art and a Fellow by Special Election of St. Catherine's College at the University of Oxford. Previously, he was a Senior Research Fellow in History of Design at the Victoria and Albert Museum and the Royal College of Art, and Douglas W. Bryant Fellow in Eighteenth-century Studies at the Houghton Library, Harvard University. He has written and curated exhibitions on various subjects including the history of the circus; the souvenir; the tree-like or dendritic form; inter-cultural and scientific themes in contemporary art; and the art of Beth Fisher. He is currently working on an exhibition about the brain as object and icon for the Wellcome Trust in London. E-mail: marius.kwint@port.ac.uk

Hushang Philsooph was a Lecturer in Cultural History and the Department of Sociology, and is now an Honorary Research Fellow of the School of Divinity, History and Philosophy, at the University of Aberdeen. He holds a PhD in social anthropology from the University of Edinburgh, and his first degrees were in philosophy and psychology. His interests include belief and thought, the structure of the mind, the history of anthropology (Tylor and Frazer), modern Persian literature, and vegetarianism. One of his latest publications is 'Hedayat, vegetarianism, and modernity: altruism, Leonardo da Vinci, and cultural desublimation', in *Sadeq Hedayat: His Work and His Wondrous World*, ed. Homa Katouzian (Routledge, 2008), pp. 144–77. E-mail: h.philsooph@abdn.ac.uk

Joan Pittock Wesson was Senior Lecturer in the English Department, University of Aberdeen, 1964–95. She was founder editor of the *British Journal for Eighteenth Century Studies* 1978–80 and President of BSECS 1980–82. She coordinated the programme for the interdisciplinary degree in Cultural History in Aberdeen with a team of colleagues from several departments. In 1986 she was a Research Fellow in the Institute for Advanced Studies in the Humanities in Edinburgh and Visiting Research Fellow at Magdalen College, Oxford. In 1990 she established the Institute for Advanced Studies in the Humanities in Aberdeen and was appointed Director. She published *The Ascendancy of Taste* (1973) and *Henry Birkhead and Foundation of the Oxford Chair of Poetry* (1999). With J. J. Carter she edited *Aberdeen and the Enlightenment* (1988) and with Andrew Wear *Interpretation and Cultural History* (1991). She has contributed articles to learned journals in the US, France and Britain and chapters to books on criticism, literary history, literature of childhood, and the history of university teaching of English. She has published some poetry and hopes to complete a history of the Oxford Chair.
E-mail: jhpittockwesson@btinternet.com

James Darrin Russell acquired an MA in Anthropology and Cultural History (2004) and an MRes in Social Anthropology, Ethnology and Cultural History (2005) from the University of Aberdeen. He then went on in 2005, again at the University of Aberdeen, to start his PhD in Social Anthropology under the supervision of David Anderson, Peter McCaffery and Robert Wishart. He has just submitted his thesis, entitled 'Savagery and civility: becoming related in seventeenth-century New France', for examination. His main research interest is how cultural encounters are facilitated through mutual miscomprehension. He is a member of the ISCH, and gave an early draft of his chapter at the ISCH *Cultures of Violence and Conflict* conference (2009) in Brisbane. He fondly remembers the inspiration as well as the enthusiasm and love for learning that Peter McCaffery imparted to all his students. E-mail: james.darrin.russell@gmail.com

William Scott was born in Stirling and attended the Universities of Caen and Oxford, where his DPhil entailed extended periods of archival research at Marseille and Paris. Appointed to the History Department at Aberdeen University in 1965, he taught French and European history, and is now an Honorary Research Fellow of the School of Divinity, History and Philosophy. He was a founder member of the Cultural History Group and helped to create and teach in most of that degree's general courses. He also taught on European and Film Studies courses. His main research activity still centres on the French Revolution,

particularly at Marseille, but has also embraced the Enlightenment. Besides writing on historiography, with a venture into the Philosophy of History, he has become increasingly interested in exploring Marseille's relations with the Ottoman Empire and its peoples. Since leaving Aberdeen in 2000 he has lived in London but is now moving to Portobello. His contribution to this volume was partly inspired by hill-walking in the Cairngorms and North-West Highlands.
E-mail: william62scott@btinternet.com

David F. Smith is Senior Lecturer in the History of Medicine in the Schools of Divinity, History & Philosophy and Medicine & Dentistry at the University of Aberdeen. When he first came to Aberdeen as a Wellcome Trust University Award Holder in 1994, he was based in Cultural History in Humanity Manse. He jumped ship to the History Department but remained involved with Cultural History, especially after Cultural History and History 'merged' in 2002. With other colleagues he organised the 'Varieties of Cultural History' conference to celebrate twenty-one years of the Cultural History programme in 2007, after which he became convenor of the provisional committee of the International Society for Cultural History, of which he is now Treasurer. His research interests are in the history of nutrition science in the twentieth century, and he has also worked on the history of the Aberdeen typhoid outbreak of 1964.
E-mail: d.f.smith@abdn.ac.uk

Norman Stockman is one of the few British sociologists with a specialised interest in China. He has worked with Chinese sociologists on several collaborative research projects. These include a comparative study of women's work and family life in China, Japan, Britain and the USA, and a project on rural-urban migration in Shanghai. He has also written on social inequality in China, and is the author of *Understanding Chinese Society*, a general survey of the sociology of Chinese society. Now retired, his teaching included a fourth-year option course on Chinese Society. He continues to contribute to the postgraduate course leading to the Master of Chinese Studies at the Universities of Edinburgh and Glasgow. He is Honorary President of the University of Aberdeen Chinese Studies Group, and was elected as Honorary Secretary of the British Association for Chinese Studies (BACS) in September 2005. He also has a long-standing interest in the theoretical and philosophical issues in sociology, on which his major publication is *Antipositivist Theories of the Sciences*. E-mail: n.stockman@abdn.ac.uk

Alex Sutherland is a Teaching Fellow at the University of Aberdeen from where he graduated in 2000 with an MA in Philosophy and Psychology. He subsequently joined the University's Cultural History Department to carry out postgraduate research under the supervision of Elizabeth Hallam and Phil Withington. He gained his PhD in 2005, which was published as *The Brahan Seer: the Making of a Legend* (Peter Lang) in 2009. He presented a paper on a topic linked to his thesis topic at the 2009 ISCH conference in Brisbane. At the dissolution of Cultural History as a separate department in 2002 he transferred to the History Department where he shared an office with Peter for several years. His interests are witchcraft, second sight and prophecy, and the cultural history of medicine. E-mail: a.m.sutherland@abdn.ac.uk

Edwin R. van Teijlingen is Professor of Reproductive Health Research at Bournemouth University. He is also Visiting Professor at Manmohan Memorial Institute of Health Sciences (Nepal) and Honorary Professor at the University of Aberdeen. Before he moved to Bournemouth in 2009 he was Reader in Public Health at Aberdeen. He is a three times University of Aberdeen graduate – MA (Hons) in 1986, PhD in 1994, and MEd in 1999. For his PhD he conducted a cross-national comparative study between Grampian (Scotland) and the Netherlands under the supervision of Peter McCaffery. He has written extensively on research related to midwifery and maternity care. He was co-editor with Peter McCaffery of *Midwifery and the Medicalization of Childbirth: Comparative Perspectives* published by Nova Science in New York, first in hardback in 2000 and later in paperback (2004). E-mail: vanteijlingen@bournemouth.ac.uk

Peter McCaffery: an appreciation

NIGEL DOWER

University of Aberdeen

I was asked to prepare this chapter by the editors, and it based largely (particularly in the first two sections) upon an interview that I conducted with Peter for the University of Aberdeen Oral History Project in the summer of 2010. I will consider, in turn, Peter's career, cultural history, and Peter as an academic. The transcript and video of the interview are held by the University's Special Libraries and Archives and readers may consult them for Peter's much fuller account of, and reflections on, the Cultural History MA programme.

AN OVERVIEW OF PETER'S ACADEMIC CAREER

Peter was born on November 11th 1935 into a Catholic family in London. He went to school at a Jesuit School in Wimbledon. He remembers particularly the teaching in classics, mainly because of the quality of his teachers. He then went on to Oxford where he studied Greats from 1954 to 1958 (a four year degree in which one studies classics followed by ancient history and ancient and modern philosophy). He recalls vividly some of his teachers at the time, such as Gilbert Ryle and his tutor Bernard Williams. But he remembers being most excited by taking part in a philosophy discussion group led by two postgraduates for both undergraduates and postgraduates. He then in 1958 became a Jesuit and took up a noviceship with a view to entering the catholic priesthood. After a period of two years he attended Heythrop College, then located in Oxfordshire, where he continued studying philosophy, taking courses in medieval philosophy, marxism, linguistic philosophy and a little existentialism, much of which went beyond the Greats syllabus – thus extending a grounding in philosophy which has always informed his theoretical and academic engagements in other areas later. He was then sent to Zimbabwe for three years to teach in schools both at St George's in Salisbury (later Harare) for whites and later at his request in Chishawasha for blacks – and his experiences there proved to be another important influence in his later interest in the third world and development. Whilst he was there he tried to learn Shona the local language (he claims with little success though as a language it fascinated him!). He also had a colleague there from South Africa who was interested in anthropology. Peter's own interest in this field was awakened though it remained in the background over the next three years when he was

Explorations in Cultural History: Essays for Peter Gabriel McCaffery,
edd. David F. Smith & H. Philsooph (Aberdeen 2010)   ISBN 978-0-9567059-0-7

concentrating on theological studies. This period included a year spent in Frankfurt in 1967–8 which to anyone who knows his or her recent European history means that he was there at the time of the Prague Spring and student riots (in Frankfurt as well as – rather better known – Paris). He found the teaching of theology there very helpful because it put more emphasis on the history of Christianity. Amongst his fellow students in Frankfurt was an American who really encouraged Peter to take up sociology and this led to Peter's doing a two-year taught BPhil in Sociology in Oxford (1969-71), with, as his supervisor, Bryan Wilson whom he found really inspiring. Peter's dissertation for that degree was on Dutch Catholic pressure groups, illustrating another of Peter's abiding interests – in the sociology of religion.

By then Peter's interest in becoming an academic was clearly established. Meantime, it should be explained, he had decided that he would not proceed to ordination as a catholic priest. The catalyst to this decision was the publication of the papal encyclical *Humanae Vitae* (July 1968), in which the Pope continued to maintain a steadfast opposition to contraception – a position Peter felt he could not uphold. By the time he came to Aberdeen in 1971 (as described below), his spiritual journey had led him to seek a rather different kind of religious community and he started to attend the Quaker meeting in Aberdeen (where I first met him), and some years later became and still remains a member of the Religious Society of Friends. But he remains deeply conscious of the debt he owes to his catholic upbringing and training for his intellectual and spiritual approach (and he sees his interest in cultural history as partly stemming from this, given the immense impact that the catholic church has had on European culture).

In 1971 he was applying for numerous academic posts, and somewhat to his surprise, partly given the problems of the postal strike at the time, he found himself called by telephone to interview in Aberdeen for a post in the fairly newly established and rapidly expanding Department of Sociology, then headed by Raymond Illsey. (It had originated out of the interest in medical sociology at Foresterhill some seven years earlier.) Peter recalls that the interview took place in Marischal College (the university administration was still located there) and that it was chaired by the redoubtable Dr Mary Esslemont (already in her 80s and a remarkable 'well kent' figure in Aberdeen). Well, he got one of the posts on offer, and the rest as they say is history, except that it wasn't, but rather sociology and cultural history (which for those in the know is not to be regarded as sub-branch of history!). He remained in the Department of Sociology for the next 19 years when he took an early retirement package when he was only 55 in 1990. He had decided in 1987 – as indeed many did both then and earlier in the 80s in response to the two university crises of 81-2 and 86-7 caused by massive funding cuts – to seek early retirement. This was not however because he wanted to give up academic work – as we will see, it continued and continues to this day twenty years on. The cuts in Sociology were deep and included the departure of all three social anthropologists (though the teaching of social anthropology was maintained for some years through the appointment of Hushang Philsooph).

He had married fairly late in life in 1983 to Teresa, and they had two boys – John and Martin – in the next few years. Teresa was a doctor and Peter says that when getting to know her 'he took good care not to mention my interest in the sociology of health and illness so as not to appear to be muscling in on her work' – though as it turned out she was also very interested in the issue of authority in medicine (see below for more on this). They had a terraced house in Erskine Street and are still there today: it has a fairly large garden with an attractive balance of flowers and vegetables – largely thanks to Teresa's efforts rather than Peter's, one should add. Interestingly Teresa was and is an active Catholic – and the combination of her liberal catholicism and Peter's Quakerism with a catholic background has proved a fruitful one. Peter says that with retirement he had hoped to spend more time of writing, but as things turned out he remained a very active teacher.

To return to the academic story, Peter reckoned that with the package and his wife's employment they could manage financially if he took early retirement, and this gave him independence to do what he most wanted. This in the next few years included of course helping with the development of cultural history. It was not however until 1990 that his decision in 1987 to retire took effect.

During his time in the sociology department Peter was involved in many aspects of the department's work. Rather soon after he arrived he found himself asked, because a member of staff left suddenly, to teach a course on the Sociology of Work and Industry – a rather different field from what he had mainly studied – but in fact this proved to be for him a fascinating area of sociology and he remained interested in it. He said he was 'very glad indeed' to have been pushed into getting into this material deeply: he found fascinating Marxist perspectives on this though he became rather critical of these.

During the 1970s he got to know members of the MRC Medical Sociology unit based at Foresterhill and attended seminars there. He recalls one particular paper by David Brewer (Edinburgh) on the sociology of knowledge which Brewer argued was a continuation of the work of the later Wittgenstein. This rather jolted Peter out of his 'somewhat Platonic' leanings in epistemology – and Peter recognised that this in particular 'sowed the seed of my later interest in cultural history'. He got started with the teaching of medical sociology in the Sociology Department in 1980 and taught it throughout the 80s. When he took over convening it, he got it renamed 'The Sociology of Health and Illness' in order to reflect more explicitly its anthropological dimension. As he remarked, he wished it to be 'about the patient experience first and foremost rather than the experience of the doctor'. He was struck by the parallel between issues of authority in medicine and those in the catholic church – especially the parallel between the experience in women in childbirth vis-à-vis the male doctor and that of young married couples vis-à-vis the celibate priest. A male student from the Netherlands Edwin van Teilingen actually did some very interesting research on the experience of child birth at that time. (Later Edwin, Peter and others co-edited a book in this area: Edwin R. van Teijlingen, George W. Lowis, Peter McCaffery and Maureen Porter (eds.), *Midwifery and the Medicalization of Childbirth: comparative perspectives* [Nova, 2000]).

Peter had also maintained his interest in the sociology of religion, partly through involvement in the British Sociological Association Religion Group of which he was secretary for two years. Indeed during the 70s he studied part-time for an Oxford DPhil in this area, developing the theme of his BPhil thesis by comparing the influences of pressure groups within the catholic church in Holland and in England, and defended his thesis successfully in 1980. In it he was rather critical of the intellectual resources of sociology in simply 'not being equipped to think about the state of modern catholicism' because of a lack of historical depth.

Another area in which he taught and developed a course was developing countries, when he took over responsibility for 'The sociology of developing countries'. It was important to him to study the sociology of countries quite different from those in Europe. In any case it chimed in with his interest in the third world, as evidenced in his involvement in the then Aberdeen World Poverty Association.

Whilst he became somewhat involved with the Cultural History group from 1985 onwards (see next section), he became rather more involved in it as it evolved after retirement in 1990 and came to teach in various courses until about 2007 when the programme was being run down (through lack of institutional support). Meantime he had in 2003 taken up an offer to teach in an MLitt in war studies on the sociology of war in the Department of Politics and International Relations, and, whilst that MLitt did not continue to run, Peter was also invited to teach in other IR courses and this continues to this day on the theme of the cultural history of war (made a hot topic, given 9/11, Afghanistan etc.). In this

Peter explores what war is like for those involved in it; that is, 'how civilians and members of the armed forces are affected in their daily lives and in their capacity to take part in society by their involvement in war'. Meantime recently he has been asked to teach a course in religious studies – which takes him full circle back to the issues which had fascinated him in his formative years.

Peter was not particularly focussed on publications – his strength lay and lies in his being an inspiring teacher, enabling colleagues and being a great inter-disciplinarian. He has however published in various fields, he is currently working on *A Reader in Cultural History* which he is co-editing with Ben Marsden, and hopes one day to write a book on the idea of reasoning and inference which takes seriously its non-cognitive and emotional dimensions.

CULTURAL HISTORY

Peter was one of the key figures in the development of the cultural history programme. Though he was not in on its origins, once he had joined the group in 1985, he put his heart and mind into it – precisely because it represented the inter-disciplinary engagement with the cultural and intellectual forces that have shaped the modern world. This inter-disciplinary engagement very much suited how his own mind – trained in various fields – liked to work. Once he had taken early retirement he was able to devote what time he wanted to it, and was not constrained by the factor that many of his colleagues in the early years of Cultural History experienced of having to combine their Cultural History interests with regular commitments in their own departments. It was only later that Cultural History was allowed to form into a group of people whose sole responsibility was the teaching of Cultural History.

As Peter recalls, the Cultural History project had a number of origins in the 1970s and early 1980s. These included the inter-disciplinary lecture series organised by Joan Pittock-Wesson, the influence of the History and Philosophy of Science which was headed by George Molland, the African Studies Group which encouraged inter-disciplinary discussion of African affairs, and ideas that Judith Hook (who sadly died before they came to fruition) and Nick Fisher had had of inter-disciplinary co-operation. By the mid-1980s a planning group led by Joan Pittock-Wesson (English department) was meeting regularly to work out a programme for an Honours course. In November 1985 Peter went along with several sociology colleagues – Norman Stockman, Mike Hepworth and Chuck Jedrez – to one such planning meeting – and he got 'hooked'! I recall vividly a conversation Peter and I had walking from Queen Mother Library back to the High Street in the spring of 1986 just after I got back from Africa when he shared his excitement about the new inter-disciplinary programme in Cultural History that was going to start!

He recalls that there were frequent planning meetings working out the details for the courses in the three terms (as we had then before semesterisation) of Junior Honours. Peter recalls that the structure that was initially decided on was something like this: the first term was on the 17th century and associated with the rise of science and the forming of the Royal Society: each week there would be a key text – it might be Descartes' *Discourse on Method* or Swift's *Gulliver's Travels* and the lecturers each week would present different aspects of the period in question. The second term (late 18th/early 19th century) was about the Enlightenment, and included consideration of music (like Mozart's operas), drama and novels, but with a special focus on the 1st edition of the *Encyclopedie* of which Aberdeen Library had a copy which students could see. The third term focused on the late 19th century and the age of decadence. What Peter remembers vividly were colleagues sitting round a table asking questions like 'on Tuesday of week 3 who will lecture on what?' where, in Peter's words, 'there were people with very different ideas of what was important in history or what were the most significant cultural developments in a decade or so'. So these meeting were intellectually demanding but 'there was enough space for everyone's ideas to get recognition'.

Amongst those whom Peter recalls as having been active in the early days of Cultural History are, apart from those already mentioned: John Dunkley (French); Mike Spiller (English); David Irvin (History of Art); Andrew Wear (History of Science); James Thrower (Religious Studies); Roger Williams (Music); Colm O'Boyle (Celtic); David Cram (Linguistics); Jennifer Carter, Bill Scott and Paul Dukes (History); Eric Mathews, Melvin Dalgarno and myself (Philosophy). (In the interview Peter comments more on the interests of most of these mentioned, but reporting here on some of these and not others would be invidious, and reporting on all too lengthy.)

By the spring of 1986 then the programme had been approved, and in the autumn of 1986 the first intake of 6 students into Junior Honours took place. They came from very different academic backgrounds. Peter recalls that Colin Melvin came from Computer Science, whereas Marius Kwint who was ' a very interesting person to teach' came from the History of Art. At any rate, perhaps because the students were very enthusiastic, 'we got through first year more easily than we had feared'. Peter recalls that this first group of students in fact did very well in the final exams. In those days the work of the Junior Honours was examined at the end of the Senior Honours year – a way of assessing students which Peter regarded as having been a 'better educational experience' than assessments per course. Roy Porter the first external examiner commented very favourably on the performance of the first cohort. Two of them – Colin and Marius – both got firsts, and whereas Colin went on to a career in financial management Marius took up an academic career in Art History and Cultural History.

Quite remarkably (by modern red tape standards) only the Junior Honours Programme had been worked out by then – what the Senior Honours Programme would consist of was yet to be decided by October 1987! As it was worked out, two Approaches to Culture courses were the core of the Senior Honours year, but students also had to do a special subject and a dissertation, each of which needed to be taken in the various participating departments.

Peter was initially more concerned with the Senior Honours programme and convened and taught in the first Approaches to Culture course in the autumn of 1987, but later did more teaching in the second Approaches to Culture course, various Junior Honours courses, as well as later on, when they were introduced in about 1995, the second year level courses on cultural anthropology and ideas of the environment. As time went on he found himself doing more teaching in the Junior Honours courses because various people dropped out either from pressure of work in their own departments or because they left (like Andrew Wear and David Cram).

Peter recalls that one of the things he taught in that first Approaches to Culture course were the ideas of Alasdair MacIntyre in his then recently published book *After Virtue* – a book Peter found immensely stimulating – perhaps not surprising given that MacIntyre also straddled the relationship as Peter does between the philosophical and the serious interest in cultural and social phenomena. As Peter put it, MacIntyre's book was a 'source of intellectual excitement', in that it combined catholic medieval thinking with other traditions such as marxism and linguistic philosophy, and provided 'an immense sweep of time and intellectual horizons', and through it he came to realise that 'looking at philosophical issues and trying to understand how society functions are enhanced by taking into account things like reading Jane Austen and a whole variety of contribution of the writers of literature'. What he found rather disappointing was that most of the students did not seem to share quite the same enthusiasm for MacIntyre as he did…! He recalls that another lecture he gave for that course was on 'the significance of computers in the context of cultural history'. Interest in the idea of a 'thinking machine' of course goes back to the 18th century and the ideas of Pascal, and Peter was much taken with the intellectual question of how far the thinking that animals do and the what computers do are related or contrasted.

By 1995 Peter was heavily involved in the programme and had an office in The Old Brewery to which it had just moved (and remained until 2002), having previously been in the beautiful if somewhat isolated Humanity Manse. He had acquired a room there in 1993 which 'meant a lot to him' (since by then he was no longer entitled to one in the Sociology Department). However this meant he got more involved in administration for cultural history. He recalls organising, for instance, several of the reading parties that went to The Burn near Edzell, and also being from 1993 to 2004 library representative with a reasonable allowance for purchasing books which he enjoyed doing. In this period the staff of the Cultural History group had come to be employed to teach Cultural History rather than as part of a job in another department. The core at that time was really Joan Pittock-Wesson, Nick Fisher, Bill Scott, Hushang Philsooph (who had come into Cultural History from Sociology with the ending of Social Anthropology in the Sociology Department), and Peter himself. Peter recalls that in 1993/1994 some doubts and criticisms in the University were being more vocally expressed about cultural history. There are always going to be detractors – those who prefer to stay inside established departments like English or History and say that cultural historians are jacks of all trades. Certainly, Peter remarked, cultural historians are faced with the challenge of what its identity is as an academic enterprise, some arguing that it is better seen as a discipline in its own right, other that the cross fertilisation of ideas from having people in different departments is part of its appeal. Anyway, given the criticisms at the time, Ian Macdonald, Dean of Arts, asked a group of 'neutral' academics to do an evaluation, and this, produced in 1994, proved very positive. (He recalls George Watson saying that he had been very impressed by what Cultural History did.)

With the move to the Old Brewery in 2005 Cultural History came to be regarded, for administrative purposes, as a sub-department within Philosophy (but for one year 2001–2 there was a School of Philosophy and Cultural History). After that it became a sub-department within History in the new School of Divinity, History and Philosophy, moved again and gradually began to lose its distinct identity. (Amongst those later involved, at different stages, whom Peter recalls are: Leigh Clayton, Colin Whatford, Elizabeth Hallam, Ben Marsden, Phil Withington, Rainer Broemer and David Smith.)

But, going back to the heyday of Cultural History in the late 80s and 90s, the growth of Cultural History was a period of great intellectual excitement. As Peter recalls, it was a period of numerous well attended conferences on Cultural History themes, including one organised by Peter on 'Explorations in Cultural History'

(1989), to which *inter alia* Stephen Kern, author of *The Culture of Time and Space 1890-1918*, was invited. Other conferences were: 'Aberdeen and Enlightenment' (organised by Joan Pittock-Wesson and Jennifer Carter 1986); 'Interpretation and Cultural History' (Joan Pittock-Wesson and Andrew Wear 1987); 'Culture and Revolution' (Paul Dukes and John Dunkley 1988, organised to mark the bicentenary of the French Revolution); 'Frontiers of European Culture' (Paul Dukes and Mike Hepworth 1991); 'Changing Organisms – Organisms and Change' (Joan Pittock-Wesson, George Rousseau, David Smith and others 1995) – the latter being a history of medicine conference which was part to the University's quincentenary celebrations.

After that period there were no more such conferences, but there was a remarkable '21st birthday' conference in 2007, organised by David Smith and others. Ironically, although by this time the commitment to Cultural History in the University of Aberdeen had waned, this conference – which was very well attended – gave rise to the formation of the International Society of Cultural History which was formally constituted a year later at a conference in Ghent. Peter had thought for some time that it would be good to have a Journal of Cultural History and the advice given by Ben Marsden was to get a Society established first which would facilitate this – and now a Journal will be launched soon. There is no doubt that in its heyday Cultural History in Aberdeen, both through these earlier conferences and through the numerous publications of its members (publications which did not, as Peter observed, get the recognition they deserved because, of course, they often fell between the cracks of the RAE's predetermined categories) was a major – if not the – catalyst to Cultural History being alive and well in other academic centres. And it is clear that Peter took immense satisfaction – even pride (if such a modest person of Quaker principles would allow himself this emotion) – in the fact that he contributed to the development of what many now see as a discipline in its own right.

PETER AS AN ACADEMIC

By the conventional standards of academic achievement – high status and a mass of publications –Peter has not been nor did he seek to be a particularly high flyer, but he is and always has been one of most genuinely academic peoples I have ever met. I count three things as central to being in this sense a genuine academic: a lively search after truth; a willingness to share that search and enthusiasm with others, whether colleague or students; and a recognition that truth is not well understood as partitioned into separate boxes corresponding to well defined disciplines. Peter has shows these qualities in high degree.

Whilst Peter might have reservations about whether there is a large timeless Truth – his interest in the sociology of knowledge and his thorough knowledge of intellectual history and of other cultures would caution him – he is not a relativist and the earnest pursuit of truth and the questioning of shallow or false views are hallmarks of his quest. But this search for truth is something he has done with both heart and mind. Certainly it is with the head by which he is guided by reason and argument and a willingness to pursue the argument wherever it takes one. But the search is one also guided by the heart in the sense that human beings matter and what one is concerned about academically should reflect the importance of understanding human beings and advancing their well being, and also in the sense that what one is looking for is, so to speak, the heart of arguments and positions – for instance in what others are saying – rather than their literal outward form. He quoted Newman who said 'cor ad cor' – 'heart speaks to heart' – as one of his favourite sayings. (I might mention in passing an interest both he and I have had in 'the heart' as a possible source of insight/intelligence/memory – something researched by e.g. the Heart Math Institute.)

Peter is a gifted communicator whether with colleagues or with students. At the heart of this gift is an acceptance of everyone as equal. Part of this means being willing to listen carefully to what others are saying. He has been a good listener in that conversations with him tend to draw thoughts out of others. Academics are not always very good at doing this, especially with regard to their students. But Peter, it strikes me, has always seen students as important sources of insight – both because, even though they may be at rather different stages in their intellectual journeys, they may well come up with insights from which one learns, and because it is important to ensure that what they are asked to learn about is grounded in their experiences and also in relevant hands-on examples taken from the real world. He sees it as part of his Quaker approach in teaching 'to bring out what is latent in students' interests'.

I recall how when in the early 2000s I convened a first year course on Global Citizenship, Peter contributed lectures and was keen to get students to look at concrete examples of global citizenship in action – for instance in ethical consuming as a stance against the pernicious effects of the global free market and big business. For this he got them to look at various web-sites. It is worth adding in passing that that although I regard myself as at an age just young enough to really get the hang of computers, Peter – just a few years older than me – has really got into the internet in a big way and uses it as academic source very successfully in tracking down interesting articles and issues. One of the things I recall over the last few years are the various emails that Peter sends to me and others with interesting links – to do with, for instance, prison reform, the sins of multinationals or little known horrors in Iraq.

This last point leads me to the third academic quality Peter has – a willingness to see academic issues as not divided into separate boxes. His own interests have been very wide ranging, as has been illustrated in what I have mentioned. He once said to me that he feared that because he has had so many interests, he was really not expert in any. But this image as a jack of all (academic) trades and master of none just does not fit Peter. His grasp of these many fields – and of their inter-connections – has been impressive. In any case we need academics – rather more in my opinion than we actually have – who are willing to straddle academic boundaries and see the big pictures. Indeed he remarked that 'he liked to see links between the way a topic is handled in different disciplines'. One can do this by oneself operating in several fields, but also, perhaps more crucially, being willing to listen to and engage with the academic perspectives coming from other disciplines – something that is crucial to the whole Cultural History ethos – which is why Peter was attracted to it like a wasp to a honey pot.

He reported to me that one of the key meta-discussions in Cultural History had been over whether it was multi-disciplinary, trans-disciplinary or an emerging new discipline in its own right. The answer which he gave at the time of the evaluation in 1994 when asked 'has cultural history a distinctive and coherent intellectual framework or methodology?' was to say 'Cultural History involves paying attention to three elements, amongst others, in a shared way of life: a) the resonance of particular symbols in a given milieu; b) how people orient themselves in time and space; and c) people's notions of human growth and decline.' This is not perhaps a direct answer to that meta-question, but it shows clearly that for Peter the input from many disciplines is needed to give an adequate account of these three elements.

If one considers some of the many areas of Peter's teaching – work and employment, health and illness, religious studies, approaches to culture and the influence of MacIntyre's *After Virtue*, and more recently issues of war and peace – they are, apart from the breadth of interests illustrated – big subjects which invite inputs from many perspectives and indeed got them, given the way Peter taught. Although most of them of course came out of Peter's training as a sociologist, they reflected other influences and interests. (Just as it is said that, once a Catholic, always a Catholic – and Peter, as I said earlier, acknowledges this influence despite his outwardly having moved quite a way from it – so, I would remark, once a Greats man, always a Greats man, in that Peter's early grounding in Philosophy has always to some extent informed – and in my opinion (being a fellow Greats man) enriched – what he has done later!) Peter is someone who is willing to take on almost any issue, and is certainly not inclined to hide behind academic specialisms! Although he might be uncomfortable with the term, given that it sometimes has connotations of secularism, he seems to me to exhibit many of characteristics of the free thinker. (When I came to the University of Aberdeen in 1967 my mother said she envied me going to a place where there would be so much exciting intellectual discussion with colleagues from many disciplines. Little did she know! But there were exceptions and Peter has been one of them (as has been Cultural History itself). She would have enjoyed talking with Peter.)

CONCLUSION

In this brief chapter I have endeavoured to give a little background to Peter's academic development, outlined his work in the sociology department, described his contribution to the development of Cultural History and reflected some of his comments on that, and assessed his academic strengths. I hope I have done justice to a person with an immense breadth of attributes and interests. When I asked him (at the end of the interview) what, in looking back on a long academic career, he took most satisfaction in, he answered without much hesitation 'my contribution both to Sociology and to Cultural History', and he added, almost as an afterthought, 'oh, and reading lots of really interesting dissertations' (including such esoteric topics as 'the cultural history of tea drinking')! These of course were the dissertations of many students who had been exposed to Peter's style of teaching which opened up their minds to new possibilities of thought. And it is perhaps this enduring influence in the minds of countless students, now all over the world, for which we should be most thankful for in Peter's academic life.

The Cultural History MA
at the University of Aberdeen, 1986–2011:
a personal reflection

NICK FISHER
University of Aberdeen

The undergraduate programme in cultural history at the University of Aberdeen began almost twenty-five years ago, but is now being discontinued. The last cultural history students will graduate next year. It is of course hard to be cheerful when writing about the last days of a programme to which so many people contributed so much care and effort, but my abiding memory will always be of the enormous enjoyment that many of us got from teaching cultural history in the early days, in the growth part of the curve, and at its peak. We all learned so much that we would otherwise not have been able to.

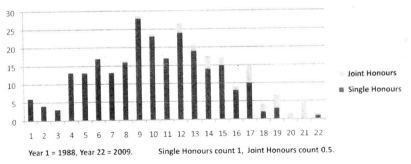

Aberdeen Cultural History Graduates 1988 - 2009

Year 1 = 1988, Year 22 = 2009.   Single Honours count 1, Joint Honours count 0.5.

My younger colleagues who have kept the flame burning in the period of decline assure me that this is still very much the case: the teaching is enormously rewarding. From the start, cultural history was a liberation from conventional disciplinary limits. Moreover, it served as a much-needed morale booster in the face of the university-wide depression caused by the Thatcher government's cuts to university funding in the 1980s, which had a severe effect on Aberdeen.

We need a word about the context, and about how the most conservative and geographically isolated of the ancient Scottish universities came to start such a unique experiment. Aberdeen University, founded in 1495, was for most of the

Explorations in Cultural History: Essays for Peter Gabriel McCaffery,
edd. David F. Smith & H. Philsooph (Aberdeen 2010)

ISBN 978-0-9567059-0-7

twentieth century an ordinary Scottish university. This means among other things that the students entered about a year younger than their English counterparts, and that they were admitted not to departments but rather to faculties (Arts, Divinity, Medicine, Science, Law), which has implications for my story: it is much easier for Scottish students than English to change their intended direction once they have sampled one or two years of university study. Moreover, the broader four-year Scottish honours degree is different from a three-year English degree. And when after the second war the other Scottish universities, St Andrews, Glasgow, and Edinburgh were forced by the conditions attached to government funding to become more aware of international comparisons and competition, Aberdeen self-consciously remained the most traditionally Scottish of the universities. It was also rather small, with 2500 students in 1960.

The 1960s saw a period of huge expansion in British education, with the foundation of many new universities. In search of the economic benefits of a more educated population, student numbers were intended to more than double in the fifteen years from 1962, facilitated by generous student grants to all who qualified for university entrance. In Scotland the number of universities was increased from four to eight. Of the older universities, Aberdeen was particularly singled out for growth. Glasgow and Edinburgh were thought by the administrators of the Scottish Education Department to be big enough already, while the little city of St Andrews was considered unable to cope with a large increase in student numbers. The target numbers for Aberdeen were raised and raised again, from the actual 2500 in 1960 to targets of 4500 for 1967, of 8180 for 1976, and finally of 10500 for 1981. These planned expansions were intended roughly to parallel the physical and economic growth of the City of Aberdeen as a result of the discovery of North Sea oil. With the encouragement, indeed the insistence, of the University Grants Committee, the distributor of British government funds to universities, the University of Aberdeen set about building the classrooms and student residences, and hiring the staff, that would be required for all these new students. Unfortunately, nobody told the students that they were expected in Aberdeen, and there were no efficient mechanisms for directing student choice. When I was appointed in 1976, the student population was around 5500, not the intended 8180. As a result, when the economic crisis for universities came in 1981, Aberdeen was found to be over-provided with both buildings and staff; and it had too many small and thus supposedly 'inefficient' departments, such as my own, History and Philosophy of Science, with its staff of 3. The cut in Aberdeen's government grant announced that summer was 19%, compared with a national average of 11%. The University's response was to announce 169 academic staff redundancies, compulsory if necessary, including all the inefficient little departments.

A vigorous academic defence was led by mass meetings of the lecturers' union, the Aberdeen Association of University Teachers (AAUT). The University meanwhile offered quite generous compensation packages for early retirement, and by April it was clear that enough academics had accepted these packages, or had left for other universities less badly affected, so that the required savings in staff costs had been achieved, and the threat of further sackings and closures was formally lifted. But it has to be said that the radicalisation and the militancy of the staff that arose during that year ensured that their attitudes towards the University, including feelings of loyalty and trust, were never the same again.

The immediate outlook for the future of teaching and learning at the University was now rather bleak. After all the work that had gone in to reducing staff costs, it was clear that it would be some time before the flow of new young lecturers could start again. How then could innovation in teaching, at little or no cost, be encouraged? One individual who gave this much thought was Dr Judith Hook of the History Department. She was a scholar of seventeenth-century English art, and of the more general history – indeed the cultural history – of Renaissance Italy. Judith's work culminated in the publication of her biography of Lorenzo de' Medici in 1984. She had been particularly active in the struggles of the AAUT, when she and I had been close comrades in arms. She was forever dreaming up new schemes, often of doubtful practicality. In early 1984 she had heard that the new British television channel, Channel 4, was seeking suggestions for new programmes, possibly some of them academic. She sat with me at my kitchen table discussing a proposal for an intellectual history series. In Britain we talk about plans being made "on the back of an envelope"; if one is talking about politics or about budgetary planning, it is rather rude and dismissive to say this. But some important plans start on the backs of envelopes, and here is the beginning of Aberdeen's cultural history.

I can't really make much sense of it after 26 years – and this is not remotely what happened. Channel 4 would certainly not have thought much of it. (Channel 4 has found its niche as the British home of 'Big Brother', and intellectual history would be entirely alien to it.) Fortunately Judith also pursued these ideas within the University, and towards the end of academic year 1983-84 organised a meeting with members of the History Department and others such as myself who had an interest in interdisciplinary teaching. That summer Judith went to Florence as usual for her research, and in August she suddenly died there of a brain haemorrhage.

Partly in memory of Judith, her colleagues in the History Department sought to carry her exploration further. The immediate occasion for the resumption of discussions was a visit by the cultural historian Roy Porter to give a lecture to the Department in March 1985. In conversation afterwards, he was most encouraging of our efforts at interdisciplinary teaching. A number of us took these forward over the summer and autumn. In the summer two significant decisions were made: to spread the invitation to talk as widely as possible by word of mouth, and to invite Joan Pittock Wesson of the English Department, who had organised a successful series of interdisciplinary seminars in the 1970s, to become convenor of the group. By the autumn 'intellectual history' had become 'cultural history', as both a more inclusive approach and more widely interdisciplinary – not to mention more modern – and detailed planning for an honours course in cultural history had begun. When the course proposal was submitted to the Arts Faculty Planning Committee in December, it was turned down on the grounds that a time of financial stringency was no time to be experimenting with new ways of teaching; this was of course the exact opposite of our argument that it was precisely because of the financial constraints that one had to come up with new ways of doing things.

So we appealed to the full Arts Faculty meeting against this initial refusal, and we won the vote, which allowed us to proceed. Apart from the intellectual arguments for the proposed cultural history course, and the emotional arguments in memory of Judith Hook, there were three other main reasons for this turnaround. The practical argument was that we had so many possible contributors that no one of us would be overburdened by the additional teaching. Translated into political terms, this same argument about numbers meant that the group and its many friends throughout the Faculty could attract enough votes to win. And the clinching political fact was that after the radical struggles of the early 1980s, nobody wanted to be told what they should do or what they should think by figures of authority such as deans and their planning committees.

Let me outline the normal structure of an arts honours degree that we were threatening to subvert. An Aberdeen arts student would typically take three courses in year 1, two in year 2, and then in years 3 and 4 ('junior and senior honours') would specialise in either those same two disciplines ('joint honours'), or only one of them ('single honours'). The overall menu was not an entirely free choice: there were rules governing permitted combinations of disciplines, and there were particular prerequisites for certain courses. And until quite recently there had been a general prerequisite that all arts students had to take at least one course in philosophy, once a characteristic of all Scottish arts degrees. The degree structure for science students was comparable, except that single honours was the norm. Overall, the expectation was that candidates for an honours degree, whether single or joint, would be prepared for their honours classes by two years of prior study in their discipline(s).

What we cultural historians were proposing was an honours degree which assumed no earlier preparation, and would thus begin from zero in Year 3. This was entirely anomalous. It was proposed that we took *any* student with the standard number of passes in earlier courses, including students from the Science Faculty (or elsewhere). We would teach them intensively a basic course in the cultural history of north-west Europe from the Enlightenment and the French Revolution, through the romanticism and nationalism of the nineteenth century, up to the onset of the First War, all over 24 weeks. This would be preparatory to more specialist courses in the senior honours year.

As students were considering their futures towards the end of academic year 1985-86, posters were circulated inviting any students interested in the new cultural history degree to contact the Convenor or any member of the core group. (It should be emphasised that altogether many more than the ten staff members named on the poster were involved.) In October 1986 our first intake was six students.

They took a single course which had 4-6 lectures a week and one or two seminars. One of the seminars would discuss the week's 'key text', an insistence from members of the English department. The first text was Francis Bacon's *New Atlantis* as part of the seventeenth-century background to the Enlightenment. Later in the year the concept of 'text' broadened to include several non-literary works; Haydn's 'Creation' as an Enlightenment text was one; the Great Exhibition of 1851 in London was another (the latter has been my chief personal research interest ever since). In keeping with the interdisciplinary nature of the course, two or sometimes even three members of staff participated in the seminars, and all for six students! This generosity could not last for very long, although many years later there were still a few seminars with staff from two different departments. The emphasis throughout was on cultural interconnexions, easily enough traced in the European Enlightenment, but also to be found throughout the nineteenth century.

Another feature of the cultural history teaching was that it involved more than the regular teaching staff. The University Archivist, Colin McLaren, gave a series of lectures on the cultural history of libraries. Other recruits included a second librarian whose PhD dissertation had been on the history of the book trade, the curator of the University's anthropological museum, the University's public relations officer who had previously worked for Scottish Opera, and a careers adviser who had an interest in the notion of the wilderness. People such as these welcomed the opportunity to teach their special interests that they would not normally have had. All at different times added to the richness and diversity of the cultural history course. (It is perhaps no coincidence that several of our students went on to work in libraries or museums.)

It should be said that in the tradition of British empiricism, the Aberdeen student's conception of cultural history was not theory-based, but was allowed to grow by slow empirical example. Such theory as we taught came later, and built on this empirical base. One result of this was an almost universal feeling among the students, maybe half-way through the introductory junior honours year, of being lost in a forest of disconnected information. "What *is* this cultural history?" they would ask. This feeling of dislocation would eventually pass, as group consciousness and solidarity reached some kind of an answer, allowing the students to make the connexions. Even among the small numbers of our initial intakes, *esprit de corps*, group solidarity, was always a striking feature.

In senior honours, our initial six students found the same generosity of staff teaching time which would be unthinkable today: eight optional courses for six students:

M.A. WITH HONOURS IN CULTURAL HISTORY: Senior Honours 1987-8
Special Options:

		Students
Death and the Family	Andrew Wear	2
Darwin and Victorian Thought	Robin Gilmour	2
Ideas of Language	David Cram	1
Russia and America	Paul Dukes	1
Structuralism and after	Michael Spiller	2
Commerce and Art	David Irwin	1
Childhood	Joan Pittock Wesson	2
The History of Sexuality	Mike Hepworth and David Oldman	1

Reading lists should be obtained from tutors before the end of this term.

And at the end of their fourth year, they took all their final exams over a few days, as was then the practice:

University of Aberdeen, 1987-88
MA with Honours in Cultural History. Degree regulations:

The examination consists of seven papers and a dissertation

Subjects of Examination

(1) General paper
(2) Reason and Enlightenment
(3) Revolution and Reaction
(4) Progress and Decadence
(5) Approaches to Culture
(6) And (7) Two options selected from a panel of topics in the senior honours
    year
(8) Dissertation: This must be on a topic approved by the Convenor

---

That first year, two of our six students achieved first class honours degrees.

I should briefly mention another activity that helped to forge a sense of common identity among the staff, and to put Aberdeen's cultural history on the map. Four successful international conferences were held in the summers of 1987 to 1990.

For a while it looked as if our enjoyment of the teaching was going to have diminishing, perhaps terminally diminishing, returns. Our class of six was followed by four, and then by three. In a naked attempt at recruitment we proposed a second-year 'feeder' course from 1988, but this was turned down – this time with no hope of appeal. But suddenly in 1989 recruitment took off, presumably due to favourable recommendations among the students: we had thirteen, thirteen, seventeen. By our ninth year of operation, we had twenty-nine graduates.

What sort of students did we get? Those with the initiative and determination to change from their original direction. Later, in the 90s, as the University made more and more effort to recruit 'mature students' (a technical term meaning those more than 23 years old when they enter) we got a disproportionate number of those. Mature students, who often turn to university to change the direction of a life they have come to see as unsatisfying, tend to opt for courses that offer cultural enrichment rather than the financial riches held out by vocational courses. At least one of our adult students used cultural history to rebuild his life more profoundly. On 6 July 1988 the Piper Alpha oil platform off Aberdeen exploded killing 167 workers; there were 59 survivors. One of these, Bob Ballantyne, entered the University as a mature student and chose to graduate in cultural history. He made a new career for himself as a community organizer and adult education teacher. Later in the 1990s, when all of our courses had been modularised (that is, they had become self-contained and graded at the end of each course, so that one could take individual cultural history courses without signing up for the whole degree), we also got much more than our share of visiting Europeans and Americans, attracted by unusual courses they could not get at home. Several of these stayed on to graduate with an Aberdeen cultural history degree. And over the years there was roughly a two to one ratio of women to men among cultural history graduates.

A major change which accompanied our success in the 1990s was the decline of our pool of teachers. It almost seemed as if staff numbers were inversely proportional to our success in attracting students. The fall-off in contributors might have been due to increasing teaching duties in a 'home' department, or transfer elsewhere in Britain, or the non-renewal of a temporary contract, or retirement, or death – all of which affected individuals among our staff. Or someone who had given a few lectures over the years would go on research leave, and on return would be unwilling to pick up the responsibility again. Or a contributor who had at the beginning given ten or twelve lectures a year was now down to two or three. By the late 1990s, more than half the teaching was done by four or five core staff, and wider contributions had become more the exception than the norm.

But there were other changes in the 1990s which may have contributed to this situation. In 1992, due to our growing numbers of students, Cultural History was for the first time granted the status of an independent academic department and the Convenor given a formal part-time appointment as Head of Department. During the following year the new department was also housed in a renovated eighteenth-century building away from the main campus, and the first appointment of a full-time Lecturer in Cultural History was made. This was the cultural anthropologist Hushang Philsooph, who planned and introduced a successful second-year feeder course, as well as a popular senior honours option, and who taught in the cultural history programme until 1996.

After two years the new arrangement was subjected to an 'Internal Teaching Review', an inquisition based on the government's official 'Teaching Quality Assessment', and like the latter requiring a mountain of paper describing every course in the smallest detail. The proceedings of the review were notable for the extremely strong support for our teaching given by our students, and also by our external examiners from past years such as Roy Porter and Peter Burke. The result of the inquisition was that – for various reasons which I need not go in to – the experiment of departmental status for cultural history was judged not to be a success. The group was to be moved back on campus to lessen any tendency of the students to consider themselves special and apart, and the administration of the group was to be under the supervision of another established department. Philosophy was chosen, chiefly in order to avoid the big guns of History and English, both of which tended to be hostile to cultural history. Powerful individuals in those two departments regarded cultural history not only as inferior as a discipline, but also as a seducer of their intended students. On the other hand, the Teaching Review recommended that full time appointments to cultural history should be extended. In early 1995 I was appointed Director, and my colleague Bill Scott, historian of the French Revolution, was made full-time Senior Lecturer. We were also given a third of the time of a Teaching Fellow, Leigh Clayton (a Lecturer in all but name, who did not have a Lecturer's research commitment), and were further supported by Peter McCaffery, a retired sociologist who was paid by the hour. Partly as a result of its success, the cultural history core group was becoming very different from the wide circle of enthusiastic volunteers who had initiated the programme.

Cultural history flourished at this time, under the most sympathetic dean we ever encountered. Now that we had secure staffing, we were able from 1996 to introduce an additional second-year course, 'The Culture of the human and natural environment', which complemented the recruiting effects of our introduction to anthropology.

At the same time, the compulsory core of courses was maintained, and indeed extended to a compulsory course on the culture of the twentieth century to be taken in fourth year. Unlike in all the other programmes in the Arts Faculty, our students were allowed a free choice only in their two optional courses. Nobody seemed to mind this lack of choice – except perhaps members of other departments, who objected that cultural history seemed always to be special case, a constant anomaly.

1995/96 Compulsory courses:

CU 3002	Reason, Enlightenment, Revolution (9)
CU 3003	Approaches to Culture 1 (3)
CU 3502	Romanticism, Progress and Decadence (9)
CU 3503	Approaches to Culture 2 (3)
CU 4012	Modern Times: Perspectives on the Twentieth Century (6)
CU 4506	Cultural History Dissertation (6)

Plus one optional course from each semester:

CU 4002	Structuralism and After (6)
CU 4003	Art and Commerce (6)
CU 4004	Race and Politics (6)
CU 4005	Women in History (6)
CU 4006	Patterns of Power and Politics in Modern French History (6)
CU 4502	Childhood (6)
CU 4503	Culture of the Renaissance and Reformation (6)
CU 4504	Music and Musical Life in the Twentieth Century (6)
CU 4505	Religion and Rejection of Religion in Western Europe (6)

I have already said that at this period of our greatest numbers of students at all three levels, the bulk of the teaching was done by four or five of us, of whom three were full time. We were desperately overworked, with ratios of students to staff which would not have been tolerated in infant school, but a now unsympathetic dean was deaf to pleas for more staff. It has been a feature of British universities since the financial crises of the 1980s and a political call for public accountability that a supposedly accurate price is put on everything from paper clips to staff salaries to tractors for the playing fields. When I was director of the programme in 1998, the figures of income and expenditure showed that cultural history's student numbers were bringing in about £200,000, but our costs were less than £100,000; we were thus subsidising the rest of the Arts Faculty. I argued strongly for the appointment of two new staff members to relieve the teaching overload, but was told that these figures were merely notional. Four years later, equally notional figures were used the other way to justify the dismantling of the programme. "Cultural History is losing money," said the new dean, without providing any evidence. Now the figures were considered not notional, but the basis for real cuts.

One other result of the success of our two second-year courses was that these were now made prerequisites for entry into cultural history honours, thus making it like all other disciplines in the Faculty, and removing an anomaly which would upset any tidy-minded dean. This meant that we could no longer freely take in refugees from English or History or wherever who had become unhappy with their original intentions. Recruitment to the honours years did suffer, although not radically so at first.

One very obvious problem with cultural history teaching being in the hands of just a few teachers was that it became vulnerable to any change in personnel. My contract was not renewed in 1999, and my colleague Bill Scott retired a year later. We were replaced by new appointments from outside, but this could be tricky. To go back a few years, before I was made Director the post had been advertised externally, but it was found that none of the outside candidates were sufficiently in tune with the existing group. Later, when replacements for myself and Bill Scott were appointed, their expertise naturally differed from ours, and so the core courses had to change. Leigh Clayton, our teaching fellow, who was now essentially full time in Cultural History, was particularly helpful in keeping the nineteenth- and twentieth-century core courses going, but the Enlightenment course, which since the very start in 1986 had been the bedrock of our programme, was replaced in 2001 by a less focused course with a much longer timespan, 'Continuity and change, 1500–1800'.

The real bombshell came in 2002, when as I have already said the Dean of Arts claimed that Cultural History was making a loss, and dissolved the group. Elizabeth Hallam, who had been my successor as Director, moved to the revived Anthropology Department. Leigh Clayton's contract was not renewed. There is a shameful suspicion that this was because after so many years teaching on fixed-term contracts, it was a legal requirement that at the next renewal the University had to give her a permanent contract. Rainer Brömer, who had been hired as a one-year replacement and kept on for a second year, was also 'let go', to use the euphemism. The remaining staff joined the History Department, with my successor Ben Marsden as Convenor of the cultural history programme. With these changes, and especially the sackings, the core of the programme fell apart. The nineteenth- and twentieth-century courses were immediately abandoned. The second-year courses did not long survive, and the prerequisites for cultural history honours became an unheard-of combination of history and religious studies and anthropology courses.

The effects on student recruitment and morale were unsurprising. The changes were announced before the end of summer term, 2002. Many of the existing junior honours students simply disappeared, and did not return for their senior honours year.

A University-wide reorganization followed a year later. Every seven years or so Aberdeen University is subjected to a major structural change, intended to transform it into the hottest university outside London, Oxford, and Cambridge. Somehow this never quite seems to work as it should. The big idea in 2003 was the abolition of faculties and departments, and the establishment of colleges and schools. History and Art History and Divinity and Philosophy became a single school, resulting in a final loss of autonomy for what little remained of cultural history. Despite his heroic efforts to keep the distinctive degree going, Ben Marsden's position as Convenor of the cultural history programme was abolished, and, as another example, the approval of dissertation topics for cultural history students was passed to the historian responsible for history dissertations. He was described to me by one colleague as clearly an enemy of cultural history.

As there came to be less and less that was distinctive about cultural history courses, so students combined them more and more with other disciplines as joint honours. Early on, we had been able to resist attempts to bring us in to joint honours combinations by using the argument that the core programme could not be broken into small parts suitable for combination, and in any case Cultural History was *the* archetypal joint honours course, since it encompassed so many diverse disciplines. As a result the great majority of the cultural history graduates over the first fifteen years, during the up curve, did single honours degrees, whereas almost all of the recent graduates have done joint.

From the other side of the argument, the side of the need for homogenization, of the avoidance of anomaly, came the claim from historians that "We're all cultural historians now." I suppose a few members of our history departments are using approaches that were once the province of the cultural historian. But they are no more true teachers of cultural history than the American teachers of English literature who were so excited by what they called 'the new historicism', otherwise known as old cultural history.

And now the end is in sight for Aberdeen's MA in cultural history. But how good it was while it lasted!

And yet all is not quite lost. A successful cultural history seminar series continues in Aberdeen, and a postgraduate MLitt in cultural history is recruiting students. And there have been very promising developments on the international scene. David Smith and other colleagues organised an international conference to celebrate 21 years of cultural history at Aberdeen in July 2007. Out of that grew the International Society for Cultural History, with a programme of annual conferences, so far meeting in Ghent, Brisbane and Turku, and with plans for a journal published by Edinburgh University Press, the first number of which will appear in 2012. And the international network so established led indirectly to a conference at the University of Mainz on 'Cultural History in Europe: Institutions, Themes, Perspectives' in March 2010, at which I gave a paper on which this chapter is based. For that audience, which included people in the process of developing undergraduate education in cultural history, I hoped that this personal account of our experiences would be helpful. For the readers of this volume it adds to the existing accounts of the programme referred to the Editors' introduction, and will provide details of the academic enterprise in which Peter McCaffery was so enthusiastically engaged during much of the latter part of his academic career.

A poem from the 1980s

JOAN PITTOCK WESSON
University of Aberdeen

During the 1980s the University of Aberdeen faced two phases of budget cuts, as described by Nick Fisher in his essay. These place much stress upon academic staff and were believed to have contributed to three suicides which received national press attention, for example David Kemp's article, 'Death on Campus' in *Scotland and Sunday*, 13 November 1988). The first of thesesuicides was that of Dr Nicola Mackie, an outstanding young classical scholar. I wrote this poem in her memory. It has not been published before, so I am glad to offer it to this volume, as a reminder of Nicola, and of the circumstances in which the MA programme in Cultural History began.

Explorations in Cultural History: Essays for Peter Gabriel McCaffery,
edd. David F. Smith & H. Philsooph (Aberdeen 2010)   ISBN 978-0-9567059-0-7

GHOST

You come to me, little cat:
There you are in my heart.

With a quick shy toss of a mane, half hiding
A bright wild eye, its glint repressing
Amused awareness of time's absurdities.

A crisp hard apple, a donnish Eve;
Adam's equal. So it was difficult
Extricating life from dead stones;
Channelling vitality through so much dust,
So much heat, trivialities, politics, without love – only
A little kindness – where social glimpses of warmth
Closed with the dead hand of affectation.

So articulate, little cat,
With that swift, sure voice as issues were clarified.
Without faith for a future there was so little hope;
For yourself no charity; no sense of your own warm voice,
Total integrity, passion for truth. Having found your ancestors
In the world's corner, where you had made your home,
There where the low headlands stood blue out to sea
(Not wine-dark, you said) the breakwater held the sunlight –
Lightness and promise. That was your good.
Too clear-sighted by far to foster illusion
Unwilling to blur existential horrors
You refused to linger with perplexities
Not susceptible of logical solution.
When dead Romans had become a commodity
Glutting the market: when not even Horace could save you
Nor the sinuous grace of his more than cat loving hold you in place
There was left the slashing shrewdness of a passion out of control
And the freedom to control what fate there was left you
Your courage and dignity seeking repose
Out of modern barbarism into a Roman resolution.

So we salute you: but more –
There is your small form, cheek turned with a chuckle,
Clear brown eye with laughter, the good white glinting,
Your shy self-mocking in the games we all played
Your steely wisdom in battle demanding
Commitment to idealism now long departed
  You could not surrender.

Is it only your ghost?
So richly alive still, so friendly and buoyant
Asserting your sweetness beyond dissolution
As love and regard fasten us to you
More closely than ever you would have imagined.
Now perhaps you wait, a little caught in the shadows,
Holding your pennies for Charon to ferry
Your darling cat spirit to the back of the moon
Where speechless affection and total devotion
Are not to be baffled with death dealing power games
And all love's simplicity lies in the intricate
Delicate empathies Horace has made.

So from the shadows you come with your laughter
With your keenness of mind and your kindness of heart
So gallant a fighter, so certain of vision
How can we have lost you? How let you depart?

The first cohort of Cultural Historians at Aberdeen: a brief memoir from a student's perspective

MARIUS KWINT

University of Portsmouth

Viewing my undergraduate course in Cultural History at Aberdeen from the mid-point of a varied and sometimes choppy academic career, I regard it as a golden moment. This is not just because of the usual nostalgia for the indolent camaraderie of student days. Cultural History at Aberdeen was a genuinely utopian endeavour that was born, as Nick Fisher has correctly characterized it, of constructive resistance as well as engagement with an international intellectual movement. It was formative and even redemptive to me, and has provided me with a robust and useful footing ever since, even though, in Aberdeen at least, the traditional disciplinary waters seem to have closed over it.

Cultural History first presented itself as an opportunity in 1986, during a period that was rather bleak not only in the history of Aberdeen University, but also in my career as a student. Though naturally inclined towards the literary and visual arts, I had gone to Aberdeen to read Geography, because I enjoyed its broad remit as an A-level student, not least its element of outdoor derring-do, and entertained notions that its mix of the social and earth sciences might offer good career prospects. However, this eclecticism became a dissatisfying fragmentation at undergraduate level. In spite of some memorably charismatic and careful teaching, especially from the late John Smith, I couldn't really see much methodological consistency between analyses of the settlement patterns of humans and accounts of the behaviour of glaciers. My performance was erratic, and at the end of the second year, I received a letter permitting me to proceed to honours level only on condition that I applied myself fully.

The problem was no doubt compounded by my disappointment with the social divisions of student life under a Thatcherism in full cry. Like other public institutions in the mid-1980s, universities were under government attack; organized labour, in particular the coal miners, had already been largely defeated. The era was polarized between a sullen, fractious Left in retreat on the one hand, and the exuberant cultural atavism of a triumphant bourgeoisie on the other, manifest in Aberdeen as cliques of 'yahs' who would congregate on King's College lawn after motoring into the city from their rented cottages and farmhouses. Most students

Explorations in Cultural History: Essays for Peter Gabriel McCaffery,
edd. David F. Smith & H. Philsooph (Aberdeen 2010)

ISBN 978-0-9567059-0-7

fulfilled neither stereotype, of course, and I certainly had some good times, but the Granite City in winter felt very far from my East Anglian home.

Rather more straightforwardly, I also faced the option of taking single honours in History of Art. I had originally opted for History of Art alongside Geography at ordinary level to keep my artistic interests alive, and thoroughly enjoyed having been taught by such respected scholars as David Mannings, John Gash and David Irwin. I especially recall one tutorial, where the late Donal Byrne coaxed us patiently through the iconographic layers of Mantegna's *Agony in the Garden* (1460, National Gallery, London), with its depiction of Jerusalem modelled on the recently fallen Constantinople.[1] It was an example of teaching and art-historical method that I have borne in mind ever since. I did not want to lose such wondrous revelations, but I also wanted a more holistic and varied picture, studying for their own sake some of the ideas, histories and societies that substantiated such images. Perhaps unfairly, I was also a little concerned about the subject's dilettantish reputation. In their ignorance, students often turn to myth and hearsay: a couple of fairly conservative historian friends at the time had, for example, taken an option in Social Anthropology in their first years, and enjoyed dismissing the entire subject; I was nevertheless somewhat envious of their set texts, which addressed the concept of 'culture' in usefully and intriguingly holistic ways that seemed well to support my art-historical interests.

The winter of 1985-86 was especially freezing, and during midnight conversations hunched over an electric radiator, I complained to my flatmate about how I wanted a more substantial and challenging curriculum. The intellectual romance and fellowship that I had expected of university had been hard to find. When I later told him about the notices advertising a new course in Cultural History being introduced at honours level only, he replied that it was 'manna from heaven', though he later suspected that it might be 'a cloak-and-dagger way of making cuts'. Another contemporary encouragingly remarked that it looked like a 'good *Mastermind* subject', referring to the BBC's then-popular and somewhat rigorous quiz programme that tested both specialist and general knowledge. The curriculum was certainly attractive, with its promise of 'Enlightenment', 'Romanticism and Reaction', and 'Progress and Decadence' in the first three terms respectively, taught through weekly 'key texts' ranging from Jonathan Swift's *Gulliver's Travels* to Beethoven's *Fidelio*, Mary Shelley's *Frankenstein* and Bram Stoker's

---

[1] Byrne had evidently been informed by Michael Vickers, 'Mantegna and Constantinople', *The Burlington Magazine*, cxviii, 883 (Oct. 1976), 680–7.

Dracula.[2] However, to embark on a new course half-way through university was by any reckoning a considerable risk, and I had a number of questions. One of these, suggested by my flatmate, was whether the novelty of the programme might make high marks harder to achieve. 'Oh come on', retorted the course convenor, Joan Pittock-Wesson, when I put it to her. 'We're not that thick!'

Duly reassured, I signed up, and was glad to begin exercising some of the interests that neither Geography nor History of Art had given full rein. Nigel Dower remarked our group of six was 'lively' after having been tackled on his interpretation of Kant's *Critique of Pure Reason* when he took a class. Thanks to the flexibility of the course, a carefully pastoral approach by Joan Pittock-Wesson, and a tuition ratio where contributing staff outnumbered the students, we were equally able to develop the interests had brought us to the doors of Cultural History. The fact that the course functioned as a kind of potlatch for staff research interests added to the general buoyancy and spirit of adventure. *Dracula*, for example, was taught by Clive Leatherdale from his recent book on the subject, while I remember discussing the significance of Mont Blanc, which I had climbed before matriculating, with Bill Scott during one of his absorbing seminars on the Enlightenment and the French Revolution. Other distinguished teachers included the organist Roger Williams and, influentially, the critical theorist and literary scholar Mike Spiller. The sheer variety was thrilling, but we were sometimes concerned to define and understand the idea of cultural history. Few were familiar with the term 'Cultural History' at the time. Simon Schama's *The Embarrassment of Riches*, which helped to exemplify and popularize a version of cultural-historical method, was not published towards the end of our course in 1988 (when my mother proudly bought it for me). And it was not until 2008 that *The Simpsons* could comfortably have an episode, set in the 1990s, in which Marge takes a college class in Cultural History, and the amorous and manipulative professor shocks her by announcing that all the American founding fathers were 'white male property-owners'.[3]

Only with the commencement of our Senior Honours dissertations and option courses (in my case 'Art and Commerce' with David Irwin and 'Ideas of Death and Destiny' with Andrew Wear) did I begin to study with proper intensity, enjoying the small group or individual tutorials in which we would report on our

---

[2] Christopher Frayling, who was then Professor of Cultural History at the Royal College of Art and later to become Rector there and Chairman of the Arts Council, complimented us on this enticing smorgasbord when he heard David Smith speak about the history of the course at the International Society for Cultural History conference in Turku in 2010.

[3] 'That 90s Show', *The Simpsons*, Season 19, Episode 11 (first broadcast 27 January 2008).

forays into the primary sources, effectively shaping our courses through dialogue with our tutors. We also embarked on some idyllic but industrious reading parties at the Burn near Edzell, an elegantly Neoclassical country house gifted to Goodenough College by the late Mr & Mrs Herbert Russell in memory of their son James, who was killed in action in 1944, aged 21. We enjoyed an astonishingly elite mode of education by any standards. Some pictures from the 1987 visit to The Burn were collected in connection with the 2007 'Varieties of Cultural History' conference and at the time of going to press are still on display the conference website. They show several shots of Peter McCaffery, who, unlike some of us, has changed very little in appearance since those days.

Peter's contribution was profound. To the exciting elements of philosophy and linguistics presented by Eric Matthews and David Cram, he added the social dimensions of ethics, theology, technology and economics that Nigel Dower mentions. It provided a keystone for the cultural-historical meta-structure that I was able to fashion, albeit provisionally, by the time that finals came along, and into which I inserted the various artefacts that I had learned. This 'meta-structure' was basically a modernization thesis. Nigel mentions that few seemed to share Peter's interest in Alasdair Macintyre's *After Virtue* (1981), but my curiosity was sufficiently aroused by his account of this important critique of modernity to offer a paper on it at the Burn.[4] In my dormitory until late the night the night before, I studied the copy that Peter had lent me, and only returned it, a little dog-eared, after finals. His teaching was remarkably learned and patient, and was where Peter could apply the rigour of his Oxford Greats education with characteristic humanity, treating the student as a co-researcher. Tutorials involved a patient, step-by-step dissection of an essay: the balances between rhetoric and substance, evidence and ideas were all thoroughly examined, and, though his attitude was always one of great respect, he would not be bamboozled by any suave undergraduate. He gently suggested that, for instance, my essay on Macintyre's treatment of Kant might have been more persuasive if I had cited the original Kantian texts rather than a dictionary of philosophy, albeit one that had been recommended by Eric Matthews, one of Kant's most authoritative translators. Few students at any university, let along Britain's most northerly, could have hoped for such a potent input of accomplished scholarly energies; it was an age away from the consumerized world of many universities today, and considerably distant from most courses then available at Aberdeen. I don't recall completing any feedback forms.

---

[4] Alasdair MacIntyre: *After Virtue: A Study in Moral Theory,* 2nd ed. (London: Duckworth, 1984).

There was, throughout, a distinct sense of common endeavour among staff and students that helped to overcome differences of personality and background, to say nothing of the challenges of interdisciplinary study. Our morale was no doubt fostered by ritual post-seminar visits to the Machar Bar and the hospitality and commensality of tutors including Paul Dukes and Joan Pittock-Wesson. As finals ended on an early June day in 1988, we emerged from the Elphinstone Hall in glorious sunshine and made our way the short distance to Nick and Beth Fisher's charming stone house in the High Street of Old Aberdeen to relax with beer in their garden. In the delicious idleness of the succeeding days, four of us students then took a camping trip by train to a midge-ridden Skye, before returning in July for the graduation ceremony at Marischal College, when Aberdeen was again at its sparkling finest. Our results were unusually strong, and we appreciated Joan Pittock-Wesson's presence, beaming with pride as she conversed with our families. That night, however, staying at a bed and breakfast near the Aberdeen Royal Infirmary, my family and I were woken up by the sound of helicopters ferrying injured and dying workers from the Piper Alpha oil platform disaster in the North Sea. And only weeks later, I was shocked to hear from a colleague on a summer job that two lecturers in History of Art and Classics at Aberdeen had taken their own lives. She didn't recall the names, but from the information she gave, I surmised that it was Donal Byrne and Nicola Mackie, the latter of whom had also contributed to the course.

So the realities of political economy caught up with us. Their jobs cut, Andrew Wear went to the Wellcome Trust Centre for the History of Medicine at University College, London, and David Cram headed, like me, to Oxford University. There, as a Fellow of Jesus College, he later told me that Cultural History 'kept us sane' during the bureaucratic enormities the staff was suffering. The course continued on its decade of success, while I adjusted to the technocratic empiricism and canonical obeisance of much of Oxford. Although there was much to learn there, and many gaps to fill, my doctoral thesis in history on the circus in eighteenth-century London in several respects hankered after the broad purview and exhilarating sense of academic totality that I recalled from Cultural History. By a happy combination of initiative, goodwill, experience, trust in their students, and sheer obstinacy, the put-upon staff at Aberdeen was able to construct a course that, for a couple of decades, challenged the modern sundering of knowledge that MacIntyre and Marx alike criticized, and engaged the fullness of the intellect as far as might be possible in an academic situation. Peter McCaffery and his colleagues showed that historical thinking could take the infinity and indivisibility of culture as its premise. They allowed Cultural History to be more than just the history of such apparently 'cultural' activities as art, literature or leisure. Culture is not wholly restricted to time and place. And we are not all Cultural Historians now.

Sociological Reflections on the History of a Sociology Department

NORMAN STOCKMAN
University of Aberdeen

PREFATORY NOTE

This chapter is a slightly revised version of a talk I was invited to give on the occasion of the celebration of the fortieth anniversary of the establishment of the department of sociology at the University of Aberdeen, at which all but one former heads of department were present. I was at the time (May 2005) the longest serving member of the department, and was about to retire from my post. Peter McCaffery was of course a lecturer in the department for nearly twenty years in the 1970s and 1980s, where he is remembered by us old ones as a stimulating and impressively knowledgeable colleague, and also familiar to many newer members through his frequent subsequent participation in seminars. I am honoured to offer the paper to this collection. I have made very few amendments to the paper as delivered, and have left it in the style of a talk.

INTRODUCTION

When John Brewer (the then head of the department of sociology) first asked me to do this talk, it was intended as the last in a series of seminars on sociology in Aberdeen, allocated to me as a *rite de passage* to mark my impending retirement. We realised only later that my retirement more or less coincided with the fortieth anniversary of the establishment of the department of sociology, where I have worked for all but three of those forty years, and the occasion expanded from a simple departmental research seminar to this celebratory occasion. For such a ritual fine words are expected, and I am pleased that we have already been able to hear such fine words earlier today. It lets me off the hook, since I am not easily given to fine words, and had all along planned to deliver myself, not of a panegyric, but of a mundane piece of sociological analysis, as befits a sociological seminar. What I would like to do is to reflect sociologically on the changing conditions of work as a sociologist, changing conditions that have been shared in many respects by all academics working in British universities since the 1960s. It's an exercise in the sociology of work and in the sociology of higher education, an attempt to stand back from our day to day work and view it sociologically.

Explorations in Cultural History: Essays for Peter Gabriel McCaffery,
edd. David F. Smith & H. Philsooph (Aberdeen 2010)   ISBN 978-0-9567059-0-7

I've had in the back of my mind while preparing this talk a model of such a 'reflexive' sociological analysis of the conditions of sociological work, and that is a paper given at a departmental seminar some time in the 1970s by a former, and late lamented, colleague Phil Strong, in whose memory the BSA Phil Strong book prize was established. Phil's paper was entitled 'Some limitations on the nature of sociological production', and I still have a yellowing copy if anyone would like to read it. I believe it's the paper of which the then head of department Michael Percy Carter (not present here today unless as an unquiet spirit) remarked that it was tantamount to 'shitting in one's own nest'. Such excremental activity was clearly to be severely deprecated at that time. However, now that faecal sociology has been given such a significant boost by one of our still extant colleagues (Inglis 2001), perhaps my modest droppings will be received more tolerantly. In any case, I promise to clear up after myself. I also promise, just in case anyone is getting anxious, not to spill any beans, always assuming there are any to be spilt. I will not, in the words of another colleague, be telling where the dead bodies are buried, all skeletons will remain firmly in their closets, no reputations, such as they may be, will be damaged. Anyone hoping for dirt to be dished has come to the wrong performance. I will, in fact, only occasionally mention names. Those not prepared to be bored may leave now. Here endeth the *leçon sur le leçon*.

DEPARTMENTS AS ORGANISATIONS

I begin, as seems appropriate, with the department as an organisational form. As the American sociologist of higher education Burton Clark proposed, and as Tim Ingold reminded us most vigorously in his lecture to inaugurate the department of anthropology (Ingold 2003), a department can be characterised as the point of intersection of an academic discipline and an institution of higher education. In the case of departments of sociology, and surely of others too, much has changed over forty years in both vectors of this intersection, the discipline and the institution, as well as the ways in which they intersect. Let me begin by sketching out some elementary features of each, beginning with the discipline.

It is difficult at this distance to realise how recent and with such shallow roots had been the development of the discipline of sociology in Britain by the 1960s. Those of us who teach the history of sociological thought have a habit of pushing back the ancestry as far as possible, and for a number of years I have amused myself (and probably no-one else) by telling third year students that the early sociologists Comte and Spencer had their forerunners in the philosophers and speculative historians of the Scottish Enlightenment and *their* predecessors such as Montesquieu and Vico; and that even that line of putative descent occupies but a brief historical moment when set against the heritage constructed for sociology in the Islamic world going back to Ibn Khaldun and Ibn Battuta or that in Chinese sociology tracing its origins back to Confucianists such as Xunzi. All well and good, at least as ancestor worship. But as an institutionalised academic discipline, sociology barely existed in Britain before the Second World War, despite the formation of the Sociological Society in 1903 and the establishment of the LSE chair in 1907 (shortly followed by that in Liverpool). When the department was founded in Aberdeen there was but a handful of departments of sociology already existing in Britain and none in Scotland (I've recently been conducting a friendly precedence dispute with Edinburgh on our behalf, and I think we're winning), the British Sociological Association (BSA) had been founded only in 1951 and the journal *Sociology* had not yet started publication. It is scarcely surprising that when Raymond Illsley, the first head of department, initially took up his appointment as MRC sociologist in the Social Medicine Research Unit under Professor Dugald Baird in 1951 he, by his own later admission, barely knew what the subject was (Aberdeen University 1985). My own first encounter with sociology, as an undergraduate student, just at the time when the Aberdeen department was being set up, gave me no inkling that the discipline had such a flimsy institutional existence (the very notion that disciplines *had* a history was one of which I only later became aware) and even the experience of being appointed to a lectureship before I had completed my postgraduate master's course did not give me a clue, innocent as I was, that the discipline was still in its infancy. By then it was growing at a tremendous rate, shortly resembling (to force the metaphor) a gangling adolescent barely able to stand upright on its spindly legs. The expansion, measured for example in terms of numbers of departments, student enrolments, and membership of the BSA, has been documented in two recent books by A. H. Halsey, Emeritus Fellow in sociology at Nuffield College, Oxford, and one of Britain's leading sociologists of education (Halsey 2004) and Jennifer Platt, Emeritus Professor of Sociology at the University of Sussex and former President of the BSA (Platt 2003), and does not need to be repeated here.

This leads me to my initial sketch of the institutions of higher education. I went up (as they used to say) from school to university in the same year that the Royal Commission on Higher Education issued its report, the Robbins Report (Great Britain Committee on Higher Education 1963). Robbins promulgated the famous principle that a university place should be available for every school-leaver qualified and willing to benefit from it, and recommended an expansion of universities to take 17 percent of the age-cohort by 1981, by contrast with the 8 percent in 1963. But in fact universities had been growing fast since the end of the war, financed by increasing amounts of state funding channelled through the UGC (University Grants Committee), and populated not only by school-leavers but also by demobilised servicemen and -women whose ambitions had been delayed or stimulated by their wartime experiences. The expansion, speeded up in the 1960s by governments' acceptance of Robbins's arguments for growth in the national interest, lasted in fact only until 1973, when it was rudely interrupted by budget cuts occasioned by the oil price crisis and even more rudely by the Thatcher cuts of 1981. Aberdeen, favoured by UGC policy, expanded faster than most and had further to fall.

It was in this so-called 'golden age' of British universities that the Department of Sociology was established in Aberdeen. This graph of the

Teaching Staff 1965-2004

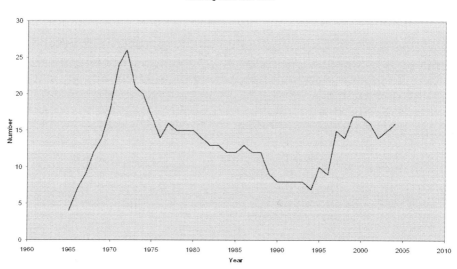

changing size of the department (lecturing staff only) shows the local manifestation of national (and in fact international) trends. The very rapid expansion in the late 1960s and early 1970s was the lagged consequence of very rapid growth in student numbers. For example, when I arrived in 1968 there were more than 500 students registered for the first year course, then called 'Ordinary Sociology', a figure that has still not been equalled in the last decade of recovery. Until the Psychology building was erected with its Arts Lecture Theatre, there was no lecture room large enough to hold such numbers and lectures had to be given twice. The explosion of sociology was quite a phenomenon at what was then still a small university, with fewer than three-and-a-half thousand undergraduate students in 1965-66, the first year of the department's teaching operations; this modest figure itself represented a three-fold increase since 1945. The student-staff ratio in sociology was well over 20:1, at a time when the UGC norm which was the basis for university funding was still 10:1. There was at that time no provision for teaching assistants, and teaching loads were much higher than now, and only kept within some limits by drafting in research staff from the medical sociology unit referred to as 'the Hut' (for further information on 'the Hut', see below and van Teilingen and Barbour 1996). The very high student demand for sociology also caused some friction with the rest of the Faculty of Arts within which the department was located (there was no body of university government specifically for the social sciences until a sub-committee of the Faculty of Arts called the Committee for Social Science was established in 1966). Five hundred students would have represented more than half of the entire first year intake into the MA degree in the late 1960s, and this rate of recruitment caused resentment among more traditional departments in a university that was not at all sure that it really wanted this new-fangled subject so closely associated in the public mind with the radical student movement. They probably thought that the rapid growth of sociology was a bubble that would soon burst, and with hindsight they were right.

Now, having given some general impression of the early days of the department, as the intersection of a newly forming discipline and a rapidly expanding HE institution, I want to turn to some analytical issues which will allow me to explore sociologically the changing organisational contexts of our work as sociologists over four decades. To help me structure this very provisional analysis, I turn again to Burton Clark who, in his book *The Higher Education System*, proposed a framework of concepts for the comparative sociological study of higher education in a variety of different societies. Clark's analysis is thorough and comprehensive, and covers many dimensions of variation in higher education systems, of which I can here take up only a few. I begin, as Clark does, with the work itself, aspects of the division of knowledge-processing labour that characterises universities.

Clark argues that the discipline is the core membership group in academic systems, that each disciplinary unit has self-evident and acclaimed primacy in its front-line tasks, and that the characteristics of core membership groups affect everything else of importance in the organisation (Clark 1983: 33-4). What varies between different higher education systems is the way in which this disciplinary activity is institutionalised and differentiated. Clark proposes to analyse this differentiation using a four-fold conceptual framework, highlighting differentiation that occurs horizontally and vertically, within institutions and among them. Horizontally differentiated units within institutions are referred to as *sections*, and vertical arrangements as *tiers*. Among institutions, horizontal separations are called *sectors*, and vertical ones *hierarchies*. I plan to concentrate mostly on differentiation *within* the institution of Aberdeen University, and mostly on horizontal differentiation, though I will say just a little about vertical differentiation later. I will return to issues connected with differentiation between institutions towards the end of this talk.

By being constituted as a department, the discipline of sociology became, in Clark's terms, a *section*, alongside others that already existed. However, as Clark mentions, disciplinary boundaries and the internal structure of knowledge tend to be more uncertain in disciplines such as sociology, and the disciplinary identity of this section has not remained stable or uncontested over time. Early on in its history (I believe in 1966), the department took on responsibility for courses in Applied Social Studies, and at least one lecturer in social work was a member of the department until a separate Department of Social Work was established in 1973, which remained in existence until courses in social work were transferred to Robert Gordon's Institute of Technology (later to be Robert Gordon's University) in 1988. In 1970, the decision was taken to extend the activities of the department to include courses in social anthropology, and between 1971 and 1977 five posts were filled with anthropologists, and a joint degree in sociology and anthropology was constructed within the department of sociology. Relations between the disciplines were much debated by interested members of staff, with a diversity of views, but with no attempt to divide the department into two. There was even some joint teaching, such as the course called 'Major Themes in Sociology and Anthropology' taught by Chuck Jedrej and myself. This arrangement was severely affected by the 1981 cuts which eventually led to a number of anthropologists leaving Aberdeen and the remaining handful in the position of having to run down the degree and see the last cohort of existing students through to graduation in 1991. More recently, of course, a similar development was attempted and implemented beginning with the appointment of a professor of anthropology (Tim Ingold) in 1999, but with the quite different outcome of the formation of a separate department of anthropology in 2003.

Another, and highly consequential, aspect of horizontal disciplinary differentiation was the internal differentiation out of medical sociology as a separate section. Clark shows how in traditional Italian and French universities, for example, departments have not existed, and sections have been constituted by chairs in specialisms that might be defined more or less narrowly. Essentially, this is what happened in Aberdeen in the case of medical sociology. As is widely known, the prehistory of the department was the existence of sociological work in the department of Obstetrics and Gynaecology under the leadership of Dugald Baird as part of a unit funded by the Medical Research Council. The unit had various names and statuses throughout the 50s and early 60s, and its renaming as the Medical Sociology Research Unit in 1964 (located in a building on the hospital campus known familiarly as 'the Hut'), with Raymond Illsley as Director after Dugald Baird's retirement, coincided with the establishment of the department of sociology. The combination of a well-funded and productive research group in medical sociology and a rapidly growing university department constituted the largest concentration of sociologists anywhere in Britain in the late 60s and early 70s, and I will come back later to reflect on the possibilities inherent in that situation. However, the estrangement of the research unit and the department that followed the transfer of department headship to the second professor, M. P. Carter, resulted in the formation of a section rather similar to the chair structure of some continental university systems, namely the Institute of Medical Sociology as a research institute with doctoral students, headed by a Professor of Medical Sociology only notionally located within the sociology department. As Bob Dingwall, one of those doctoral students who became a research fellow in the institute on his way to higher things (currently Professor in the Institute for Science and Society at the University of Nottingham), remarked in his own contribution to this seminar series, eventually the institute and the department had very little to do with each other apart from some personal contacts.

Finally on the disciplinary make-up of the department, the Department of Education, which had a long history dating back to the nineteenth century, was dissolved into the Centre for Educational Research in 1997 and the remaining staff incorporated into the department of sociology. So far as I am aware, there has been little if any discussion within the department concerning the relation between sociology and education as disciplinary fields.

It seems that Clark's view of sociology as a weakly defined discipline with uncertain boundaries with others is at least partly borne out by the experience in Aberdeen over forty years. And yet the boundaries with most other disciplines, including other social sciences, have remained rather rigid and impermeable. At the department's lowest point in 1990, the proposal from the then Dean that sociology should merge with the department of politics and international relations was met with determined opposition from both sides. There has been rather little collaborative research spanning departments (though this may be changing), and (so-called) joint degree programmes have generally been constructed, as is typical in Aberdeen at least in the arts and social sciences, by each department laying down required courses in its own field, with little if any attention paid to possible disciplinary interrelationships.

A section identified in disciplinary terms is deemed to be 'authoritative in its own field of learning' (Moodie and Eustace 1974: 61). Just as in any other department, this was formally the case with the department of sociology, and in principle has remained so. Nobody else apart from sociologists has any license to pronounce on sociological knowledge, to say what should be taught in sociology courses or what topics should be studied by sociologists in their research. This does not preclude the fact that requirements emanating from outwith the department have increasingly impinged on *how* teaching and research should be carried out, and I will return later to this large topic.

Another aspect of horizontal institutional differentiation that Clark discusses concerns the way disciplinary sections are combined into larger groupings such as faculties, schools and colleges. Here the experience of the department of sociology has been somewhat unstable. The department has been part, successively, of the following groupings: the Faculty of Arts, the Committee for Social Science within the Faculty of Arts, the Faculty of Arts and Social Sciences, the Faculty of Social Sciences, the Faculty of Economic and Social Sciences, the Faculty of Social Sciences and Law, the School of Social Sciences, and most recently the School of Social Sciences within the College of Arts and Social Sciences. The first four of this list reflected the growing importance and autonomy of the social sciences, culminating in the Faculty of Social Sciences as a recognised distinct sectional interest group; the last four, with shifting combinations of departments and the new terminology of schools and colleges, reflect the managerial reorganisation of the university from the late 1980s, to which I will return. The early faculties were relatively self-governing collegiate bodies of the traditional type, with elected Deans holding office for short periods and representing the faculty as *primus* (seldom *prima*) *inter pares*. The later faculties, schools and colleges, as we all know, are levels in the hierarchical line management system, headed by appointed Deans and Heads with executive powers.

One might wonder whether involvement in such wider sections of the university might expand the notion of membership beyond the core group of the discipline. I have no systematic evidence with which to test such a hypothesis, nor, curiously, have I yet found any discussion of the topic in the sociological literature on higher education. However, my speculative response would be to doubt it. Participation in academic bodies beyond the department has been a minority activity throughout the forty years of the department's existence. Partly this is because only nominated or elected representatives have been eligible to attend the relevant committees, but even the radical move taken in the 1970s by the Faculty of Arts and Social Sciences to open attendance and voting membership to all full-time permanent members of the component departments did little to increase participation and may even have decreased it. In more recent times, attendance and active participation at the open forums at faculty, school or college levels seems to have been quite weak, a fact that I would interpret in relation to the line-management structure into which these forums are inserted, on which more later. In general there seems to have been little interest in the department in the wider committee structure of the university, and representatives have often not been required to report back to their constituency. As for inter-disciplinary academic activities, these too have been sporadic and only occasionally generative of wider membership involvement. Speaking personally, the high-points of inter-disciplinary discussion that some think is the very point of universities came early on in my career at Aberdeen, with the History and Philosophy of Science Seminar promoted by the now defunct department of the same name, and the lecture series on great thinkers of the twentieth century organised by Joan Pittock-Wesson (which eventually resulted in the Cultural History programme, where Peter McCaffery found a congenial home after leaving the sociology department). Such academic activities, however, did little to break down disciplinary boundaries as the key feature of horizontal differentiation of the institution. In the case of sociology, I think this structural feature may have been accentuated by a kind of bunker mentality as a response to being a pariah discipline. Sociology has never been taken seriously as a discipline by members of more traditional arts departments, let alone those in the natural sciences, and even (or perhaps especially) other social sciences have not been particularly welcoming. Sociology has of course been replaced as chief rubbish subject in the columns of such papers as *The Daily Telegraph* by media studies, but nonetheless I find that the level of disparaging humour of which sociology is the butt from representatives of other disciplines has not markedly reduced over the years.

The one area in which involvement with members of other disciplines has at times been more intense is trade union activity in relation to general employment conditions in the university. The department has always had a very high rate of membership in the AUT (now the UCU), although active membership, as in other departments, has tended to flourish only at times of great anger and tension over worsening employment conditions, which leading scholars such as Halsey refer to as 'the proletarianisation of academic labour' or 'the decline of donnish dominion' (Halsey 1995). Most obviously, this heightened activity has occurred during pay disputes and especially those that have provoked strike action, in which departmental AUT members have distinguished themselves on the picket-lines alongside sisters and brothers from other departments. However, there was also one specific episode that took place more than twenty years ago and so may not be well known to more recent members of the department. The letters sent by the UGC to universities on 1st July 1981 set out the reductions that universities had to make in the light of drastically lower funding for higher education in the Expenditure White Paper of March that year. All over the country the AUT mobilised to try to defend the jobs of its members. In Aberdeen, where the level of cuts imposed by the UGC was particularly high, a 'ginger group' (wrongly called a 'splinter group' in Kogan and Kogan 1983: 74) emerged to encourage the AAUT towards more determined opposition to the plans of the Principal, Court and Senatus to implement reductions in staffing, by compulsory redundancy if necessary. This group published a weekly newsletter entitled 'Alternatives' and sub-titled 'The Campaign Newsletter of the AAUT'. The title 'Alternatives' was chosen as a deliberate reference to the Thatcher slogan 'TINA' – 'There Is No Alternative'. The group consisted of members of AAUT from several departments, but the location of the writing and duplicating activities was the offices of the department of sociology, and members of the department played a prominent role. Every week, including weekends, for several months, the group gathered to collect information about developments in Aberdeen and other universities, and to write stirring editorials to mobilise the membership and encourage the AAUT committee. I still proudly possess a virtually complete run of this scurrilous publication. 'It was the worst of times, it was the best of times.' This trade union activity did more to cement some personal friendships and solidarities across departmental boundaries than any of the inter-disciplinary academic work or committee work on faculty boards that I have just mentioned. Its consequences in that sense were long-lasting, and in fact the group revived 'Alternatives' in the years 1986-88 to aid campus-wide discussion of plans for the university being proposed by the Principal, Court and Senatus. However important it was in the lives of activists, though, it clearly did nothing in the long run to affect the sectional boundaries between departments. If anything, the new management structures and funding procedures set up in the wake of the Thatcher cuts have made relationships between sections of the university - departments, faculties, schools and colleges - more competitive and conflictual than they ever were, as the struggle for scarce resources takes on more of the character of a zero-sum game.

Surveys of university academics, in Britain and internationally, have repeatedly shown that they are far more attached to their discipline than to their employing institution. This is hardly surprising. As many writers have pointed out, commitment to the discipline is the result of deliberate choice and many years of hard work, whereas employment in a particular institution is often, perhaps usually, the outcome of the fleeting vagaries of the academic labour market. An academic is far more likely to change institution in pursuing a disciplinary career than to change discipline within the same institution. Given everything I have just said about disciplinary boundaries in Aberdeen, there is no reason to doubt that the same reasoning would apply to most of the members of the sociology department over the years and decades.

WORK IN A DEPARTMENT

And so I turn to the division of labour within the department. Several different categories of staff work in a department, but I first concentrate on the lecturing staff. As we all know, and as is often pointed out in the research literature, the work of university lecturers is very imprecisely specified and comprises a wide range of apparently disparate activities. Contracts for university lecturers are usually framed in general terms and do not really make it clear what staff are expected to do or how much of it they are supposed to do. This state of affairs is actually not at all uncommon in a variety of occupations. Before he was famous, the sociologist who in my opinion did most to analyse this characteristic of occupations was Ulrich Beck who, together with his colleagues Michael Brater and Hansjürgen Daheim, wrote a series of books (e.g. Beck *et al* 1980) on the social conditions in which occupations, and the occupational form itself, were historically constituted. They conceived of occupations as bundles of activities that are packaged in such a way that they can be bought and sold on the labour market, and they conducted a series of specific studies of the economic, political and cultural conditions in which such packages come about, a process for which they coined the wonderful word '*Verberuflichung*' or 'occupationalisation'. I can't here do more than suggest programmatically that such an approach would be very valuable in understanding the occupation of university lecturer. All I want to do here is to make a few stabs at summarising how the package of activities that lecturers in the department are expected to undertake has shifted over the last forty years, and outline some of the strains that have emerged between components of the package.

We have become used to summarising the duties of university lecturers under the three heads of teaching, research and administration. In principle one could have used the same three categories in the early years of the department's existence. However, I think it can be argued that the character and balance of the three components was significantly different at that time, for a variety of structural, cultural and technical reasons. (The technical factors relate mostly to the IT revolution, and the changing division of labour between lecturers and secretaries, but I'm afraid I don't have space to do justice to that fascinating aspect of the department.) The department of sociology was most unusual (compared with departments in other disciplines in the arts and social sciences) in having been, as it were, born out of a pre-existing research unit, and one located in a faculty, namely the Faculty of Medicine, whose research culture was much closer to that of the natural sciences. Not only the first Professor of Sociology, but also some of the early appointed staff, had considerable research experience in that medical environment. It is not surprising, therefore, that early research plans for sociology were conceived as a continuation and expansion of the research programme of the medical sociologists who pre-dated the department, with an emphasis on policy-related, epidemiological and demographic projects. In his inaugural lecture, incendiarily entitled 'The explosion of sociology', Raymond Illsley made a distinction that would have been easily understood within the university at the time, between this kind of research, that is best carried out by full-time researchers within a research institute, and 'scholarly research' that is more congenial to lecturers whose primary task is teaching. He argued that, although people pursuing these two types of inquiry can profitably learn from each other, the conditions that favour each type remain very different. The basis was therefore laid for a distinction, and an institutional differentiation, of research on the one hand and teaching and scholarship on the other.

I think it can be said that the department was, at that time, and to put it in Northern Irish terms, the teaching wing of the research unit. In a document setting out 'The Research Programme of the Department of Sociology and the Medical Sociology Research Unit' dated August 1967, the list of the department's membership is divided into 'Teaching Staff' and 'Research Staff', and the Unit's membership are listed as 'Director' and 'Research Staff'. (In fact, the distinction between research staff in the Department and those in the Unit was merely a matter of the source of their funding; most research staff were located at Foresterhill in 'the Hut'.) Although the 'Regulations for the Appointment of Senior Lecturers, Lecturers and Assistant Lecturers' dated October 1967 (the nearest thing I had to a contract when I was appointed) do lay down in paragraph 4 that lecturers 'will be required to engage in research or higher study', this requirement seems to be subsidiary to paragraph 1, according to which a lecturer 'shall undertake, in addition to lecturing, such duties as may be required in the Department to which he is attached'. (Note, incidentally, the gendered language, an issue I'll come back to briefly later.) Aberdeen in the 1960s was not yet much of a research university. Historians of the university have pointed out that, although one can identify several important scientific contributions made by Aberdeen professors over the years, the university was much more oriented towards undergraduate teaching in the standard range of disciplines found in traditional Scottish universities. A story told me by a friend in a traditional department, whose first appointment dated to around 1960, illustrates the point. On appointment as an assistant lecturer, he was allocated his teaching duties, and duly went on to prepare and give his lectures, conduct his tutorials, mark essays and exam scripts, and generally to perform 'such duties' as were required of him in his department. After a couple of years of this, he went to his head of department and enquired whether, in addition to his teaching responsibilities, there might not be something called 'research' of which he had heard mention, and whether perhaps he should be doing some of it, whatever it was. He received the reply: 'If you want to make a name for yourself, laddie, that's your business. Your job here is to teach students'. Several years later, when there was far more talk of research and the beginnings of moves to monitor the amount and quality of research done in departments, one response of some members of traditional arts departments was to make jokes about whether the word concerned was correctly pronounced '*ree*-search' or 're-*search*' (the OED kindly allows both).

This emphasis on teaching and research as separate activities took a more specific form in the discipline of sociology in Aberdeen. The fact that the same person (Illsley) was both head of a teaching department and director of a research institute, coupled with the fact that these units had different institutional and geographical locations and to a great extent different personnel, suggests a complex differentiated structure very different from the current assumption of the integration of teaching and research in the same unit and same staff. The argument was pushed even further by Phil Strong in his excremental paper I referred to earlier. In that paper, the 'limitations of production of sociological knowledge' that Phil Strong discussed were essentially the limitations placed on research by the requirements of teaching. He argued that the work of a department was entirely structured around the timetables and rhythms of undergraduate teaching, with its far-reaching demands on the time of lecturers, which made commitment to large-scale and extensive research projects very difficult. The logical consequence was drawn by Raymond Illsley, that individuals who wanted to conduct or take part in such research projects should have the opportunity to be withdrawn from teaching altogether for periods of time determined by the needs of the research. Nowadays, the same end can be pursued as a personal project by individuals buying themselves out of teaching and using part of their research grant to pay for substitute teachers. As head of both department and research institute, Illsley attempted a more far-reaching structural solution which in principle would have allowed a new kind of career path, by providing opportunities for teachers from the department to move to the research institute for a period of years and then to return to the department once the research project had been brought to fruition. It was an imaginative approach to a deep-rooted structural problem, but it foundered on the estrangement of department and institute following the appointment of the second professor as head of department[1]. One can only speculate what might have happened to sociology in Aberdeen had this opportunity not thereby been lost.

Be that as it may, the climate has changed very considerably since those days. One should not over-emphasise the change, of course. Research and publication had long been one of the main criteria for promotion in Aberdeen as elsewhere, and that in itself provided an incentive for lecturers to do 'some of it, whatever it was'. But not very much happened to lecturers who didn't publish, apart from not getting promoted (and there were notable exceptions to that rule). It was very much as if 'making a name for oneself' was an optional extra, and the career grade of lecturer was primarily a teaching job. With the introduction of research selectivity and eventually the RAE as we have learned to know and love it, senior personnel in Aberdeen as elsewhere began to talk much more of the mission of the university as conducting 'teaching in an atmosphere of research'. This was a new Humboldtean conception for Aberdeen, which had traditionally cleaved closer to Newman's idea of a university. It has changed the 'package of activities' that is expected of a university lecturer. Now, as we know, lecturers are expected to devote themselves to research and publication, as much as possible and of as high a quality (as measured by developing criteria) as possible. Yet the problems of combining teaching and research identified by Phil Strong have not gone away. The main way in which these problems have been tackled has been by relieving lecturing staff of the burden of high teaching loads to make time for research. And the way this has been done, in the face of student-staff ratios that have become steadily worse over the decades, and are now in sociology even worse than at the height of the explosion of sociology in the late 1960s, has been by the creation of new categories of staff in the department, namely teaching assistants and teaching fellows.

---

[1] In a private communication of May 2005, Raymond Illsley told me that he had tried in 1983 to raise the strategic issue of the relationship of teaching and research on the ESRC, but could not provoke interest in the matter. He sent me copies of position papers he wrote at the time.

There is now a considerable literature on the growth of what some call the new academic 'underclass' of teaching assistants, because it is such a widespread phenomenon. Since about the mid-90s, universities including Aberdeen have put increasing budgetary resources into employing teaching assistants with the primary aim of improving the RAE performance of lecturing staff. I don't have statistics of the numbers of TAs in the department, but no doubt course co-ordinators, heads of department and head of school keep records of who is employed each year and statistics would be easy enough to compile. What is significant is that enough TAs are employed to relieve lecturing staff of virtually all tutorial classes in first and second year courses, a considerable transformation in the way these courses are delivered, and with important consequences for how teaching is done. The point of calling TAs an underclass relates to their conditions of employment and their career prospects. As we know, they consist of a variety of categories of people: some are post-graduate students who take on teaching to earn money to pay their way through graduate training and to build up their CVs; others have completed doctorates but cannot find more permanent academic positions; others still have withdrawn from graduate study and take on tutoring as a temporary source of income which as the years go on may become less temporary. They are often hourly paid, at rates that are well above the statutory minimum wage but well below other work for similarly qualified employees. Recent legislation based on European court rulings have given some teaching assistants rights to permanent contracts once they have worked for a certain number of years, but I have heard that some universities' response is to evade their commitments to such employees by abolishing their jobs. From a perspective drawn from theories of labour market segmentation, it is difficult to avoid the conclusion that the armies of teaching assistants across the country have many of the characteristics of a secondary labour force. Their orientations, social location, and life chances would repay investigation.

In addition to this group of employees specialised in teaching, there is of course also a category of staff specialised in research. Because of the genesis of the department in medical research, in the early years of the department there was a large number of staff in this category. A couple of graphs illustrate the changes over the years. Research staff contractually located in the department appear in substantial numbers in the first ten years of the department's existence, then fall back to negligible numbers from the mid-1970s. I haven't had time to extend the series beyond 1994, when my main sources, university calendars and staff lists, ceased to publish such information. The last ten years will have seen a small increase in comparable numbers, mainly through the addition of the Centre for

Research Staff - Department plus Institutes 1965-1994

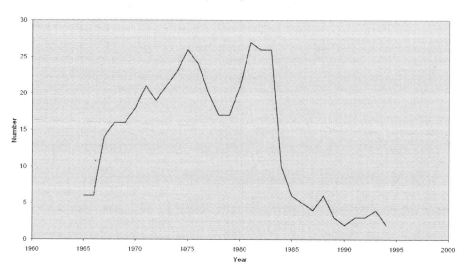

Educational Research and the later Rowan Group[2]. A second graph shows totals of research staff located in the department and in sociological research institutes,

Research Staff - Department 1965-1994

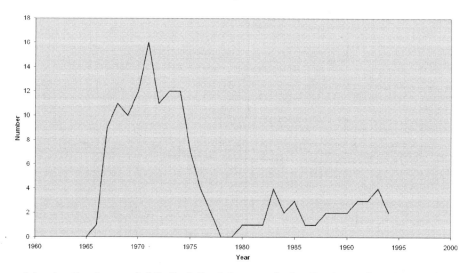

mainly the Institute of Medical Sociology and the Institute for the Study of Sparsely Populated Areas. Here the high numbers last until the closure of the

---

[2] The Rowan Group was a group of staff and postgraduate students with primary interests in education. It derived ultimately from the earlier merger of the Department of Education into the Department of Sociology.

Institute of Medical Sociology in 1984-85 and the transfer of most of its staff to Glasgow.

In terms of the structure of the department, it seems clear that there has developed a differentiation of levels of membership. Full membership of the department is held by the permanent lecturing staff, who are supposed to combine teaching and research, and who have established customary rights to attend staff meetings and to participate in collective decision-making. Staff who have exclusive responsibilities for either teaching or research are not usually included in staff meetings and are not treated as full members of the department. Once again, adherents of dual labour market analysis would see here a distinction between a core and a peripheral labour force.

Before I leave this sketch of the internal differentiation of the department, I want to touch briefly on two other aspects of it. One of these was stressed by Phil Strong in the excremental paper, and it has become an important theme in the research literature on higher education. As Burton Clark argues, although the discipline can be seen to be the core membership group for academics, disciplines themselves undergo continual processes of differentiation into sub-disciplines. This can easily be demonstrated in sociology, by referring to the proliferation of specialist journals, specialist conferences, sub-disciplinary study groups within the BSA and research committees within the ISA, and so on. A teaching department offering a wide range of courses will necessarily employ a variety of specialists in different branches of the discipline. These specialists will tend to be oriented for intellectual stimulation and competition more to their colleagues within their sub-discipline, who will be scattered throughout the country and indeed the world in 'invisible colleges', than they are to their immediate colleagues within the department. The internet and e-mail have made it increasingly easy to carry on intense intellectual discussion and exchange of information within sub-disciplines across the globe. To put it strongly, namely in the manner of Phil Strong, members of a department may have little interest in each other's work and little to talk to each other about apart from the administrative banalities and personal gossip of everyday departmental life. By contrast, members of a research group or institute, such as the Rowan Group in the department, are far more likely to share interests, even if their particular research projects diverge in detail. Anyone who's spent time in a research institute as opposed to a teaching department will recognise this distinction. A consequence is that the quality of academic intercourse in the two settings is quite different. It seems to me, for example, that this process of 'sub-disciplinisation', together with the increasing emphasis on individual research productivity, underlies the difficulty the department has had in sustaining an active research seminar over the years. It also means that, in the context of teaching, each lecturer is treated as 'authoritative in his or her own field of learning', just as each disciplinary section is so treated in the wider university context. This increases the tendency for the degree curriculum to be balkanised rather than integrated.

The second aspect of differentiation that I want to mention briefly is that of gender. For much of the history of the department, staff meetings, which are attended by full members of the lecturing staff, have been almost a female-free zone. This chart shows the breakdown of the total lecturing staff into male and

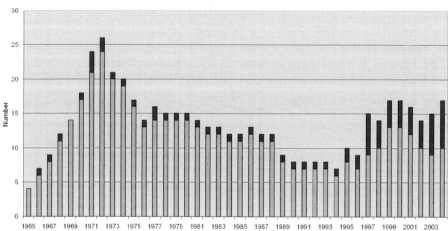

Lecturing Staff by Gender

female. For many years, the small red column represents just one female person. Only well into the 1990s did this situation begin to change. Aberdeen University has been much criticised for its failure to employ women, and it remains quite close to the bottom of the league table of the proportions of professors who are female. Until the appointments this year (2005), there has never been a female professor in the sociology department[3]. There is much that could be said about this state of affairs, which has been thoroughly investigated in a large-scale comparative survey of the academic careers of women in several countries of the European Union. Information about it can be found on its website, www.women-eu.de. One of the most interesting findings is worth reporting here, relating to a marked difference between top male and female academics (equivalent to full professors) in their family and household circumstances. Especially in more

---

[3] In the years since 2005, there have been several appointments of females to departmental staff, including two professors, and the gender balance is now much more even.

conservative countries such as Germany, whereas male professors were very likely to live in conventional 'cornflake packet' households with a wife (often not economically active) and children, female professors were markedly more likely to be either unpartnered or childless or both. This supports the argument often advanced in such contexts, that women are faced with a much starker choice between family and career than men are. It is interesting that a quick and unsystematic recollection of the household circumstances of the people who have held full lecturing posts in the sociology department over forty years would, without mentioning names, provide some partial corroboration of this pattern.

I have said a lot about the dimension of differentiation of the higher education system that Burton Clark calls 'sectional', the horizontal differentiation within institutions. I said that I would say just a little about vertical differentiation within the institution, which Clark refers to as a division of the institution or its sections into 'tiers'. What Clark has in mind here is the existence in some higher education systems of cleavages within the institution that divides it into lower and higher tiers. From a student's point of view, this cleavage can appear as a hurdle that has to be overcome before progress up the degree programmes can be achieved. From the teacher's point of view, it can appear as a division between staff who mostly (or exclusively) teach in the lower tier and those who teach in the upper tier or tiers. The prime example he mentions is the division in large American universities between the undergraduate 'College of Arts and Sciences' and the graduate or vocational schools. Students are rigorously selected before they can proceed to the higher tier, and the teachers employed in each tier are often quite different, with much undergraduate teaching being done by teaching assistants and fellows, while graduate education is undertaken by active researchers. British universities have traditionally been single-tiered, with little in the way of a cleavage of this kind. As in many other aspects of the internal structure of universities, I think a tendency towards increased vertical differentiation can now be seen. I have already pointed to the tendency in Aberdeen and elsewhere for an increasing amount of first- and second-year undergraduate teaching to be taken by the 'underclass' of teaching assistants and fellows, while honours teaching is done by full teacher-researchers. In addition there is the new 'threshold' for progression from foundation courses to the honours programme. There has always been strict selection for progression or admission to post-graduate studies; the next development in vertical differentiation, if it were to take place, would be the formation of graduate schools and a restriction on the kind of lecturing staff who were eligible to work in them. We will have wait and see.

UNIVERSITIES AS ORGANISATIONS

Most of what I've said so far relates to the level of the department, its external relations with other departments and its internal structure. I want now to turn to the university, and how changes at the university level and beyond have affected work within the department. There has been much sport in the literature on higher education in attempting to characterise what a university is. There is the old joke attributed to Chicago President Hutchins about a university being a collection of schools and departments held together by a central heating system, and the variant from Clark Kerr in California, that a university is a collection of departments held together by a common grievance over parking (Kerr 1972: 20). There is the suggestion that a university is a bit like a holding company, a paper financial umbrella for a set of disparate and relatively independent enterprises. A more sociological way of making the point of these jokes and images is to say that universities in the past were not much in the way of collective actors. There was not much that universities 'did' that was not in fact the doing of its component parts, in British universities especially, its departments. To a great extent this was true of Aberdeen University at the time the department of sociology was established. Departments were to a considerable extent autonomous from central control, and made all sorts of decisions for themselves with scarcely any reference to a central authority. Of course they couldn't spend money they didn't have, and were dependent for resources on allocation from central university funds, but many of their teaching and research activities could be decided internally according to internal procedures. New courses were proposed to the relevant Faculty where they were more or less rubber-stamped. Departments even had completely different internal assessment procedures and marking scales, and managed the assessment of joint degrees by ad hoc agreements between the two departments concerned. And so on. In terms of systems theory, departments had relatively powerful boundary-maintaining mechanisms, as if surrounded by relatively impermeable membranes and equipped with strong immune systems capable of warding off intrusion from the organisational environment or beyond. In the 1960s, and for some time before that, the main decisions that had to be taken at university level were those concerned with expansion: the establishment of new departments, the planning of new buildings to house the extended activities of the various departments, and the provision of some new facilities, such as student residences.

The spur to change this state of affairs, and to the attempt to turn the university into a powerful collective actor, was change in the external environment of the university. Once again I turn to Burton Clark to get a handle on these changes. In a chapter of his book entitled 'Integration', Clark advanced his famous 'Triangle of Coordination' which sets out the three principles by which the higher education institutions within a society might be linked into something that might, or might not, look like a higher education system. This overhead

The Triangle of Coordination

State authority

USSR

Sweden

France   United States   Market

Canada

Japan

Britain

Italy

Academic oligarchy

Source: Burton Clark, *The Higher Education System*. Berkeley: University of California Press, 1983, p.143

reproduces his diagram. The three principles, as you can see, are entitled 'State authority', the 'Market', and 'Academic oligarchy' (Clark 1983: 143). In extreme types, higher education institutions could be linked by one of those principles alone. The societies that come closest to those extremes were, according to Clark: the USSR, where higher education institutions were integrated into a unified state-administered system; the USA, where there was no central coordination of colleges and universities but rather a series of differentiated open markets in which various kinds of higher education institutions competed for students, financial resources and reputations; and Italy where, in the absence of market competition and state authority, a relatively small oligarchical group of powerful chair-holders exercised control in notionally state bodies responsible for higher education finance, personnel, curricula and research. Most systems exhibit combinations of these three principles. As you see, Clark places Britain closest to the 'academic oligarchy' pole, though with admixtures of state authority and market competition, since the unified funding system which allocated public funds to universities was in fact controlled by the senior professors who sat on the UGC, which managed the competition between universities for finance and allowed universities to compete for students. Within the parameters set by the UGC, universities were free to make their own decisions for development.

Clark developed this 'triangle' in the 1970s, when the Cold War made the contrast between state and market a particularly powerful analytical device. In many of the societies Clark studied, things changed considerably over the subsequent thirty years. Concentrating on the British system for present purposes, I have seen two different attempts to modify Clark's triangle to pin down the key changes that have taken place. The first comes from the recent work of Reinhard Kreckel, a former colleague of ours in this department who unfortunately couldn't be with us today but who sends his good wishes. Reinhard returned to Germany in 1978

Tafel 3: Verschiebungen im Clark'schen Dreieck: Momentaufnahme 2000

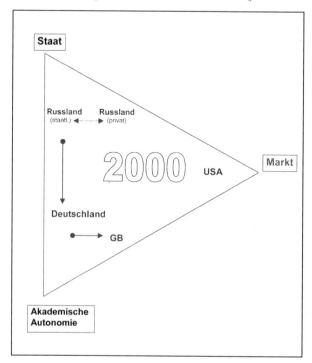

where he rose to become Rektor of the Martin Luther University of Halle-Wittenberg. Semi-retired from the Institute of Sociology there, he is now Director of the Institute for Higher Education Research at Wittenberg, where he presumably spends his time nailing theses to university doors. I reproduce (below) his adaptation of Clark's triangle, according to which the British system has moved towards the 'market' corner (Kreckel 2004: 187). The second is put forward in a book on change in universities by Henry Miller (I kid you not), who is more struck by the shift in Britain (and in Australia and Canada) towards greater state control,

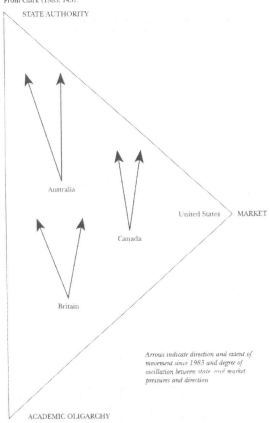

Figure 1 Systems of university control and direction of change, 1983–93. From Clark (1983: 143).

STATE AUTHORITY

Australia

United States   MARKET

Canada

Britain

Arrows indicate direction and extent of movement since 1983 and degree of oscillation between state and market pressures and direction

ACADEMIC OLIGARCHY

Source: Henry D. R. Miller, *The Management of Change in Universities: Universities, State and Economy in Australia, Canada and the United Kingdom.* Buckingham: The Society for Research into Higher Education & Open University Press, 1995, p. 71.

though he also recognises the growth of market pressures (Miller 1995: 71).

Without going into a lot of detail on British government policy on higher education since Thatcher, I think it is clear that both Kreckel's and Miller's adaptation of Clark's triangle capture part of the truth. Under the watchwords of 'accountability', 'audit', 'efficiency' and 'enterprise', governments have created a state-regulated and state-administered market in higher education in which universities are forced to compete for resources mediated through various quasi-currencies, such as RAE ratings and teaching quality scores. Even a sketch of the economic and political conditions in which this state-imposed market emerged would take us too far afield today, so I bracket these out of consideration, even though aware that a fuller account of them would be desirable. The main point I want to stress is that this drastic transformation of the external environment of universities laid the conditions for change in their internal structure and process. Universities were encouraged to reorganise themselves so as to be able to operate as coherent collective actors. Aberdeen, along with many other universities, duly proceeded to transform its internal processes of government in the direction of a system of line management, which has had profound consequences for the work of academics within departments.

We have become so used to the language of 'management' that it is difficult to remember a time when it was not common currency. But it is certainly the case that the words 'management' and 'manager' were scarcely if ever used in Aberdeen before the later 1980s. A dean or a head of department was not thought of as a 'manager' nor were their responsibilities seen as part of a process of 'management'. If academics thought about the structure of decision-making in the university at all, which most probably did not, they would have used the word I just mentioned, namely government. The higher governing bodies of the university were the Court, responsible under the 1860 Universities of Scotland Act for financial matters and the legal employer of the university's employees, and the Senatus, responsible for academic matters. The composition of the Senatus consisted of the Principal, the holders of established chairs, and some elected lecturers and readers. Below that came, as I mentioned earlier, the Faculties, with a membership of *ex officio* professors and elected lecturers. Faculties were self-governing collegiate bodies which elected their deans to organise faculty business and to represent the faculty at university levels of government. Within Faculties were their component departments. At each level there were what I called boundary-maintaining mechanisms allowing a unit considerable autonomy from higher levels.

This stress on collegiality shouldn't be exaggerated, however. In practice, no doubt, groups of senior professors exercised oligarchical influence in Faculties, while at the departmental level the tradition of the autocratic professor had support both in contract and custom. Nonetheless, this form of professional self-government (as in the case of other professions especially in the public sector) was anathema to the Conservative government under Thatcher. It was seen as the expression of a producer interest incapable of accounting for the efficient use of public funds and of delivering services that represented value for money. Universities were pressured to set up a committee under the auspices of the CVCP, which recommended the introduction of systems of management and of financial planning and control that were thought to be best practice in the private sector. This was the famous Jarratt Report of March 1985, the foundational document of everything that has happened in universities over the past twenty years, but which quite possibly newer generations of colleagues have never heard of. Even at the time it was a shadowy document, spoken about in hushed tones. Universities, with greater or lesser enthusiasm, moved to adopt its proposals. The Court of Aberdeen University commissioned a consultancy from the British Association for Commercial and Industrial Education on how to implement Jarratt, which reported in May 1988. The National Audit Office also reported later that year using Jarratt's proposals as the benchmark against which to test whether universities had reorganised their management structures to ensure that public expenditure was giving value for money. From this stem all the procedures that are now familiar to us in Aberdeen: a system of strategic planning and accountability; rolling institutional plans regularly reviewed (supposedly) in the light of outcomes; the Principal as Chief Executive of the university; joint committees of Court and Senate linking academic decision-making to financial planning; budget delegation to departments, and now to schools; development of performance indicators with greater awareness of costs; the appointment of heads of departments and of deans (now heads of schools and colleges) with line management powers and responsibility for the use of resources; arrangements for staff appraisal and development; and so on.

All of this has meant a considerable expansion in the operation of universities as collective actors. If a university is to flourish in this new competitive environment, it has to bind its component parts to collective goals to a much greater extent than hitherto. And this in turn has meant a considerable weakening in the boundary-maintaining mechanisms of sections such as departments. The membranes surrounding departments have been penetrated so that they can be made subject to requirements emanating both from central agencies of the university itself, now usually referred to as 'senior management', and from outside the university. In fact the senior management of universities now act primarily as transmission belts for externally generated imperatives, either those imposed directly or indirectly by agencies of the state, or those necessitated by the demands of market competition.

There is an enormous amount more that can be said about the consequences of this new system of management in the university, but I am already outstaying whatever welcome I might have had. Most of it has already been said; soon after the Jarratt report and the subsequent implementation there was an outpouring of publications on the changes that were taking place in universities. For example, the Society for Research into Higher Education published a vast number of monographs and edited collections, most of them stemming from the early and mid-1990s. I simply want to end by reflecting briefly on the impact of this changed management system on the ordinary academic staff of the university, by going back to something I said much earlier on the basic orientation of academics. Following Burton Clark and a host of surveys of academics in various countries, I repeated the generalisation that academics are more closely attached to their disciplines than to their universities. A consequence that might be drawn from this is that authority within universities will be more legitimate when it is based on disciplinary prowess and is exercised as disciplinary leadership. Managerial control used to bind groups and individuals to collective goals imposed by heteronomous powers is less likely to be accepted as legitimate. This is hardly surprising; matters are essentially no different in relations between clinicians and managers in the health service. Not does it mean that there is incessant warfare between academics and managers. In the early days of Jarrattism, it would be scarcely an exaggeration to describe academic attitudes towards the new system of line management as a mixture of derision and disbelief, but academics soon came to realise that management was here to stay. Fifteen years on, it seems to me that an appropriate term to capture academic attitudes to managerialism in universities is the one popularised by Michael Mann in his writings from the 1970s on working class consciousness: 'pragmatic acceptance' (Mann 1973). I suspect such an attitude is not uncommon among academic managers themselves. It is not a strong basis for legitimate authority, but it is enough to maintain the peace. It does not promote commitment of academics to the organisational fortunes of their university; academics remain primarily committed to their discipline or their sub-discipline, and are not overly enamoured of moves to abolish the department as the organisational form of the discipline.

I end with a final comment on the main theme of my reflections, differentiation. I suspect we are heading for a period of increasing differentiation in the higher education system, and I have touched on some aspects of this already. The Westminster government clearly wishes to push through a form of institutional differentiation in England, and has commissioned consultancies whose reports reject a basic plank of conventional conceptions of the university, that teaching must always be combined with research. It may well get its way, with the backing of the Russell Group. Things may turn out differently in Scotland, but I wouldn't bet on it. I'm no crystal ball gazer, but I suspect there is trouble ahead.

References

Aberdeen University 1985. Interview with Raymond Illsley, 12 June, 1985. University of Aberdeen Oral History Archive, GB 0231 Aberdeen University, Special Libraries and Archives. Available online at: http://calms.abdn.ac.uk/DServe/dserve.exe?dsqServer=Calms&dsqIni=Dserve.ini&dsqApp=Archive&dsqDb=Catalog&dsqCmd=show.tcl&dsqSearch=(RefNo==%22MS 3620/1/25/1%22), accessed 14 September 2010.

Beck, Ulrich, Brater, Michael and Daheim, Hansjürgen 1980. *Soziologie der Arbeit und der Berufe*. Reinbeck bei Hamburg: Rowohlt Taschenbuchverlag.

British Association for Commercial and Industrial Education (BACIE) 1988. *Consultancy on Management and Budgetary Development for Aberdeen University – March to May 1988*. London: BACIE.

Clark, Burton 1983. *The Higher Education System*. Berkeley: University of California Press.

Committee of Vice Chancellors and Principals (CVCP) 1985. *Report of the Steering Committee on Efficiency Studies in Universities* (Jarratt Report). London: CVCP.

Great Britain. Committee on Higher Education 1963. *Higher education : report of the committee appointed by the Prime Minister under the chairmanship of Lord Robbins, 1961-63*. London : H.M.S.O.

Halsey, A. H. 2004. *A History of Sociology in Britain*. Oxford: Oxford University Press.

Halsey, A. H. 1995. *The Decline of Donnish Dominion: the British Academic Professions in the Twentieth Century*. Oxford: Oxford University Press.

Inglis, David 2001. *A sociological history of excretory experience : defecatory manners and toiletry technologies*. Lewiston, N.Y. : Edwin Mellen Press.

Ingold, Tim 2003. Anthropology at Aberdeen. Text of a lecture delivered at King's College Conference Centre, on Friday 31st October 2003, to celebrate the inauguration of the Department of Anthropology at the University of Aberdeen. Accessed through http://www.abdn.ac.uk/anthropology/about.php on 14 September 2010.

Kerr, Clark 1972. *The Uses of the University. With a "Postscript — 1972"*. Cambridge, Mass.: Harvard University Press.

Kogan, Maurice with Kogan, David 1983. *The Attack on Higher Education*. London: Kogan Page.

Kreckel, Reinhard 2004. *Vielfalt als Stärke: Anstöße zur Hochschulpolitik und Hochschulforschung*. Bonn: Lemmens.

Mann, Michael 1973. *Consciousness and Action among the Western Working Class*. London: Macmillan.

Miller, Henry D. R. 1995. *The Management of Change in Universities: Universities, State and Economy in Australia, Canada and the United Kingdom*. Buckingham: The Society for Research into Higher Education & Open University Press.

Moodie, Graeme C. and Eustace, Rowland 1974. *Power and Authority in British Universities*. Montreal: McGill-Queen's University Press.

Platt, Jennifer 2003. *The British Sociological Association: a Sociological History*. Durham: sociologypress.

van Teijlingen, E. and Barbour, R. S., 1996. The MRC Medical Sociology Unit in Aberdeen: its development & legacy. In: Adams, A., Smith, D. and Watson, F., eds. *'To the Greit Support and Advancement of Helth': Papers on the History of Medicine in Aberdeen, Arising from a Conference Held During the Quincentenary Year of Aberdeen University*. Aberdeen: Aberdeen History of Medicine Publications, pp. 54-63.

Section Two: Varieties of Cultural History

The polymath:
a cultural and social history of an intellectual species[1]

PETER BURKE

Emmanuel College, Cambridge

This paper offers a brief historical sketch of the rise and decline of the polymath and to a lesser extent of the complementary opposite topic, the rise of intellectual specialization. A serious history of specialization has not, as far as I know, been written.[2] The conclusions that follow are therefore premature - but readers cannot expect too much expertise from a discussion of the ideal of the non-specialist.

The narrative will be emplotted as tragedy, as decline and fall, or more exactly as a story of a long retreat accompanied by a number of significant rearguard actions. To sum up the conclusion in advance: both the rise and the beginning of the decline of the polymath occurred in the same century, the seventeenth, even if the decline was a gradual one of which the last chapter has not yet been written even now. The idea of the polymath arose as a reaction against increasing specialization, just as in the 20th century, the idea of interdisciplinarity arose in an age of disciplines.

In the ancient and medieval worlds, scholars did not yet need to specialize. Aristotle, now remembered as a philosopher, wrote on natural history, physics and rhetoric as well as on ethics, politics and metaphysics. Claudius Ptolomaeus, best known today as an astronomer and a geographer, also wrote on music and optics. The scholar Alexander of Miletus was nicknamed 'polyhistor' for the breadth of his learning.

In the Middle Ages, encyclopaedias were compiled by single individuals, such as Isidore of Seville, Vincent of Beauvais or Hugh of St Victor. Other wide-ranging authors included Gerbert, Thomas Aquinas, Albertus Magnus, Roger Bacon and Ramon Lull, for whom the unity of knowledges, branches on a common tree, reflected the unity of the cosmos. The arts course at the medieval university, ranging as it did from rhetoric to astronomy, offered institutional support for this kind of encyclopaedism. So did the *quodlibet*, an academic occasion on which a scholar would prepare questions for disputation in all

---

[1] This essay began as a lecture, delivered in Brighton, Cambridge, Gotha, Madrid, Montreal and Sheffield. My thanks to the audiences for some pertinent questions.

[2] For a longer sketch, see Peter Burke, *A Social History of Knowledge from the Encyclopédie to Wikipedia* (Cambridge, forthcoming), ch.6.

Explorations in Cultural History: Essays for Peter Gabriel McCaffery,
edd. David F. Smith & H. Philsooph (Aberdeen 2010)   ISBN 978-0-9567059-0-7

disciplines.

The intellectual range of medieval scholars should not be exaggerated. What they mastered was the academic knowledge of their day, which was only one form of knowledge, alongside the practical knowledges of peasants, of artisans, of merchants, of knights, of midwives, and so on. All the same, in the Middle Ages it was possible for an individual to make original contributions to widely separated branches of the common tree of knowledge. A similar point might be made for the Islamic world at this time, about scholars such as Ibn Sina (known in the West as Avicenna), Al Biruni and Ibn Rushd (known as Averroes). Indeed, the Arabs already had a word for many-sidedness: *tafannun*.[3]

It remained possible to work in this way in the Renaissance. I should like to stress the word 'remained', thus disagreeing with Jacob Burckhardt.[4] Burckhardt's well-known suggestion that the 'many-sided man' — sometimes described at the time as an *uomo universale* - was a new phenomenon is actually somewhat misleading, at least as far as intellectual many-sidedness (leaving aside dancing or athletics) is concerned. The humanists were continuing the tradition of medieval encyclopaedism. For instance, the intellectual tournament which the humanist Giovanni Pico della Mirandola proposed at Rome in 1486, defending 900 theses in many disciplines, followed the medieval practice of the *quodlibet*, even if Pico's performance was planned on a grander scale and with more publicity.

Whether they worked inside and outside the university, some Renaissance scholars certainly ranged widely. The Spaniard Michael Servetus, who owes his place in history to his denial of the Trinity, lectured on geography and wrote on astrology, theology and medicine. Giambattista della Porta of Naples, now best known for his plays, 'wrote on cryptography, horticulture, optics, mnemonics, meteorology, physics, astrology, physiognomy, mathematics and fortification'.[5] The Florentine humanist Cosimo Bartoli wrote on architecture, ethics, history, literature, mathematics, music, sculpture and theology.[6] The interests of the Elizabethan Englishman John Dee included mathematics, navigation, alchemy and magic. The Swiss Konrad Gesner wrote on natural history and linguistics as well as compiling a bibliography of the learned works available in print in his day.

By the sixteenth century, however, there were signs of a coming crisis of knowledge. One French historian, Lancelot Voisin de La Popelinière, criticized

---

[3] George Makdisi, *The Rise of Humanism in Classical Islam and the Christian West* (Edinburgh, 1990).

[4] Jacob Burckhardt, *Cultur der Renaissance in Italien* (Basel, 1860: English trans. *The Civilization of the Renaissance in Italy*, 1878, rpr Harmondsworth, 1990), ch.2. Cf. Joan K. Gadol, 'Universal Man', *Dictionary of the History of Ideas*, ed. Philip Wiener, (4 vols., New York, 1973), vol.4, 437-43.

[5] Louise G. Clubb, *Giambattista della Porta*, Dramatist (Princeton, 1965), xi.

[6] Judith Bryce, *Cosimo Bartoli, 1503-72; the career of a Florentine polymath* (Geneva, 1983).

what he called 'les esprits universels', such as François de Belleforest and André Thevet, as if their attempt at breadth resulted in lack of depth.[7] More famous are the examples of Rabelais and Faust.

François Rabelais was a humanist, a physician and a scholar who was well-read in a variety of subjects. The educational programme for Gargantua that he described in his romance has often been read literally in the light of the idea of the so-called 'Renaissance Man'.[8] However, it is always risky to take Rabelais literally. His description of a gargantuan educational programme, including 9999 theses is surely both a parody and a critique of the intellectual claims made by Pico.

Again, Faust demonstrated an insatiable thirst for knowledge, but this unlimited curiosity of his was condemned as an example of spiritual pride in the German *Faustbuch* - or at least in its French translation - as well as in Christopher Marlowe's *Dr Faustus* (1594). The protagonist was not presented as a hero, but as a warning. In any case, if Dr Faustus could not attain his encyclopaedic ideal without the help of the devil, something had surely gone wrong.

THE AGE OF ANXIETY

Changes in vocabulary are often sensitive indicators of broader or deeper changes in a given culture. Despite a few earlier instances, it was only in the seventeenth century that the terms 'polymath' and 'polyhistor' came into regular use in a number of languages – Latin, French, English and German, as did the term 'pansophia', associated with the Bohemian scholar Jan Amos Komenský (Comenius) and his followers. Robert Burton, for example, referred to 'Polymathes and Polyhistors' in his *Anatomy of Melancholy* (1621). In French, the scholar-librarian Gabriel Naudé and the philosopher Nicolas Malebranche both used the term 'polymathie'.[9]

In Central Europe, a treatise on the subject was published in 1603, Johann von Wower's treatise *De polymathia*.[10] The Polish physician Johannes Jonstonus's *Polyhistor* (a work on world history) dates from 1660; his *Polymathia* (on philology) from 1667. The first edition of the German librarian Daniel Morhof's *Polyhistor* – a thorough and successful guide to the world of learning which continued to be

---

[7] Lancelot Voisin de La Popelinière, *Histoire des histoires* (Paris, 1599), 371.

[8] For example, by Emile Durkheim, *L'évolution pédagogique en France, des origines à la Renaissance* (Paris, 1938).

[9] For English, here and subsequently, I depend on the *Oxford English Dictionary* (1888: revised ed., online, 2000); for French on Emile Littré, *Dictionnaire de la langue française* (1863: revised edn, 7 vols., Paris 1956-8).

[10] Luc Deitz, 'Joannes Wower', *Journal of the Warburg and Courtauld Institutes* 58 (1995), 132-51.

revised and republished for nearly a century – dates from 1687. According to Morhof, *polymathia* was concerned with the relations between disciplines, *scientiarum cognatio et conciliatio*.[11] Related concepts were *scientia universalis* and 'General Learning'.[12]

The invention of the new words was an indication of the growing consciousness of a problem. The problem might be described as a 'crisis of knowledge', forming part of the famous 'general crisis' of the seventeenth century. The rapid rise of new knowledge of the natural world, like the entry into Europe of increasing information about the world beyond it, was making it increasingly difficult for individual scholars to master as many fields or disciplines as before.

The printing-press made the crisis more acute by allowing knowledge to circulate more rapidly and more widely. The multiplication of books was already causing alarm by the middle of the sixteenth century. An Italian writer complained in 1550 that there were 'so many books that we do not even have time to read the titles'. Books were described as a 'forest' in which readers could lose themselves, an 'ocean' through which readers had to navigate, or even a 'flood' of printed matter in which it was hard to escape drowning.[13]

Discussions of the polymath reveal this 'information anxiety', a sense of a threat to the ideal. As a Master of Trinity College Cambridge, Isaac Barrow, put it in his treatise *Of Industry* (1700) 'he can hardly be a good scholar, who is not a general one'. General knowledge was made necessary by what Barrow called the 'connection of things, and dependence of notions', so that 'one part of learning doth confer light to another'.

In this century of unstable equilibrium or transition between traditional encyclopedism and the rise of specialization, the ideal of the polymath was exemplified by a few remarkable individuals. The Calvinist cleric Johann Heinrich Alsted for example, compiled a seven-volume encyclopaedia by himself.[14] The interests of the French nobleman amateur Nicolas Fabri de Peiresc extended – as

---

[11] Françoise Waquet (ed.) *Mapping the World of Learning* (Wiesbaden, 2000), 35-6.

[12] Meric Casaubon, *Generall learning: a seventeenth-century treatise on the formation of the general scholar*, ed. Richard Serjeantson (Cambridge, 1999).

[13] Quoted in Giovanni Cavallo and Roger Chartier (eds.) *A History of Reading in the West* (Cambridge, 1999), 234; H. H. M. van Lieshout, 'Dictionnaires et diffusion de savoir', *Commercium Litterarium*, ed. H. Bots and F. Waquet (Amsterdam and Maarssen, 1994), 134. Cf Ann Blair, 'Reading Strategies for Coping with Information Overload, c. 1550-1700', *Journal of the History of Ideas* 64 (2003), 11-28.

[14] Howard Hotson, *Johann Heirich Alsted between Renaissance, Reformation, and universal reform* (Oxford, 2000).

[15] Peter N. Miller, *Peiresc's Europe: learning and virtue in the seventeenth century* (New Haven, 2000).

his extensive correspondence reveals – to law, history, mathematics, numismatics and Egyptology.[15] The Jesuit Athanasius Kircher, originally a protégé of Peiresc's, and a fellow-enthusiast for Egyptology, also wrote on China, magnetism, mathematics, mining, music and on *scientia universalis* itself. He has been described as 'the last man who knew everything'.[16] The Swede Olaus Rudbeck was active in the fields of anatomy, botany and medicine as well as history and antiquities.[17] It would be easy to extend the list to include (among others) the Italian Ulisse Aldrovandi, the Frenchman Pierre Gassendi, the Dutchman Hugo Grotius, the Englishman John Selden, the German Johann Kepler and the Dane Ole Worm. There was at least one female polymath of note, the Dutchwoman Anna Maria Schuurman.

The most famous example of a seventeenth-century polymath is of course Gottfried Wilhelm Leibniz. He is remembered today – like Aristotle – as a philosopher, but this label is little more than a symptom of our own propensity to fit scholars into single fields. In his own day, Leibniz was known for his calculating machine and for his studies of medieval German history, not to mention his interests in law, theology, sinology, geology and linguistics.[18]

According to Morhof, polymathy was still possible.[19] However, Peiresc did not publish. The reputations of both Kircher and Rudbeck went into a rapid decline after their deaths and they came to be viewed retrospectively as charlatans or cranks. Even Leibniz seems to have felt the strain of keeping up his different knowledges, and he was unable to finish many of his projects.

The first lament about the fragmentation of knowledge known to me was expressed in the middle of the seventeenth century, by the Puritan divine Richard Baxter, 'We parcel arts and sciences into fragments, according to the straitness of our capacities, and are not so pansophical as *uno intuitu* to see the whole'.[20] There is of course a danger of taking this remark out of context. Baxter was making a point about the human condition and contrasting 'us' with God and perhaps the angels. All the same, the date of his comment is surely significant, like his reference to the *pansophia* of Comenius.

It was at much the same time that Meric Casaubon, the son of the great scholar Isaac Casaubon, admitted to a 'sad apprehension … of the decay of learning, and great danger of approaching barbarism'.[21] In similar fashion, later in

16 Paula Findlen (ed.) *Athanasius Kircher. The Last Man Who Knew Everything* (London, 2003).
17 Gunnar Eriksson, *The Atlantic Vision: Olaus Rudbeck and Baroque Science* (Canton, MA, 1994).
18 Maria Rosa Antognazza, *Leibniz: an intellectual biography* (Cambridge, 2009).
19 Waquet, *Mapping*, 62.
20 Richard Baxter, *Holy Commonwealth* (London, 1659), 493.
21 Casaubon, *Generall learning*, 88.

the century, the French librarian Adrien Baillet expressed his fear that the multiplication of books would bring with it a new age of barbarians.[22]

To sum up so far: the seventeenth century was the age of the polymath. Before that time the concept was scarcely necessary, while after that time the ideal was becoming increasingly unattainable. It is intriguing to discover that a leading sinologist has dated the shift in China from the Ming amateur ideal to that of the Qing specialist to about the same time, the later seventeenth century.[23]

The remainder of the story to be told here is the story of an intellectual retreat, from knowledge in every field to knowledge in several fields, and from making original contributions in many fields to a more passive consumption of what has been contributed by others. It is a rearguard action punctuated by a few remarkable feats of intellectual heroism.

THE EIGHTEENTH AND EARLY NINETEENTH CENTURIES

During the Enlightenment many-sided intellectual interests were not uncommon, as in the case of Montesquieu, revealed by the contents of both his library and his notebooks. Again, the ambition of Giambattista Vico, according to his autobiography, was to unite all human and divine wisdom (*tutto il sapere umano e divino*).

However, it was becoming more and more difficult to see the whole. Diderot was able to edit the *Encyclopédie* because his interests were encyclopaedic, but the book itself was the collective work of some 140 authors. As the article on 'gens de lettres' in the *Encyclopédie* put it, 'Universal knowledge is no longer within the reach of man' (*la science universelle n'est plus à la portée de l'homme*). In similar fashion the biographer of James Tytler, the editor of the supplement to the *Encyclopaedia Brittanica*, remarked in 1805 that 'No man, however astonishing his talents and intense his application, can ever reasonably expect to be a walking encyclopaedia'.[24]

If universality was no longer attainable, it remained possible to make original contributions to several fields. In France the Comte de Buffon, for instance, was active as a mathematician, a geologist, a biologist, a palaeontologist and a physiologist. The Russian scholar Mikhail Lomonosov was a chemist, linguist,

---

[22] Adrien Baillet, *Jugements des Savants sur les principaux ouvrages des anciens* (4 vols, Paris, 1685-6), preface.

[23] Benjamin A. Elman, *From Philosophy to Philology: Intellectual and Social Aspects of Change in Late Imperial China* (1984; revised edn, Los Angeles 2001), ch.4.

[24] Quoted in Richard Yeo, *Encyclopaedic Visions: scientific dictionaries and Enlightenment culture* (Cambridge, 2001), xi.

poet and historian, as well as helping to organize and describe the Great Northern expeditions. The leading figures of the Scottish Enlightenment were active in more than one field apiece. David Hume was not only a philosopher but a historian as well. Adam Smith wrote on ethics, law, rhetoric and the history of astronomy as well as on the wealth of nations.

Another series of examples come from the activities of the members of the Lunar Society in late eighteenth-century Birmingham. Erasmus Darwin, Matthew Boulton, Josiah Wedgwood, Joseph Priestley, James Watt and their circle made discoveries in physics, chemistry, geology and botany, as well as inventing many ingenious machines. Darwin, for instance, was active as a physician, a poet and an inventor. Priestley was perhaps the most polymathic of the group, writing as he did on theology, philosophy, education, history and physics.[25]

Even in the nineteenth century it remained possible for a creative individual to make original discoveries in several different domains. Take the case of Thomas Young of Emmanuel College Cambridge. 'Phenomenon Young', as his contemporaries called him, was trained as a physician and pursued medical research but he also published important papers calculating life insurance and describing his experiments in physics. In addition, Young contributed to the decoding of Egyptian hieroglyphics, although he was overtaken by Champollion.

Like Athanasius Kircher, Young has been described as 'the last man who knew everything'.[26] However, a generation later, William Henry Fox-Talbot, best known today for his contribution to the development of photography, wrote on mathematics, physics, chemistry, astronomy and etymology as well as being one of the first to decipher Assyrian cuneiform texts. Francis Galton was a mathematician, statistician, meteorologist and eugenicist. John Lubbock, a banker and a Member of Parliament, wrote on archaeology and anthropology as well as taking an interest in geology and natural history. In the United States, Joseph Leidy, a third scholar described as the 'last man who knew everything', worked in the middle years of the nineteenth century on anatomy, natural history and palaeontology at the very moment that these fields were drifting apart.[27]

It is not difficult to find nineteenth-century scholars who might be described as 'passive polymaths', reading widely though not making original contributions to different fields. Young's Cambridge colleague, William Whewell, like Barrow a Master of Trinity College, wrote on mathematics, mechanics, mineralogy, astronomy, philosophy, theology and architecture. He confessed to a 'desire to

[25] Jenny Uglow, *The Lunar Men* (London, 2002).
[26] Andrew Robinson, *The Last Man Who Knew Everything: Thomas Young* (New York, 2005).
[27] Leonard Warren, *Joseph Leidy: the last man who knew everything* (New Haven, 1998).

read all manner of books at once'.[28] Coleridge was another passive polymath whose interests included astronomy, botany, chemistry, geology and medicine as well as the humanities. Mary Somerville wrote on mathematics, astronomy and geography as well as on the connexion between the sciences. George Eliot once declared that 'I enjoy all subjects', knew seven foreign languages, wrote on a wide range of topics in the *Westminster Review*, translated Spinoza and completed a study of psychology by her late partner G. H. Lewes.[29]

Turning from Britain to the German speaking world, Goethe had a Faustian desire for knowledge of many kinds, criticized Newton's optics and offered contributions to the natural sciences (anatomy, botany, zoology and mineralogy) as well as to literature.[30] What have been described as 'polymath theses' survived in German universities into the 1820s.[31] Alexander von Humboldt offers a quite extraordinary example of *polymathia*, since his interests included geology, astronomy, meteorology, botany, physiology, chemistry, geography, archaeology, political economy and ethnography. In all these fields, incredible as it may now seem, he was able to make contributions to knowledge, thanks to his exploration of South America.[32]

Later in the century, Hermann von Helmholtz, described as a 'universal genius' made contributions to medicine, physiology, mathematics and physics as well as keeping up an interest in the humanities and corresponding with the ancient and modern historians Theodor Mommsen and Heinrich von Treitschke.[33] Ernst Haeckel spanned the fields of anatomy, zoology and ecology (a discipline that he named), as well as writing on the philosophy of science. Rudolph Virchow made contributions to biology, medicine, anthropology, sociology and statistics.

THE RISE OF DISCIPLINES

However, the intellectual climate – in other words, European culture – was becoming more hostile to polymaths. Young sometimes published anonymously so that narrower colleagues would continue to take him seriously as a physician. Sidney Smith said of Whewell that 'omniscience is his foible'. Coleridge was mocked by Thomas Peacock in the novel *Headlong Hall* (1816) as 'Mr Panscope',

---

[28] Richard Yeo, *Defining science: William Whewell, natural knowledge, and public debate in early Victorian Britain* (Cambridge, 1993), 57.

[29] Pauline Nestor, *George Eliot* (Basingstoke, 2002), 2-3. Cf. Diana Postlethwaite, 'George Eliot and Science', in George Levine (ed.) *The Cambridge Companion to George Eliot* (Cambridge, 2001).

[30] Frederick Amrine et al., *Goethe and the Sciences* (Dordrecht, 1987).

[31] William Clark. *Academic Charisma and the Origins of the Research University* (Chicago, 2006), 222.

[32] Helmut De Terra, *Humboldt* (New York, 1955).

[33] Lorenz Krüger (ed.), *Universalgenie Helmholtz* (Berlin, 1994).

'who had run through the whole circle of the sciences, and understood them all equally well'.[34] Humboldt complained that 'People often say that I'm curious about too many things at once'.

The nineteenth century was of course a crucial period in the development of intellectual specialization as well as in the division of labour in general, part of the rise of industrial society. To return to philology: in the eighteenth century the term 'versatile' was used to mean someone who could turn easily from one intellectual pursuit to another, as if this was a trait worthy of admiration. In the nineteenth century, on the other hand, the term *dilettante*, which like *amateur* had referred to someone who took pleasure in something, usually one of the arts, became associated with superficiality. In English and in German the pejorative terms 'dilettantism', 'dilettantish', *dilettantisch*, *dilettantenhaft*, *Dilettantismus* and *Dilettantentum* date from this time. Other new English words included 'expert' (1825) and 'expertise' (1868).[35] The word 'scientist' goes back to 1834. The term 'specialist' was coined a little later, originally in a medical context (1856), though it soon came to be used more widely (1862).

These new words are clues to what has been called the 'rise of professional society'.[36] The three traditional professions were now joined by many others such as architect, engineer, accountant and surveyor, each with its own association and its own formal qualifications, demarcating fields and putting up fences.

The proliferation of specialized departments or institutes in the nineteenth-century university, first in Germany, then in the USA and later elsewhere, may be seen as a part of this trend.[37] Incidentally, the phrase 'department of knowledge', like the terms 'department of history', and so on, is modelled on 'department of state' and dates from the mid-nineteenth century. At the end of the century, Max Weber declared that 'Limitation to specialized work, with a renunciation of the Faustian universality of man which it involves, is a condition of any valuable work in the modern world'.[38]

This was the formative age of academic tribes and territories.[39] Subjects such as philosophy shrank as areas which had traditionally been part of philosophy,

---

[34] Quoted in Yeo, *Encyclopaedic Visions*, 249. Cf Yeo, *Defining Science*, 58.

[35] Roy M. MacLeod (ed.) *Government and Expertise: Specialists, Administrators and Professionals, 1860-1919* (Cambridge, 1988).

[36] Harold J. Perkin, *The Rise of Professional Society: England since 1880* (London, 1989).

[37] Gérard Lemaine et al (eds.) *Perspectives on the Emergence of Scientific Disciplines* (The Hague, 1976); Martin Guntau and Hubert Laitko (eds.) *Ursprung der Modernen Wissenschaften* (Berlin, 1987); Ian F. McNeely with Lisa Wolverton, 'The Disciplines', *Reinventing Knowledge* (New York, 2008), 161-204.

[38] Max Weber, *The Protestant Ethic and the Spirit of Capitalism* (1904: English trans. London 1930), 180.

[39] Tony Becher, *Academic Tribes and Territories* (Milton Keynes, 1989).

psychology for example, became independent. The amateur study of antiquities fragmented into professions such as archaeology and folklore. The reform of the Royal Society (1847) limited membership to natural scientists. The variety of subjects available for students to study at the university increased, but a price had to be paid, the gradual but irresistible division between what has been known, since C. P. Snow's famous lecture, as the 'two cultures'.[40]

All the same, resistance to specialization continued. At this point we may return to Jacob Burckhardt and his idea of the Renaissance many-sided man. Burckhardt himself was a many-sided man at the very time that this identity was becoming an anachronism. He sketched, he wrote poetry, he played the piano, he taught art history as well as history, and despite his association with the Renaissance he did not confine himself to that period. He also wrote about ancient Greece, the age of Constantine, and Rubens as well as reflecting on world history. No wonder that Burckhardt was drawn to figures like Leonardo da Vinci whose breadth of interests and abilities symbolized a kind of paradise lost. He liked to present himself as a dilettante, his habitual self-mockery only half-concealing a critique of the professionalism and specialization of his time.[41]

In Britain, too, there was resistance to intellectual professionalism. Both John Ruskin and Herbert Spencer, different as they were, had a foot on each side of Snow's notorious divide: Ruskin was an enthusiast for geology, while Spencer had been trained as an engineer. The ideal of the 'all-rounder' was formulated in the environment of the reformed public school on the model of Arnold's Rugby. The term was first used, in the 1860s, to refer to the complete cricketer, but by the 1870s it was being employed to refer to intellectual attainments as well. Another word that came into use in English at this time was 'pundit', originally referring to an Indian scholar but now employed in a pejorative sense to mean a pseudo-expert, as in the phrase 'the shallowness of contemporary Punditship' (1879). The British cult of the gentleman-amateur, and distrust of the so-called 'expert' is also apparent in Macaulay's report on the British Civil Service at the time of its reform (1854). No wonder that British civil servants were and are called 'mandarins'.

THE AGE OF SURVIVALS

The pressures towards specialization and fragmentation have continued to increase over the last century, and even the British are unable to resist what has

---

[40] Charles P. Snow, *The Two Cultures* (Cambridge, 1959).

[41] Peter Burke, 'Introduction', to Burckhardt, *Civilization*; Urs Breitenstein, Andreas Cesana and Martin Hug, *'Unerschöpflichkeit der Quellen': Burckhardt neu editiert - Burckhardt neu entdeckt* (Basel and Munich, 2007), 49, 52.

been described as 'expertocracy'. The term 'polymath' has been diluted to refer to people who have mastered two or three disciplines. The explosion of secondary literature makes it difficult to study big subjects and move between them as Burckhardt did. The idea of general knowledge has been trivialized into a subject for television shows rather than for scholars. Some universities (notably Sussex in the 1960s), broke with the tradition of specialized education, but Sussex recently abandoned the ideal of multidisciplinarity.

In any case, work on the borders between disciplines, valuable as it is, is not the same as polymathia. Indeed, such interdisciplinary research sometimes results in new specializations. Historians who engage in dialogue with demographers, for instance, have created a new field or sub-field, historical demography, and risk losing touch with the main body of historians.

All the same it remains possible even now to swim against the stream, at least under certain conditions. The dream of the unity of knowledge has not been abandoned completely, as books such as Edward O. Wilson's *Consilience* (1998) bear witness. What of the reality?

Looking back over the twentieth century, a few distinguished examples come to mind of that endangered species whose collective biography I have been trying to trace. These polymaths generally spanned fewer disciplines than their colleagues in the seventeenth or even the nineteenth century, but their achievements were remarkable all the same. It may be useful to present a typology of polymaths, dividing twentieth-century examples into four broad groups or sub-species.

The first group is that of the passive polymaths, who read widely but make their reputation in one discipline alone. In the English-speaking world, the most famous of the passive polymaths is surely Aldous Huxley, who was said to have read the *Encyclopaedia Britannica* from cover to cover. Huxley's successors include Ernst Gombrich and George Steiner, both of whom have ignored the gap between the 'two cultures'. Gombrich regularly read the *Scientific American*, and took a particular interest in zoology and experimental psychology. Steiner has written about philosophy, linguistics and history as well as comparative literature (his vast 'field') and is like Gombrich well-read in science, at least for a humanist.

The second group is that of limited polymaths, active in a small cluster of neighbouring disciplines. Despite his remark about the need for specialization, Max Weber himself was as much a historian, philosopher and economist as he was a sociologist, in addition to drawing ideas from law and theology. Anther polymath of this kind was Benedetto Croce, described by Antonio Gramsci as 'the last Renaissance man'. Croce was, like Leibniz, best known as a philosopher but he also played an important role as a literary critic and as a historian, especially of his native Naples. Other examples include José Ortega y Gasset, philosopher, essayist, sociologist and historian; Gilberto Freyre, sociologist, anthropologist and historian; and more recently Michel Foucault, who spanned philosophy, sociology and history.

On the analogy with polygamy, a third group might be described as serial polymaths, whose interests gradually shifted from one discipline to others. In the case of France, one thinks of Gustave Le Bon, who began his career in archaeology and anthropology, then turned to the natural sciences and finally to social psychology; or of Antoine Cournot, who began in mechanics and moved over to mathematics and then to economics. In the USA, Lester Ward took degrees in medicine and law, worked as a geologist and palaeontologist and made contributions to botany before his appointment to a chair in sociology at Brown University in 1906.

In Britain, Karl Pearson studied law, went on to teach German literature at Cambridge but became famous as a geneticist and as a statistician. Patrick Geddes was originally a biologist but turned philosopher, sociologist, geographer and town planner. Gregory Bateson (named 'Gregory' by his father, a biologist, in homage to Mendel), was an anthropologist turned psychologist, as well as an 'intellectual nomad' who drew ideas from biology, mathematics and systems theory.[42] Joseph Needham switched in mid-career from biochemistry to the history of science and civilization in China. The Hungarian émigré Michael Polanyi, who has been described, like Needham, as 'a contemporary Renaissance man', was active as a physical chemist before he turned to philosophy.[43]

It is worth noting that a few academic institutions have shown themselves flexible enough to accommodate these unusual individuals. In Cambridge, Joseph Needham remained on the university payroll when his interests shifted from embryology to the history of science in China. Herbert Fleury continued to teach at the University College of Aberystwyth, while moving from the department of geology to that of zoology and then to geography and anthropology. At the University of Manchester, a chair of social studies was created for Polanyi, the former head of the department of physical chemistry.

Most remarkable of all, though, is a fourth group, proper polymaths who have continued to work in several fields and to make serious contributions to all of them, keeping several balls in the air at the same time rather than picking them

---

[42] R. W. Rieber, 'Bateson', *American National Biography* (24 vols., New York 1999), vol. 2, 339.

[43] Struan Jacobs, 'The Life of a Renaissance Man: Michael Polanyi', *Sophia* 45 (2006), 117-20; Maurice Goldsmith, *Joseph Needham: 20th-century Renaissance man* (Paris, 1995).

up one by one. The Russian Roman Jakobson, for instance, wrote - in several different languages – on linguistics, literature, folklore and psychology. The American Lewis Mumford, critic of literature, architecture and society, used to describe himself as a 'generalist' and surely merited that title, since he 'bridged the seemingly disparate disciplines of architecture and planning, technology, literary criticism, biography, sociology and philosophy'.

In Britain, Herbert Simon won a Nobel Prize in economics, but 'never held a position in a department of economics' and also worked on public administration, psychology and mathematics.[44] The French Jesuit Michel de Certeau was trained as a philosopher, theologian and psychoanalyst but also made original contributions to history, sociology and anthropology. The American Jared Diamond is a physiologist who moved into ornithology and ecology but is perhaps most widely known today for his essays on world history, to say nothing of his lifelong interest in languages. He has moved from a chair in physiology to a chair in geography while remaining at UCLA.

Let us hope that these are not the last of the dinosaurs. Within the current division of intellectual labour we still need generalists in the sense of individuals who are able to perceive what Barrow called the 'connection of things, and dependence of notions'. We need them not only for synthesis, to paint the big picture, but also for analysis, since it takes a polymath to mind the gap and to draw attention to what has fallen into the spaces between disciplines. In an age of specialization, we need such people more than ever before. Yet this species will surely become extinct if governments and universities do not do something to maintain an intellectual habitat in which it has a chance of survival.

---

[44] Mattei Dogan and Robert Pahre, *Creative marginality: innovation at the intersections of social sciences* (Boulder, CO, 1990), 112.

What is mediaeval Gaelic poetry?

DAVID N. DUMVILLE
University of Aberdeen

A full answer to my question cannot be given here. This is the first of a series of essays in which the problem will be approached from different angles, with subsidiary questions being asked at each turn. I am writing in the conviction that unless this question is answered we must have grave difficulty both in grasping the essentials of the mediaeval Gaelic poetic tradition as a whole and in approaching any individual poem with a realistic chance of understanding it.

FRAMEWORK

What are the assumptions on which our sense of the history of mediaeval Gaelic poetry rests? Dominant in the record of more than a thousand years of observable poetic creativity, as its largest and most coherent element, is the Classical 'bardic' poetry of an approximate half-millennium, *ca* 1200 – *ca* 1700,[1] with its attendant normative works of grammatical and metrical exegesis explaining a system of usage established in detail by the beginning of the thirteenth century.[2] The functions of the aristocratic poets who created the public, political poetry of that period were socially determined. We have a generalising anthropological explanation, provided by Marshall Sahlins, the leading Neo-evolutionist scholar of his generation, of the fundamental socio-political structure of the type of culture in which such literature was produced.[3] More local colour and detailed explanation must be provided by understanding of three long-term cultural inheritances – the

---

[1] For the scale and nature of the corpus see Katharine Simms, *From Kings to Warlords. The Changing Political Structure of Gaelic Ireland in the Later Middle Ages* (Woodbridge 1987). See also the bardic-poetry database at http://bardic.celt.dias.ie and cf. n. 288, below.

[2] For the normative works, see: *Irish Grammatical Tracts*, ed. Osborn Bergin (Dublin 1915–55); *Bardic Syntactical Tracts*, ed. Lambert McKenna (Dublin 1944). For the origins of the system, see B. Ó Cuív, 'Linguistic terminology in the mediaeval Irish bardic tracts', *Transactions of The Philological Society* (1965) 141–64, and 'A mediaeval exercise in language planning', in *Progress in Linguistic Historiography*, ed. Konrad Koerner (Amsterdam 1980), pp. 23–34, as well as 'The linguistic training of the mediaeval Irish poet', *Celtica* 10 (1973) 114–40. See further P. Ó Macháin, 'The early Modern Irish prosodic tracts and the editing of Irish verse', in *Metrik und Medienwechsel. Metrics and Media*, ed. Hildegard L.C. Tristram (Tübingen 1991), pp. 273–87; D. McManus, 'Teanga an dána agus teanga an phróis', *Léachtaí Choilm Cille* 24 (1994) 114–35, and 'Classical Modern Irish', in *Progress in Medieval Irish Studies*, edd. Kim McCone & K. Simms (Maynooth 1996), pp. 165–87.

[3] M.D. Sahlins, 'The segmentary lineage: an organization of predatory expansion', *American Anthropologist* 63 (1961) 322–45.

Explorations in Cultural History: Essays for Peter Gabriel McCaffery, edd. David F. Smith & H. Philsooph (Aberdeen 2010)   ISBN 978-0-9567059-0-7

colonial pressures provided by Francophone and Anglophone involvement in the Gaelic world from the twelfth century;[4] the characteristics, both general and particular, of Gaelic society as they are observable over the long haul, perhaps back to *ca* 500 B.C. but as attested in written sources beginning in the fifth century A.D.;[5] and the yet longer-term Celtic linguistic and cultural heritage.[6] These provided a fundamental structure whose character allowed, indeed encouraged, the production of this formal literature.

Scholars have uneasily acknowledged that formal public poetry, of the type characteristic of the Classical period, *ca* 1200 – *ca* 1700, is on the whole not present in the corpus of Gaelic literature surviving from the previous 650–750 years. The unease arises from the fact that the received scholarly history of mediaeval Gaelic literature has for more than a century insisted on the essential continuity of the public and political role of the poet from a remote Celtic antiquity.[7] That has rested above all on arguments from the vocabulary of poets and poetry in the Celtic languages, and their etymological analysis using the techniques of comparative Indo-European philology, which have created a picture of the imagined forbear in Celtic prehistory of the later mediaeval Gaelic public poet, the court-poet as he is commonly known.[8] In sum, a line has been strung between pre-christian Celtic society and the world of the Classical Gaelic poet of the thirteenth to seventeenth century.

What has happened, therefore, in Celtic scholarship at large is that a pursuit of origins, not unreasonable in itself, produced results which have provided an excessively dominant structure of explanation of the poet and his role in society, leaving too little room for the reception and assessment of difficult questions

---

[4] For a general, rounded introduction to these matters, see *A New History of Ireland*, gen. edd. T.W. Moody *et al.*, II–III (Oxford 1987 and 1976).

[5] For archaeology, see Barry Raftery, *Pagan Celtic Ireland. The Enigma of the Irish Iron Age* (London 1994). On the early Middle Ages, see T.M. Charles-Edwards, *Early Christian Ireland* (Cambridge 2000); for the central Middle Ages, see Donncha Ó Corráin, *Ireland before the Normans* (Dublin 1972).

[6] E. Knott, 'Irish Classical poetry commonly called bardic poetry', *apud* Eleanor Knott & G. Murphy (ed. J. Carney), *Early Irish Literature* (London 1966), pp. 19–93. See also, for a yet larger comparative (literary) context, H. Munro Chadwick & N.K. Chadwick, *The Growth of Literature* (3 vols, Cambridge 1932–40), I.

[7] For early specimens of this kind of exposition, see (for example) *Cours de littérature celtique*, ed. H. d'Arbois de Jubainville (12 vols, Paris 1883–1902).

[8] M. Dillon, 'The archaism of Irish tradition', *Proceedings of The British Academy* 33 (1947) 245–64; Knott, 'Irish Classical poetry'; J.E.C. Williams, 'The court poet in medieval Ireland', *Proceedings of The British Academy* 57 (1971) 85–135; P. Mac Cana, '*Regnum* and *sacerdotium*: notes on Irish tradition', *Proceedings of The British Academy* 65 (1979) 443–79; J. Carney, 'Society and the bardic poet', *Studies* (Dublin) 62 (1973) 233–50. On etymology in this context, see L. Breatnach, 'Poets and poetry', in *Progress*, edd. McCone & Simms, pp. 65–77, at p. 76. On the use of the term 'court-poet', see below, n. 299.

arising from the evidence (or absence of evidence) from the early and central Middle Ages. That broad expanse of historical time – extending from the death-throes of the Roman empire in the West and (locally) the arrival of christianity in Gaeldom to the end of the Viking-Age, the rise of a militantly reformist papacy transforming into a so-called 'papal monarchy', the development of an anti-Islamic crusading ideology, and a broad movement of European internal colonialism which in its northwesternmost dimension made Francophone culture politically dominant in Britain and then, in varying degrees, in Ireland – amounts to some eight centuries.[9] Until the 1960s, the historiography of the Celtic-speaking peoples had in many respects a markedly unhistorical character, often not acknowledging change over time; and in some measure – especially in its social dimension – literary history fell into the same trap of timelessness.[10]

In sum, scholarship and teaching in this field have offered an answer to the question 'What *was* mediaeval Gaelic poetry?' This was and is an entirely reasonable question for a literary historian to pose. How one achieves a satisfying answer is what is at stake, however.

An altogether different approach has emerged from the work of those literary scholars, beginning with Kuno Meyer and Robin Flower, who placed the poetry of the Old- and Middle-Irish periods, approximating to the early and central Middle Ages, at the centre of their characterisation of mediaeval Irish literature.[11] From their more popularising work, providing translations in anthology-form[12] (as too did Julius Pokorny in the German-speaking world in the generation after Meyer's death)[13] and accessible literary history written closely around translated poetry,[14] has

[9] On the last issue, see in particular Robert Bartlett, *The Making of Europe. Conquest, Colonization and Cultural Change, 950–1350* (London 1993).

[10] I have commented on this elsewhere: see, for example, D.N. Dumville, 'Kathleen Winifred Hughes, 1926–1977', *Studia Celtica* 14/15 (1979/80) 387–91, at p. 388, and *apud* Christopher N.L. Brooke, *The Church and the Welsh Border in the Central Middle Ages* (Woodbridge 1986), pp. xi–xiii, at p. xi.

[11] R.I. Best, 'Bibliography of the publications of Kuno Meyer', *Zeitschrift für celtische Philologie* 15 (1924/5) 1–65; Seán Ó Lúing, *Kuno Meyer 1858–1919. A Biography* (Dublin 1991) and *Celtic Studies in Europe and Other Essays* (Dublin 2000); *Bláithín: Flower*, ed. Mícheál de Mórdha (An Daingean 1998).

[12] *Selections from Ancient Irish Poetry*, transl. Kuno Meyer (London 1911; 2nd edn, 1913). For a selection of Flower's collected poetry to 1928, see Robin Flower, *Poems and Translations* (London 1931; rev. imp., Dublin 1994); for a summation of his views on mediaeval Irish literature, see *The Irish Tradition* (Oxford 1947), published posthumously.

[13] *Die älteste Lyrik der grünen Insel*, transl. Julius Pokorny (Halle a.S. 1923); *Altkeltische Dichtungen aus dem Irisch-Gälischen und Cymrischen*, transl. Julius Pokorny (Bern 1944).

[14] See, for example, *Early Irish Poetry*, ed. James Carney (Cork 1965), and *Seven Centuries of Irish Learning, 1000–1700*, ed. Brian Ó Cuív (Dublin 1961); *Medieval Irish Lyrics*, ed. & transl. James Carney (Dublin 1967), and *A Golden Treasury of Irish Poetry, A.D. 600–1200*, edd. & transl. David Greene & F. O'Connor (London 1967). A rather different emphasis, based on his own particular experience, was given in the interesting paper of R.T. Meyer, 'Early Irish poetry', *Annuale Mediaevale* 2 (1961) 31–54.

arisen a radically different image of mediaeval Gaelic poetry.

One of the most famous generalising observations about this poetry was provided in 1911 by Kuno Meyer, in particular in his characterisation of nature-poetry.[15]

In Nature poetry the Gaelic muse may vie with that of any other nation. Indeed, these poems occupy a unique position in the literature of the world. To seek out and watch and love Nature, in its tiniest phenomena as in its grandest, was given to no people so early and so fully as to the Celt. Many hundreds of Gaelic and Welsh poems testify to this fact. It is a characteristic of these poems that in none of them do we get an elaborate or sustained description of any scene or scenery, but rather a succession of pictures and images which the poet, like an impressionist, calls up before us by light and skilful touches. Like the Japanese, the Celts were always quick to take an artistic hint; they avoid the obvious and the commonplace; the half-said thing to them is dearest.

Meyer's own 'artistic hint', pointing to Japan for a striking comparison, has led to invocation of the haiku (although I have not seen evidence that that is what Meyer intended), especially by editors of anthologies.[16] The combination of characteristics remarked here – no sustained description, a succession of images, impressionism, hints, the half-said – and reïterated by successors who were less widely read in Gaelic poetry has produced a distortion, quite unintended by Meyer, which has remained essentially unchallenged as a generally applicable description of the Gaelic poetry of the earlier Middle Ages.

The tension between these two images of mediaeval Gaelic poetry has, when felt, been resolved in two ways. Chronology has been invoked, the view attributed to Meyer being held to characterise the poetry of the earlier Middle Ages, that of the Classical 'bardic' poetry being taken to represent the later period. However, both of these generalisations are grotesque distortions. Just as the former is highly partial, there is much late mediaeval Gaelic poetry which does not represent the world invoked by summoning up the court-poet at his most formal and

---

[15] *Selections from Ancient Irish Poetry*, transl. Meyer, pp. xii–xiii, where one should note also his reference to W. Lewis-Jones, 'The Celt and the poetry of nature', *Transactions of The Honourable Society of Cymmrodorion* (1892/3) 46–70. This passage has been quoted also by M. Dillon, 'Early lyric poetry', in *Early Irish Poetry*, ed. Carney, pp. 9–27, at 10–11, and by J. Carney, 'Introduction', *apud* Knott & Murphy, *Early Irish Literature*, pp. 1–17, at p. 5, and in *Medieval Irish Lyrics*, ed. & transl. Carney, p. xx; for its quotation in a slightly different context, see S. de Búrca, 'Aspects of transmission', *Éigse* 15 (1973/4) 51–65, at p. 59.

[16] The Japanese pop up again (with Gilbert and Sullivan) in *A Golden Treasury*, edd. & transl. Greene & O'Connor, p. 137. Cf. also *Medieval Irish Lyrics*, ed. & transl. Carney, pp. xx–xxi (*haiku*).

'Classical'.[17] The second means of resolution of tension, first enunciated by Meyer for other reasons, was to divide the earlier poetry into two categories defined by authorship.[18]

The purely lyrical poetry of ancient Ireland may be roughly divided into two sections – that of the professional bard attached to the court and person of a chief; and that of the unattached poet, whether monk or itinerant bard.

Yet, as we have seen, some scholars have remarked the substantial absence of formal public poetry from the Old- and Middle-Gaelic corpus.

There are indeed too many tensions, contradictions, misunderstandings here. We might reasonably ask how different the picture could look if we were to park the assumptions on which the received histories rest. I suggest that we can do this by parking the underlying question 'What *was* mediaeval Gaelic poetry?' Let us ask instead 'What *is* mediaeval Gaelic poetry?', commencing with what we have rather than seeking to begin with an excessively large historical hypothesis. The answers are at once liberating and increasingly troublesome.

KUNO MEYER'S LAST THOUGHTS (1919)

Let us begin with the last work sent to the press (on 10 July, 1919) by that greatest-ever publicist, editor, and (often poetic) translator of mediaeval Gaelic poetry, especially of the period before 1200. This was, of course, Kuno Meyer, and the work in question was the first of two projected parts of his 'Bruchstücke der älteren Lyrik Irlands'.[19] The second was never completed, and I do not know whether Meyer's plan for its contents survives in manuscript. A formal analysis of this publication (72 large-quarto pages long, containing editions and translations of 168 texts) reveals Meyer changing his mind – even as the work went to press in the very difficult circumstances of immediately post-war Berlin[20] – in respect of the answer to the fundamental, existential questions about the character of the Gaelic poetic tradition. Let us consider how he arranged his last work. And let us start with his table of contents, placed (in the 'French' tradition) on the very last page.[21]

---

[17] Flower, *The Irish Tradition*, pp. 142–64; cf. *Dánta Grádha. An Anthology of Irish Love Poetry of the Sixteenth and Seventeenth Centuries*, ed. Thomas F. O'Rahilly (Dublin 1916). See especially Seán Ó Tuama, *An Grá in Ambráin na nDaoine* (Dublin 1960) and *An Grá i bhFilíocht na nUaisle* (Dublin 1988), as well as chapters in his *Repossessions. Selected Essays on the Irish Literary Heritage* (Cork 1995), especially pp. 159–95, 282–3.

[18] *Selections from Ancient Irish Poetry*, transl. Meyer, p. xi.

[19] K. Meyer (ed. & transl.), 'Bruchstücke der älteren Lyrik Irlands. Erster Teil', *Abhandlungen der preussischen Akademie der Wissenschaften, phil.-hist. Klasse* (1919), Nr. 7.

[20] Some flavour of this has been given by Ó Lúing, *Kuno Meyer*, pp. 201–17.

[21] Meyer, 'Bruchstücke', p. 72.

I. Aus Gedichten auf Personen
        A. Loblieder 1–58
        B. Spott- und Schmählieder 59–88
        C. Totenklagen 89–131
II. Aus Gedichten auf Örtlichkeiten 132–147a
III. Vermischtes
        A. Aus Naturgedichten 148–159
        B. Aus Liebesgedichten 160–162
        C. Aus Liedern der Freundschaft 163–167

If, however, we turn to the body of the work, the headings have a somewhat different character. The first is 'Gedichte auf Personen'.[22] The second is 'Gedichte auf Örtlichkeiten'.[23] The subdivisions of the third section are, however, as printed in the contents-table. The theory, which we see becoming entrenched (with the generalisation of *Aus* in the headings) in Meyer's last thinking on the subject, is clearly in favour of the concept of what Rolf Baumgarten rather elegantly described in 1986 as 'isolated or alienated poetry': all this verse is flotsam and jetsam of the Gaelic poetic corpus of the earlier Middle Ages.[24]

On this basis, we may reasonably suspect Meyer's preface of having been written last, itself not an unusual situation. It begins uncompromisingly.[25]

Die große Masse der älteren Lyrik Irlands ist uns, wie diejenige Griechenlands und Roms, nur in Bruchstücken erhalten, welche sich als Zitate in verschiedenartigen Werken zerstreut finden. Manche von ihnen werden als Belege in Glossaren, andere in metrischen und grammatischen Abhandlungen als Beispiele angeführt; wieder andere stehen in den Annalen zum Gedächtnis berühmter Personen und Ereignisse. Auch als Randeinträge in den Handschriften finden wir sie, manchmal mit Bezug auf den dabeistehenden Text, öfter bloße Einfälle und Erinnerungen, wie sie dem Schreiber gerade in den Sinn kamen. (Einige der Vierzeiler, die einen abgeschlossenen Sinn geben, mögen auch von den Schreibern selber verfaßt sein.)

Meyer then turned to some of the difficulties which he faced.[26]

Alle diese *disiecta membra* einer untergegangenen großen und blühenden Literatur zu sammeln, übersteigt die Fähigkeit des Einzelnen .... So kann ich auch keine umfassende und planmäßig angelegte Sammlung bieten, sondern nur das Ergebnis einer langjährigen Lektüre, die meist auf ganz andere Zwecke gerichtet war. Vor allem aber mußte ich mir eine zeitliche Grenze setzen, da im Laufe der Jahrhunderte das Material schier ins Uferlose wächst. (Davon geben

---

[22] *Ibid.*, p. 5.

[23] *Ibid.*, p. 59.

[24] Rolf Baumgarten, *Bibliography of Irish Linguistics and Literature, 1942–71* (Dublin 1986), pp. xi–xii, 532–4 (cf. 318–20). James F. Kenney, *The Sources for the Early History of Ireland: Ecclesiastical. An Introduction and Guide* (New York 1929; rev. imp., by L. Bieler, 1966), p. 481, referred to commentary on *Félire Oenguso* as containing 'the debris of history and literature'.

[25] Meyer, 'Bruchstücke', pp. 3–4 ('Vorwort'). I have added the text of p. 3, n. 1, in brackets at the end of the quotation.

[26] *Ibid.*, p. 3 (I have inserted the text of n. 3, in brackets, into the body of the quotation).

die vielen Zitate aus mittelirischen Gedichten in dem … grammatischen Traktate einen Begriff.) Ich liefere also eine Auswahl, bei der ich besonders bisher überhaupt nicht oder unkritisch edierte und übersetzte Stücke drucke. Der Zeit ihrer Entstehung nach reichen sie vom Anfang des 8. bis zum 11. Jahrhundert, gehören also der alt- und frühmittelirischen Sprachperiode an. Ihr Inhalt ist ungemein bunt. Ich habe mich bemüht, sie in gewisse Gruppen zu zerlegen, die aber nicht immer ganz reinlich zu scheiden sind.

After some remarks about his methods of presentation, Meyer returned to his earlier theory of two different categories of poet.[27]

Die überwiegende Mehrzahl rühr von Berufsdichtern her, von denen wir zwei Klassen zu unterscheiden haben, die der hochangesehenen *filid* (studierte Dichter, Kunstdichter, Hofdichter) und die der weniger geachteten Barden.

Finally, he looked forward to presenting further categories of such verse.[28]

Ich hoffe, diesem ersten Heft bald ein zweites folgen zu lassen, welches Bruchstücke von geistlichen Liedern, von Gedichten auf besondere Ereignisse, von solchen, die aus Sagen stammen, und von Gelegenheitsdichtung aller Art enthalten soll.

It was not to be. Part I was published on 27 August, 1919; Meyer died suddenly on 11 October, at the age of 61.[29] No such collection as he envisaged has ever since been published.

SOURCES AND EXAMPLES OF MEYER'S 'BRUCHSTÜCKE'

It is well, given an argument which I wish to advance, to examine the source-texts of Meyer's first collection of *Bruchstücke*. The 168 items therein divide as follows between sources.

Mittelirische Verslehren and *Trefhocal* (tracts on metrics) account for 105 items in the collection.[30] Irish chronicles account for 37 items. 7 derive from glossaries. 3 come from commentary on *Félire Oenguso*. 2 have been plucked from the margins of manuscripts. 12 emerge from different combinations of source. 2 derive from other sources.[31]

There are many wonderful poems or poem-fragments in this collection,

---

[27] *Ibid.*, p. 4.

[28] *Ibid.*

[29] Ó Lúing, *Kuno Meyer*, pp. 215–17.

[30] Meyer, 'Bruchstücke', Nr. 1–4, 6, 8–14, 16–18, 20–76, 79–88, 120, 129, 136–7, 139–41, 144, 147, 147a, 149–50, 153–4, 160, 164–5, 167 (one hundred items). To these should be added excerpts from the *Trefhocal*-tract: Nr. 7, 19, 135, 138, 163 (five items).

[31] From the chronicles, *ibid.*, Nr. 5, 89–92, 94, 97–105, 107–18, 121–8, 142, 145 (37 items). From the glossaries, *ibid.*, Nr. 93, 119, 134, 148, 152, 157, 158 (seven items). From commentary on *Félire Oenguso*, *ibid.*, Nr. 130, 131, 162 (three items). From margins, *ibid.*, Nr. 151, 161 (two items). From combinations of source, *ibid.*, Nr. 15, 77, 78, 95, 96, 106, 133, 146, 155, 156, 159, 166 (twelve items). Two other items are of different origins: Nr. 132 (Leinster genealogical book), 143.

interesting for a remarkably wide range of reasons. I offer ten, five of them drawn from the metrical tracts published by Rudolf Thurneysen in 1891. I simply reproduce Meyer's edited texts and German prose translations.[32]

4.[33]   Fó sén dia ngab Óengus Alpain,
             Alpu thulchach trethantríathach;
             ruc do chaithrib costud clárach
             cossach lámach lethanscíathach.

'Es war eine günstige Stunde, als Oengus Alba in Besitz nahm, Alba, das hüglichte, voll mächtiger Fürsten. Er brachte den Städten Krieg mit Brettern, mit Füßen und Händen und breiten Schilden.'

This is a representative of a number of poems having reference to, or originating in, North Britain which are found in the tracts on metre and in Irish chronicles, the principal sources from which Meyer derived the *Bruchstücke* which he assembled into such an interesting collection. In Metrical Tract II, §7 (in which this *Bruchstück* is quoted as an example) opens *Ocus dian midthrom .v., ut est Gruibni eces di Alpain cecinit.*[34] The poet Grúibne had his own legendary place in Gaelic literature. We meet him in a text which has been given the editorial name *Longes Chonaill Chuirc*, 'The Exile of Conall Corc', of which the unique copy survives

---

[32] In these quotations I have replaced macrons over vowels by acute accents and suprapuncted *f* and *s* by *fh* and *sh*.

[33] Meyer, 'Bruchstücke', p. 6, from *Mittelirische Verslehren*, ed. Rudolf Thurneysen (Leipzig 1891), p. 33 (II.7). This quatrain shows no *dúnad* (see below, pp. 110–12).

[34] *Ibid.* There is an abbreviated twelfth-century text of II.3–8 (used by Thurneysen, *ibid.*, pp. 32–3), followed by III.26 (*ibid.*, p. 71), Meyer's Nr. 51 (see below, pp. 94–6); for separate publication, under the heading *Dian airing*, see *The Book of Leinster formerly Lebar na Núachongbála*, edd. R.I. Best *et al.* (6 vols, Dublin 1954–83), I.175–6. It occurs in a section (folios 37–8; *ibid.*, I.165–79) devoted to matters of metre and *filidecht*, containing (i) the *Trefhocal*-tract, (ii) the poem of Cellach Ua Ruanada (Thurneysen's Text IV), (iii) *Dian airing*, (iv) *De dúlib feda*, and (v) a short anecdote of Nédi *fri grádaib filed*. The section concludes, perhaps *zur Seitenfüllung* (see below, n. 122), with (vi) three quatrains (without *dúnad*) on the deaths of the three Cairpri:

Marb Cairpre Músc co n-áne
ac fiaduch na fordáme
iar ngabáil a duaine dó
ic eolchaib Muman ní immargó.

Atbath Cairpe Baschain bunaid
de galur i nIarmumain
ica doenib ba dis sin
ní fetatar a muntir.

Gai meic Cruind Badruí ro-briss
druim Cairpri Riatai ind rigliss
co torchair fond na fagla
la Cond catha Congabla.

acephalously in *Leabhar na Nuachongbhála*, otherwise 'The Book of Leinster', written in the second half of the twelfth century. There he is *Grúibne éices, fili Feradaig ríg Alban*.[35] Although we know of some Gaels of North Britain called Feradach,[36] this 'king of [North] Britain' is probably a legendary, prehistoric Pictish ruler, Uuradech.[37]

The first question must therefore be whether this association implies that the Oengus of the poem has the same status. This was indeed the opinion of Rudolf Thurneysen and Kuno Meyer,[38] who took the view that the Oengus in question was a brother of that Fergus mór who in Gaelic legend was one of the various hypothetical Irish prehistoric invaders and conquerors of what is now northwestern Scotland.[39] While we need not be at all shy of adopting a more recent general hypothesis, that Gaelic praise-poetry might be produced for a historical Pictish king[40] – and the favoured candidate in this instance has been Onu(i)st son of Uorgu(i)st (Oengus mac Forguso/Ferguso in Old Gaelic), king of Fortriu and then overking of Picts 729–61 –,[41] that very sensible general

---

[35] V. Hull (ed. & transl.), 'The Exile of Conall Corc', *Publications of The Modern Language Association of America* 56 (1941) 937–50; cf. *The Book of Leinster*, edd. Best *et al.*, V.1249–51. For a further dimension of the relationship of the Eoganacht of Munster with Pictland, see *Corpus genealogiarum Hiberniae*, I, ed. M.A. O'Brien (Dublin 1962; 2nd edn, rev. by J.V. Kelleher, 1976), pp. 186–99; there is brief commentary by Marjorie O. Anderson, *Kings and Kingship in Early Scotland* (Edinburgh 1973; 2nd edn, 1980), pp. 187–8, and more by D. Sproule, 'Politics and pure narrative in the stories about Corc of Cashel', *Ériu* 36 (1985) 11–28. Grúibne makes two appearances in this connexion in *Sanas Chormaic* (see n. 79, below), §§598 and 688 (ed. Meyer, pp. 49, 56); cf. William J. Watson, *The History of the Celtic Place-names of Scotland* (Edinburgh 1926), pp. 218–19.

[36] Anderson, *Kings*, pp. 185, 187, 189, 232, 296, 301, for a Feradach taken prisoner by the eighth-century King Onu(i)st (n. 41, below) in 736 and possibly the father of Ciniod, overking of Picts 763–75.

[37] *Ibid.*, pp. 90, 142, 187–8.

[38] R. Thurneysen, 'Zu irischen Handschriften und Litteraturdenkmälern. [Erste Serie]', *Abhandlungen der königlichen Gesellschaft der Wissenschaften zu Göttingen, philosophisch-historische Klasse*, N.F., 14 (1912/13), Nr. 2, p. 84 (*ad* II, 7); Meyer, 'Bruchstücke', p. 6 (Nr. 4).

[39] David N. Dumville, *Celtic Essays, 2001–2007* (2 vols, Aberdeen 2007), II.35–71, at pp. 35–47. On Cairpre Riata (n. 34, above), see *ibid.*, pp. 36–9.

[40] *The Triumph Tree. Scotland's Earliest Poetry, 550–1350*, ed. Thomas Owen Clancy (Edinburgh 1998), p. 15.

[41] *Ibid.*, pp. 14–15 and 144. On this king, see K. Forsyth & J.T. Koch, 'Evidence of a lost Pictish source in the *Historia regum Anglorum* of Symeon of Durham', in *Kings, Clerics and Chronicles in Scotland, 500–1297. Essays in Honour of Marjorie Ogilvie Anderson on the Occasion of her Ninetieth Birthday*, ed. Simon Taylor (Dublin 2000), pp. 19–34; Forsyth has endorsed Clancy's identification, *ibid.*, pp. 27–8. So has James E. Fraser, *From Caledonia to Pictland. Scotland to 795* (Edinburgh 2009), pp. 287, 302.

hypothesis neither validates nor is validated by this particular example.[42]

Meyer's collection has some other items which may have a North British or eastern Gaelic connexion. One such (and, alas, rather undistinguished) quatrain is derived from a chronicle, the so-called 'Fragmentary Annals of Ireland', for the year 858.

104.[43]   Nad mair Cináed co lín scor
fodera gol i cach thig:
óenrí a lóga fo nim
co bruinne Róma ní fil.

'Daβ Cinaed mit einer Menge von Reiterscharen nicht mehr am Leben ist, ruft Klage in jedem Hause hervor: bis hin an die Grenze Roms gibt es keinen einzigen König seines Verdienstes unter dem Himmel.'

There are three translations into English. Here is John O'Donovan's, published in 1860.[44]

     'That Cinaedh with the number of studs liveth not,
Is the cause of weeping in every house.
Any one king under heaven of his worth
To the borders of Rome there is not.'

That produced by Joan Newlon Radner in 1978 made the first line more intelligible and the whole somewhat less literal:[45]

     'Because Cináed with many troops lives no longer
there is weeping in every house;
there is no king of his worth under heaven
as far as the borders of Rome.'

---

[42] Some notes are necessary on translation of the poem extolling King Oengus. Clancy's English version very closely follows Meyer's German. (i) To take *cathair* as *Stadt*, 'town', is silly, given the sociopolitical structures of early mediaeval North Britain: 'fortress' would be much more apposite. (ii) I see no justification for rendering *costud*, 'arranging' (etc.), as *Krieg*, 'war'; to gain such meaning, one would have to emend to disaggregate *chathrachaib costud* into *chaithrib* (Meyer's emendation) and *cath(a)*, 'battle(s)', or *cocad*, 'war'. (iii) It is not clear to me that any useful sense has been got from *clárach. mit Brettern*, 'with boards', simply produces bafflement – the suggestion in *Dictionary of the Irish Language, based mainly on Old and Middle Irish Materials. Compact Edition*, gen. ed. E.G. Quin (Dublin 1983), p. 119 (C:221), *s.v.* **1. clárach**, 'a defence-mechanism made of boards(?)' is ingenious but still thoroughly baffling: how are we to take this poem, as a celebration of defence or of aggression or as something altogether different?

[43] Meyer, 'Bruchstücke', p. 47.

[44] *Annals of Ireland. Three Fragments, copied from Ancient Sources by Dubhaltach Mac Firbisigh*, ed. & transl. John O'Donovan (Dublin 1860), p. 151. It was reproduced in *Chronicles of the Picts, Chronicles of the Scots, and Other Early Memorials of Scottish History*, ed. William F. Skene (Edinburgh 1867), p. 404.

[45] *Fragmentary Annals of Ireland*, ed. & transl. Joan Newlon Radner (Dublin 1978), p. 113 (§285, annal 858.1).

In 1998 the poem made its first appearance in a Scottish anthology of verse, rendered into English by Thomas Owen Clancy:[46]

> 'That Cinaed with his hosts is no more
> brings weeping to every home:
> no king of his worth under heaven
> is there, to the bounds of Rome.'

One is tempted to say that this is rather better than the original! The quatrain follows a notice of the king's death:[47]

Cionaodh mac Ailpín, rex Pictorum, *mortuus est*.
Conadh dhó do ráidheadh an rann.

'Cionaodh son of Ailpín, king of Picts, died.
It was of him that the [following] quatrain was uttered.'

It is uncertain whether this verse can be taken as a contemporary utterance. There is little which would establish that on linguistic grounds. Textual history can only get us to the eleventh century at best.[48] There is no anchorage in any specific historical reference in the stanza. Indeed, it could have been composed in respect of any Gaelic king called Cinaed and used to embellish this annal-entry. This is a poor historical return for the labours of one who has been since perhaps the late tenth century one of Scotland's most famous rulers![49] We shall return to a chronicle-poem which has something to say about one of his sons and which throws up further and more interesting problems.[50]

We turn next to a *Bruchstück* with a somewhat different – and perhaps also rather tenuous – connexion with North Britain.

---

[46] *The Triumph Tree*, ed. Clancy, pp. 15–16, 144, where some of the historical commentary is extraordinary, being by turns exaggerated, outdated, and inaccurate – for example, 'Cinaed son of Ailpín, the Gael who took over the kingdom of the Picts, and whose dynasty continued to rule a united kingdom of Picts and Gaels throughout the Middle Ages'!

[47] The text is constructed from those of O'Donovan and Radner; the translation is mine.

[48] *Fragmentary Annals of Ireland*, ed. & transl. Radner, pp. vii–xxxiv. Cf. C. Downham, 'The good, the bad, and the ugly: portrayals of vikings in "The Fragmentary Annals of Ireland"', *The Medieval Chronicle* 4 (2004) 27–39.

[49] The legend of Cinaed mac Alpín as Gaelic conqueror of the Picts is first found in an acephalous chronicle which one can see developing from the late tenth century to the early thirteenth, and whose textual layers are still a matter of discussion: cf. D.N. Dumville, 'The Chronicle of the Kings of Alba', in *Kings, Clerics*, ed. Taylor, pp. 73–86.

[50] See below, pp. 133–5.

40.[51]   Bendacht úaim for Ethni n-ollguirm,
            ingen Domnaill dáiles bir,
            ica n-esbius, íar cúairt chathrach
            fo neim nathrach
            eire ochtair cethrair bachlach
            sithchenn srathrach, srúaim de mid.

'Segen von mir auf die glorreiche Ethne, die Tochter des speereverteilenden Domnall, bei der ich nach einer Runde durch die Stadt, wo ich nichts als Schlangengift erhielt, einen Metstrom getrunken habe, der eine Last für vier und zwanzig langköpfige Kerle mit Packsätteln gewesen wäre.'

It has been rendered in English and given a title by David Greene and Frank O'Connor.[52]

'*The Thirsty Poet*
A blessing from me on glorious Eithne, daughter of Domnall who casts a spear, with whom, after searching through a poisonous town, I have drunk a stream of mead that was load enough for thirty-two wry-necked haltered hauliers.'

In Text II of Thurneysen's *Mittelirische Verslehren* we encounter first the legendary *albanach* Grúibne éces and 'his' troublesome quatrain on King Oengus.[53] Immediately following it (§8), we read: *Ocus dian iartrom .vi. ut est Eochu echbél di Albain cecinit*, with a reference to a *Bendacht Dé for Eithne nollguirm ingin nDomnaill* (I give this reference from the earliest and fullest of the three witnesses, 'The Book of Leinster').[54] Fortunately, the whole is preserved in Thurneysen's Text III – albeit from partly different witnesses, neither of which is earlier than the later fourteenth century. There the attribution to Eochu echbél is not found.[55]

---

[51] Meyer, 'Bruchstücke', p. 20.

[52] *A Golden Treasury*, edd. & transl. Greene & O'Connor, pp. 202–4 (no. 53.2).

[53] *Mittelirische Verslehren*, ed. Thurneysen, pp. 29–66, at p. 33. The witnesses to the whole are 'The Book of Ballymote' (Dublin, Royal Irish Academy, MS. 536 [23.P.12]: Thomas F. O'Rahilly *et al.*, *Catalogue of Irish Manuscripts in The Royal Irish Academy* [28 fasciculi & 2 index-volumes, Dublin 1926–70], XIII.1610–55), 'The Book of Pottlerath' (Oxford, Bodleian Library, MS. Laud misc. 610 [*S.C.* 1132]: Brian Ó Cuív, *Catalogue of Irish Language Manuscripts in The Bodleian Library at Oxford and Oxford College Libraries* [2 vols, Dublin 2001/3], I.62–87 [no. 22]). For this section of the text, see also *The Book of Leinster*, edd. Best *et al.*, I.175 (cf. n. 34, above), lines 5297–5301.

[54] *Ibid.*, I.175, lines 5302–5.

[55] *Mittelirische Verslehren*, ed. Thurneysen, pp. 67–105, at p. 72 (§28), from 'The Book of Ballymote' and Dublin, Trinity College, MS. 1308 (H.2.12, no. 8). Cf. Thurneysen, 'Zu irischen Handschriften', I, p. 62 (*ad* §28).

Whether Eithne ingen Domnaill lived or was a poetic fantasy we can hardly know.[56] The *albanach* Eochu echbél ('horse-mouth') was no doubt fictional:[57] nor is this the only occurrence of a figure of that name in Gaelic literature. The poem has been nicely described by Thomas Clancy, when cleverly versifying and anthologising it, 'as a plausible example of an early Gaelic pub-crawl poem':[58]

> 'A blessing from me on excellent Eithne,
> daughter of Domnall
> who deals out spears,
> with whom I've drunk (after touring towns,
> on top of snake-poison)
> a load for an octet and quartet of peasants
> (long-headed, and hauling pack-saddles)
> of streams of mead.'

Thurneysen's Text III has at least one further poem with an apparent relationship to North Britain, but it was not included in Meyer's collection and I shall therefore not allow it into the present sequence.[59] Furthermore, tracts on metrics which were not available to Meyer have since been brought into print and have

---

[56] *Ibid.*, p. 84 (*ad* II, 8), Thurneysen identified her, for better or worse, as the wife of Bran ardchenn, overking of Leinster, who was killed with him in 795: *The Annals of Ulster (to A.D. 1131)*, I, edd. & transl. Seán Mac Airt & G. Mac Niocaill (Dublin 1983), pp. 250/1 (795.1), 'Bran arddcenn rex Lagenentium occisus est, et regina eius, Eithne ingin Domnaill Midhe. Fínshnechta cetarderc mac Ceallaigh occidit eos hi Cill Chúle Dumai in sexta nocte post kalendas Maii, id est quarta feria'.

[57] He is to be found in the introduction to the ninth-century text *Imaccallam in dá thuarad*, §§I–V: *The Colloquy of the Two Sages*, ed. & transl. Whitley Stokes (Paris 1905), pp. 8–11 (the earliest surviving copy also names Grúibne éces and Crechduile), and in *Sanas Chormaic* (see n. 79, below: ed. Meyer, pp. 47–8, *s.v.* **fír**, §585). Cf. Watson, *The History*, pp. 157–8.

[58] *The Triumph Tree*, ed. Clancy, p. 145. Here, *cathair* as 'town' is presumably less troublesome than in n. 42, above.

[59] *Mittelirische Verslehren*, ed. Thurneysen, p. 104 (III.203). The connexion is seemingly provided by the name of the metre which it exemplifies: the heading reads *Ettal sheisidach Cruitheantuath inso i cloich Locha Comru*. *Cruithentuath* is a standard Gaelic expression for Pictland, although of course it might in principle refer to the Cruithni of northeastern Ireland. The stanza reads as follows:

> Gilla Pádraig plagh mellghaile
> noconhuair slan troid seanmaire
> tlam dotharr agmuilt fhithnaigi
> cisdi nach roichet foglaidi
> adarc bó rodraide
> cornaire istí ibraighi.

For 'a tentative translation' of 'an extremely obscure piece', see *The Triumph Tree*, ed. Clancy, p. 145:

> 'Gille-Phádraig, plague of versecraft,
> has not found the musicians' sound measure:
> a handful of a wether's belly-wool for bedding;
> a treasure-chest bandits can't get at;
> the horn of a cow, snarling fiercely;
> a horn player, inside, on a yew-wood vessel.'

yielded poetry of historical and literary importance for the study of early twelfth-century Scotland.[60]

Meyer's collections, both from the tracts on metre and from Irish chronicles, give us a remarkable range of evidence (some fourteen poems) for Viking-Age Gaelic-Scandinavian contacts, not only in the politico-military sphere, but in settlement, material culture, and religion, as well as in displaying a Gaelic poet uttering verse praising a Scandinavian king of Dublin.[61] One example must stand for all these.

22.[62]   Amláib airchingid   átha airtheraig   Érenn íathaige,
             dagrí Duiblinne   déne dúthaige   tréne tríathaige.

'Olaf, der Vorkämpfer der östlichen Furt des länderreichen Irland, der edle König von Dublin, dem gewaltigen, ererbten, starken, beherrschenden.'

51.[63]   Brigit búadach,
             búaid na fine,
             siur Ríg nime,
             nár in duine,
             eslind luige
                    lethan breó.

             Rosíacht nóibnem
             mumme Góidel,
             ríar na n-óiged,
             óibel ecnai,
             ingen Dubthaig,
             duine úallach,
             Brigit búadach
                    bethad beó.

---

[60] *Irish Grammatical Tracts*, ed. Bergin, p. 269; on the very interesting source-manuscript, see in particular J. Carney, 'The Ó Cianáin Miscellany', *Ériu* 21 (1969) 122–47. For edition and discussion, see T.O. Clancy, 'A Gaelic polemic quatrain from the reign of Alexander I, ca. 1113', *Scottish Gaelic Studies* 20 (2000) 88–96. For translation and brief commentary, see *The Triumph Tree*, ed. Clancy, p. 184 (and cf. p. 18).

[61] Meyer, 'Bruchstücke', pp. 14 (Nr. 25), 20–1 (Nr. 43), 24 (Nr. 53), 25 (Nr. 56), 28 (Nr. 61), 34 (Nr. 79), 54 (Nr. 119), 57–8 (Nr. 129), 64 (Nr. 147). If we add those contexts of survival point in the same direction, we should add *ibid.*, pp. 13 (Nr. 22), 55–6 (Nr. 123), 56 (Nr. 124), 57 (Nr. 128).

[62] Meyer, 'Bruchstücke', p. 13, retaining Meyer's layout; *Mittelirische Verslehren*, ed. Thurneysen, pp. 14–15 (I.32) and 44 (II.58). This shows no *dúnad*.

[63] Meyer, 'Bruchstücke', p. 23; *Mittelirische Verslehren*, ed. Thurneysen, p. 71 (III.26). See also (for an English translation) Kuno Meyer, *Miscellanea Hibernica* (Urbana, IL 1917), p. 45 (595). For a text with facing English translation, see *Dánta Ban. Poems of Irish Women, Early and Modern*, ed. & transl. P.L. Henry (Cork 1991), pp. 50–1.

'Die glorreiche Brigitta, der Ruhm ihres Geschlechtes, Schwester des Himmelskönigs, hehr ist die Frau, gefahrvoll bei (falschem) Eidschwur, eine breite Flamme.

'Sie hat den Himmel erreicht, die Pflegemutter der Gälen, den Fremden willfährig, der zündende Funke der Weisheit, die Tochter Dubthachs, eine stolze Frau, die glorreiche Brigitta, die Lebendige des Lebens.'

Much could be said about this remarkable poem. While it is undoubtedly a celebration of the principal female saint of the Gaels, and thus very certainly a religious poem, its language is nonetheless steeped in secular panegyric convention,[64] praising not only the victorious glory of the saint but her familial relationships, genetic and adoptive, and her social roles. While the poem has no regular *dúnad*,[65] it would be preposterous not to accept the equivalence of lines 1 and 13 as an indication of poetic completion. Brigit came to stand in an important fictive relationship both to God and to her people: so did other female saints, notably St Íte as suckler of Jesus,[66] but none achieved the relationship with the whole Gaelic nation which was early asserted for Brigit and eventually left her as one of the *trias thaumaturga* of Gaeldom. On the one side, Brigit was *siur ríg nime*, 'the sister of the king of Heaven'; on the other, she was *mumme Goídel*, 'the fostermother of the Gaels'. It is not needful to labour the importance of fosterparents in mediaeval Gaelic society.[67] Rather, I wish to draw attention to the role of the *mu(i)mme* in relation to Gaelic poetry. It is part of a very much larger issue, that of the woman's witness in mediaeval Gaelic poetry, on which there is still almost everything to do.[68]

As an example (by no means isolated) I offer the well known pair of quatrains about Cú Chuimne of Iona, recorded in 'The Annals of Ulster', *sub anno* 746, which accompany the bare notice of his death, *Cú Cuimne sapiens obiit*.[69] They were written in the lower margin of the manuscript-page by the chronicle's principal scribe, *H*.[70]

---

[64] Cf. the poem *Bairri bréo bithbúadach*: Meyer, 'Bruchstücke', pp. 23–4 (Nr. 52); *Mittelirische Verslehren*, ed. Thurneysen, p. 57 (III.107).

[65] As defined in the quotations below (pp. 110–12).

[66] As manifested in the now famous poem of six quatrains (with *dúnad*), *Ísucán*, 'Jesukin': *Medieval Irish Lyrics*, ed. & transl. Carney, pp. 64–7 and 99 (no. XXVI).

[67] Fergus Kelly, *A Guide to Early Irish Law* (Dublin 1988), pp. 86–90. See also a fine study by F. Kerlouégan, 'Essai sur la mise en nourriture et l'éducation dans les pays celtiques d'après le témoignage des textes hagiographiques latins', *Études celtiques* 12 (1968–71) 101–46.

[68] For one approach, see Joanne Findon, *A Woman's Words: Emer and Female Speech in the Ulster Cycle* (Toronto 1997).

[69] *The Annals of Ulster (to A.D. 1131)*, I, edd. & transl. Mac Airt & Mac Niocaill, pp. 200/1 (747.5). There is a very interestingly different version in *Annala rioghachta*, ed. & transl. O'Donovan, I.342–5.

[70] On all this, see below, pp. 114–20, and, on the situation of attribution, especially n. 164.

1.   Cu Chuimne
        Ro legh suithi co druimne,
        A lleth n-aill hiaratha
        Ro leici ar chaillecha.

2.   Ando Coin Cuimne ro-mboi,
        im-rualad de conid soi,
        ro leic caillecha ha faill,
        ro leig al-aill arith-mboi.

Unusually, these are followed (rather than preceded) by an attribution: *Muime Chon Cuimne cecinit*, 'Cú Chuimne's fostermother recited this'.

The verses are humorous, even satirical. That his foster-mother could have outlived him to recite this is (in the circumstances envisaged) decidedly unlikely, and the attribution is perhaps also part of the humour – unless one might allow that an authorised critical voice raised about an eminent cleric might be that of a woman in such an important relationship.

These stanzas, which show no *dúnad* and may therefore be part of a larger original whole, have gained more celebrity in a remarkable version by John V. Kelleher, first published in 1954 and entering oral tradition.[71]

'Cú Chuimne in youth
Read his way through half the Truth.
He let the other half lie
While he gave women a try.

'Well for him in old age.
He became a holy sage.
He gave women the laugh.
He read the other half.'

72.[72]   Rocúala
        ní tabair eochu ar dúana:
        dobeir aní as dúthaig dó:
        bó.

'Ich habe gehört, daß er keine Pferde (zum Lohn) für Lieder gibt. Er gibt was ihm naturgemäß ist – ein Rind.'

Meyer may have known this text for a quarter-century before he published it, with an English prose translation (in America in 1916/17).[73] Apparently he had

---

[71] Printed here from John V. Kelleher, *Too Small for Stove Wood, too Big for Kindling. Collected Verse and Translations* (Dublin 1979), p. 12. On the oral tradition, cf. *Medieval Irish Lyrics*, ed. & transl. Carney, p. xxi. The original publication was in *Teangadóir* (Toronto) 2 (1954/5) 39.

[72] Meyer, 'Bruchstücke', p. 32; *Mittelirische Verslehren*, ed. Thurneysen, p. 67 (III.3). This shows no *dúnad*.

[73] Meyer, *Miscellanea Hibernica*, p. 44 (594).

challenged his friends and colleagues in Liverpool by telling them that he thought the metre unreproduceable in English.[74] John Sampson teased him back by producing a lengthy, cheeky encomium for Meyer's fiftieth birthday, in 1908, entitled "'A Clap on the Back" for Kuno Meyer'.[75] Walter Raleigh, on the other hand, had already produced a sonorous poem (embedded in an occasional piece) which yet lives.[76] Meyer's warm relationship with fellow literary scholars gave rise to much thought about and engagement with metres used by mediaeval Gaelic poets.[77] We see Meyer here as a precursor to Robin Flower, an ideal ambassador for Gaelic literature to an English-speaking public. It was left to Vivien Mercier in 1962 to create and publish a metrical imitation and translation, a justly celebrated rendering of a much appreciated stanza:[78]

> 'I know him;
> He'll give no horse for a poem;
> He'll give you what his kind allows,
> Cows.'

The next comes from a glossary, *Sanas Chormaic*,[79] attributed to the king-bishop of

---

[74] John Sampson, *In Lighter Moments. A Book of Occasional Verse and Prose* (Liverpool 1934), p. 95, n. 1.

[75] *Ibid.*, pp. 95–7 (eighteen stanzas). The poem's title refers to the name of the Gaelic metre in question, *Deibide baise fri tóin*, 'Slap-on-the-buttocks *deibide*' (*Mittelirische Verslehren*, ed. Thurneysen, p. 67 [III.3]): Kuno Meyer, *A Primer of Irish Metrics* (Dublin 1909), p. 18 (§30); *Early Irish Lyrics*, ed. & transl. Gerard Murphy (Oxford 1956; rev. imp., 1962), pp. 90/1 and 215 (no. 38); Gerard Murphy, *Early Irish Metrics* (Dublin 1961), p. 69 (§128); *Early Irish Satire*, ed. & transl. Roisin McLaughlin (Dublin 2008), pp. 104–262, at 134/5, 190. Sampson's poem begins, 'Halfway house! / To Walhalla where carouse / Zeuss and Zumpf: where Pott and Bopp / Stop.', and ends 'May none carp / When you take the biggest harp! / May the cloud on which you sit / Fit!'. (The account and quotation by Dillon, 'Early lyric poetry', p. 18, are erroneous.) Sampson (1862–1931) was a pupil of Meyer and became Liverpool's University Librarian (1892–1928).

[76] Walter Alexander Raleigh (1861–1922) was Professor of Modern Literature & English Language at Liverpool, 1890–1900. For his correspondence, see *The Letters of Sir Walter Raleigh (1879–1922)*, ed. Lady Raleigh (2 vols, London 1926; 2nd edn, 1926). For his poem in this metre, see Walter Raleigh, *Laughter from a Cloud* (London 1923), pp. 216–18 (a poem dated 21.12.1901): 'Though our songs / Cannot vanquish ancient wrongs; / Though they follow where the rose / Goes; // And their sound, / Swooning over hollow ground, / Fade and leave the enchanted air / Bare; // Yet the wise / Say that not unblest he dies / Who has known a single May / Day. // If we have laughed, / Loved, and laboured in our craft, / We may pass with a resigned / Mind.' These are stanzas 8–11 of a sixteen-stanza poem otherwise occasional and frivolous. As with Sampson's poem (n. 75), the quotation by Dillon, 'Early lyric poetry', p. 19, is erroneous and suggests oral tradition (cf. n. 71, above).

[77] See, for example, W.P. Ker, 'On a lyric stave called in Irish *ochtfhoclach bec*', in *Miscellany presented to Kuno Meyer*, edd. Osborn Bergin & C. Marstrander (Halle a.S. 1912), pp. 327–32.

[78] Vivien Mercier, *The Irish Comic Tradition* (Oxford 1962), p. 115.

[79] K. Meyer (ed.), 'Sanas Cormaic. An Old-Irish Glossary compiled by Cormac Úa Cuilennáin, king-bishop of Cashel in the tenth century, edited from the copy in The Yellow Book of Lecan', in *Anecdota from Irish Manuscripts*, edd. O.J. Bergin *et al.* (5 vols, Halle a.S. 1907–13), IV.

Cashel, overking of Munster, Cormac mac Cuilennáin (†908).[80]

95.[81]   Gúaire: Cían ó thibi do gáiri,
                  is ar n-aire fri dóini,
                  atchíu for indaib t'abrat
                  is tind galgat nochóini.

        Órnait: Dethbir dam ceni antais
                  adám abrait di bréissi,
                  ní bad fáilid Laidgnén clam
                  cid é maras tarm éissi.

'Guaire: Lang ist's her, seit du gelacht hast, – wir geben auf Leute acht, – ich sehe es an deinen Augenwimpern, schmerzlich ist der Verlust, den du beklagst.

'Órnait: Es wäre nur Recht, wenn meine Wimpern nie aufhörten von Tränen zu tropfen: (denn auch) Laidgnén der Aussätzige würde nicht froh sein, wenn er es wäre, der mich überlebte.'

In fact, Meyer constructed this from two widely separated entries in *Sanas Chormaic*.[82] He had previously edited, and translated into English verse, the second of these stanzas (the first in order of occurrence in the Glossary).[83]

    'Meet for me, though my two eyelashes
    Should not cease from flowing:
    Laidgen the leper would not be joyous
    Though he were living after me.'

The three following items come from Irish chronicles.

101.[84]   Mallacht ort, a Challainn chrúaid,
                  a shrúaim amal ceó do shléib,
                  dorimmart éc do cach leith
                  for dreich níthaig níamguirm Néill.

[80] No major study of Cormac, whether of his life or of the great body of texts attributed to him, has ever been published: in these circumstances, none of these attributions can be deemed credible – cf. D.N. Dumville, *Peritia* 11 (1997) 451–68, at p. 456. For discussions of the authorship of *Sanas Chormaic*, see Meyer, 'Sanas', pp. xvii–xviii, with reference to K. Meyer, 'Miscellen. 1. Die Autorschaft von Cormac's Glossar', *Zeitschrift für celtische Philologie* 8 (1910–12) 178, and above all to *Three Irish Glossaries*, ed. Whitley Stokes (London 1862), pp. ix–xviii. See further R. Thurneysen, 'Zu Cormacs Glossar', in *Festschrift Ernst Windisch* (Leipzig 1914), pp. 8–37, and *Zeitschrift für celtische Philologie* 10 (1914/15) 454–5. On the risk of frivolity in modern attributions of texts to Cormac, see D.N. Dumville, 'A dangerously disturbed Irish manuscript: Oxford, Bodleian Library, MS. Rawlinson B.502 (*S.C.* 11849), folios 19–89', *The Journal of Celtic Studies* 6 (2006) 1–40, at p. 30, n. 83.
[81] Meyer, 'Bruchstücke', p. 40. Neither stanza shows *dúnad*.
[82] Meyer (ed.), 'Sanas', pp. 62 (§726) and 17 (§180).
[83] *King and Hermit. A Colloquy between King Guaire of Aidne and his Brother Marban, being an Irish Poem of the Tenth Century*, ed. & transl. Kuno Meyer (London 1901), p. 30 (cf. p. 9).
[84] Meyer, 'Bruchstücke', p. 45. Neither stanza shows *dúnad*.

Ní caraim in n-usce ndúabais
immethéit sech tóib m'árais,
a Challainn, ce nomóide,
macc mná báide robádais.

'Fluch über dich, grausamer Callinnfluβ, du Strom wie Nebel vom Gebirge; du hast von allen Seiten den Tod auf das tapfere glanz- und ruhmvolle Antlitz Nialls gezwängt.

'Ich liebe das unheilvolle Wasser nicht, das zur Seite meines Wohnsitzes vorbeiflieβt; o Callinn, ob du dich gleich (deiner Tat) rühmst, du hast den Sohn einer liebenden Mutter ertränkt.'

Because of their different metres, Meyer deemed these stanzas to be excerpts from different poems, even though the same person is addressed in both.[85] Both are found together in 'The Annals of The Four Masters', only the second in 'The Annals of Ulster'.[86]

The next item is quite unusual in its attribution, and it stands here as a representative of a small body of verse attributed to its royal author, Aed Allán mac Fergaile of the Northern Uí Néill, king of Tara (†743), which (in so far as it survives) is transmitted almost wholly in chronicles.

---

[85] *Ibid.*: 'Aus zwei metrisch verschiedenen Gedichten'. In this context, it is perhaps important to remember the following comment about a group of so-called 'epigrams': 'Notice, too, that though the textbooks do not mention it, the first three are in a form that seems uniquely Irish [viz, Gaelic], that of the double epigram with verses in contrasting metres' (*A Golden Treasury*, edd. & transl. Greene & O'Connor, p. 107).

[86] The second stanza is found in Dublin, Trinity College, MS. 1282 (H.1.8), folio 41r, in the upper margin as a single long line with a prefixed *signe de renvoi* matching one at the end of 41rb1. Cf. *The Annals of Ulster (to A.D. 1131)*, I, edd. & transl. Mac Airt & Mac Niocaill, pp. 304/5, *s.a.* 845 (=846.3); the hand is that called 'H¹' by the editors. For the pair together, albeit separated by the words *Acus bheós* (implying, I take it, either that the two stanzas were drawn from different sources or that the two stanzas were not contiguous in a source-poem – or even both!), see *Annala rioghachta Eireann. Annals of the Kingdom of Ireland, by The Four Masters, from the Earliest Period to the Year 1616*, ed. & transl. John O'Donovan (2nd edn, 7 vols, Dublin 1856), I.470–3 (844.9). It should be noted that, after the two stanzas edited by Meyer, two more are given in the annal. These are introduced by the statement *Maonghal alithir ro ráidh*. The text reads:

Beir lat leir imcomort Néll,
na badh brithem condal céill,
Do rígh nimhe taibhredh réir,
condibh reidh do cech naimhreid.

Niall do baa,
Niall fo bá
Niall i mmuir,
Niall i tein,
Niall cen naidhidh.

99.[87]   Int Áed isind úir,
              in rí isind rúaim,
              int énán dil déin
              la C<é>rán i Clúain.

'Aed ist unter der Erde, der König ist im Friedhof, das liebe saubere Vögelchen ist bei Cérán in Clúain.'

The King Aed in this quatrain is Aed mac Colgen, overking of the Leinstermen, killed by the forces of Aed Allán at the battle of Áth Senaig in 738. In 'The Annals of The Four Masters', *s.a.* 733, in 'The Annals of Tigernach' for 738,[88] and in the chronicle *Do fhlaithiusaib Érenn* attached to *In lebor gabála* at the end of 'The Great Book of Lecan',[89] this quatrain is attributed to him. But there was clearly much story attached to his reign and its battles.[90] We have also (albeit in different sequence) in the first two chronicles just mentioned a quatrain uttered in anticipation of the battle and attributed to a female poet Samthann, presumably the saint of Cluain Brónaig (Clonbroney, Co. Longford), who died in 739; it begins *Ma conrísat in dá Aed*.

As Kuno Meyer was mopping up after the completion of his 'Bruchstücke', I, he assembled the verse attributed to these two, Aed and Samthann, each singing of the other.[91] He wrote of Samthann 'die selbst als Dichterin auftrat' and printed 'ein ganzes, kleines Gedicht' – of three stanzas with (irregular) *dúnad* – attributed to Aed Allán, which is about St Samthann. He held this to be genuine work of the first half of the eighth century. What makes it unique within this little corpus, however, is that it is found, in the same shape, as a marginale in 'The Book of Leinster', part of a sort of liminal verse commentary on 'The Martyrology of Tallaght'.[92] What the nature of the relationship between these two manifestations of the poem and a hypothetical original might be remains to be discovered. Finally here, one item can be added to Meyer's corpus, however dubiously: in 'The

---

[87] Meyer, 'Bruchstücke', p. 44.

[88] Only the first line is given in this text: *Aedh Allán féin doróne so, 'In t-Áed issin úir', 7rl.* See *The Annals of Tigernach*, ed. & transl. Whitley Stokes (2nd edn, 2 vols, Felinfach 1993), I.242.

[89] The reference was provided in *Annala rioghachta*, ed. & transl. O'Donovan, I.334, naming '*Lib. Lec.* fol. 311'. See O'Rahilly *et al.*, *Catalogue*, XIII.1551–1610: Dublin, Royal Irish Academy, MS. 23.P.2 (535).

[90] I have discussed this briefly elsewhere: D.N. Dumville, 'Genre and function in mediaeval Irish chronicles', *The Journal of Celtic Studies*, forthcoming. For the saga-literature about the period and the interaction of Uí Néill and the Laigen, see Myles Dillon, *The Cycles of the Kings* (London 1946), pp. 99–114, and *Cath Almaine*, ed. Pádraig Ó Riain (Dublin 1978).

[91] K. Meyer (ed. & transl.), 'König Aed Allán als Dichter', *Zeitschrift für celtische Philologie* 13 (1919–21) 143–4.

[92] *The Book of Leinster*, edd. Best *et al.*, VI.1646, n. 3: it is in the upper margin of facs. p. 365. Cf. *The Martyrology of Tallaght*, edd. & transl. R.I. Best & H.J. Lawlor (London 1931), pp. 124–5.

Annals of The Four Masters', *s.a.* 600, and 'The Annals of Inisfallen' is a quatrain introduced in the latter text with the words *Inde dixit Aed Alláin*.[93] (This was another era of contending kings called Aed, one of whom indeed was an Aed mac Colgen who died at Clonmacnoise:[94] it may be that false associations were made.) The late eleventh-century Southern text reads:[95]

Ba romór in ruadchumma	'Very great was the red slaughter
for rígraid Hérend huile,	Of the kings of all Ireland,
Aed Sláne co sochaide	Aed Sláine with an army,
Aed Róin ocus Aed Buide.	Aed Róin and Aed Buide.'

The next and last item, the longest given here, Meyer pieced together in a heroic (re)construction from five different sources in three different genres: the unattached marginal quatrain;[96] the glossary *Sanas Chormaic*;[97] and three chronicles, 'Fragmentary Annals of Ireland',[98] 'The Annals of The Four Masters',[99] and 'The Annals of Inisfallen' (the last being preserved in a manuscript of the end of the eleventh century).[100] Such a range of attestations is decidedly unusual in Meyer's

[93] *Annala rioghachta*, ed. & transl. O'Donovan, I.226/7 (600.4), where it is anonymous; *The Annals of Inisfallen (MS. Rawlinson B 503)*, ed. & transl. Seán Mac Airt (Dublin 1951), pp. 82/3 ([607].1). The alleged poet was of course alive a century and more later.

[94] *Annala rioghachta*, ed. & transl. O'Donovan, I.232/3 (606.3).

[95] The Four Masters' text is different in line c: after the name, it reads *fa shluagh glonnach*.

[96] London, British Library, MS. Harley 5280, folio 46v, used for quatrain 5 by Meyer, seems to have escaped Robin Flower: see Standish Hayes O'Grady *et al.*, *Catalogue of Irish Manuscripts in The British Museum* (3 vols, London 1926–53), II.314–15.

[97] Meyer (ed.), 'Sanas', pp. 34 (§419 = quatrain 6, introduced *ut Colmán mac úi Clúasaigh dixit*) and 54 (§673 = quatrain 7, introduced *unde dixit Colmán mac húi Clúasaigh hi marbhnaidh Cuimine Fotæ*).

[98] *Annals of Ireland. Three Fragments*, ed. & transl. O'Donovan, pp. 60–3 (*s.a.* 661=662.1); *Fragmentary Annals of Ireland*, ed. & transl. Radner, pp. 12/13 (*s.a.* 661=662.1[§19]), 186. A poem of five stanzas (= quatrains 1, 2, 4, 8, [Vab=?], [Vcd=]7ab) is introduced after the annal-entry by *unde Colman úa Clúasaigh, aide Chuimin, cecinit.*

[99] *Annala rioghachta*, ed. & transl. O'Donovan, I.270–3 (*s.a.* 661.2). Here we have a poem of three stanzas (= quatrains 3, 4, 5). No stanza shows *dúnad*: there is no way of reärranging the three quatrains to achieve such an effect.

[100] *The Annals of Inisfallen*, ed. & transl. Mac Airt, pp. 94/5 ([661].1–2) = quatrain 2, the one which summarises the notable deaths recorded in the annal. The quatrain is anonymously introduced: *De illis dictum est.* The same quatrain is to be found in 'The Annals of Ulster' but has been overlooked by the editors of the *marbnad*:

Marbain inna bliadna-sa
nibo chointi ni oco,
Mæl Duin, Bécc mac Fergusso,
Conann, Cumméne foto.

In TCD MS. 1282 (H.1.8), folio 24r, this quatrain stands in a long line at the right-hand end of the lower margin; verse d stands above that line, hemmed in by a line-divider. In *The Annals of Ulster (to A.D. 1131)*, I, edd. & transl. Mac Airt & Mac Niocaill, p. 132, n. b *ad an.*, it is attributed to hand 'H²(?)'.

'Bruchstücke'. The poem is presented as a *marbnad*, elegy, composed by Colmán mocu Chluasaig for the famous bishop of Clonfert, Cummíne fota, who was held to have died in the plague of the 660s.[101]

96.[102]

1   Marb frimm andess, marb antúaid,
níptar inmuini athshlúaig,
tofóir, a Rí nime glaiss,
a ndochairte tatharlais.

2   Marbáin inna blíadna-so,
nírbo chúinti nech occo:
Máel Dúin, Bec macc Ferguso,
Conaing, Cuimmíne Foto.

3   Ní beir Luimnech for a druimm
de shíl Muimnech i lLeth Cuinn
marbán i nnói ba fíu dó,
do Chummíniu macc Fhíachno.

4   Ma dotéiged nech dar muir
seissed i suide nGriguir,
mad a hÉre, ní búi dó,
inge Cummíne Foto.

5   Mo chuma-sa íar Cummíniu
ón ló rofoilged a árc,
cói m'ocuil nísningaired,
dord Gaill íar ndérach a bárc.

6   Ní maid cride ce chíë
marb teinn, coich bé a díë,
inná róimdetar íar Clíu
óä béo íar Cummíniu.

7   Úäe Corpri, úäe Cuirc,
ba súi, ba án, ba airdirc,
dirsan marbán i mmí gam,
ní líach ní d'écaib íaram.

8   Sech ba hepscop som ba rí,
ba macthigern Cummíni,
tendál Érenn ar shoäs,
ba hálaind mar adchoäs.

---

[101] There were multiple prominent persons called Cumméne/Cummíne (Latin Cummianus) in those years, and no clear statement exists in modern scholarship to help understanding of where evidence about each one begins and ends. Cf. D.N. Dumville, 'Two troublesome abbots', *Celtica* 21 (1990) 146–52, at pp. 146–9.

[102] Meyer, 'Bruchstücke', pp. 41–3. No stanza shows *dúnad* with any other.

'1   Ein Toter im Süden von mir, ein Toter im Norden, – es war keine willkommene Auflösung einer Kriegerschar – o König des blauen Himmels, hilf dem schlimmen Pakt, den du (uns) geschickt hast (?), ab!

'2   Die Toten dieses Jahres – im Vergleich mit ihnen ist keiner zu beklagen: – Máel Dúin, Bec, Sohn des Fergus, Coning, Cummíne der Lange.

'3   Der Luimnech trägt vom Geschlechte derer von Munster auf seinem Rücken keinen Toten zu Schiffe nach Leth Cuinn, der Cummíne dem Sohne Fíachnas an Wert gleich käme.

'4   Wenn jemand übers Meer käme, um den Sitz Gregors einzunehmen, – wenn er aus Irland sein sollte, so gab es außer Cummíne dem Langen niemand dafür.

'5   Mein Schmerz um Cummíne von dem Tage an, da sein Leib zugedeckt worden ist, – das Weinen meines Auges konnte ihn nicht bewahren, (es ist wie) der Klagegesang eines fremden Händlers, dem man seine Schiffe geplündert hat.

'6   Ein Herz bricht nicht, wenn es auch einen Toten schmerzlich beweint, um wen immer seine Klage gehen mag, da die Ohren der Lebenden westwärts von Cliu durch das Wehklagen um Cummíne nicht zerbrochen sind.

'7   Der Nachkomme Corbres, der Nachkomme Corcs, er war ein Weiser, war herrlich, war berühmt. Ach über den lieben Toten im Wintermond!   nach ihm ist nichts was stirbt beklagenswert.

'8   Außer daß er Bischof war, war Cummíne ein König, war ein Jungherr, ein Leuchtfeuer Erins an Weisheit, war schön, wie man berichtet hat.'

Unlike some of these poems, this one has been subjected to a vigorous reänalysis and become a subject of controversy between major scholars.[103] It is clear that there are significant aspects of Meyer's poem-building which cannot stand, the most obvious being the inclusion of his stanza 2 which is tightly yoked to the chronicling genre.[104]

The sources which supplied the specimens for Meyer's 'Bruchstücke', I, exemplify some significant parts of Gaelic literary tradition. The metrical tracts carry a certain authority as reference-works. *Sanas Chormaic* and other glossaries are reference-works with much potential for mutation and, particularly, expansion.

[103] For reëdition, see G.S. Mac Eoin (ed. & transl.), 'The Lament for Cuimine fota', *Ériu* 28 (1977) 17–31; F.J. Byrne (ed. & transl.), 'The Lament for Cummíne foto', *Ériu* 31 (1980) 111–22. This matter is intimately related to a literary cycle about King Guaire, about which see Dillon, *The Cycles*, pp. 75–98; S. Ó Coileáin, 'The structure of a literary cycle', *Ériu* 25 (1974) 88–125, and 'The making of *Tromdám Guaire*', *Ériu* 28 (1977) 32–70.

[104] This quatrain is found alone in 'The Annals of Inisfallen' and 'The Annals of Ulster' (cf. n. 100, above). It is with qq. 1, 4, 7, and 8 in 'Fragmentary Annals of Ireland' (cf. n. 98, above). It is not found in 'The Annals of The Four Masters'. Nor does it (or any verse) appear at the relevant place in 'The Annals of Tigernach' and *Chronicum Scotorum*.

The commentaries on major vernacular (or bilingual) poetic works are also sources of further poetry.[105] Gaelic chronicles (themselves often bilingual texts) are in varying degrees encrusted with or penetrated by verse items, the quatrains being either distributed in margins or incorporated into the text: they share such characteristics whether they were written in Gaeldom or abroad.[106] The last source of Meyer's 'Bruchstücke', I, needing mention at this point is simply the margins of manuscripts written, used, or owned by literate Gaels, whether at home or abroad, from the first evidence of Gaelic manuscript-culture to at least the end of the seventeenth century. The volume of such marginal literature from more than a millennium of manuscript-use is quite extraordinary and has scarcely been treated as a literary and cultural phenomenon.[107]

What was not laid under contribution in Meyer's 'Bruchstücke', I, was partly advertised as intended for inclusion in the second part of the collection, notably, religious poetry and poems found embedded in the prose saga-literature.[108] These are two large bodies of text. However, they by no means make adequate allowance for the vast array of metrical marginalia mentioned above, a literature better known to Meyer than to any other scholar. To suspect that Meyer would have had to publish more than two volumes of his 'Bruchstücke' is perhaps to avoid the difficult question of just what, by the end of his life, Meyer thought about the literature of margins.

One other corpus must be mentioned before we proceed further. In Meyer's writing in English we read of 'ancient' or 'early' Gaelic literature, terminology redolent of an era of scholarship which in its own professional diction and terminology can itself seem archaic. The word 'mediaeval' rarely found itself at the tip of Meyer's pen: we may suspect that, as in much Insular scholarship of the period, 'the Middle Ages' would have been understood by him as coming to the

---

[105] *Amre Coluimb Chille*, *Félire Oenguso céli Dé*, and 'The Irish *Liber hymnorum*' are particularly significant in this respect.

[106] The outstanding example from the world of Gaelic ecclesiastical emigration is the Chronicle of Marianus Scottus, written in the 1070s and 1080s. For an edition (none is adequate), see *Mariani Scoti, poetæ, mathematici, philosophi et theologi eximii, monachi Fuldensis, historici probatissimi, Chronica*, ed. Iohannes Herold (Basel 1559). For commentary, see B. MacCarthy, *The Codex Palatino-Vaticanus, No. 830* (Dublin 1892), and B. Ó Cuív, 'The Irish marginalia in Codex Palatino-Vaticanus No. 830', *Éigse* 24 (1990) 45–67. For a recent study, see P. Verbist, 'Reconstructing the past: the chronicle of Marianus Scottus', *Peritia* 16 (2002) 284–334.

[107] We owe to Charles Plummer an admirable and delightful introduction to two such outstanding features of the Gaelic manuscript-tradition: C. Plummer, 'On the colophons and marginalia of Irish scribes', *Proceedings of The British Academy* 12 (1926) 11–44. But what should have been a generally seminal paper has had more effect on manuscript-cataloguing practice than on Gaelic literary studies, for which it is nonetheless perpetually pregnant.

[108] Meyer, 'Bruchstücke', p. 4: cf. p. 87, above.

islands with Francophone culture after 1066. In his German-language writing, however, he made matters easier for us with a more precise range of expression. The *Abhandlungen* of the Prussian Academy for 1913 carried an earlier two-part publication by him, 'Über die älteste irische Dichtung'.[109] Suddenly we can see a progression: *die älteste Dichtung* in 1913, *die ältere Lyrik* in 1919. Was he contemplating a further series of chronological moves towards and into modernity – to *die alte Dichtung*, and then perhaps to *die neue, die neuere*, and (no doubt least likely) *die neueste Lyrik*?

Die älteste irische Dichtung comprised the poetic elements contained in that section long known as *An Leabhar Laighneach* of what has since 1962 been called *Corpus genealogiarum Hiberniae*. Both generically and prosodically it has a different character from *die ältere Lyrik* of Meyer's second collection. The function of the poetry in the genealogical book may however be held to be essentially similar to that in *Sanas Chormaic* and the metrical tracts, providing authority and illustration for reference-texts which developed their own authority (but were nonetheless subject to revision) over time.[110]

Meyer had increasingly come to regard Gaelic verse literature of the earlier Middle Ages as comprising largely *disiecta membra*.[111] In opening his 'Bruchstücke' by observing that 'Die große Masse der älteren Lyrik Irlands ist uns … nur in Bruchstücken erhalten …' he had already gone too far;[112] his comparison with Classical Greek and Roman literature gives much too dark a picture of what survives thence; and his further specification that these Gaelic poetic *Bruchstücke* 'sich als Zitate in verschiedenartigen Werken zerstreut finden'[113] begs very important questions about what they were doing there. Yet in all this the margin is not a topic of central discussion, even though it is probably the site of the preservation of the largest body of short Gaelic poetry. Is it possible to imagine that Meyer had not thought through the total significance of the body or bodies of material which he was editing, translating, and commenting on in the 1910s?

---

[109] K. Meyer, 'Über die älteste irische Dichtung', *Abhandlungen der königl. preuss. Akademie der Wissenschaften, phil.-hist. Classe* (1913), Nr. 6 & Nr. 10.

[110] *Corpus*, I, ed. O'Brien, pp. 1–116 (and cf. 334–57); cf. Dumville, 'A dangerously disturbed Irish manuscript'. For interesting remarks about the character of this poetry, see J. Corthals, 'The rhymeless "Leinster poems": diplomatic texts', *Celtica* 24 (2003) 79–100, at p. 82.

[111] Meyer, 'Bruchstücke', p. 3.

[112] *Ibid.*

[113] *Ibid.*

LITERARY CRITICISM AND LITERARY HISTORY IN THE HEROIC AGE OF CELTIC STUDIES

In the liveliest and most stimulating, most original and most insightful, and (for many scholars) most irritating bilingual anthology of Gaelic verse of the earlier Middle Ages – I refer to *A Golden Treasury of Irish Poetry, A.D. 600 to 1200*, edited and translated by David Greene and Frank O'Connor –, the introduction ends thus:[114]

All but one of the poems have been edited elsewhere – the majority by Kuno Meyer, whose combination of flair and scholarship first brought early Irish poetry to the notice of the outside world – and this has allowed us a freedom of emendation that would be inappropriate in a purely scholarly work.

The great bulk of the mediaeval Gaelic literature published in modern editions in the two generations from 1860 to 1920 was edited (and translated) by two men, Whitley Stokes (1830–1909) and Kuno Meyer (1858–1919).[115] From 1860 to 1880, Stokes set the pace.[116] When the young Meyer contacted him and announced his desire and intention to be a celticist, he was embraced and nurtured by Stokes who exercised a profound – but far from controlling – influence on him.[117] Both had a wide literary range, but the polymathic Stokes commanded by far the greater sweep. Meyer's interests settled down into Gaelic literature of the early and central Middle Ages, although he enjoyed a much wider knowledge of Celtic studies. Meyer had a significantly shorter life-span than Stokes, and by the time of Stokes's death Meyer had only a decade left. The 1910s were not an easy decade to live through, especially for someone who at its beginning was a German occupying a public position in the United Kingdom and very much committed to Ireland's struggle to take control of its own destiny. Even by comparison with the exacting régime of teaching, scholarship, and travel with which Meyer had lived since his first appointment to Liverpool in 1882, the 1910s were for him an era of extraordinary effort, upheaval, stress, and achievement, lived to the full until the very last moment.[118]

Stokes had set the tone, discovering, editing, translating, and publishing Celtic texts at a furious pace. He worked fast and between continents for a significant slice of his adult life: from 1862 to 1882 he held appointments in India at the

---

[114] *A Golden Treasury*, edd. & transl. Greene & O'Connor, p. 17.

[115] K. Meyer, 'Whitley Stokes, 1830–1909', *Proceedings of The British Academy* 4 (1909/10) 363–7; R.I. Best, *Whitley Stokes (1830–1909). A Memorial Discourse* (Dublin 1951); Ó Lúing, *Kuno Meyer*. Best also prepared bibliographies of both men: see above, n. 11 (Meyer), and below, n. 116.

[116] R.I. Best, 'Bibliography of the publications of Whitley Stokes', *Zeitschrift für celtische Philologie* 8 (1910–12) 351–406.

[117] Ó Lúing, *Kuno Meyer*, pp. 1–15, 72.

[118] *Ibid.*, pp. 81–217.

instance of Sir Henry Maine. He made errors in his work but never shied from publishing lists of corrigenda. He took an interest in comparative legal, literary, and mythological studies from a secure base in comparative Indo-European philology and extensive reading, and he was aided by communication with a wide circle of friends and colleagues. He had views about literature and reäctions to it, but these were for the most part treated as personal and not to be luxuriated in in public. Meyer shared this outlook, perhaps having imbibed it from Stokes's example. While we can gain glimpses into, or read brief statements of, his outlook on matters of literary critical interest, we find no extended expositions in that vein. While his sense of literary history – of prosody, of the origins of the written tradition, of genre, of transmission and reception – can be captured, there is again rarely more than summary statement of views which could only have been developed on the basis of an almost incomparable knowledge of the subject.

It is striking that Meyer's published oeuvre contains only a handful of general essays on Celtic (and of course, more specifically, Gaelic) literary history, even though he is known to have lectured widely on such matters.[119] It is as if an austere self-denial in face of larger issues was preferred or required when the priority was seen to be to make the literary culture visible to and respected by an international public. It is arguable that this deprived Meyer of the opportunity to think harder and more deeply about the issues which his work of edition and translation was forcing to the fore. An anecdote told by Myles Dillon about Meyer's pupil and younger colleague Osborn Bergin in relation to the 1920s catches well, I think, the legacy of Stokes and Meyer in this regard, intensified as scholars with very different backgrounds and personalities came to the fore in

---

[119] *Ibid.*, pp. 15, 26–30, 93–7, 131, 230–1, for example, for the lectures. The essays in question are: (i) 'On the study of Celtic languages and literature', *Transactions of The Liverpool Welsh National Society* 1 (1885/6) 17–33; (ii) 'Problems in early Irish and Welsh literature', *University College of Wales Magazine* 22 (1899/1900) 411–33; (iii) 'Ancient Gaelic poetry', *Transactions of The Gaelic Society of Glasgow* 3 (1895–1906) 1–28; (iv) 'Die irisch-gälische Literatur', in *Die Kultur der Gegenwart, ihre Entwicklung und ihre Ziele*, ed. Paul Hinneberg, Teil I, Abteilung xi.1, *Die romanischen Literaturen und Sprachen, mit Einschluss des Keltischen* (Berlin 1909), pp. 78–97.

Celtic studies. In a lecture published in 1965, Dillon wrote:[120]

Forty years ago, when I was a young student, I went one night to a lecture by Osborn Bergin on 'The Exile in Irish Poetry' at the Irish Literary Society. I had not yet met Bergin then, I suppose, and it was a rare occasion, *for he seldom ventured into literary discussions, although he had a fine sense for literature.* The society met in a room over Crane's music shop in Upper O'Connell Street, and they were quite a distinguished company. Bergin's plain delivery added to the tension as he recited the poems, and I have always remembered the lecture as one of the stages in my conversion. One of the poems that he read was Columcille's 'Farewell to Ireland'.

I have heard versions of the italicised statement from scholarly personalities as different as James Carney and Kenneth Jackson, both of whom had sat at Bergin's feet. It must be said that this reluctance remained the dominant manner in Celtic literary studies until change began in the 1960s. Part of its legacy is still with us in that there are large issues of literary history which remain to be addressed, even though some of the more historical questions concerning Gaelic literature were being discussed in print by Meyer's contemporary Rudolf Thurneysen (1857–1940) – with now limpid, now penetrating clarity – already in the years on either side of 1900.

QUESTIONS OF RECEPTION, INTEGRITY, LIMINALITY, AND FUNCTION

If all the short poetry assembled by Meyer in his two collections of the 1910s and in his earlier publication of stray or collected quatrains is fragmentary or excerpted, 'isolated or alienated',[121] what of its reception? If the mediaeval scholar/scribe read his metrical tracts, was he then prone to write in the margins of his manuscripts the canonical examples embedded therein, or to fill up with the customary – inbred – *horror uacui* what would otherwise have been empty

---

[120] Dillon, 'Early lyric poetry', pp. 16–17 (my italics). For Bergin's outlook, see D.A. Binchy, *Osborn Bergin* (Dublin 1970). For an important observation on Bergin and Classical Gaelic bardic poetry, see Carney, 'Society', p. 233. After the passage reproduced here, Dillon quoted the first five stanzas of the 22-quatrain poem from *Selections from Ancient Irish Poetry*, transl. Meyer, pp. 85–7: Meyer's title for it was 'Colum Cille's *greeting* to Ireland', but it is easy to see how either is applicable. For the text used by Meyer, see *The Life of St. Columba, Founder of Hy; written by Adamnan, Ninth Abbot of that Monastery*, ed. William Reeves (Dublin 1857), pp. 285–9 (24 quatrains), from an unspecified source. Quatrain 5 of that version occurs in the commentary on *Amre Coluimb Chille* in *Leabhar na hUidhre*: see *Lebor na Huidre. [The] Book of the Dun Cow*, edd. R.I. Best & O. Bergin (Dublin 1929; 2nd rev. imp., 1992), p. 11. For further complications, see *Betha Colaim Chille, Life of Columcille, compiled by Maghnas Ó Domhnaill in 1532*, edd. & transl. A. O'Kelleher & G. Schoepperle (Urbana, IL 1918), pp. 198–201 (§201).
[121] Baumgarten, *Bibliography* (as n. 24, above).

spaces at the end of manuscript-columns?[122]

One has only to turn the pages of mediaeval and early modern Gaelic manuscripts, or modern catalogue-descriptions thereof, to discover how widespread is the phenomenon of liminal poetry. Is there a satisfying explanation, both literary and functional in character, waiting to be enunciated?

As I have already remarked,[123] the publication of these items, both piecemeal and in anthologies, whether in the original or (above all) in translation, has created a new reception-phenomenon which expects such literary artefacts to be intelligible or emotionally acceptable as if they were complete authorial emanations.

Supposedly the oldest pieces of surviving Gaelic verse are what have been described as the fragments (seven in number) attributed to Colmán mac Lénéni, abbot of Cloyne (Co. Cork), who died in 604.[124] These stand close to the origins of written vernacular Gaelic poetry. It is relatively easy to accept the categorisation of them as fragmentary.

Other poems are fragmentary in different ways – a poem might be superficially complete but on analysis revealed to be a pastiche reörganised from a previous poem or poems on the same subject: the well known 'Nun of Beare' seems to be a case in point, the creation of 'a dotty eleventh-century editor'.[125]

When we read of 'a bitter little fragment of a poem …, the metre of which is probably eleventh century', whose thought at least can be taken as complete, there is reason to halt to ask further questions.[126] A 'fragment from a poem about the sea in flood', perhaps of the twelfth century, and a 'fragment about the blackbird

---

[122] For discussion of early mediaeval Gaelic attitudes to the book, see M.B. Parkes, *Scribes, Scripts and Readers. Studies in the Communication, Presentation and Dissemination of Medieval Texts* (London 1991), pp. 1–18. For modern practice, compare R. Thurneysen, 'Zur Seitenfüllung', *Zeitschrift für celtische Philologie* 20 (1933–6) 363, 367, 381; cf. Dumville, 'A dangerously disturbed Irish manuscript', pp. 37–8.

[123] See above, pp. 83–5.

[124] R. Thurneysen, 'Colmán mac Lénéni und Senchán Torpéist', *Zeitschrift für celtische Philologie* 19 (1931–3) 193–207, and cf. 'Zu Verslehre II', *ibid.*, 17 (1928) 263–76; *A Golden Treasury*, edd. & transl. Greene & O'Connor, p. 3; J. Carney, 'Three Old Irish accentual poems', *Ériu* 22 (1971) 23–80.

[125] *A Golden Treasury*, edd. & transl. Greene & O'Connor, pp. 9–10, 48–55 (no. 9); cf. also pp. 161–4 (no. 40). On the reception of this text, see the important article by B. Murdoch, 'In pursuit of the *Caillech Bérre*: an early Irish poem and the medievalist at large', *Zeitschrift für celtische Philologie* 44 (1991) 80–127.

[126] *A Golden Treasury*, edd. & transl. Greene & O'Connor, p. 11 (cf. 12 on its metre). The poem, not identified there, is *Canas ticc macc léginn?* (two quatrains, without *dúnad*): for text, see *Mittelirische Verslehren*, ed. Thurneysen, pp. 93–4 (III.142), and (with discussion, localisation, and dating) C. Ní Mhaol-Chróin, 'Macalla as Cluain-mhac-Nóis A.D. 1050', *Galvia* 1 (1954) 15–17.

by Belfast Lough', of the same century, provoke similar questions.[127] That 'this little lyric [*M'airiuclán hi Túaim Inbir*] is all that remains of a ninth-century version of the story of Suibne' is ambiguous in respect of our immediate concerns.[128]

When one or two quatrains only constitute the extant poem, it might be held that '[i]t is often impossible to tell what some of the hundreds of fragments scattered through annals, textbooks, and romances really are'.[129] This might be put another way: 'Again we have no method of knowing what the origin of these verses is'.[130] No method(s) at all? When one throws in the towel so rapidly, unsubstantiated assertion is the next step: three poems, of a collection of eleven single quatrains, 'are probably genuine epigrams';[131] why?

One simple test, though by no means wholly determinative, deserves to be a starting point of any critical probing of short poetic texts, as of longer ones. The introductions to Gaelic metrics by Kuno Meyer (1909) and Gerard Murphy (published in 1961, two years after his death) both contain a section entitled 'How to conclude a poem'.[132] Murphy's account begins thus:[133]

In Irish syllabic verse, and also often in the older poetry, the last word or syllable of the *íarcomarc* ('final stanza') echoes the first word or syllable of the first line of the poem. A poem in which this echo does not occur is said to lack a *dúnad* ('conclusion').

The importance of such a *dúnad* is stressed in a Middle Irish poem preserved in the early-fifteenth-century Book of Ballymote ....

The following stanza ... classifies the three main types of conclusion as **saigid**, **ascnam**, **comindsma**. The same three types are referred to also in [a stanza of instruction].[134]

> **Comindsma** do Dondchad *dó*;
> **ascnam** *dond*, im cach degló;
> **saighid** so (is é in slicht amra)
> *Dondchadh* int ainm ollamda.

---

[127] *A Golden Treasury*, edd. & transl. Greene & O'Connor, pp. 13–14, 126–9 (no. 29); and pp. 14, 16. The latter is *Int én bec*: *Early Irish Lyrics*, ed. & transl. Murphy, pp. 6/7 and 174 (no. 5), and *Medieval Irish Lyrics*, ed. & transl. Carney, pp. xx–xxi; cf. *Mittelirische Verslehren*, ed. Thurneysen, p. 99 (III.167). The former is *ibid.*, p. 38 (III.24), *Fégaid úaib*: *A Golden Treasury*, edd. & transl. Greene & O'Connor, pp. 205–7 (no. 54.1).

[128] *Ibid.*, pp. 100–1 (no. 22).

[129] *Ibid.*, p. 107.

[130] *Ibid.*, p. 111.

[131] *Ibid.*, pp. 111–14. On the epigram, see further below, pp. 112–13 and n. 140.

[132] Meyer, *A Primer*, p. 12 (§28); Murphy, *Early Irish Metrics*, pp. 43–5.

[133] *Ibid.*, pp. 43–4 (incorporating p. 44, nn. 1–2). For an essential supplement to Murphy's discussion, see D. McManus, '*Úaim do rinn*: linking alliteration or a lost *dúnad*?', *Ériu* 46 (1995) 59–63.

[134] *Auraicept na n-Éces, The Scholars' Primer*, ed. & transl. George Calder (Edinburgh 1917), p. 164 (lines 2199–2202); cf. *Mittelirische Verslehren*, ed. Thurneysen, pp. 29–31 (Text II, Introduction), for discussion of terminology. I have quoted the stanza from the text given by Murphy, *Early Irish Metrics*, p. 44 (but I have replaced his macrons by acute accents).

This means that if a poem begins with the name *Dondchad* it may be concluded: (*a*) by a weak type of *dúnad*, known as **comindsma** ('riveting together'), in which the first consonant and vowel (*do*) – vowel length is disregarded in the *dúnad* of a poem – of the first syllable of *Dondchad* form the last syllable of the last line of the *íarcomarc*; (*b*) by a stronger type of *dúnad*, known as **ascnam** ('approach'), in which the whole first syllable (*dond*) forms the last syllable of the last line of the *íarcomarc*; (*c*) by a still more excellent type of *dúnad*, known as **saigid** ('attainment'), in which the whole opening word *Dondchad* is repeated as the last word of the last line of the *íarcomarc*.

In 1912, Thomas P. O'No(w)lan, referring to the Psalm-glosses preserved in the mid-ninth-century Irish manuscript at Milan, wrote as follows in the *Festschrift* for Kuno Meyer:[135]

We have in Ml. 26 b 10 what may I think be taken as a reference to the native custom of ending a poem with the same words with which it begins.

Almost a half-century later, Francis Shaw encouraged Gerard Murphy to reïnvent this particular wheel.[136]

… the following reference to the custom … is contained in an Old Irish gloss on Psalm VIII, which begins and ends with the words 'Domine, Domine noster, quam admirabile est nomen tuum in universa terra': *Amal as hó molad ocus adamrugud in Choimded in-tinscana in salmsa, is [s]amlaid for-centar dano, amal dund-gniat ind filid linni cid in sin* ('As this psalm begins with praise and admiration of the Lord, it is thus moreover that it is concluded, even as the poets do with us') ….

The concept has a long history, therefore, certainly well back into the Old-Gaelic period, and its practice and perceived importance are well attested. Murphy provided some greater specification of its practical usage.[137]

A glance through a collection such as [my *Early Irish Lyrics* (1956)] shows that **saigid** is the commonest type of *dúnad*, at least in the Old and Middle Irish period[s]. As a rule such a **saigid** includes opening unstressed syllables, as in no. 7, where opening *A ben* is answered by concluding *a ben*, or no. 30, where opening *Robad mellach* is answered by concluding *robad mellach*. Occasionally, however, an opening unstressed syllable is disregarded, as in no. 22, where opening *In Spirut* is answered by concluding *do Spirut*. Occasionally, too, different grammatical parts of the same word correspond, as in no. 10, where opening *Día* is answered by concluding *Dé*, or no. 44, where opening *Gáir* is answered by concluding *gáire*.

Instead of ordinary **saigid** the whole of the first line (nos. 14, 18, 23, 52, 56), or the whole

---

135 T.P. O'No(w)lan (ed.), 'Imchlód aingel', in *Miscellany presented to Kuno Meyer*, edd. Bergin & Marstrander, pp. 253–7, at p. 253. For the date of the manuscript, see David N. Dumville, *Three Men in a Boat. Scribe, Language, and Culture in the Church of Viking-Age Europe* (Cambridge 1997), pp. 21–3, 33–4. For the gloss in the context of the rest of the vernacular glossing in Milano, Biblioteca Ambrosiana, MS. C.301 inf., see *Thesaurus Palaeohibernicus. A Collection of Old-Irish Glosses, Scholia, Prose and Verse*, edd. & transl. Whitley Stokes & J. Strachan (2 vols, 2nd edn, Dublin 1975), I.44–51 (Psalm VIII), at p. 51.

136 Murphy, *Early Irish Metrics*, pp. 43–4.

137 *Ibid.*, p. 44.

of the first two lines (nos. 26, 36, 46), may be repeated at the end; and occasionally this repetition is not absolutely perfect, as in no. 33, where opening *Is scíth mo chrob ón scríbainn* is answered by concluding *dían scíth mo chrob ón scríbonn*.

After giving some examples of **ascnam** and **comindsma**, the two other subtypes of *dúnad*, Murphy stated an editorial rule.[138]

> Absence of *dúnad* in a verse text, unless it be a short epigram, may be taken as a sign that the poem has not been preserved in its entirety.

There is some ambiguity in Murphy's expression, which must engender extra caution in one's reäction to his rule as stated. That said, however, there appears to be much to disagree with.[139] It is far from clear, on Murphy's evidence, that *dúnad* was compulsory rather than customary. What the rule needs to say (and perhaps this was indeed what Murphy intended) is that a reader or editor, asking (as what should be a matter of routine) whether a poem as transmitted is entire, should weigh absence of *dúnad* as one factor in coming to a judgment on the matter. If formal *dúnad* is at length shown to have been a compulsory embellishment of the structure of a poem from the beginnings of written Gaelic poetry to about 1700, or in period-divisions of those eleven or twelve centuries, the matter becomes in principle much more straightforward.

Murphy's caveat, or allowance of an exception, to his rule raises issues which are absolutely crucial in the context of the present discussion. Leaving aside the implied concept of a long epigram, we may wonder whether we are confronted with an invitation to circularity of thought. How is a mediaeval Gaelic 'short epigram' to be defined? Do we know that it existed as a category in that cultural context? As I have already remarked, it could be held to be a genre created by modern anthologising reception.[140] An irony in this is that Kuno Meyer, who might be held responsible for presenting an anthology which initiated such

---

[138] *Ibid.*, p. 45. The preceding comments on the other two subtypes are as follows: 'Examples of **ascnam** in EIL are *Tórramat … tor* (19); *Cen áinius … cena* (35); *Ránacsa … ránac* (42); *Géisid … géis* (49). In 20 (*A Maire … mair*) and 25 (*A Choimdiu … choim*) we have **ascnam** with neglect of an opening unstressed syllable. | Examples of **comindsma** in EIL are *Dúthracar … dú* (12); *I mebul … is mé* (17); *Tuc … tú* (27); *Do bádussa … do bá* (58).'

[139] Gerard Murphy has (at least posthumously) acquired something of a reputation as an over-zealous editor, emending too freely. He has also been taken to task for allowing his interpretations of poems to be coloured by accompanying prose, whatever its date. For all this, see J. Carney, 'The so-called "Lament of Créidhe"', *Éigse* 13 (1969/70) 227–42, and 'Notes on early Irish verse', *ibid.*, pp. 291–312.

[140] See above, pp. 83–5, 108–10. But the verse epigram had already been enunciated as a genre in Irish literature and with an Irish name, and the impact of that classification needs to be assessed: see *Dánfhocail. Irish Epigrams in Verse*, ed. Thomas F. O'Rahilly (Dublin 1921). Cf. Flower, *The Irish Tradition*, p. 48, on seventeenth-century English 'Ejaculations'.

reception, had by the end of the same decade come to the conclusion that the fragment was almost the usual condition of survival of Old- and Middle-Gaelic poetry.[141]

A crucial element in any attempt to understand this fragmentary and/or epigrammatic verse in its cultural context is a recognition of the importance of liminality, of marginality, in the mediaeval Gaelic book. The manuscript-book, particularly the vernacular manuscript-book, is one of the least well studied elements of Gaelic culture. This may seem surprising when one considers that the cataloguing of vernacular Gaelic manuscripts has been one of the great academic achievements of modern Celtic studies. Since 1926, when Robin Flower's volume of the *Catalogue of Irish Manuscripts in The British Museum* and the first fascicule, by Thomas F. O'Rahilly, of the *Catalogue of Irish Manuscripts in The Royal Irish Academy* were published,[142] almost all such manuscripts have been catalogued, a remarkable scholarly triumph.[143] But the study of Gaelic palaeography and codicology has not kept pace, the history of the Gaelic book is an almost unknown concept, and discussion of the relationship of book and text remains (with some few outstanding exceptions by remarkable scholars) at the level of banalities.

One must ask questions which may themselves risk sounding banal. Why was the margin a seat of poetry in Gaelic literary culture (as it may indeed have been in Welsh too in the ninth, tenth, and eleventh centuries)?[144] How did such liminal

---

[141] Compare *Selections from Ancient Irish Poetry*, transl. Meyer (1911), with Meyer, 'Bruchstücke' (1919).

[142] These two completed works are: O'Grady *et al.*, *Catalogue*; O'Rahilly *et al.*, *Catalogue*.

[143] For a guide to the whole, see Pádraig de Brún, *Lámhscríbhinní Gaeilge: Treoirliosta* (Dublin 1988). Mopping up continues: Cornelius G. Buttimer, *Catalogue of Irish Manuscripts in The University of Wisconsin – Madison* (Dublin 1989); Breandán Ó Conchúir, *Clár Lámhscríbhinní Gaeilge Choláiste Ollscoile Chorcaí: Cnuasach Uí Mhurchú* (Dublin 1991); Pádraig Ó Macháin, *Catalogue of Irish Manuscripts in Mount Melleray Abbey, Co. Waterford* (Dublin 1991); William Mahon, *Catalogue of Irish Manuscripts in Villanova University, Pennsylvania* (Dublin 2007). The two substantial collections on which work is still needed are those of The National Library of Ireland – cf. Nessa Ní Shéaghdha & P. Ó Macháin, *Catalogue of Irish Manuscripts in The National Library of Ireland* (13 fasciculi, Dublin 1961–96) – and Trinity College, Dublin (where a draft-catalogue had been undertaken by Anne O'Sullivan before her death in 1984).

[144] On Wales in this context, see Ifor Williams, *The Beginnings of Welsh Poetry* (Cardiff 1972; 2nd edn, 1980), pp. 89–121, 181–9. Cf. further J.C.T. Oates, 'Notes on the later history of the oldest manuscript of Welsh poetry: the Cambridge Juvencus', *Cambridge Medieval Celtic Studies* 3 (1982) 81–7. Old-English examples are few and may be directly attributable to Gaelic influence: cf. the extensive marginal additions to Cambridge, Corpus Christi College, MS. 41, on which see first N.R. Ker, *Catalogue of Manuscripts containing Anglo-Saxon* (Oxford 1957), pp. 43–5 (no. 32). There is other potentially relevant matter. (1) In Winchester, Cathedral Library, MS. 1 (of unknown English origin, perhaps *ca* 1000), there is a bilingual Latin and Gaelic colophon to a copy of Bede's History: *Venerabilis Baedae opera historica*, ed. Charles Plummer (2 vols, Oxford 1896), I.cix–cxi; David N. Dumville, *English Caroline Script and Monastic History: Studies in Benedictinism, A.D. 950–1030* (Woodbridge 1993), pp. 118–19. (2) See H. Meroney, 'Irish in the Old English charms', *Speculum* 20 (1945) 172–82, and D. Stifter, 'A charm for staunching blood', *Celtica* 25 (2007) 251–4.

verse interact with other inhabitants of such space and of course with the contents of the text-block? What kinds of poetry existed *in limine*, *in limite* (not to say *in limbo*), and *in margine*? And to what extent did what lived in the margin have another life (perhaps in more extensive form) in the text-block? A half-way house between centrality and liminality is column- and page-end where more or less modest blank spaces received additions. Such additions are not uncommonly short pieces of poetry. Furthermore, one can see from comparable textual collocations how such addenda in one manuscript were not rejected when that book in its turn served as an exemplar for copying; what was liminal might now be safely central,[145] and we can easily imagine therefrom how such absorption of liminal additions could be cumulative with each act of copying in a manuscript-culture of this kind. It was Charles Plummer's achievement, also in 1926, to point to margins and rubrics, especially colophonic rubrics, in Gaelic books as constituting a site which had its own conventions, where a certain freedom of expression and performance might be tolerated.[146] Such ideas have long since been taken up more generally by art-historians in relation to mediaeval Western manuscript-culture as well as other art-forms.

TWO CASE-STUDIES: (1) VERSE IN CHRONICLES

The margin in Gaelic literature and manuscript-culture is the subject for a whole book, perhaps even two books. Before that, there are various articles to be written, probing aspects of the question, in search of definition. Meanwhile, I wish to consider briefly two areas in which margins are of great but uncertainly understood importance in our studies. The first involves manuscripts from the late eleventh century to the seventeenth but may have an earlier and therefore longer textual history. The second will be restricted to the ninth century but is of much broader applicability.

I turn first therefore to Gaelic chronicles, of which the extant examples are all Irish in origin save the earliest, that of Marianus Scottus (a Gaelic emigré),[147] written at Mainz in the 1070s and 1080s, which shows equally keen interest in contemporary Ireland and Gaelic North Britain.[148] We have a quasi-autograph of

---

[145] See, for example, the description (by Robin Flower) of London, British Library, MS. Additional 30512: O'Grady *et al.*, *Catalogue*, II.470–5.

[146] Plummer, 'On the colophons'.

[147] Cf. I. Sperber, 'Lives of St Finnian of Movilla: British Evidence', in *Down: History and Society*, ed. Lindsay Proudfoot (Dublin 1997), pp. 85–102, at p. 100, n. 19, on the question of his provenance (his origin being unknown).

[148] Kenney, *The Sources*, pp. 614–16 (no. 443). Cf. also n. 106, above.

Marianus's work, as well as a copy executed in England a generation later.[149] Unlike the English manuscript, Marianus's margins are full of varied fare and have been made the subject of special study,[150] although much remains to be done. The earliest native chronicle-manuscript to survive from Ireland contains 'The Annals of Inisfallen', written in Munster in 1092 and thereafter continually augmented into the fifteenth century (although the whole picture cannot be seen because of some physical lacunae).[151] The margins here too offer interesting material, including a limited amount of verse, as is true also of some chronicle-manuscripts of the later twelfth, thirteenth, and fourteenth centuries. This manuscript-background is important, for it is a witness of the early sixteenth century which offers us rich pickings. What we now call 'The Annals of Ulster' (there are better titles available)[152] is attested in a number of recensions of late fifteenth- and sixteenth-century date (and another can be deduced from 'The Annals of The Four Masters') and in two manuscripts of that period.[153] What has been taken as the principal witness – Dublin, Trinity College, MS. 1282 (H.1.8) – carries a significant quantity of verse in its margins.[154]

The precise character of almost all Gaelic texts in this genre is that of the annalistic chronicle.[155] In other words, its major building block is the record of a single year, an annal, a form inherited from Classical antiquity. The annal's constituent elements are syntactically separable units of record of an event in the year in question: these have been called 'entries' or 'items' or 'units'.[156] We can see

---

[149] Elizabeth Duncan, *Catalogue of Latin and Vernacular Manuscripts written by Gaelic Scribes, A.D. 1000–1200* (Aberdeen, forthcoming), no. 43; *The Chronicle of John of Worcester*, edd. & transl. R.R. Darlington *et al.* (3 vols, Oxford 1995–).

[150] See above, n. 106.

[151] *The Annals of Inisfallen reproduced in Facsimile from the Original Manuscript (Rawlinson B 503) in The Bodleian Library*, facs. edd. R.I. Best & E. MacNeill (Dublin 1933); Duncan, *Catalogue*, no. 36; *The Annals of Inisfallen*, ed. & transl. Mac Airt.

[152] Sir James Ware (1594–1666), who acquired one of the manuscripts, referred to its text as 'The Annals of the North' until he deferred to the (now received) title given by Archbishop James Ussher (1581–1656) who adopted 'The Annals of Ulster'. See W. O'Sullivan, 'A finding list of Sir James Ware's manuscripts', *Proceedings of The Royal Irish Academy* 97 C (1997) 69–99, at p. 71.

[153] Dumville, 'Genre and function'.

[154] *Annala Uladh, Annals of Ulster, otherwise, Annala Senait, Annals of Senat; a Chronicle of Irish Affairs from A.D. 431, to A.D. 1540*, edd. & transl. William M. Hennessy & B. MacCarthy (4 vols, Dublin 1887–1901); *The Annals of Ulster (to A.D. 1131)*, I, edd. & transl. Mac Airt & Mac Niocaill.

[155] D.N. Dumville, 'A millennium of Gaelic chronicling', *The Medieval Chronicle* 1 (1999) 103–15, and 'What is a chronicle?', *ibid.*, 2 (2002) 1–27. I have reprinted the latter: Dumville, *Celtic Essays, 2001–2007*, II.1–24.

[156] *The Chronicle of Melrose Abbey. A Stratigraphic Edition*, I, edd. Dauvit Broun & J. Harrison (Woodbridge 2007), pp. 36–7; Nicholas Evans, *The Present and the Past in Medieval Irish Chronicles* (Woodbridge 2010), p. xi.

annals being augmented, corrupted, or shrunk by the addition or withdrawal of entries or elements of entries. One type of addition, and perhaps subtraction, is of verse. It is important that we appreciate that the situation of verse is not identical in all Gaelic chronicles. In this, as in all other respects, it is crucial that we avoid the formula 'the [Irish] Annals',[157] a device long used to avoid citation of precise reference and information;[158] Gaelic chronicles are a large and varied corpus of texts, and the place and role of verse within them are likewise quite various.

In the Dublin-manuscript of 'The Annals of Ulster' the verse is distributed across much, but by no means all, of the chronological span (A.D. 431–1504) of the text as originally copied there. It is generally in the margins, written in long lines of one quatrain each. (Some years ago, a little more verse emerged from new study of the book.)[159] Much of the verse is written in an additional hand, that of a scribe who made other significant additions:[160] this script is by no means of a lower status which might seem appropriate to additions – there is even some highlighting of initials. In other words, there is nothing casual about this significant addition to the book.

No analysis of the verse in 'The Annals of Ulster' has ever been published. Some certainly is Old-Gaelic in character, some is later. Some 'poems' are of a single quatrain, others in varying degrees longer: the two longest are each of five quatrains.[161] Some are merely versified lists of those persons whose deaths are recorded in a given annal. In contrast, there are some outstanding verses within the corpus. Some poems are satirical. More are laudatory in character. There are

---

[157] Employed recently as a book-title by Daniel P. McCarthy, *The Irish Annals, their Genesis, Evolution and History* (Dublin 2008).

[158] On this, see Kathryn Grabowski & D. Dumville, *Chronicles and Annals of Mediaeval Ireland and Wales. The Clonmacnoise-group Texts* (Woodbridge 1984), p. viii.

[159] The range of the annals with attached verse is 516–1099, 1207, 1343–65. For the new discovery, see F.J. Byrne, *apud* M. Byrnes, 'The Árd Ciannachta in Adomnán's *Vita Columbae*: a reflection of Iona's attitude to the Síl nÁeda Sláine in the late seventh century', in *Seanchas. Studies in Early and Medieval Archaeology, History and Literature in Honour of Francis J. Byrne*, ed. Alfred P. Smyth (Dublin 2000), pp. 127–36, at p. 130; cf. F.J. Byrne, 'Chiasmus and hyperbaton in The Annals of Ulster', in *Ogma. Essays in Celtic Studies in Honour of Próinséas Ní Chatháin*, edd. Michael Richter & J.-M. Picard (Dublin 2002), pp. 54–64, for other poetic elements of Gaelic chronicling.

[160] *The Annals of Ulster (to A.D. 1131)*, I, edd. & transl. Mac Airt & Mac Niocaill, pp. viii–ix. Cf. Ó Cuív, *Catalogue*, I.153–63 (no. 33), whose starting point was the manuscript of the B- (or R-)text.

[161] (1) *Sinsit faebra, sinsit fir* (no *dúnad*) on folios 20v–21r at 563.1 (hands *H²* and *H¹*): *The Annals of Ulster (to A.D. 1131)*, I, edd. & transl. Mac Airt & Mac Niocaill, pp. 82/3. (2) *Easbaidh Hua Calman 'n-a cill* on folio 56vb (apparently complete, with *dúnad*) at 1207.2 (but quatrain 3 is not in text B/R): *Annala Uladh*, edd. & transl. Hennessy & MacCarthy, II.244–7.

only two 'poems' within the text-block, in annals 857 and 921.[162] It is not always clear how many poems (as opposed to a simple count of quatrains) pertain to a single year. A conservative tally reveals about eighty 'poems', occasionally with more than one belonging to a given year, amounting to some 120 quatrains. One quatrain (at 1080) is given twice.[163] In a number of instances the placing of the poems is unexplained: for example, what has been taken to be (at 980) a single three-quatrain poem – the third stanza may carry an attribution to Mac Coissi – is divided between three separate locations, and a single-quatrain 'poem' concerning 669 has been displaced from folio 24v to 25r, even though the margins of the former page are blank.[164]

In sum, there are many problems to be addressed in this particular body of chronicle-verse. Once one adds the evidence of other chronicle-manuscripts and the interrelated texts, the complexity multiplies and requires more solutions.

In related chronicles, the verse may be found within the body of the text. One is left to wonder how much migration of these 'poems' had occurred and in how many directions, and whether there was at any moment an original corpus which might now be reconstructable. We certainly seem to see development between chronicles, with one chronicle containing more (or less) of a given 'poem'. But how much of this is to be explained by losses in transmission, by scholarly recovery of text from collating more witnesses, or by creative composition or recomposition? Or to what extent might there have been organic growth, beginning in the sixth- to eighth-century early history of Gaelic

---

[162] *The Annals of Ulster (to A.D. 1131)*, I, edd. & transl. Mac Airt & Mac Niocaill: (1) pp. 314/15 (857.5), a single quatrain (without *dúnad*), *Cellach dixit, Ó baí senath finn fótail* ... ; (2) pp. 372/3 (921.10), a single quatrain (without *dúnad*), *Cudú andud indbais huaigh* .... Is it conceivable that these two embedded poems are unintended residue of an exemplar in which all the verse was part of the body of the text (as in 'The Annals of Tigernach')?

[163] *Ibid.*, pp. 514/15 (1080.7), a single quatrain with *dúnad*, assigned to hand *H²*:

> Áth Ergail
> i ndiongnat lacich a terbhaid;
> sochaidhe bes cen inmhain
> d'iomguin Átha Ergail.

Both copies are on folio 61vb.

[164] On poetry attributed to one or more poet(s) called Mac Coissi, see A.M. O'Leary, 'The identities of the poet(s) Mac Coisi: a reinvestigation', *Cambrian Medieval Celtic Studies* 38 (1999) 53–71. The poem (if that is what it is) stands on folio 52rb, at 980.2: it is attributed at the outset to *Maccán mac Scolaigi, rí Delbna*. The attribution to *Mac Coissi* stands at the end, an unlikely position for an attribution which refers to (part of ?) what precedes (but cf. pp. 95–6, above). It might, I suppose, pertain to the single quatrain *Ó genair <Mac> Dé de nim* at 980.3. For all this, see *The Annals of Ulster (to A.D. 1131)*, I, edd. & transl. Mac Airt & Mac Niocaill, pp. 414–17. No *dúnad* is evident anywhere in these four stanzas. The stanza at 669.1 (*ibid.*, pp. 138/9), *Ní diliu ... ina geimnen do Dhairiu*, might be held to show weak *dúnad*. The text is written in hand *H*, the attribution (*Cenn Faelad cecinit*) in hand *H²*.

chronicling, and then extended from time to time, sometimes contemporaneously with events or with acts of poetic composition?

In 1972, Kathleen Hughes baptised the ultimate common source of the main stream of mediaeval Gaelic chronicling as 'The Chronicle of Ireland'.[165] Thomas F. O'Rahilly had already in 1946 identified the last annal of that source as 911, and this has been confirmed by subsequent work.[166] Recognition of such a source-chronicle has potential implications for the verse-components of the various texts. Kathleen Hughes acknowledged this:[167]

The Chronicle of Ireland was already itself glossed when the texts diverged. The H.1.8 manuscript of *AU* has a number of marginalia, including quatrains in early forms. In *Tig.* the quatrains start at 490 and they are especially frequent in both [chronicles] until the end of the seventh century. Between 490 and 695 there are nineteen quatrains in the margins of *AU* which are [in the body of] the text of *Tig. AU* also has sixteen quatrains in these years (all in the margins) which are not in *Tig.* And *Tig.* has seventy-three quatrains (all in the text) which are not in *AU*. At least the nineteen quatrains common to both [chronicles] are likely to have been in the exemplar, probably as marginalia. *Tig.* incorporated them into the text; a scribe went through *AU* after the manuscript was written, copying them into the margins. (These quatrains might repay study.)

In Hughes's view, therefore, the original site of the verse in annals 490–695 was the margins. In the textual tradition which led to text A/H of 'The Annals of Ulster' this situation was maintained (but she did not ask where the verse stood in text B/R of that chronicle).[168] On the other hand, in the tradition of 'The Chronicle of Clonmacnose' (created in the period 911×954 by developing a copy of 'The Chronicle of Ireland')[169] the verse was embedded in the text. What Hughes did not do was to ask whether the marginal verse in text H of 'The Annals of Ulster' was separate from the mass of other secondary material added to the text and/or was itself of a single immediate source (given the complication

---

[165] Kathleen Hughes, *Early Christian Ireland: Introduction to the Sources* (London 1972), p. 101.

[166] Thomas F. O'Rahilly, *Early Irish History and Mythology* (Dublin 1946), p. 258; Grabowski [& Dumville], *Chronicles and Annals*, pp. 53–6; Evans, *The Present*, pp. 2–3, 67–72, 225.

[167] Hughes, *Early Christian Ireland*, pp. 103–4. Her sigla *AU* and *Tig.* mean, respectively, 'The Annals of Ulster' and 'The Annals of Tigernach'. I have made two square-bracketed emendations to avoid confusion: '[chronicles]' stands for Hughes's 'manuscripts'; and '[in the body of]' replaces Hughes's 'copied into'.

[168] For the interrelationships of the various witnesses to 'The Annals of Ulster', see Dumville, 'Genre and function'. 'B' or 'R' is the text in Oxford, Bodleian Library, MS. Rawlinson B.489 (*S.C.* 11836), written by the same scribes as the H-text and usually (but not necessarily correctly) held to be derivative of it as augmented: Ó Cuív, *Catalogue*, I.153–63 (no. 33).

[169] The crucial evidence for the later terminus is provided by Welsh chronicles: [Grabowski &] Dumville, *Chronicles and Annals*, pp. 207–26. This evidence has been entirely ignored by Evans, *The Present*.

that more than one scribe was responsible for marginal verse).[170] Nor did she concern herself with verse, in either chronicling tradition, attached to annals 696×911.[171]

In an important brief contribution published in 1998, Patrick Sims-Williams assessed Robin Flower's treatment of the early development of the Irish literary tradition, including chronicling and its verse.[172] Commenting on Flower's observation that Cenn Faelad mac Ailello 'is the first poet quoted in the Annals' [*sic*][173] and George Calder's that 'His poems, dealing to a large extent with the wars of his kinsfolk, the Northern Uí Néill, are quoted largely in the annals' [*sic etiam*],[174] Sims-Williams noted:[175]

One problem is that most of these attributions are found in the Annals of Tigernach and its cognate *Chronic[um] Scotorum* alone. Only three quatrains are attributed to Cenn Faelad in the other early [chronicles]. One of them, found in the Annals of Ulster (and the Four Masters), commemorates a king buried in Derry in 669, which in time and space suits Cenn Faelad well (although strictly speaking the king was of the Airgialla rather than the Northern Uí Néill); the attribution may be late, however, since it is not supported by [the Annals of] Tigernach. The two quatrains attributed to Cenn Faelad both in the Annals of Ulster and (in the latter case) in the Annals of Tigernach concern battles in Meath between the *Southern* Uí Néill and Uí Fhailge of Leinster in 510 and 516. They should be read consecutively and, as [Eoin] MacNeill recognized, must have been extracted from some lost historical poem attributed (rightly or wrongly) to Cenn Faelad. These quatrains are quoted as early as [annals] 510 and 516 because that was when the battles were supposed to have occurred, not because Cenn Faelad was a pioneer in vernacular poetry! Between 490 and 695 there are nearly a hundred quatrains in the Annals of Ulster or Annals of Tigernach and nineteen of these are common to both and arguably therefore come from the lost 'Chronicle of Ireland' (if we make the large assumption that the quatrains had the same line of transmission). It is presumably just a coincidence that the first ones not given anonymously are ascribed to Cenn Faelad.

---

[170] If the separation of scribal hands offered in *The Annals of Ulster (to A.D. 1131)*, I, edd. & transl. Mac Airt & Mac Niocaill, is correct, there were at least five scribes (H, H¹, H², H³, H⁴) writing in the margins and/or making additions within the text-block of Dublin, Trinity College, MS. 1282 (H.1.8), creating text 'A' or 'H'. However, *ibid.*, I.viii–ix, no criteria for separation of the hands were offered, and the statement that 'One of the interpolating hands (H²) is that of Cathal Mac Maghnusa' was left entirely undocumented.

[171] As mentioned in n. 162, above, annal 857 (as also annal 921) of 'The Annals of Ulster' is part of the main text. In 'The Annals of Ulster' 696–911 there are twenty-eight 'poems'.

[172] P. Sims-Williams, 'The medieval world of Robin Flower', in *Bláithín: Flower*, ed. de Mórdha, pp. 73–96.

[173] Flower, *The Irish Tradition*, p. 11. On 'the Annals', see above, p. 116 and nn. 157–8.

[174] *Auraicept*, ed. & transl. Calder, p. xxvii.

[175] Sims-Williams, 'The medieval world', pp. 89–90 (and pp. 95–6, nn. 49–50). The two bracketed clauses in the penultimate sentence are from p. 96, n. 50. The reference to 'MacNeill' is to E. MacNeill, 'A pioneer of nations', *Studies* (Dublin) 11 (1922) 13–28 and 435–46. On Cenn Faelad mac Ailello, see most recently Evans, *The Present*, pp. 221, 227–8 (but without reference to Sims-Williams).

'Large assumption' is exactly right. Nicholas Evans has recently made an important point that, in view of their complex distribution across the corpus of chronicles,[176] 'The textual history of each poem, therefore, should be studied on an individual basis' – and, of course, in relation to any external attestation. But this does not absolve us from studying their place within the chronicles' text-histories.

Thomas Charles-Edwards, in his pioneering realisation of 'The Chronicle of Ireland', published in 2006, explained that[177]

> I have almost always omitted the poems which occur in the annals (an exception is 548, where it is part of a sequence of entries discussed below because it is one of the clearest examples of a later addition). In the Annals of Ulster such poems are additions to the original text copied [in] the first hand; none of them meets the primary test for ascription to the Chronicle of Ireland, and, therefore, they have normally been omitted [hence].

We have seen that in the H-text of 'The Annals of Ulster' almost all the verse is marginal. But one of the (at least) three scribes who wrote this marginal poetry was the principal scribe of the chronicle itself.[178] There is as a result at least a question whether copying in the margin was an act of addition to rather than completion of the chronicle's original execution. In mediaeval Gaelic literary culture the role of a manuscript's margins was by no means exclusively to receive addenda.

Nevertheless, the larger contexts provided by the character of the individual chronicles and by their interrelated textual histories are important elements in our appreciation of the functions of verse in Gaelic chronicles. Charles-Edwards's treatment of annal 548 offers significant lessons.[179]

> There is another major issue ..., whether the differences in coverage between the Clonmacnois group and the Annals of Ulster arise principally from abbreviation or expansion. ...

548

AU, AT, CS

> ... This is an extreme case, in which the two witnesses, the Clonmacnois group and the Annals of Ulster, ... share only the initial 'Kalends of January'. ... The retrospective character of part of the annal is revealed by the phrase 'which gave rise to the saying' (548.2). The whole entry about the killing of Tuathal Máelgarb has a doublet at 544, an entry which

---

[176] *Ibid.*, p. 220.

[177] *The Chronicle of Ireland*, transl. T.M. Charles-Edwards (2 vols, Liverpool 2006), I.2. His cross-reference is to I.16–17 (this is quoted below, at n. 179).

[178] The scribe called simply *H* in *The Annals of Ulster (to A.D. 1131)*, I, edd. & transl. Mac Airt & Mac Niocaill.

[179] *The Chronicle of Ireland*, transl. Charles-Edwards, I.15–17. The bracketed penultimate sentence is his n. 3 (p. 17).

was undoubtedly part of the original Chronicle of Ireland, since it is in both branches of the [textual] tradition. The rest of the annal, apart from the final entry, has to do with St Ciarán of Clonmacnois; and the final entry is again a doublet. ... The whole of this material in the Clonmacnois texts may thus be seen as a single hagiographical argument designed to buttress an alliance between Clonmacnois and the Southern Uí Néill, the descendants of Diarmait. (Compare 663.2 where AU records merely the death of Guaire Aidne, a king famous in the traditions of Connaught, but both AT and CS add that he was buried in Clonmacnois.) If this is correct, these entries will have been added to the Chronicle of Ireland after the [text-historical] split in 911; and what is worse, they may well not have been drawn from an annalistic source, so that their being dat<ed> to 548 would have no value.

This is as elegant and illuminating a dissection of an annal as one could desire. It shows one way (probably the major visible route) by which specific pieces of verse entered the Gaelic chronicling tradition. In that sense we owe a very great deal – of both gain and grief – to the clerics of Clonmacnoise in the central Middle Ages.

With these questions in mind, I propose to examine three poems, each attested by a different chronicle, which will open up questions about origins and sources, function and transmission, as well as their use by modern scholars. It is not wholly accidental that they concern North Britain as well as Ireland.

Let us begin with three quatrains known from four chronicles, *Chronicum Scotorum*,[180] 'The Annals of The Four Masters',[181] 'The Annals of Tigernach', and 'The Annals of Ulster', situated in an annal perhaps intended for A.D. 625. I give first the text from the earliest manuscript-witness, that of 'The Annals of Tigernach', of the second half of the fourteenth century.[182]

K. .i.

[1.] Annus tenebrosus.

[2.] Aedhá(i)n mac Cumascaigh *et* Colmán mac Comgelláin ad Dominum migra<n>t.

[3.] Babtismum Etu<in> ma*i*c Elle, qui primus credidit in reghionibus Saxonom.

[4.] Cormacc caem *et* Illand m*ortui* <sunt>.

[5.] Rónán mac Tuathail, rí na nAirrther, m*ortuus* est.

[6.] Mongán mac Fiachna Lurgan, ab Artúir filio Bicoir Pretene lapite percussus, interit. Unde (dictum est) Béc Boirche dixit:

---

[180] *Chronicum Scotorum. A Chronicle of Irish Affairs, from the Earliest Times to A.D. 1135; with a Supplement, containing the Events from 1141 to 1150*, ed. & transl. William M. Hennessy (London 1866).

[181] *Annala rioghachta*, edd. & transl. O'Donovan.

[182] *The Annals of Tigernach*, ed. & transl. Stokes, I.177–8. One is bound to wonder whether in item 6 an original formula *dictum est* introducing [b] + [c] was replaced by the attribution to Bécc Boirche after his poem was introduced as [a]. The conventions used here are the usual ones: italics indicate resolved abbreviations carrying some element of ambiguity; angle-brackets < > mark editorial emendation; round brackets ( ) indicate editorial deletion. For the manuscript, Oxford, Bodleian Library, MS. Rawlinson B.488 (*S.C.* 11835), folios 1–26, see Ó Cuív, *Catalogue*, I.141–53 (no. 32). The Latin orthography is well worthy of remark as a not uncharacteristic specimen of late mediaeval Gaelic Latin.

[a]   Is (f)uar in gaeth dar Íle.
          Dofuil óca i Cind Tíre
          dogéna<t> gním amnus de:
          m<a>ir<b>fid(h) Mongán mac Fiachnae.

[b]   Land Cluana Airrthir indiu,
          amra in ceathrar forsr'iadhad:
          Cormac caem fri im<fh>ochidh
          ocus Illand m*ac* Fiach<n>a<ch>.

[c]   *Ocus* in dias ele,
          dia foghnonn mór do t<h>uathaib,
          Mongán mac Fiachna Lurgan
          ocus Rónán m*ac* Tuathail.

[7.]   Cathal mac Aeda, rí Muman.

[8.]   Maedóc Ferna quieuit.

I have given the entire annal in view of the following discussion where the interrelationship of elements will be an issue.

The closely related Clonmacnoise-group text known as *Chronicum Scotorum* – as it stands, a product of the mid-seventeenth century – has a much shorter and rather differently structured annal.[183]

Kl. .vii.

[1.]   Maodhóg Ferna quieuit.

[2.]   Mac Fiachna, .i. Mongán, ab Arthúr filio Bicuir Britoni lapide percussus, interiit. Unde Bécc Bairce dixit:
          As uar an gaoth dar Íle
          Dusfail óga Cinn Tíre.
          Dogénait gníom namnus de:
          Mairbfid Mongán mac Fiachna.

[3.]   Cormac caom ocus Iollann mac Fiachach moriuntur.

[4.]   Rónán mac Tuathail.

[5.]   [a]   Lann Cluana Airtir indiu
          Amra cethrur forsfiadh
          Cormac caem friu imochid
          Ocus Illann mac Fiachach.

          [b]   Ogus an dias aile
          Dia fognaid mór do thuataibh
          Mongán mac Fiachna Lurgan
          Ocus Rónán mac Tuathail.

[6.]   Aengus mac Colmáin móir, rí Mide, do marbadh.

[7.]   Cathal mac Aedha, rí Muman, mortuus est.

---

[183] *Chronicum Scotorum*, ed. & transl. Hennessy, pp. 78/9 (Kl. .vii.). On the mid-seventeenth-century author of this chronicle, see Nollaig Ó Muraíle, *The Celebrated Antiquary Dubhaltach Mac Fhirbhisigh (c. 1600–1671), his Lineage, Life and Learning* (Maynooth 1996; 2nd edn, 2002), pp. 97–107, 308–9. On the textual affiliations of this chronicle, see [Grabowski &] Dumville, *Chronicles and Annals*, chapters II–III.

In *Chronicum Scotorum*, item 6 is a duplicate of an entry four annals earlier.[184] What is the last item in 'The Annals of Tigernach' is here the first, perhaps reflecting the more ecclesiastical character of the former and the greater secularity of the latter chronicle,[185] or perhaps indicating that the entry was a marginale in their common source. Items 1–3 in 'The Annals of Tigernach' are not in *Chronicum Scotorum*, a distribution which is in line with the criteria separating the two chronicles.[186] The sequence 4, 5, 6 (in which last all three verses are gathered) in 'The Annals of Tigernach' compares with 2, 3, 4, 5, with Mongán advanced to the top, accompanied by one quatrain, and the other verses separated below 3–4. Finally, the last two entries seem to be outside the scheme which unites 4–6 in 'The Annals of Tigernach' and 2–5 in *Chronicum Scotorum*.

The quatrains provide the essential keys to our comprehension of the development of the annal. Bécc Boirche was a poet of the Ulaid, a member of a royal line.[187] Mongán mac Fiachnai was a prince of Dál nAraidi, a Cruithin people; the death of his father, King Fiachna Lurgan, in the battle of Leithet Midind against Dál Riata, is recorded in the following annal in both chronicles.[188] Nothing is quite what it seems, however. Whether a quatrain of this sort is what a royal *fili* of the seventh century would have composed as a eulogy is very uncertain. Bécc Boirche was probably not alive in 625: his recorded activities extend from a killing in 674 to his own death in 718.[189] Whatever Mongán was at his death, by the tenth century (and perhaps well before that) he had become not merely a figure of legend but of mythology, enjoying some sort of relationship with Manannán mac Lir, a heathen Gaelic deity, and Find mac Cumaill, the central figure in a major

[184] *Chronicum Scotorum*, ed. & transl. Hennessy, pp. 76/7 (with erroneous editorial date '621' [item 1]).

[185] For these characterisations, see [Grabowski &] Dumville, *Chronicles and Annals*, chapter III, especially pp. 157–8.

[186] *Ibid.*

[187] *Corpus*, I, ed. O'Brien, p. 517, *s.n.*, referring to pp. 322, 410–11. For comment on his appearance in the list of overkings of the Ulaid, see *The Chronicle of Ireland*, transl. Charles-Edwards, I.160, n. 4.

[188] For the historical Mongán, see *Corpus*, I, ed. O'Brien, p. 702, *s.n.*, referring to pp. 282–4 (a most interesting poem, *A Fhiachnae ná-ráid in gae*, of twenty-three quatrains, with *dúnad*, headed *Mongán mac Fiachna cecinit do thecosc a athar*), 409. For King Fiachna's death, see *The Annals of Tigernach*, ed. & transl. Stokes, I.179 (K.i.1), and *Chronicum Scotorum*, ed. & transl. Hennessy, pp. 80/1 (K.i.1).

[189] *The Chronicle of Ireland*, transl. Charles-Edwards, I.160 (674.1), 163 (679.3), 182 (707.6: entry into religion), 189 (714.7: sons), 192 (718.2: died).

developing category of Gaelic literature.[190] And there are aspects of Mongán's literary history which suggest a connexion with Arthurian legend, as here. Whether *Pretene* as a description of Artúr or Bicor (perhaps not recognised in and certainly edited out of 'The Annals of Tigernach' by Whitley Stokes) is to be taken as epithet or ethnic descriptor, it is clearly a word of great interest.[191] In sum, the entry draws us into a rich and complex literary world.

By contrast, the two following quatrains are a classic annalistic verse performance. They memorialise collectively those of note to the annalist and already recorded in prose in that annal.[192] They can have no intentional point of connexion with the first quatrain. Those enumerated are four, their deaths recorded in items 4–5 of 'The Annals of Tigernach' and items 2–4 of *Chronicum Scotorum*. We should take these as being the persons of interest to the chronicler: they fit best with the text of *Chronicum Scotorum*, when compared with 'The Chronicle of Ireland' and 'The Annals of Tigernach'. If the obit of St Moling were originally marginal, we could recapture a text-historical stage at which the enumerative stanzas are likely to have originated. In 'The Annals of Tigernach' all three stanzas ended up together, all attributed to Bécc Boirche and pretending to be a single poem.

Matters are not so simple, however. Let us turn to the H-text of 'The Annals of Ulster', executed at the beginning of the sixteenth century. The annal as originally written is brief.[193]

Kl. Ian*air*. Anno Domini .dc°.xx°.iiii°.

[1.]   Annus tenebrosus.

[2.]   Aedhán mac Cumuscaigh et Colmán mac Comgelláin ad Dominum migrant; et Rónán mac Tuathail rex na nAirther et Mongán mac Fiachae Lurgan moriuntur.

---

[190] Kuno Meyer & A. Nutt, *The Voyage of Bran son of Febal to the Land of the Living. An Old Irish Saga* (2 vols, London 1895/7), I.42–58, for text and translation of a series of short works about Mongán; K. Meyer (ed. & transl.) & A. Nutt, 'The Colloquy of Colum Cille and the Youth at Carn Eolairg', *Zeitschrift für celtische Philologie* 2 (1897/8) 313–20, and P. Grosjean (ed. & transl.), 'S. Columbae Hiensis cum Mongano heroe colloquium', *Analecta Bollandiana* 45 (1927) 75–83; E. Knott (ed. & transl.), 'Why Mongán was deprived of noble issue', *Ériu* 8 (1915/16) 155–60; Flower, *The Irish Tradition*, pp. 1–23; P. Mac Cana, 'Mongán mac Fiachna and *Immram Brain*', *Ériu* 23 (1972) 102–42; J. Carey, 'On the interrelationships of some *Cín Dromma Snechtai* texts', *Ériu* 46 (1995) 71–92; Sims-Williams, 'The medieval world', p. 88; John Carey, *A Single Ray of the Sun. Religious Speculation in Early Ireland* (Andover, MA 1999), pp. 3–6; T.M. Charles-Edwards, *Early Christian Ireland* (Cambridge 2000), pp. 201–2.
[191] Cf. K. Meyer, 'Zur keltischen Wortkunde. II', *Sitzungsberichte der königlich preussischen Akademie der Wissenschaften, philosophisch-historische Klasse* (1912) 1144–57, at pp. 1153–7 (§§39–40).
[192] For other examples, see above, pp. 101–3, and below, pp. 133–5.
[193] In *The Chronicle of Ireland*, transl. Charles-Edwards, I.133, item 2 has been reported as two separate entries, nos 2 and 5, with two Clonmacnoise-group entries sandwiched between.

Now if this be taken as *prima facie* an indication of the text of 'The Chronicle of Ireland', we can see that all four persons enumerated and memorialised in the pair of quatrains are incorporated within AU 624.2. It would therefore be possible to argue that these quatrains could have belonged to this annal (or even item) in either 'The Chronicle of Ireland' or the first stage of development of 'The Chronicle of Clonmacnoise'.

The plot thickens. The H-text does indeed contain the two quatrains, entered in marginal position by scribe *H* who copied the main text.[194] If we were to take the view that physical marginality does not by definition indicate text-historical posteriority, here would be the *prima facie* evidence required to establish the presence of this verse text in 'The Chronicle of Ireland'. Here is the H-text of the two quatrains.[195]

> [a] Lann Cluana Airthir indiu
>   amhra cethrar fors-riadhat,
>   Cormac – fri imochaidh –
>   *ocus* Illann m*acc* Fiachach.
>
> [b] In dias aile –
>   fos-gniat mór di thuathaib –
>   Mongán m*ac* Fiachnai Lurgar
>   *ocus* Rónán m*ac* Tuathail.

A certain addition, at the end of the annal, is item 3, written by scribe *H²*,

Maedhóicc Fearna quieuit.

We can see that this represents the position in 'The Annals of Tigernach' and is almost certainly derivative in 'The Annals of Ulster' of a text belonging to the Clonmacnoise-group of chronicles. Lastly, we may observe that there is no sign in 'The Annals of Ulster' of the quatrain on Mongán alone, attributed to Bécc Boirche, and therefore no formal reason to think it to have been part of this annal in 'The Chronicle of Ireland'.

We cannot conclude without the evidence of 'The Annals of The Four Masters', a chronicle which its authors announced as having been compiled by using a good many other chronicles – nine were specified –, a project which took just over four and a half years, 22 January 1632 to 10 August 1636, to see to completion.[196] Their criteria of inclusion and exclusion and for use of technical

---

194 These were written across the lower margins of (first) 23r and (then) 22v.
195 *The Annals of Ulster (to A.D. 1131)*, I, edd. & transl. Mac Airt & Mac Niocaill, p. 112.
196 *Annala rioghachta*, ed. & transl. O'Donovan, I.lv–lxxi.

language have been deduced in part.[197] Here the relevant annal is dated 620.[198]

Aois Criost, sé céd a fiche. An deachmhadh bliadhain do Suibhne.
[1.]   Seanach garbh, abb Cluana Ferta Brénainn, décc.
[2.]   Colmán mac Coingelláin décc.
[3.]   Rónán mac Tuathail, tigherna na nAirther, dég.
[4.]   Corbmac caomh et Iollann mac Fiachrach décc.
[5.]   Mongán mac Fiachna Lurgan do mharbhadh do cloich la hArtúr mac Bicair do Bretnaibh. Conid dó ro ráidh Bécc Boirche:

    [a]   As huar an gaeth dar Ili.
        Do fail ócca i cCiunn Tíre
        do génsat gnímh namhnus de:
        mairfit Mongán mac Fiachnae.

    [b]   Lann Cluana hAirthir indiu
        amhra cethrar forsriadhadh:
        Corbmac caemh fri imfochidh
        agus Iollann mac Fiachrach.

    [c]   Agus an dias aile –
        dia fognad mór do thuathaibh –,
        Mongán mac Fiachna Lurgan
        agus Rónán mac Tuathail.

[6.]   Cathal mac Aodha, rí Mumhan, décc.

This agrees more closely with 'The Annals of Tigernach' than with any other chronicle but is nonetheless by no means identical with it. What it does particularly share is the grouping together of the three quatrains with an attribution of them all to Bécc Boirche. Bécc is not the first author whom we have seen gaining extra work by editorial or scribal manipulation.[199]

Our next specimen comes from a single chronicle, the so-called 'Fragmentary Annals of Ireland' surviving only in a late seventeenth-century copy of a mid-century (1643) manuscript of An Dubhaltach Mac Fhir Bhisigh (the author of *Chronicum Scotorum*) who derived his text from a chronicle in a then broken parchment-manuscript of Giolla na Naemh Mac Aedhagáin: that Giolla na Naemh was either a teacher of Dubhaltach or an ancestor (*ca* 1400) of that teacher.[200]

In an annal apparently for 704, the fourth item (§165) begins thus:[201]

Mors Flainn Fiona meic Ossa, rí Saxan, an t-eagnaid amhra, dalta Ad<a>mnáin. De quo Riaguil Beanncuir cecinit:

---

[197] Cf. K.M. McGowan, 'The Four Masters and the governance of Ireland in the Middle Ages', *The Journal of Celtic Studies* 4 (2004) 1– 41.

[198] *Annala rioghachta*, ed. & transl. O'Donovan, I.242–5.

[199] See above, pp. 100–3.

[200] *Fragmentary Annals*, ed. & transl. Radner, p. vii.

[201] *Ibid.*, pp. 54/5. We are given the poet's name in the genitive case: if he was an ecclesiastic, it is much more likely that the name was Mac Riaguil, otherwise attested.

When one turns to the following poetry, however, a difficulty rapidly becomes apparent: it is quite inappropriate for a death-notice of one who is intended to be Aldfrith, king of the Northumbrians 685/6–704/5.[202] As was deduced by W.F. Skene, the verse has been wrongly positioned,[203] no doubt by a compiler or scribe who relied on the poem's repeated *mac Os(s)a*, 'the son of Oswiu', for identification. Where it must belong is in annal 685, the death of King Ecgfrith, son of Oswiu, on 20 May at the battle of *Dún Nechtain / Linn Garan / Nechtanesmere* (Dunachton, in Badenoch, Invernessshire) in Pictland,[204] where his opponent was King Bridei/Bruide. Here is the same chronicle's entry (§96) for that event:[205]

Cath Dúin Neachtain i ttorc<h>*air* mac Ossu. Bruite mac Bile uictor fuit.

'The battle of Dún Nechtain, in which the son of Oswiu was killed. Bruide son of Bile was the victor.'

And here is the poetry which should be attached to it.[206]

[a] Iniu feras Bruide cath
im forba a senathar,
manad algas lá mac Dé
conid é ad-génathar.

[b] Iniu ro-bíth mac Ossa
a ccath fria claidhmhe glasa;
cia do rada ait<h>irge,
is hí ind Hí iar n-assa.

[c] Iniu ro-bíth mac Osa,
las(a) mbidis dubha deoga;
ro-cuala Críst ár nguidhe
roisaorbut Bruide bregha.

The alleged poet, 'Riaguil' of Bangor, is otherwise known, if barely, but we have no death-date for him.[207] The mistaken location of these stanzas leaves open the

---

[202] On this difficulty, see Dumville, 'Two troublesome abbots', pp. 149–52. Cf. Sims-Williams, 'The medieval world', pp. 90 and 96, n. 51.

[203] *Chronicles*, ed. Skene, p. 402, n. 1.

[204] A. Woolf, 'Dún Nechtain, Fortriu and the geography of the Picts', *Scottish Historical Review* 85 (2006) 182–201.

[205] *Fragmentary Annals*, ed. & transl. Radner, pp. 36/7 ([686].4).

[206] *Ibid.*, p. 54.

[207] In *Chronicles*, ed. Skene, p. 402, n. 1, a false death-date is given for him on the basis of a wild misidentification. For a Riagal (cf. n. 201, above), see Eugene O'Curry, *Lectures on the Manuscript Materials of Ancient Irish History* (Dublin 1861), pp. 423–30, 634; M. Miller, 'Eanfrith's Pictish son', *Northern History* 14 (1978) 47–66, at p. 53 and n. 24, with mention of correspondence with James Carney.

possibility that he was the author of a poem on Aldfrith (or on Flann Fína)[208] intended for quotation here (or once quoted but then lost) rather than of these three quatrains. This chronicle is the only known witness to both the attribution and these three quatrains.

Once one considers the 'poem' itself, another difficulty becomes apparent. But we must begin with a translation. Here is the first published version (1860), by John O'Donovan:[209]

> [a]   'This day Bruide fights a battle
>   for the land of his grandfather,
>   Unless the Son of God wish it otherwise,
>   he will die in it.
> [b]   'To-day the son of Oswy was killed
>   in a battle with green swords,
>   Although he did penance,
>   he shall lie in Hi after his death.
> [c]   'This day the son of Oswy was killed,
>   who had the black drinks;
>   Christ heard our supplications,
>   they spared Bruide the brave.'

Here is Radner's tentative but rather different version (1978):[210]

> [a]   'Today Bruide fights a battle
>   over the land of his ancestor,
>   unless it is the wish of the Son of God
>   that restitution be made.
> [b]   'Today the son of Osw[iu] was slain
>   in battle against gray swords,
>   even though he did penance
>   and that too late in Iona (?).
> [c]   'Today the son of Osw[iu] was slain,
>   who used to have dark drinks;
>   Christ has heard our prayer
>   that Bruide would save the hills (?).'

We may compare a more recent and more confident anthology-version by Thomas Clancy.[211]

---

[208] Cf. Dumville, 'Two troublesome abbots', pp. 149–52.

[209] *Annals of Ireland. Three Fragments*, ed. & transl. O'Donovan, p. 111: his text and translation were each published in six long lines (which I have broken up here) in which he was followed in *Chronicles*, ed. Skene, p. 402.

[210] *Fragmentary Annals*, ed. & transl. Radner, p. 55.

[211] *The Triumph Tree*, ed. Clancy, pp. 114–15 (cf. 14, 331).

[a]   'Today Bruide gives battle
       over his grandfather's land,
       unless it is the command
       of God's Son that it be restored.

[b]   'Today Oswiu's son was slain
       in battle against iron swords,
       even though he did penance,
       it was a penance too late.

[c]   'Today Oswiu's son was slain,
       who used to have dark drinks:
       Christ has heard our prayer
       that Bruide would save Breo.'

The last word is a reflection of Clancy's idea that 'rhyme and other sources indicate that we should posit an unknown place-name in eastern Scotland'.[212]

What becomes apparent from a reading of these verses in that, in spite of the stanzas' shared opening formula, *Iniu*, 'Today',[213] there is a marked difference of perspective between stanza a and the other two. Stanza a anticipates a battle but allows the possibility that it will be averted, 'that restitution be made' / 'unless it be restored', the subject being Bruide's ancestral land. On the other hand, in stanzas b and c the poet looks back on the battle, secure in the knowledge that King Ecgfrith has been slain. Unless we are to take the probably unnecessary step of disassembling this group of stanzas, which would involve thinking of two source-poems (perhaps part of a saga) or an addition to an original poem containing either a or b–c, we must allow that we have here the remains of a narrative poem, where stanza a was placed some distance before b and c.

This poem has recently been dated 'c. 685'[214] – rather bizarrely, given that it can hardly be earlier than that year. No formal linguistic argument has yet been presented to suggest that it is (a single) work of the late seventh century.[215] We need to be clear whether an event described in Gaelic poetry as occurring *indiu*, 'today', was necessarily composed on that very day or whether we are dealing with an artistic convention. If these stanzas were drawn from a narrative poem, a possibility which I entertained in the last paragraph, we should need to be comfortable with the existence of such a genre at that time in Gaelic poetry. In other words, there is still much work to do.

I labour this since I detect in recent scholarship a desire for this poem to be

---

[212] *Ibid.*, p. 331. We await enlightenment: how can rhyme indicate that we should do any such thing?

[213] Old-Gaelic *indiu*, accented on the second syllable: *Dictionary*, gen. ed. Quin, p. 402 (I:230).

[214] *The Triumph Tree*, ed. Clancy, p. 115.

[215] James Carney indicated that he thought it not later than 900: Miller, 'Eanfrith's Pictish son', p. 53, n. 24.

prematurely anchored on 20 May, 685.[216] Particularly at stake too is the understanding of line 1*b*, *im f<h>orba a s<h>enathar*. When the verse was first published, *forba* was translated 'the land',[217] an entirely acceptable and perhaps wisely vague rendering, given that certain context for his motive was (and still is) not readily available. The reference might be to a kingdom or to patrimonial property inherited or simply to real estate as possession (Old-Gaelic *orb[b]a*, Middle-Gaelic *forba*).[218] James Fraser has recently insisted on the translation 'legacy'[219] which might, while perhaps excluding the last option, seem sufficiently vague. Imagine, however, that the word is Old-Gaelic *forbba(e)*, verbal noun of *for-ben*, therefore 'smiting'.[220] *forba* is followed by a dependent genitive of a definite noun, *a s<h>enathar*. The first translator (1860) took this, on the basis of Modern Irish, to mean 'of his grandfather',[221] which is certainly a possible rendering of the Old Gaelic.[222] However, as with other such terms of human blood-relationship – *aue*, *bráthair*, *mac(c)* –, the meaning can be narrower or broader, or more or less distant:[223] in the case of *senathair*, 'ancestor' or 'family-founder' is also appropriate[224] and might (given that it offers more genealogical options) be wiser in our state of relative ignorance of context.

We may be reasonably confident then that Bruide is here represented as preparing to fight for something, whether real property or kingship or both, which at least one of his ancestors had held (and which, given that he was in 685 defending his own [over]kingdom, had presumably come into his own hand). This would work, however we might translate *forba*. If we were to take it as 'smiting', we could imagine that, between those two periods of possession, someone – probably Oswiu or Ecgfrith, perhaps Edwin or Oswald (and, less likely in this context, perhaps even a non-English enemy) had smitten one of his ancestors, and that honour, not only possession, was at stake.

The matter is made more troublesome still by another short poem, much quoted nowadays, preserved in a tenth-century Life of St Adamnán where it is

---

[216] See, for example, Fraser, *From Caledonia*, p. 215 (cf. pp. 134–5, 202). In this connexion, it is worth recurring to Alfred P. Smyth, *Warlords and Holy Men. Scotland, A.D. 80–1000* (London 1984), pp. 64–5.

[217] *Annals of Ireland. Three Fragments*, ed. & transl. O'Donovan, p. 111; *Chronicles*, ed. Skene, p. 402 (and cf. pp. cxix–cxxii).

[218] *Dictionary*, gen. ed. Quin, pp. 491–2 (O:152–3), *s.v.* **orb(b)a**.

[219] Fraser, *From Caledonia*, pp. 134–5, 202, 215.

[220] *Dictionary*, gen. ed. Quin, p. 328 (F:314), *s.v.* **forbba(-e)**.

[221] *Annals of Ireland. Three Fragments*, ed. & transl. O'Donovan, p. 111.

[222] *Dictionary*, gen. ed. Quin, p. 536 (S:176), *s.v.* **senathair**.

[223] *Ibid.:* p. 618 (U:1–3), *s.v.* **ua** (earlier *aue*); p. 81 (B:163), *s.v.* **bráthair**; p. 447 (M:1–8), *s.v.* **1 mac**.

[224] *Ibid.*, p. 536 (S:176), *s.v.* **senathair**.

attributed to the saint himself.[225] Since *Mór do ingantu do-gní* is not a chronicle-poem, here I pass over it relatively quickly. It offers a eulogy of King Bridei, who died in 693. What has particularly excited historical commentators on *Iniu feras Bruide cath* has been the identity of the Pictish king's *senathair*. In the Pictish king-lists his father is named, *Bredei filius Bili* (and derivative forms),[226] as he is also in 'The Annals of Ulster' at his death: *Bruide mac Bili, rex Fortrend, moritur.*[227] (In Clonmacnoise-group chronicles, these particulars about Bruide have been introduced into other annal-entries naming him.)[228] This led, especially in a context of scholarly acknowledgment of Pictish exogamous matriliny, to rather careless identification of his father as Beli, a Briton of the royal family of Dumbarton.[229] But the two-quatrain poem *Mór do ingantu do-gní* has been trumpeted more recently as 'the unique witness to the fact that Bruide was the son of Beli of Dumbarton'.[230] This suggests confusion of hypothesis and fact. The dating and source of the poem are crucial – all we have been offered so far is

[225] R.I. Best (ed.), 'Betha Adamnáin', in *Anecdota from Irish Manuscripts*, edd. Bergin *et al.*, II.10–20 (poem at p. 17, §10); M. Joynt (transl.), 'The Life of Adamnan', *The Celtic Review* 5 (1908/9) 97–107 (poem on p. 100); *Betha Adamnáin. The Irish Life of Adamnán*, edd. & transl. Máire Herbert & P. Ó Riain (London 1988), pp. 58/9 (§14), with notes on p. 82.

[226] Anderson, *Kings*, p. 248 (List A).

[227] *The Annals of Ulster (to A.D. 1131)*, I, edd. & transl. Mac Airt & Mac Niocaill, p. 154 (693.1a).

[228] *The Annals of Tigernach*, ed. & transl. Stokes, I.169, and *Fragmentary Annals*, ed. & transl. Radner, pp. 36/7 (§96), in the account of the battle of *Dún Nechtain*.

[229] For the most straightforward account of this view, unintentionally revealing the utter weakness of the proposition, see A. Macquarrie, 'The kings of Strathclyde, c. 400–1018', in *Medieval Scotland, Crown, Lordship and Community. Essays presented to G.W.S. Barrow*, edd. Alexander Grant & K.J. Stringer (Edinburgh 1993), pp. 1–19, at p. 7. The rather minimal genealogy of the royal line as it was in the late ninth century is preserved in a Welsh genealogical collection probably datable 954×988 (but surviving in a manuscript of about 1100 – London, British Library, MS. Harley 3859 – in which *Annales Cambriae* [A] and these 'Harleian Genealogies' are found incorporated within a version of *Historia Brittonum*). For this genealogy in tabular form, see David N. Dumville *et al.*, *Saint Patrick, A.D. 493–1993* (Woodbridge 1993), p. 110 (and pp. 107–31 more generally). The name Beli appears twice: the later (*Beli map Elfin*) is presumed to be the king whose death is recorded for 722 in *Annales Cambriae* and 'The Chronicle of Ireland': *Annales Cambriae, A.D. 682–954: Texts A–C in Parallel*, ed. & transl. David N. Dumville (Cambridge 2002), pp. 4/5 (*an.* 722); *The Chronicle of Ireland*, transl. Charles-Edwards, I.195 (722.3*b*). The earlier, three generations above his namesake, is *Beli map Neithon* who would have died in 722–75×111 years = 611×647. (There is a suggested – but very uncertain – identification with a *Belin* whose death is recorded in *Annales Cambriae* in the 620s.) The first problem is that we have no idea whether the earlier Beli of the genealogy was himself king of Dumbarton: the text is not a regnal list. The second is chronological: it is far from certain that someone who was dead before (and perhaps thirty years before) 642 (when we find one Owain in the kingship, presumably the son of Beli in the genealogy) is a likely father for a king who ruled 672–93. If we are to think of Bridei's father as belonging to the royal line of Dumbarton, it might be better to take him to be another dynast of that name (given that it was recurrent in the family) who is unknown to us, whether he was king or not. Cf. Miller, 'Eanfrith's Pictish son', p. 52.

[230] *The Triumph Tree*, ed. Clancy, p. 115.

this:[231] 'The source of the tale is Iona, and the poem may well be early, but it is not clear whether as it stands it can be as early as Adomnán's time' (or Bridei's, one might add). Here is Clancy's version (1998) alongside that of William F. Skene (1867).[232]

'Great the wonders he performs,	'Many wonders doth he perform,
the King who is born of Mary:	The King who was born of Mary,
the life of little sheaves in Mull,	He takes away life,
death for Bruide mac Bili.	Death of Bruide son of Bile:
'It is strange,	'It is rare, [it is rare,]
after ruling a kingdom:	After ruling in the northern kingdom
a small ruined hollow of oak	That a hollow stick of withered oak
about the son of Dumbarton's king.'	is about the son of the king of Al Cluaith.'

It is inevitable that, for us, the two poem-fragments discussed here will be taken together. Study of them is still in a very primitive condition; yet Scottish historians and literary historians are alarmingly eager to bend them to their designs. Why was Bridei son of Beli fighting about Beli's father's or more remote ancestor's *forba*? What could the kingdom of Dumbarton have directly and particularly had at stake in the conflict between Northumbrians and Picts in 685? The useful obsession with the kingdom of Dumbarton (then a.k.a. Strathclyde) which Alfred Smyth developed in writing his history of first-millennium Scotland, published in 1984,[233] delivered what has turned out to be a rather long-lived idea, albeit now sustained by poetry rather than speculative analyses of genealogical tracts: 'Such an hypothesis would hold that princes of the house of Neithon of Strathclyde were the true overlords of southern Pictland in the seventh century, and that their position there was seriously challenged by the expanding Northumbrian rulers to the south-east'.[234] This is not the place for pursuing that matter, save to say that the specific hypotheses used to explain what the two little (fragmentary) poems on King Bridei are failing to convey to us across the centuries fall on simple issues of chronology. And, until these poems are adequately dated and understood in terms of literary context as well as linguistic detail, hypotheses based on them will fail too.

---

[231] *Ibid.*, 'may well' is a clear indicator of special pleading and does not advance a case, which needs detailed investigation and argument. For Smyth, *Warlords*, pp. 62–3, it is 'a very early poem', 'Old Irish verse'.

[232] *The Triumph Tree*, ed. Clancy, p. 115 (where note the retention of Gaelic *mac* in line 4); *Chronicles*, ed. Skene, p. 409. In the latter I have made two alterations: (i) I have square-bracketed Skene's addition to the text in *b*1, and (ii) I have divided his 'Alcluaith' in *b*4.

[233] Smyth, *Warlords*, pp. 62–83, 120–1, 150, 179, 191–208, 215–38, 276–7.

[234] *Ibid.*, p. 65.

I turn finally in this section to another chronicle-poem, one which has acquired an unexpected celebrity over the last fifteen years. It may be found – uniquely, I think – in annal 877 (= A.D. 878) of 'The Annals of Ulster'. This annal comprises eleven entries: we shall begin with the first four, and then add the eleventh.[235]

Kl. Ian*air* .xxᵃ.iiiᵃ. luna. Anno Domini .dcccᵒ.lxxᵒ.viiᵒ.

[1.] Ruaidhri m*ac* Muirminn, rex Brittonum, a Saxonibus interemptus.

[2.] Aedh m*ac* Cinadan, rex Pictorum, a soci`i´s suis occisus est.

[3.] Garfith m*ac* Mael Bri*gte*, rex Conaille, decollatus est ó Auib Echach.

[4.] [a] Ruaidrí Manann, minn n-áine,   'Ruaidrí of Manu, symbol of glory,
        Aed a críchaib Cinn Tíre,   Aed from the lands of Cenn Tíre,
        Donnchad, domna finn flatha,   Donnchad, lustrous stuff of sovereignty,
        Garbs<h>íth, minn Macha mine.   Garbshíth, diadem of smooth Macha.
      [b] Ó do-ralaim ar m'aire,   'Whenever I bring it to mind,
        fu-geir crícha mo cridhe,   It inflames the limits of my heart,
        lecca huara iar n-aire,   Cold flags over temples,
        baile for Barrfhinn Bile.   distress on Barrfhinn of Bile.'

        ...

[11.] Scrín Coluim C*hille* ocus a minna olchena du t<h>iachtain dochum nÉrenn for teicheadh ria Gallaibh.

878 was a year of radical political change in Britain – in Wales, in North Britain, and in England – which is reflected in the events noted in this annal.[236] Nor was it quiet in Ireland.

The two quatrains here, written by scribe H^1 in the upper margin of the manuscript-page, have recently received an excellent discussion by Alex Woolf.[237] The origins attributed to Aed son of Cinaed, king of Picts, and Rhodri ap Merfyn, king of Greater Gwynedd, have excited controversial comment.[238] Essential to an understanding of the contents of these quatrains is comprehension of the

---

235 *The Annals of Ulster (to A.D. 1131)*, I, edd. & transl. Mac Airt & Mac Niocaill, pp. 332–5 (nine entries). Items 3 and 6 in that edition need to be divided after their first sentence, thus giving eleven entries. In item 4, the poem, I have given a modified version of those editors' translation.

236 David N. Dumville, *Wessex and England from Alfred to Edgar* (Woodbridge 1992), pp. 1–23, *Britons and Anglo-Saxons in the Early Middle Ages* (Aldershot 1993), essays XV–XVI, and *Celtic Essays, 2001–2007*, I.103–22. For Pictland and the events leading to the birth of the kingdoms of Alba and Muréb, see D. Broun, 'Dunkeld and the origin of Scottish identity', *Innes Review* 48 (1997) 112–24.

237 Alex Woolf, *From Pictland to Alba, 789–1070* (Edinburgh 2007), pp. 116–17, albeit without reference to P. Sims-Williams, 'Heroic need and literary narrative: a caveat from ninth-century Wales', *Welsh History Review* 17 (1994/5) 1–40, at pp. 11–20, and David E. Thornton, *Kings, Chronologies, and Genealogies. Studies in the Political History of Early Medieval Ireland and Wales* (Oxford 2003), pp. 88–96. Cf. *The Chronicle of Ireland*, transl. Charles-Edwards, I.327–8.

238 For the Second Dynasty of Gwynedd, see the work of Sims-Williams and Thornton mentioned in the last note. On Aed son of Cinaed, see T.M. Charles-Edwards, 'Picts and Scots', *Innes Review* 59 (2008) 168–88, at pp. 169–74 and (on the poem) especially 171–2.

chronicling genre and its poetry. Woolf's exposition takes us some way down that path.

This is an enumerative poem of a sort which we have already encountered.[239] While (in the absence of *dúnad*) one cannot be absolutely certain that the two stanzas originated together, there are two factors which point in that direction: some repetition of rhyme and vocabulary;[240] and the need for a second stanza to complete the sense. Thomas Charles-Edwards has written that this 'seems to be a contemporary poem',[241] although it is hard to see how this can be established. He and Woolf have agreed that *Mag mBili*, Movilla (Co. Down), is the probable place of composition, on the evidence of reference to its patronal saint in *b*4, and Woolf has further noted the suitable centrality of Movilla in reference to the people and events enumerated.[242] We are left, however, to deduce why in particular St Bairrfhind (Finnbarr) should be distressed.[243]

It is certain that the quatrains were not written for the annal in its present form. The third person enumerated in the verse, Donnchad, is not to be found in this annal in any chronicle. It is striking that the other three obits enumerated in the poem are found only in 'The Annals of Ulster' (and 'The Annals of The Four Masters', whose authors used a closely related product of the same workshop);[244] item 3 and the subsequent unique items 5–6 all record events in northeastern Ireland. One proximate Donnchad is to be found in 'The Annals of Ulster' as the second item in the preceding annal, for 877: *Donnchad mac Aedhaccáin maic Conchobuir ó F<h>launn mac Mael S<h>echnaill per dolum occisus est.*[245] Consultation of 'The Annals of The Four Masters' reveals that item at 874[=877].6 and another Donnchad in the tenth item: *Donnchadh mac Maoileachloinn do ghuin la*

---

[239] See above, pp. 101–3, 121–6.

[240] And note the identical position of *crích* in *a*2 and *b*2.

[241] For the metrical reasons which would allow but do not require this, see Charles-Edwards, 'Picts and Scots', p. 172, n. 10.

[242] *Ibid.*, p. 172; Woolf, *From Pictland*, p. 117. On Movilla and the cult of St Uinniau / Finnbarr / Bairrfhinn, see D.N. Dumville, 'St Finnian of Movilla: Briton, Gael, ghost?', in *Down*, ed. Proudfoot, pp. 71–84. McCarthy, *The Irish Annals*, pp. 85, 146, 157–9, 162–3, 167–85, 188, 196–7, 276–9, 284, 292, 301–2, 309, 313, 356, has made it a centre of chronicling for a brief period (approximately 743×753), which is very doubtful; but the annals which suggested this theory are well worth pondering.

[243] In a state of frenzy (*baile, buile*), indeed: *Dictionary*, gen. ed. Quin, p. 63 (B:16), *s.v.* **2 baile**.

[244] Dumville, 'Genre and function', for the interrelationships of these two chronicles. For the entries unique to 'The Annals of Ulster', see the layout in *The Chronicle of Ireland*, transl. Charles-Edwards, I.327–8.

[245] *Ibid.*, Charles-Edwards has identified this Donnchad as the missing person: see especially p. 327, n. 2, and p. 327(–8), n. 6.

hÉlibh.[246] While each Donnchad would deserve our verse's description of blue blood, *domna finn flatha*, 'lustrous stuff of sovereignty', it is apparent from comparison of the two chronicles at this point that the essential difference between them is The Four Masters' incorporation of a Southern (Leinster and Munster) chronicle into theirs:[247] Donnchad mac Maíl Shechlainn belongs to that strand of The Four Masters' text and therefore must be rejected as the candidate for 'the missing Donnchad of 878'. What caused the displacement of the obit of Donnchad mac Aedaccáin to the preceding annal in 'The Annals of Ulster' remains to be discovered. Woolf has demonstrated that 'the poet associates the dead kings with an ancestral homeland and not with the kingdom[s] they had ruled at their deaths, perhaps to emphasise the transience of earthly power'.[248] He rather spoilt this point by continuing thus: 'If this is a genuine ninth-century lament it may bear witness to two facts about Áed [king of Picts]. His kindred were no longer ruling in Kintyre but it was believed that they had done so in the past.'[249] Whatever the date of the poem, the 'two facts' would remain the same. The implied alternative of 'a bogus ninth-century lament' is a very interesting idea. But, before going down that route, we might do better to think of (say) an eleventh-century eulogy and restrain ourselves from describing a lament of such a date as 'bogus': there is nothing in the content of these verses to show either that the poet lived in the late ninth century or that he was passing himself off as a contemporary. Indeed, may not the implication of the last line (*b*4) be that Finnbarr himself, now an eternal saint, was the author?

We may wonder, then, whether we are corrupted in our appreciation of the poetry by our very necessary concern with the chronicles' textual history, on which historians rely in their assessment of the chronicles' evidential value (both in general and at any given point), or whether lack of concern with all the specific issues raised here is corrupting our understanding of the nature of the chronicle-poetry.

It is arguable that one could categorise all the verse in a single hand in a single chronicle-manuscript as constituting a single text. But it is as certain as anything can be that the sources were various. Nevertheless, occasionally there surfaces a

---

[246] *Annala rioghachta*, ed. & transl. O'Donovan, I.520–3 (annal 875[=878]).

[247] I hope to publish the results of an investigation arising from this observation.

[248] Woolf, *From Pictland*, p. 117.

[249] *Ibid.*; Charles-Edwards, 'Picts and Scots', pp. 171–4 (the quotations which follow are from p. 171), has made recognition of 'the notion that there was … a link' between Clann Chináeda and Cenél nGabráin' the starting point of an unacceptable argument in favour of the view that Ciniod son of Alpin was a Gael from Dál Riata who conquered Pictland.

hypothesis that this or that type of verse derives from a much longer text applying a particular approach to a lengthy stretch of chronicling time: after all, one 'synthetic' Middle-Irish poet is known to have versified the whole of Bede's *Chronica maiora* from *De temporum ratione*.[250]

Kuno Meyer included some forty poems witnessed by chronicle-texts in his first collection of 'Bruchstücke'.[251] But, as we have seen, from one version of 'The Annals of Ulster' alone there are more than twice that number available. It will be useful for scholars to attempt to divine his principles of selection.

TWO CASE-STUDIES: (2)

NINTH-CENTURY GAELIC MANUSCRIPTS ON THE EUROPEAN CONTINENT

AND THE IMPLICATIONS OF THEIR VERNACULAR POETIC CONTENT

I wrote some years ago about these emigrants' books and some implications of their script, structure, contents, and dating.[252] Here I wish briefly to retrace my steps somewhat. Let us begin with the so-called 'Reichenau Schoolbook', now and for two centuries past at Sankt Paul im Lavanttal in Austria. After I published my previous study, in which I remarked that this single-quire *encheiridion* 'occupies an exalted place in the Irish-studies pantheon, although it is doubtful if any living [in 1996] celticist has ever examined it in the flesh',[253] Patrick Sims-Williams informed me that, while I was no doubt correct on that point when I wrote, before the lecture's publication my remarks had been rendered void as Marged Haycock and he had made the necessary pilgrimage: happily, they are both still with us! The five Old-Gaelic texts which this manuscript contains, not as glosses or marginalia,[254] include two clearly complete poems (one of which is the famous eight quatrains of *Pangur bán*), but others which show no *dúnad* and could be excerpts from or reminiscences of longer poems – in one case, a poem attributed in the manuscript to [St] Moling, a complete text is known from later manuscripts,

---

[250] For the use of 'synthetic' for a category of poets and poems, see Eoin MacNeill, *Celtic Ireland* (Dublin 1921; rev. imp., by D. Ó Corráin, 1981), pp. 25–42.

[251] See above, n. 31. To the thirty-seven listed there, we can add nos 15, 96, 106, and 146 as also deriving from sources other than chronicles.

[252] Dumville, *Three Men*.

[253] *Ibid.*, pp. 48–51, at p. 49.

[254] *Thesaurus*, edd. & transl. Stokes & Strachan, II.293–5. Texts II and V show *dúnad*. Cf. L.C. Stern, 'Ueber die irische Handschrift in St. Paul', *Zeitschrift für celtische Philologie* 6 (1906–8) 546–55; H. Oskamp, 'The Irish material in the St. Paul Irish codex', *Éigse* 17 (1977–9) 385–91; H. Tristram, 'Die irischen Gedichte im Reichenauer Schulheft', in *Studia Celtica et Indogermanica. Festschrift für Wolfgang Meid zum 70. Geburtstag*, edd. Peter Anreiter & E. Jerem (Budapest 1999), pp. 503–29.

beginning with 'The Book of Leinster'.[255] Yet they have all been given essentially the same status in modern reception.

It is the same story with the marginal poems in the glossed Irish manuscript of Priscian's *Institutiones grammaticae*, now preserved in the Stiftsbibliothek at Sankt Gallen in Switzerland.[256] Whether we think of the two quatrains of 'The Scribe in the Woods' or 'Writing out-of-doors', *Dom-fharcai fidbaide fál*, with its recurrent *fom-chain*,[257] or the single-quatrain 'Viking Times', *Is acher in gáith innocht*,[258] we are looking at poems with no *dúnad* which may be quotations. There has been a tendency, especially in the case of the latter, to argue that the content of the poem proves the manuscript to have been written in Ireland and the poem to be complete: neither is logical or justified by the evidence of the codex itself.[259]

It is worth remarking that we know of the habit of writing Gaelic vernacular non-gloss text in margins from exile-manuscripts of the ninth to twelfth centuries and from manuscripts of Gaelic provenance (not always necessarily Gaelic origin) from the later eleventh century to the seventeenth. In the context of western and central continental Europe in the former period, the practice is so unusual that we have no difficulty in understanding it as a transplanted aspect of Insular, and

[255] The complete poems are: (1) *Messe ocus Pangur bán*, first published in *Irische Texte mit Wörterbuch*, ed. Ernst Windisch (Leipzig 1880), p. 316; (2) *Aed oll fri andud n-áne*, first published in 1872 by Whitley Stokes with translation by Eugene O'Curry – not in the latter's *Lectures*, pp. 47–8, as stated by R.I. Best, *Bibliography of Irish Philology and of Printed Irish Literature to 1912* (Dublin 1913; rev. imp., 1992), p. 131 – but in *Goidelica. Old and Early-Middle-Irish Glosses, Prose and Verse*, ed. & transl. Whitley Stokes (2nd edn, London 1872), pp. 175–6, 177–9. The poem attributed to [St] Moling, *Is én immoniada sás* (two quatrains), was already on its first publication shown to be an extract (quatrains 2 and 1, where 1c is quite different in the full text) of *Is ór glan is nem im gréin* (eight quatrains where qq. 6–8 might be additions) known (with prose introduction) from 'The Book of Leinster' and various later manuscripts: *Goidelica*, ed. & transl. Stokes (2nd edn), pp. 177, 179–82; *Thesaurus*, edd. & transl. Stokes & Strachan, II.xxxiii–xxxiv, 294; *Félire Óengusso Céli Dé. The Martyrology of Oengus the Culdee*, ed. & transl. Whitley Stokes (London 1905), pp. 150–7 (commentary on the Feast of St Moling, 17 June); *Selections from Ancient Irish Poetry*, transl. Meyer, pp. 39–40; *Dánfhocail*, ed. O'Rahilly, p. 114 (*ad* §119; cf. pp. 24, 74); *The Book of Leinster*, edd. Best *et al.*, V.1238–40, part of a collection of six prose-and-verse texts about Moling (*ibid.*, V.1236–42). Its appearance in 'The Book of Ballymote' is marked by a source-reference to 'The Book of Glendalough'.

[256] *Thesaurus*, edd. & transl. Stokes & Strachan, II.xix–xxiii, 290: three verse-texts, the third of which, *Gaib do chuil isin charcair*, has gained no celebrity at all. The chances are that that is so because it does not fit a Romantic image of 'the Celt'. On the codex and its dating, see P.P. Ó Néill, 'Irish observance of the three Lents and the date of the St Gall Priscian (MS 904)', *Ériu* 51 (2000) 159–80.

[257] First publication: Johann Caspar Zeuss, *Grammatica Celtica* (2nd edn, by H. Ebel, Berlin 1871), pp. 953–4.

[258] First publication: *ibid.*, p. 953.

[259] Dumville, *Three Men*, pp. 34–6. Cf. the remarks (more cautious than the usual fare) by R.T. Meyer, 'Early Irish poetry', pp. 39–41, on *Pangur bán*: 'One fine day an Irish scholar, sitting on the shores of Lake Constance, tired of his work on his Vergil commentary, either composed or wrote from memory this poem in his native language' (p. 40).

particularly Gaelic, ecclesiastical culture, even though the manuscript-evidence is hardly available from the Gaelic world itself to demonstrate that point conclusively for the period before 1050×1100.[260]

My principal concern here is, however, with another of these exile-manuscripts – now at Dresden (Germany) – and where its evidence may lead us. It has 'fragments' of Latin verse in a couple of margins.[261] It contains the very famous Old-Gaelic stanza on pilgrimage, *Techt do Róim*. This is found on the lower margin of folio 23r of the *Codex Boernerianus*, a bilingual Greek-Latin biblical manuscript. But following it is another quatrain (*Mór báis mór baile*) standing in an uncertain physical relationship to its predecessor.[262] Some editors and translators have taken the two together, some have not; anthologists have invariably rejected the second stanza.[263] An extended discussion of the physical context of these two

---

[260] London, British Library, MS. Harley 1802, is a gospel-book written (apparently at Armagh) in 1138 by one Maelbrigte hua Maeluanaig: O'Grady *et al.*, *Catalogue*, II.428–32; Duncan, *Catalogue*, no. 29. Apparently in the context of bilingual commentary added in blank spaces in the book, nine poems were written, but the single-quatrain pieces of verse are found in the margins. For text, see W. Stokes (ed. & transl.), 'The Irish verses, notes and glosses in Harl. 1802', *Revue celtique* 8 (1887) 346–69. The bilingual manuscript containing 'The Annals of Inisfallen' (Oxford, Bodleian Library, MS. Rawlinson B.503 [*S.C.* 11850]), begun in 1092 and continued thereafter for more than three centuries, has verse in its margins (notably, extratextual matter by Scribe 1 on folio 1r/v; then by Scribe 9 by annals 1098 and 1104, and perhaps by Scribe 13 by annal 1111): *The Annals of Inisfallen*, facs. edd. Best & MacNeill; Duncan, *Catalogue*, no. 36. *Leabhar na hUidhre* (Duncan, *Catalogue*, no. 5), a wholly vernacular codex, has verse in its margins (by one of the original scribes, B, on MS. pp. 5*a*, 11*a*, 50*a*, all in the upper margins, the last headed *Mac Lonan dixit*; by the revising Scribe H, on MS. pp. 21*b*, 38*b*, 87–89, 116*a* – one in a lower margin – with three attributions; by two sixteenth-century annotators, MS. pp. 69a, 83a, both in lower margins): for the texts see *Lebor na Huidre*, edd. Best & Bergin, footnotes on pp. 11, 28, 56, 92, 124, 178, 208, 216, 289. 'The Book of Leinster' (*Leabhar na Nuachongbhála*), of the second half of the twelfth century, another wholly vernacular codex, has verse in its margins – as, for example, the verses attributed to King Aed Allán mentioned above (pp. 99–101): *The Book of Leinster*, edd. Best *et al.*, VI.1646, n. 3. For a full description, see Duncan, *Catalogue*, no. 11.

[261] It is no doubt with such latinate (and therefore less unusual) activity in mind that R.T. Meyer ('Early Irish poetry', pp. 34–5) advanced the interesting but uncertain proposition that the *probatio pennae* ('pen-trial') was the context of writing Gaelic verse in manuscript-margins. He also defined that context more happily (p. 42): 'The man who wrote[,] "Pleasant is the glint of the of the sun today upon these margins, because it flickers so," on the top of a page of Cassiodorus' *Commentary on the Psalms*, was of a poetic temperament'.

[262] These two quatrains were first published by W. Reeves, *Irish Ecclesiastical Record* 5 (1868) 138, and then in 1872 in *Goidelica*, ed. & transl. Stokes (2nd edn), p. 182; see also *Thesaurus*, edd. & transl. Stokes & Strachan, II.296. For facsimiles of folio 23r, see *Der Codex Boernerianus der Briefe des Apostels Paulus (Msc. Dresd. A.145*b*)*, facs. ed. Alexander Reichardt (Leipzig 1909), and Walter Berschin, *Eremus und Insula. St Gallen und die Reichenau im Mittelalter – Modell einer lateinischen Literaturlandschaft* (Wiesbaden 1987), plate 8 (cf. pp. 23, 132).

[263] It was no doubt *Selections from Ancient Irish Poetry*, transl. Meyer, p. 100 ('The Pilgrim at Rome'), which established the anthologists' tradition by omitting the second stanza. For the two together in translation, see Flower, *The Irish Tradition*, pp. 39–40.

quatrains' mid-ninth-century preservation is the first requirement of any attempt to consider their relationship. For my present purpose, however, I turn in another direction.

The second quatrain of this pair is unusual among all this exile-poetry – the only other known example being the pair of quatrains attributed to St Moling in 'The Reichenau Schoolbook' – in making a reäppearance in Ireland. London, British Library, MS. Additional 30512 is a complex codex: folios 2–9, 19–71 were written by the well known scribe Uilliam Mac an Leagha in the second half of the fifteenth century and contain mostly texts composed before 1200.[264] There is also a rich collection of marginalia,[265] as well as some suspected former marginalia (from an exemplar or exemplaria) now part of the main body of original contents of the manuscript.[266] Among the former is a series of eight quatrains which fill the lower margins of folios 32v and 33r. The fourth of these is *Mór ndrúiss, mór mbaoes, <mór> mbaile* :[267] it is a version of the second quatrain written, six hundred years earlier, on folio 23r of the manuscript preserved at Dresden. The gap in time is remarkable but is an illustration of the continuity of the literary and manuscript tradition of mediaeval Gaeldom. While it is not impossible that this poem was composed on the Continent by a Gaelic exile in the mid-ninth century and carried thence to Ireland, it is no doubt more likely that it was copied from memory into *Codex Boernerianus* and derived from a text already known to its scribe in his homeland, whether or not that text also included *Techt do Róim* ; it then proceeded by a different and lengthy route to lie beneath the eyes of the scribe who made the marginal collection of quatrains at the end of the Middle Ages.

In this same manuscript of Uilliam Mac an Leagha, there occurs in the middle of folio 34v a series of quatrains printed in 1913 by Kuno Meyer as a single poem.[268]

> 1   \<Is\> saoth lem in t-aos léigind
>   do dul ind ifern píanach,
>   is indtí nát lég ecna
>   do dul hi parrthus ngríanach.

---

[264] O'Grady *et al.*, *Catalogue*, II.470–4. The manuscript was repeatedly augmented in the sixteenth century.

[265] *Ibid.*, II.504–5 (art. 114).

[266] *Ibid.*, II.486 (art. 56).

[267] *Ibid.*, II.483 (art. 43). (Cf. n. 243, above.) For this later witness, see K. Meyer (ed.), 'Ein altirischer Spruch', *Archiv für celtische Lexicographie* 3 (1905–7) 215.

[268] K. Meyer (ed.), 'Ein Gedicht aus Additional 30512, fol. 34*b*2', *Zeitschrift für celtische Philologie* 9 (1913) 470; cf. K. Meyer (ed.), 'Mitteilungen aus irischen Handschriften', *ibid.*, 12 (1918) 358–97, at p. 385, for another printing of the whole, but with the derivative copy in Dublin, Trinity College, MS. 1285 (H.1.11), folio 143r, taken into account.

2   Is ed is dech do senóir,
     érge romoch ón dedóil,
     cétul na salm dia eráil,
     éccna<irc> na marb do gabáil.

3   Érlam grind <is> manach mín,
     eccluiss dalta co nglanbríg,
     combrugaid is deorad Dé,
     úadib dlegar apdaine.

4   Fogluim feallsamnacht<a> is fás,
     léig<e>nd Gáideilg<e> 7 glúas,
     litirdacht léir 7 rím,
     is becc a mbríg is tig thúas.   As

The *dúnad* is feeble – indeed, visual rather than aural – but was evidently acceptable to the scribe who rightly took the first word to be Early Modern-Gaelic *as*, Old- and Middle-Gaelic *is*.[269] However, Robin Flower deconstructed this poem, identifying three of its four quatrains elsewhere,[270] one of them in a law-text where Meyer himself would later find it.[271] It is highly probable that Flower was correct, but (if so) we have here an indication of how a poem might be created more or less by accident. The suspicion must be that these quatrains were copied from a margin of a manuscript which served as an exemplar for BL Add. 30512 (and therefore for Uilliam Mac an Leagha, the presumed father of the new poem). Here is an indication that even a short poem with *dúnad* (however feeble) must be subjected to harsher tests before being admitted as a unity. The translator-anthologists have been pulling it apart, however, for quatrain 1 alone has appealed for that purpose. Here is Robin Flower's fine version.[272]

> 'Tis sad to see the sons of learning
> In everlasting Hellfire burning
> While he that never read a line
> Doth in eternal glory shine.

Amen.

---

[269] Cf. above, pp. 110–12, for the rules.

[270] O'Grady *et al.*, *Catalogue*, II.486 (art. 56).

[271] *Ibid.*, Flower printed a version of this quatrain from Bruxelles, Bibliothèque royale, MS. 5100–5104 (507), folio 88v. Cf. K. Meyer, 'Zur keltischen Wortkunde. IX', *Sitzungsberichte der preussischen Akademie der Wissenschaften, philosophisch-historische Klasse* (1919) 374–401, at p. 389 (§212), where he showed no recognition of having twice printed this quatrain.

[272] Flower, *The Irish Tradition*, p. 46.

Economy has been a watchword of commentary on Old- and Middle-Gaelic verse, especially among the anthologists. Another way of putting it is: 'This famous little poem ["Winter"] from the ninth century is the last word in compression'.[273] It undoubtedly has its first and last stanzas and is presumed complete.

Scél lem dúib:	'I have news for you:
dordaid dam,	the stag bellows,
snigid gaim,	winter snows,
ro fáith sam.	summer has gone.
Gáeth ard úar	'The wind is high and cold,
ísel grían;	the sun is low;
gair a rrith,	its course is brief,
ruirthech rían.	the tide runs high.
Rorúad raith,	'The bracken has reddened,
ro cleth cruth,	its shape has been hidden;
ro gab gnáth	the wild goose has raised
giugrann guth.	his customary cry.
Ro gab úacht	'Cold has caught
etti én;	the wings of birds;
aigrid ré –	it is the time of ice –
é mo scél.	these are my news.'

Comment on Old- and early Middle-Gaelic narrative prose (to say nothing of, for example, Old-Gaelic legal prose) has likewise stressed its radical economy of diction.[274] This has seemed particularly problematic to those scholars who have, over the decades, wished to see close reflexes of oral literature in the written tales.[275] That concern may now seem otiose, but the stylistic phenomenon remains very deserving of study and explanation. Might it not be useful to take prose and verse together, to consider this shared quality – I do not recall having seen the parallel mentioned – as a possible reflex of a shared milieu?[276] It is, after all, rather unlikely that the texts had radically different types of author.

---

[273] *A Golden Treasury*, edd. & transl. Greene & O'Connor, pp. 98–9 (no. 21). Cf. R.T. Meyer, 'Early Irish poetry', pp. 45–6: 'the following little gem is preserved only because it is quoted as a gloss on the Old Irish word *rian*, "sea"', in *Amre Coluimb Chille*; see *Lebor na Huidre*, edd. Best & Bergin, p. 30.

[274] A very economical, and penetrating, assessment of such prose is that of G.S. Mac Eoin, *Studia hibernica* 4 (1964) 244–9, at pp. 244–6. For legal prose (and its implications) see T.M. Charles-Edwards, 'The *Corpus iuris hibernici*', *ibid.*, 20 (1980) 141–62, at pp. 146–56.

[275] Cf. important discussion by de Búrca, 'Aspects of transmission'.

[276] But cf. *A Golden Treasury*, edd. & transl. Greene & O'Connor, p. 93, on *Fingal Rónáin*.

NARRATIVE AND VERSE

Another remark by Kuno Meyer has proved a challenge, provided a provocation, to various scholars:[277]

The Celtic nations stand almost alone in this, that they did not employ poetry for epical narrative. There are no ancient Irish epics or ballads.

We know that this is not true of the Middle-Gaelic period. There, one can speak relatively freely of the ballad, as did David Greene and Frank O'Connor in describing *Truaghán sin, a Rí na Ríogh*, a probably twelfth-century poem about King Cormac mac Cuilennáin, who was killed in the battle of Belach Mugna (Ballaghmoon, Co. Kildare) in 908:[278] 'This poem is a ballad from a romance about Cormac's death', a subject and a figure of great interest in Irish literature.[279] So the hunt has been taken up for that yeti of our studies, the *Old*-Gaelic ballad. In 1976 the subject was discussed with characteristic brilliance by Peter Dronke in a wide-ranging paper on 'Learned lyric and popular ballad in the early Middle Ages'.[280] He focused on what we might call 'The Ballad of Fothad Canainne', published by Kuno Meyer in 1910, dated by him *ca* 900.[281] The subject has received much impetus from studies by Donald Meek and, most recently, in the Meek *Festschrift*, by Thomas Clancy.[282]

It is worth saying, however, that narrative verse was by no means alien to Old-Gaelic literature, despite Meyer's strictures. An author whose remarkable work in the mid-eighth century came to light long after Meyer's death is Blathmac mac Con Brettan.[283] He has been correctly described as enjoying 'a superb

[277] *Selections from Ancient Irish Poetry*, transl. Meyer, p. xi.

[278] *A Golden Treasury*, edd. & transl. Greene & O'Connor, pp. 176–8 (no. 45), at p. 176.

[279] *Ibid.*; cf. n. 80, above.

[280] P. Dronke, 'Learned lyric and popular ballad in the early Middle Ages', *Studi medievali*, 3rd series, 17 (1976) 1–40, at pp. 15–17 in the context of a longer discussion of the idea of the lover's ghost.

[281] *Fianaigecht, being a Collection of hitherto inedited Irish Poems and Tales relating to Finn and his Fiana*, ed. & transl. Kuno Meyer (Dublin 1910), pp. 1–21, for *Reicne Fothaid Canainne* ('A ben nachamaicille'). Cf. V.E. Hull (ed. & transl.), 'The Death of Fothath Cananne', *Zeitschrift für celtische Philologie* 20 (1933–6) 400–4. See also *A Golden Treasury*, edd. & transl. Greene & O'Connor pp. 86–92 (no. 19). Cf. E.P. Hamp, 'Fian^{L?}', *Studia Celtica Japonica*, new series, 8 (1996) 87–95. More generally, cf. the remark about 'Fenian ballads which were popular from the twelfth century on': B. Ó Cuív, 'Literary creation and Irish historical tradition', *Proceedings of The British Academy* 49 (1963) 233–62, at p. 249.

[282] D. Meek, 'The banners of the fian in Gaelic ballad tradition', *Cambridge Medieval Celtic Studies* 11 (1986) 29–69; 'Development and degeneration in Gaelic ballad texts', *Béaloideas* 54/55 (1986/7) 131–60; 'The Gaelic ballads of medieval Scotland', *Transactions of The Gaelic Society of Inverness* 55 (1986–8) 47–72; 'Gaelic heroic verse', *Newsletter of The School of Celtic Studies* 8 (1995) 26–30. T.O. Clancy, 'Before the ballad: Gaelic narrative verse before 1200', *Scottish Gaelic Studies* 24 (2008) 115–36.

[283] *The Poems of Blathmac Son of Cú Brettan together with the Irish Gospel of Thomas and a Poem on the Virgin Mary*, ed. & transl. James Carney (London 1964).

narrative sense and a sensitive and lucid style': 'Bláthmacc, retelling the Bible stories, and never taking his eyes off the object[,] is the born narrative poet'.[284]

For all that, prose remained the natural medium for Old-Gaelic narrative. Nevertheless, there is scarcely a narrative prose text which lacks verse content. Comment on the phenomenon has been rather repetitive, but a starting point may be taken in some of the always sharp observations offered by David Greene and Frank O'Connor:[285]

> The new 'literary' saga, whether lay or ecclesiastical, is of considerable interest to us, for much good verse appears in it. Although prose – and usually excellent prose – is the true medium of the saga proper, it was customary to use heightened language at dramatic moments – often for a dialogue between two characters – and in the later sagas this heightened language takes the form of verse. ... Sometimes it is difficult to decide whether the prose and poetry are really by the same hand; the situation is even worse when the prose has been lost, or is reduced to a cryptic and garbled introduction to the poem.

Moving beyond the usual remarks about employment of verse at emotionally heightened moments and especially for speech, we are fortunate to have a recent study by Gregory Toner which has taken us into much more precisely focused, finer-grained considerations of the interactions of prose and verse in Middle-Gaelic literature.[286] The roles of verse in prose (or prose-and-verse) literature may now be recognised as varied. The analysis needs to be broadened out by date and genre. What kind of definition of 'prosimetric' is to be allowed, as this word becomes more popular in our studies, and therefore what roles are to be allowed for prose in fundamentally verse texts and for verse in essentially prose texts?[287] One has only to start asking such questions to realise that we have a long way to go.

---

[284] *A Golden Treasury*, edd. & transl. Greene & O'Connor, pp. 36, 44.

[285] *Ibid.*, p. 7. An example specified there is 'the poems which terminate "Fingal Rónáin"'; cf. *ibid.*, pp. 93–7 (no. 20). And cf. n. 276, above.

[286] G. Toner, 'Authority, verse, and the transmission of *senchas*', *Ériu* 55 (2005) 59–84. Cf. R.M. Scowcroft, '*Leabhar gabhála*', *Ériu* 38 (1987) 81–142 and 39 (1988) 1–66, at pp. 91–2.

[287] In 1985 Jenny Rowland called 'for a general reappraisal of the use of verse in Celtic narrative, since few works conform to the all too brief descriptions of the classic prose-verse saga in general handbooks': J. Rowland, 'The prose setting of the early Welsh *Englynion chwedlonol*', *Ériu* 36 (1985) 29–43, at p. 29. P. Mac Cana, 'Notes on the combination of prose and verse in early Irish narrative', in *Early Irish Literature – Media and Communication. Mündlichkeit und Schriftlichkeit in der frühen irischen Literatur*, edd. Stephen N. Tranter & H.L.C. Tristram (Tübingen 1989), pp. 125–47; Peter Dronke, *Verse with Prose from Petronius to Dante. The Art and Scope of the Mixed Form* (Cambridge, MA 1994), with treatment of 'Liadain and Curithir' on pp. 59–62 and 66; *Prosimetrum. Crosscultural Perspectives on Narrative in Prose and Verse*, edd. Joseph P. Harris & K. Reichl (Cambridge 1997).

THE QUANTITY OF SURVIVING VERSE (AND QUESTIONS OF CLASSIFICATION)

The last generation has seen the beginnings of efforts at quantification of Gaelic verse texts, from the beginnings of the written tradition, not later than the second half of the sixth century, to the end of the formal, public tradition of 'Classical' Gaelic poetry in the period from the mid-seventeenth century to the mid-eighteenth. These exercises have identified larger-than-expected corpora, whether for the centuries spanning the Archaic, Old-, and Middle-Gaelic linguistic periods (to approximately A.D. 1200) or for the Early Modern (*ca* 1200 – *ca* 1700).[288] What particularly remains to be quantified for the Early Modern period is the amount of verse not in Classical *dán díreach*. The effort for the preceding 650 years was admittedly very provisional and largely avoided engagement with the 'isolated or alienated' verse which has loomed so large in the present paper.

In 1961 Robert T. Meyer recorded the views of one of his teachers:[289]

Professor Michael A. O'Brien … estimates that there are still about 12,000 poems from the Middle Irish period still in manuscript awaiting editors. About 2,000 have been edited up to now. The *Irish Grammatical Tracts* [edited serially by Osborn Bergin from 1915 to 1955] quote from about 4,500 Irish poems, only 220 of which have so far been identified.

Nor was the search over:[290]

One never knows when he may stumble quite by accident upon a perfect quatrain embedded in a prose text. When that happens … [h]e runs to his teacher, or he fastens upon the first library attendant[,] to announce his discovery; the verse count is perfect – seven syllables to a line; it falls off into four-line (verse) stanzas; alliteration and assonance clinch the matter.

Robert Meyer indeed had such experience.[291] So too did James Carney, discovering (for example) a stanza unexpectedly among prose glosses on a Latin manuscript of Patristic text or another in a prose tale in which other such verse had long been

---

[288] The first published results of a modern exercise to quantify formal *dán díreach* of the Early Modern-Gaelic linguistic period were reported by Simms, *From Kings*, p. 4; cf. P. Mac Cana, 'Praise poetry in Ireland before the Normans', *Ériu* 54 (2004) 11–40, at pp. 11–12. The total was some 2,000 poems amounting to more than 250,000 lines of verse. For further developments, cf. n. 1, above.

[289] R.T. Meyer, 'Early Irish poetry', p. 35.

[290] *Ibid.*, p. 34. For the current state of identification of source-poems, see D. McManus, '*IGT* citations; more identifications', *Ériu* 58 (2008) 181.

[291] See, for example, R.T. Meyer, 'Scraps from the law books', *Irisleabhar ceilteach* 1.2 (1953) 22 and 2 (1953/4) 19.

identified.[292]

Almost thirty years ago, James Carney (1914–89),[293] the leading student of mediaeval Gaelic poetry after the death of Gerard Murphy and always a voice of high originality,[294] in many ways indeed the intellectual heir of Kuno Meyer,[295] laid out a periodised list of verse texts (and thereby authors) in thirteen sections extending across approximately A.D. 500–1090 and comprising 22,801 lines of poetry.[296] Carney explained his method of compilation thus:[297]

Considerable thought has been given as to what poems ascribed to particular authors should be included, and which, at least temporarily, excluded.

The list could be added to at every stage, but to add to it excessively might only succeed in making it cumbersome and unusable, and already, as I think will be conceded, it forms a formidable reading programme. I conceive of it as an instrument, perhaps blunt, but withal capable of sharpening, that can help us to assess the dates of other compositions. At some points there will be argument, but this also is part of its purpose.

We may hope to find two things in such a list: firstly a credible progression in linguistic development from the beginning to the end, and secondly, at every stage, or almost every stage, a historical anchorage of some kind. The historical anchorage is fundamental to dating, but, unfortunately[,] is not always clearly and unambiguously present at the points where we need it most.

Inevitably, given what we have already seen, the bulk of this corpus is ecclesiastical in authorship, inspiration, and subject-matter. But it is not wholly so.

---

[292] For the former, see *Medieval Irish Lyrics*, ed. & transl. Carney, pp. 10/11 and 98 (no. V); for its manuscript-context, see *Thesaurus*, edd. & transl. Stokes & Strachan, II.1–9, at p. 7 (17v1: 'on the upper margin without any reference to the text'). The manuscript is Karlsruhe, Badische Landesbibliothek, MS. Aug. perg. 195. For the second example, from *Esnada tige Buchet*, see Carney, 'Three Old Irish accentual poems', pp. 59–60; for the saga, see *Fingal Rónáin and Other Stories*, ed. David Greene (Dublin 1955), p. 28.

[293] For Carney's work, see his *Festschrift – Sages, Saints and Storytellers. Celtic Studies in Honour of Professor James Carney*, edd. Donnchadh Ó Corráin *et al.* (Maynooth 1989) – and the volume of studies in his memory published as *Celtica* 23 (1999), in which the appreciation by Terence McCaughey on pp. 188–92 was by some oversight not placed at the head of the volume.

[294] From across the course of his publishing career, from the 1930s to 1989, one may identify the following items as of preëminent importance and quality in this regard: 'A Chrínóc, cubaid do cheól', *Éigse* 4 (1943/4) 280–3; *The Poems of Blathmac* (1964); 'The deeper level of early Irish literature', *Capuchin Annual* 36 (1969) 160–71; 'Two poems from *Acallam na senórach*', in *Celtic Studies. Essays in Memory of Angus Matheson (1912–1962)*, edd. James Carney & D. Greene (London 1968), pp. 22–32; 'The so-called "Lament of Créidhe"', *Éigse* 13 (1969/70) 227–42, and 'Notes on early Irish verse', *ibid.*, pp. 291–312; 'Three Old Irish accentual poems' (1971); 'The dating of early Irish verse texts, 500–1100', *Éigse* 19 (1982/3) 177–216; 'The dating of archaic Irish verse', in *Early Irish Literature*, edd. Tranter & Tristram, pp. 39–55.

[295] Cf. the remark about Kuno Meyer in *A Golden Treasury*, edd. & transl. Greene & O'Connor, p. 17 (quoted above, p. 106), the core of which could be applied, *mutatis mutandis*, to James Carney.

[296] Carney, 'The dating of early Irish verse texts', pp. 177–81.

[297] *Ibid.*, pp. 181–2.

Proinsias Mac Cana rightly emphasised the importance of the poetry of Dallán mac Móire, who was active in the early tenth century.[298] Here is a poet who can be seen as a secular practitioner, in some sense antecedent to the court-poets of the thirteenth century and later.[299]

Another Viking-Age poet may have had a similar profile, Flann mac Lonáin:[300] he (if correctly identified) has a curious memorial in a marginale – perhaps more celebrated than closely read – in 'The Book of Leinster', *Leabhar na Nuachongbhála*.[301] In it, a Bishop Find, attributed to Kildare in a gloss, wrote to Aed Mac Crimthainn, coarb of St Colum of Tír da glas (Terryglass, Co. Tipperary): *Tucthar dom duanaire Meic Lonáin co-faiccmis a cialla na nduan filet ann*, 'Let the poem-

---

[298] Mac Cana, 'Praise poetry', pp. 19–20; cf. Carney, 'The dating of early Irish verse texts', pp. 179, 187–8.

[299] Carney, *ibid.*, p. 187: 'He is the earliest recognisable court or household poet whose poems have survived in some quantity; in style and approach he anticipates and is ancestral to the type of poet that we know well from the fourteenth century onwards to the end of the Bardic Order', quoted in part by Mac Cana, 'Praise poetry', p. 20. It is as well to remember in this context Carney's very heavy involvement for much of his career with editing and discussing Classical Gaelic poetry. The term court-poet (with close variants thereof) has a lengthy history in modern scholarship: *Selections from Ancient Irish Poetry*, transl. Meyer, p. xi ('the professional bard attached to the court and person of a chief'); Joseph Vendryes, *La poésie de cour en Irlande et en Galles* (Paris 1932); Eleanor Knott, *Irish Classical Poetry, commonly called Bardic Poetry* (Dublin 1957; 2nd edn, 1960), reïssued in Knott & Murphy (ed. Carney), *Early Irish Literature*, pp. 19–93; Williams, 'The court poet'; P.A. Breatnach, 'The chief's poet', *Proceedings of The Royal Irish Academy* 83 C (1983) 37–79; Enrico Campanile, *Die älteste Hofdichtung von Leinster. Alliterierende reimlose Strophen* (Wien 1988); G. Mac Eoin, 'Poet and prince in medieval Ireland', in *The Court and Cultural Diversity*, edd. Evelyn Mullally & J. Thompson (Cambridge 1997), pp. 3–16. Carney, 'Society', p. 233, complained about Williams, 'The court poet': 'Quite recently … Williams has … substitut[ed] the term "court poet" for "bardic poet". I am less than enthusiastic about this change in terminology. There are, it is true, reasonable objections to the use of the term "bardic", but at least it has been sanctioned by usage. The term "court poet" has implications of sycophancy that are not fully justified.' Carney had evidently forgotten that the term was used by Knott in her standard introduction to the subject (which Carney had republished in 1966); and by 1983 he himself ('The dating of early Irish verse texts', p. 187, quoted above) was quite cheerfully using the phrase.

[300] For a relatively lengthy treatment, see Flower, *The Irish Tradition*, pp. 68–72. For Flann and his mother as 'literary figments', see C. O'Lochlainn, 'Poems on the battle of Clontarf', *Éigse* 3 (1941/2) 208–18 and 4 (1943/4) 33–47, and Ó Cuív, 'Literary creation', p. 251 (and see my next note). On another curious dimension, see H. Meroney, 'A druidic liturgy in *Ogam Bricrend*?', *Modern Language Notes* 62 (1947) 187–9. For an attribution of a marginal quatrain as *Mac Lónán dixit*, see *Lebor na Huidre*, edd. Best & Bergin, p. 124 (cf. n. 260, above). A Middle-Gaelic prose-and-verse text about Flann has recently been given thorough study: D. Clifford (ed. & transl.), 'Bó bithblicht meic Lonán: eagrán de scéal faoi Fhlann mac Lonáin', *Celtica* 25 (2007) 9–39. For an intervention of critical importance, see K. Simms, 'The Donegal poems in The Book of Fenagh', *Ériu* 58 (2008) 37–53.

[301] O'Curry, *Lectures*, pp. 186, 571; Brian Ó Cuív, *The Irish Bardic Duanaire or "Poem-book"* (Dublin [1973]), pp. 15–16; S.L. Forste-Grupp, 'The earliest Irish personal letter', *Proceedings of The Harvard Celtic Colloquium* 15 (1995) 1–11; D.N. Dumville, 'Frivolity and reform in the Church: the Irish experience, 1066–1166', *Studies in Church History* 48 (2011).

book of Mac Lonáin be brought to me so that we may discover the meaning of the poems which are in it'. If a tenth-century secular poet was represented in the third quarter of the twelfth century by a *duanaire* about which two senior ecclesiastics might correspond (and perhaps meet), we need not suppose such a significant divide between the literary cultures of the Middle- and Early Modern-Gaelic periods as has sometimes been supposed.[302] The issue would then be one of transmission and survival rather than differing cultures of production.

This has recently been given brief consideration by Liam Breatnach, and we shall turn to other aspects of his article in a moment. His approach was to measure survival of formal public eulogy (and satire) against the general pattern of evidence of survival and loss of Gaelic literature (including that written in Latin).[303] He offered biblical and legal literature in particular as comparanda. However, the difficulty with pursuing this is that very substantial amounts of both biblical and legal literature survive, even though losses are admittedly heavy. But when we turn to formal panegyric in especial – whether directed to lay or ecclesiastical recipients, men or women[304] – the surviving quantity is vanishingly small. 'Vanishing' may indeed be the operative word. Consider the following extract from the so-called 'Fragmentary Annals of Ireland', *s.a.* 855, for A.D. 859, about a military expedition led by Cerball mac Dúnlainge, king of the Osraige, into Mide:[305]

Is sochaidhe trá d'f<h>earaibh dána Éireann dorónsat duana mholta do C<h>earbhall, agus taithmead gach cosgur rug inntibh; agus as mó doríne Aongas an t-áirdeaghnaidh, comarba Molua.

This was translated in 1860 by John O'Donovan thus:[306]

'Many of the literati of Erin composed laudatory poems for Cearbhall, in which they commemorated every victory which he gained, and Aenghus, the high wise man, successor of Molua, did so most [of all]'.

It was rendered less exuberantly by Joan Radner in 1978:[307]

'Many of the poets of Ireland made praise-poems for Cerball, and mentioned in them every victory he had won; and Óengus the scholar, successor of MoLua, made the most [of all]'.

---

302 The question almost inevitably arises whether, in addition to the poet's *duanaire* which is hypothesised here for the mid-twelfth century, we might imagine a patron's *duanaire* and a family's *duanaire* before the late Middle Ages. For the terminology, cf. Ó Cuív, *The Irish Bardic Duanaire*.

303 L. Breatnach, 'Satire, praise and the early Irish poet', *Ériu* 56 (2006) 63–84, at pp. 81–2.

304 *Ibid.*, pp. 68–71. The same situation obtains for eighth- to eleventh-century Wales: Williams, *The Beginnings*, p. 45, n. 12.

305 I have constructed this text from the two published editions.

306 *Annals of Ireland. Three fragments*, ed. & transl. O'Donovan, pp. 140/1.

307 *Fragmentary Annals*, ed. & transl. Radner, pp. 104/5 (§265).

This of course provides a context for the work of Dallán mac Móire, one of those *fir dána*. We may note in passing that early use of 'literati' by O'Donovan in this context, a foolish locution which has become ever more prevalent in mediaeval Gaelic studies. But what of Abbot Oengus, *comarba* ('heir', hence 'successor') of St Molua, patronal saint of Cluain ferta Molua (Clonfertmulloe, Co. Laois)? He died in 860, the year after the campaign recorded above, and was himself memorialised in 'The Annals of The Four Masters':[308]

Oengus, abb Cluana fearta Molua – agus ba heccnaid tocchaidhe é dna –, agus Colmán, abb Doimhliacc, décc.

'Oengus, abbot of Clonfertmulloe – and he was an excellent scholar –, and Colmán, abbot of Duleek, died.'

Would he too have been called *fer dána*, or was his praise-poetry formally or qualitatively different from that of the many *fir dána Érenn* whose mostly vanished poems gain brief celebrity here?

Where we have only 'isolated or alienated' stanzas, it has proved very hard to judge their status – and, indeed, their genre (modern scholarly work on mediaeval Gaelic poetic genre is itself notably exiguous) –, and when a complete poem (of eight stanzas) can be held up for examination, *Aed oll fri andud n-áne* being the totemic item, its precise generic status is by no means agreed.[309] It may be that Breatnach has acknowledged this in his remark, 'Even in the case of this complete poem, however, not to mention the many illustrative verses extracted from others and cited in the metrical tracts, it is difficult to be sure that it was composed by a *fili* rather than a *bard*'.[310] And, on this scale of nomenclature, what was an ecclesiastical poet to be called?[311] If those who were not court-poets were 'non-professionals',[312] what would they be called by the 'professionals'? Another way, then, of posing one of our crucial questions is to ask how we should describe surviving poetry which cannot convincingly be attributed to a court-poet. But if we are to allow that *Amre Coluimb Chille* does indeed belong to the aftermath of the death of St Columba of Iona (597) and that its author, steeped in christian Latin learning, was a professional

---

[308] *Annala rioghachta*, ed. & transl. O'Donovan, I.492/3 (858.1).

[309] For the text, see most conveniently *Thesaurus*, edd. & transl. Stokes & Strachan, II.295 (no. V). Cf. n. 254, above. For discussion, see G. Murphy, 'Bards and filidh', *Éigse* 2 (1940) 200–7; Flower, *The Irish Tradition*, pp. 27–8; Knott [& Murphy], *Early Irish Literature*, p. 71; Mac Cana, 'Praise poetry', pp. 32–5.

[310] Breatnach, 'Satire, praise', p. 81.

[311] Introductions to quoted verse in chronicles and genealogical tracts, for example, suggest that *poeta* or *senchaid* might be appropriate answers! Cf. Toner, 'Authority'.

[312] *Selections from Ancient Irish Poetry*, transl. Meyer, p. xi. (Cf. n. 18, above.)

court-poet,[313] we are returned to troublesome questions about the interrelationship of *fili*, *filidecht*, and transmission of poetry of praise in the earlier Middle Ages. And, as so often, we are reminded of the necessity of thinking about relationships between oral performance and manuscript-culture.

THE PRACTITIONERS: PROBLEMS OF PERCEPTION

There is indeed a large and interesting problem surrounding the secular professionals who have been identified – and who in some measure can be seen presenting themselves – as the bearers of their society's inherited knowledge of itself. Once again, we find that we can see them in action from the thirteenth century to the seventeenth (and of course we have some quantity of their technical professional literature of instruction).[314] We can also see what colonial administrators and settlers found politically troublesome and culturally offensive about them in the sixteenth and seventeenth centuries.[315]

At the beginning of this paper, I observed that we could, with the aid of an anthropological definition, invoke a generalising explanation which would help us in examining various aspects of Gaelic society crucial for our understanding of ritual public literary production.[316] The segmentary lineage has indeed long been stressed by Donnchadh Ó Corráin as an appropriate definition of the sociopolitical entity which provided the structural dynamic of mediaeval Gaelic royal and aristocratic martial activity.[317] The relevant work of Thomas Charles-Edwards has essentially cohered with this.[318] We should note before proceeding further that for Sahlins the segmentary lineage is to be understood as 'an organization of predatory expansion'.[319] It seems to me to be important to grasp that this characteristic defines the secular political culture of Gaeldom from our first fragmentary

---

[313] On dating, see especially Thurneysen, 'Colmán mac Lénéni', and Charles-Edwards, *Early Christian Ireland*, pp. 285–90 (cf. 180, 192–3, 306). See also Meyer, *Miscellanea Hibernica*, pp. 25–7 (575–7), on the character of the opening lines of *Amre Coluimb Chille* as verse.

[314] Cf. n. 2, above.

[315] T.F. O'Rahilly, 'Irish poets, historians, and judges in English documents, 1538–1615', *Proceedings of The Royal Irish Academy* 36 C (1921–4) 86–120.

[316] Cf. n. 3, above.

[317] Ó Corráin, *Ireland before the Normans*, pp. 37–42, and with development in various other publications.

[318] T.M. Charles-Edwards, 'Early medieval kingships in the British Isles', in *The Origins of Anglo-Saxon Kingdoms*, ed. Steven Bassett (London 1989), pp. 28–39, 245–8; *Early Irish and Welsh Kingship* (Oxford 1993); *Early Christian Ireland*, chapters 2–3.

[319] Cf. n. 3, above.

glimpses of it in the later sixth century[320] down to its last gasp in mid-eighteenth-century Scotland.[321] This is in no way an insistence that the history of Gaeldom was timeless or unchanging – which would be a wholly unhistorical proposition – but a plea for scholars to acknowledge some fundamental characteristics of a culture which showed remarkable resilience across at least a millennium from the dawn of the Middle Ages to within about a generation of the American and French revolutions which have defined the politics of the modern world. That, as a historical argument, is a topic for larger exposition on another day. But it does offer a suggestion that we might privilege a corresponding argument about the relationship of poets and royals across the same period.

All commentators have been agreed that it is against a particular socio-political background that one should understand formal panegyric, satire, and eulogy, and the poets who produced and offered these in a public context. We might attribute the initial explorations of this phenomenon – as something needing to be explained to those who did not participate in it – to English administrators in early modern Ireland.[322] From that beginning it has taken much time and a more dispassionate and yet sympathetic approach, as well as a very considerable amount of work, to achieve the establishment of the present scholarly paradigm. That has been able to be achieved as a result of (above all) the survival of a very considerable (if obviously incomplete) body of primary evidence.

When we turn to the earlier Middle Ages, we find an evidential context very different from that of the period 1200–1750. We have, in the early mediaeval *Bretha nemed* and *Uraicecht na ríar*, law-tracts which speak to us variously about training, rights, responsibility, and status of members of this very political literary profession, and in some measure about important status-divisions within it.[323]

---

[320] Or perhaps even in the later fifth century through the works of Bishop Patrick: D. Ó Corráin, 'The Church and secular society', *Settimane di studio della Fondazione Centro italiano di studi sull'alto medioevo* 57 (2009) 261–324.

[321] Dillon, 'The archaism', p. 262, on poems of 1715 and 1738: Alexander Cameron, *Reliquiæ Celticæ. Texts, Papers, and Studies in Gaelic Literature and Philology* (2 vols, Inverness 1892/4), II.248–59, 274–81. See now, for a poem probably datable in 1746, M. Scott, 'Poetry and politics in mid-eighteenth-century Argyll: "Tuirseach andiugh críocha Gaoidhiol"', in *Rannsachadh na Gàidhlig 2000*, edd. Colm Ó Baoill & N.R. McGuire (Aberdeen 2002), pp. 149–62.

[322] Cf. n. 315, above.

[323] E.J. Gwynn (ed. & transl.), 'An Old-Irish tract on the privileges and responsibilities of poets', *Ériu* 13 (1940–2) 1–60 and 220–36; *Uraicecht na ríar. The Poetic Grades in Early Irish Law*, ed. & transl. Liam Breatnach (Dublin 1987); Breatnach, 'Satire, praise'.

There are questions still needing answers about this legal literature.[324] Whose law was this? – whose in Gaelic society was the authoritative voice in this area? were there regional or other differences which allowed significant variations between one territory or people and another?[325] And how much change was there over time?

In attempts at explication of some of this, we find clear (but, it seems to me, partial) thinking in important publications by Gerard Murphy and Donncha Ó hAodha.[326] In the last few years there has been a spurt of attention to these matters, which is partly due to a clash of larger theories about the nature(s) of literary production and the character and interaction of those responsible for it. Proinsias Mac Cana successfully deconstructed Gerard Murphy's history of the relationship of *fili* and *bard*:[327] nevertheless he continued to hold that before the later twelfth century the practice of 'formal eulogy did in fact flourish'[328] – while allowing nonetheless that in that era 'the scribes and redactors ... did not regard formal panegyric as coming directly within their own professional ambit'.[329]

Mac Cana's contribution seems to have been taken as a provocation by Liam Breatnach: 'The role of the *fili* in the composition of praise-poetry in the pre-Norman period has been questioned'.[330] Whether that is what Mac Cana did may itself be questioned, but in any case Breatnach has agreed with Mac Cana in his judgment of Murphy's analysis of the history of the relationship of *fili* and *bard*. Although we have the unedifying spectacle of Breatnach continuing to pursue his old master with negative feeling, this time beyond the grave,[331] his article nonetheless contains much of interest and importance, notably including an analysis (which is of significance for the present discussion) of the sources of illustrative stanzas in the *Trefhocal*-tract.[332]

Some problems remain, however. The first is the question of the history of

---

[324] Cf. Kelly, *A Guide*, pp. 225–86, is the natural starting point, but he there – like most writers on the subject – has taken for granted that some of these big questions have answers of such self-evident simplicity that they do not need discussion.

[325] Cf. D.A. Binchy, '*Bretha nemed*', *Ériu* 17 (1955) 4–6.

[326] Murphy, 'Bards and filidh'; D. Ó hAodha, 'The first Middle Irish metrical tract', in *Metrik und Medienwechsel*, ed. Tristram, pp. 207–44.

[327] Mac Cana, 'Praise poetry', pp. 32–6.

[328] *Ibid.*, p. 11.

[329] I wonder exactly what he meant by using the word 'redactors'. If it is a step back from regarding scribes as redactors, that is very welcome. But it might be a nativist formula for 'authors'.

[330] Breatnach, 'Satire, praise', p. 63. It seems to me unwise to take 'the pre-Norman period' as a singular.

[331] *Ibid.*, pp. 79–80. Cf. my comments in *Peritia* 11 (1997) 451–68, especially pp. 465–6. I may say that we should note what awaits any of us who may have the fortune to predecease Professor Breatnach; my recommendation is, adopting the modern politician's phrase, to get in one's retaliation first.

[332] Breatnach, 'Satire, praise', pp. 80–1, and cf. pp. 68–71.

the learned classes after the period of the Old-Gaelic legal literature and before 1200, one of the issues which Murphy sought to address in 1940. Breatnach has here been less than clear about how he would interpret that history. From the Middle-Gaelic linguistic period – the central Middle Ages more or less – we have the metrical tracts which delivered such a high proportion of the 'isolated or alienated' verse gathered by Kuno Meyer into his first collection of *Bruchstücke*. Here, Breatnach has rightly felt the need to discuss possible answers (or, perhaps rather, expound a single response) to 'the not insignificant question of who the Early Irish metrical tracts … were intended for. Texts such as the four included in [Thurneysen's *Mittelirische Verslehren*] are, after all, written texts, and the second of these is set out in the form of a twelve-year curriculum for the *filid*, with various metres illustrated for each year.'[333] Where did these texts originate, and among whom did they circulate? Did they have authority and status in the profession of *filidecht* itself? And what was the relationship of the professionals with those non-professionals who were certainly producing literature of their own?

Across the long history of mediaeval and early modern Gaelic written literature we find stories about the producers and performers of secular poetry and story. One recurrent theme is of *filid* and *baird* as extortionists, now extracting political concessions, now eating their hosts out of house and home, now requiring extravagant gifts or rewards, with satire as an implicit or explicit inducement to deliver benefits.[334] Given the strongly self-interrogatory nature of the mediaeval Gaelic literary tradition, it is noteworthy that these narratives are characteristically presented as pertaining to periods or moments of crisis and transition in the relationships between tradition-bearers and the elevated ranks of society who lived in a structurally determined symbiotic relationship with them. A question must always be who produced such stories – and to what purpose. It is noteworthy that *Tromdám Guaire*, for example, is itself a satire on unreasonable behaviour by members of this poetic corporation.[335]

---

[333] *Ibid.*, p. 80.

[334] On the story (not attested contemporaneously) about the interaction of Colum Cille and Dallán Forgaill in the later sixth century, see Flower, *The Irish Tradition*, pp. 1–3, and Knott, 'Why Mongán was deprived', p. 155, n. 1; cf. John Bannerman, *Studies in the History of Dalriada* (Edinburgh 1974), pp. 157–70, and D.A. Binchy, 'The background of early Irish literature', *Studia Hibernica* 1 (1961) 7–18, at pp. 17–18.

[335] Carney, 'Society', p. 237; Ó Coileáin, 'The structure'. For an important recent contribution, see L. Breatnach (ed. & transl.), '*Araile felmac féig don Mumain*: unruly pupils and the limitations of satire', *Ériu* 59 (2009) 111–36, presenting a hilarious short Middle-Gaelic tale in the context of other stories in which poets are central figures. We may suspect legal instruction as the text's function, but inadequately penetrating questions about audience, authority, and origin are being put to this and other *fili*-centred literary texts.

Another set of relationships between Gaelic learned institutions has been invoked in relation to the actual or apparent watershed in the evidence for production of secular public poetry on either side of A.D. 1200. In discussions by Robin Flower, Gerard Murphy, and Proinsias Mac Cana we have been offered socio-historical explanations of this change in the character of the evidence.[336] Two great processes of the Gaelic twelfth century, ecclesiastical reform and francophone political and military intervention, have inevitably been interrogated as to their possible responsibility for or share in this change.[337] But whether the nature of the change has been properly conceptualised is open to question. And one is bound to wonder, in view of changing estimates of the character and degree of success of ecclesiastical reform in Ireland at least, whether that movement could have provoked the changes hypothesised.[338]

These issues are all matters for fuller consideration on other occasions. But the question remains: does the change in the nature of the evidence signify a major transition in the nature of the institutions responsible for literary production or is it merely a reflex of changes in the character of evidence over time, to which long-lasting patterns are particularly prone? It is important, once again, that the questions 'What *is* …?' and 'What *was* mediaeval Gaelic poetry?' should be kept apart and answered separately.[339]

---

[336] Flower, *The Irish Tradition*, pp. 67–93 (chapter III, 'The rise of the bardic order'); Murphy, 'Bards and filidh', especially pp. 206–7; Mac Cana, 'The rise'.

[337] On the interaction of the two processes, see (most concisely and incisively), Maurice P. Sheehy, *When the Normans came to Ireland* (Cork 1975; 2nd edn, 1998). On the external military intervention from the later 1160s, see *A New History of Ireland*, gen. edd. T.W. Moody *et al.*, II.1–126. On ecclesiastical reform, see most recently *Ireland and Europe in the Twelfth Century. Reform and Renewal*, edd. Damian Bracken & D. Ó Riain-Raedel (Dublin 2006).

[338] For scholars debating the literary historical issues, the subject seems to be stuck in the condition in which it was left with the summation of an outstanding life's work by Aubrey Gwynn, *The Irish Church in the Eleventh and Twelfth Centuries* (Dublin 1992); that understanding had already been gravely undermined, however, by a movement of thought beginning with Canice Mooney, *The Church in Gaelic Ireland: Thirteenth to Fifteenth Centuries* (Dublin 1969).

[339] I am indebted to my colleague Patrick Crotty – whose very remarkable work, *The Penguin Book of Irish Verse*, ed. Patrick Crotty (London 2010), was published as I was completing this article – for reading and commenting on a draft of my paper, to Rachel Howie and Aideen O'Leary for discussion of some of the ideas, and to Peter Dronke, Colm Ó Baoill, Pádraig Ó Macháin, and Pádraig Ó Riain for specific and much valued help. It is a pleasure to be able to dedicate this article to Peter McCaffery, an inspiring and learned colleague and friend with whom one can discuss any subject and always come away wiser.

Nature's Perils:
Mountains, Enlightenment and the French Revolution

WILLIAM SCOTT
University of Aberdeen

In 1791, Laurent-Gaspard Gérard proposed the establishment of a theatre of national education. Inspired by Buffon's study of nature, from the smallest grain of sand to "the immensity of the celestial orbs", Gérard would show "the majestic brilliance of a rising sun, the imposing elevation of the Alps, the happy climates of India, the burned earth of Africa, the ice of the poles, volcanoes, earthquakes, tempests, shipwrecks …". The spectator, eyes and ears struck with a force beyond history books and travellers' accounts, would hold his or her breath as a mountaintop tree resisted the gale, but would also draw a moral lesson, applicable in real life. Before the stage, and an hour before the performance, a screen would provide information and explanation to occupy the mind and furnish the memory. The first scene, Systems of the World, saw philosophers – Thales, Anaxagoras, Epicurus, Descartes, Newton and Buffon – together with geographers and astronomers, demonstrate visually the essentials of their system. Descartes would juggle soap bubbles to illustrate his *tourbillons*. Buffon would heat balls, whose cooling would indicate the age of the world …. They would explain their fundamental principles to a rather truculent child: despite the sight of Epicurus's brilliant atoms whizzing around against a black backcloth, he remained unsatisfied till Moses, hitherto lurking in the wings, came forward, presenting the Creation, whereupon the philosophers, child and Moses were joined by an angelic choir hymning the glory of the Creator.

Subsequent scenes, including Tableaux of Nature and Moral Scenes from History and Fable, were not described but there can be no doubting the excessive ambition of this multi-media, multi-cultural project.[1]

The idea of a Creation was not, of course, universally accepted (angels notwithstanding). Nature, as everything that exists, has existed and will exist, might be self-sufficient and eternal but also active and creative, with will and feeling. Nor, for some *philosophes*, did man need a "supernatural" being. God was man-made, a political invention of some men, to dupe others into accepting gross inequalities of power and wealth. Passed off by those who enjoyed that power as

---

[1] Laurent-Gaspard Gérard, *Mémoire sur le théâtre de l'éducation nationale*, (Paris, August 1791). BL, F568(1).

Explorations in Cultural History: Essays for Peter Gabriel McCaffery,
edd. David F. Smith & H. Philsooph (Aberdeen 2010)   ISBN 978-0-9567059-0-7

"natural", such inequalities were challenged by those for whom an early, now idealised nature, of liberty, equality and fraternity, had been perverted by powers both secular and profane. The Church, in turn, branded the "nature" of these subversives, animated by a pervasive "Spinosisme", as mere animality – that "concupiscence" excoriated in so many sermons.[2] What revolutionaries saw as a regeneration in 1789 was a further fall into chaos and barbarism (in which, regrettably, many priests collaborated).

The natural disasters featuring so spectacularly on Gérard's stage, could be understood by both the religious and the scientifically inclined (not always opposites of course) as having beneficial effects – volcanoes as "safety valves", storms as "purifying the air". But leading churchmen also regarded them as salutary warnings from the Deity, punishment for man's presumptuous pride. For them, mere physical explanations were inadequate. Scientific reason could not penetrate the God-given, God-guarded secrets of the universe. Hence, the Revolution as a natural force was, for them, a divine punishment, to strike terror into sinful hearts and minds. But, like natural catastrophes, this one had been long prepared and the irreligiously irresponsible had already been damned. The Sorbonne's blistering condemnation of Raynal comprehensively rubbished Enlightenment values, notably its "scientific" pretensions.[3] The abbé Barruel, soon to be a leading ideologist of the counter-revolution, mercilessly, and sometimes humorously, exposed the contradictions of Enlightenment luminaries on all matters concerning man, nature and religion.[4]

***

Theories of the Earth proliferated in 18th century France.[5] Given the power of the Catholic Church, controlling the Sorbonne, being responsible for the banning or burning of many works of philosophy and history, the clash between *Genesis*

---

[2] Yves Citton, *L'Envers de la liberté. L'invention d'un imaginaire spinoziste dans la France des lumières*, (Paris, 2006): Y. Citton and Frédéric Lordon, *Spinoza et les Sciences sociales*, (Paris, 2008): Anne Dalsuet, *Philosophie et écologie*, (Paris, 2010).

[3] *Censure de la Faculté de Théologie de Paris* - against *Histoire philosophique et politique des établissements des Européens dans les Deux Indes* of GT Raynal, (Paris, 1782). BL, R91(2).

[4] Augustin Barruel, *Les Helviennes*, 4 vols, (1784-1788).

[5] The main body of this essay was given as a paper at the Varieties of Cultural History Conference, held at Aberdeen University, 5-8 July 2007. I wish to thank the Conference organisers for giving me the opportunity to talk on a topic which reflects my outside, indeed outdoor, interests, rather than my purely academic ones. I also want to reiterate how rewarding I found participation in the Cultural History degree programme at Aberdeen. I recall with pleasure the amical enthusiasm of staff and students.

and non- or anti-Biblical accounts of the Earth's history was inevitably acrimonious.[6]

Mountains had a key role in this clash.[7] Their interpretation posed acute problems. Their very existence challenged beliefs across a wide spectrum of concerns – for mountains, and the sea from which some believed they emerged to provide support for early life, were so prominent and possibly permanent a feature of the physical world, perhaps even holding that world together. They had witnessed the whole of man's existence. To understand mountains was to understand man's history but, increasingly, man's history was seen as only a very small part of the world's. The task of understanding <u>both</u> histories and their linkages, was, many thought, essentially secular. It could be considered separately from "religion". One could insert a disclaimer, claiming that physical truths did not affect revealed religious Truth. Clearly, however, the Church was not fooled by this, even if some disclaimants were probably sincere.

Mountains aroused admiration and astonishment even from "scientists". They could be benevolent: they attracted clouds and so provided the water fertilising the plains. As a churchman noted, in a treatise on physics: "It is therefore a folly, I might even say an impiety, to see mountains as the effects of chance, as <u>faults</u> in Creation". God had ensured that "the Earth is not a confused mass, composed of bits piled up in disorder, regardless of beauty and symmetry…".[8]

Other clerics, however, held to the view that God had created the world perfect, smooth and fertile. Mountains, like the Flood, were a punishment for man's sins. Both religious and secular writers agreed that the Earth had endured many "revolutions" – cataclysms which some secularists thought may even have exterminated the whole human race, cataclysms which the religious mind attributed to man's inveterate sinfulness but which secularists used to refute the

---

[6] Among works on the so-called Counter-Enlightenment, Didier Masseau, *Les Ennemis des philosophes*, (Paris, 2000).

[7] Among the numerous works on mountains: Claire-Elaine Engel, *La Littérature alpestre en France et en Angleterre aux XVIIIe et XIXe siècles*, (Chambéry, 1930); CE Engel and Charles Vallot, *"Ces monts affreux…", (1650-1810)*, (Paris, 1934); Numa Broc, *Les Montagnes au siècle des Lumières*, (Paris, 1991); Philippe Joutard, *L'Invention du Mont Blanc*, (Paris, 1986); a challenging work, Barbara Maria Stafford, *Voyage into Substance. Art, Science, Nature and the Illustrated Travel Account, 1760-1840*, (Camb. Mass., 1984). Two inspirational works: Robert Macfarlane, *Mountains of the Mind, A History of a Fascination*, (Granta Books, 2003) and Nan Shepherd, *The Living Mountain*, (Canongate, 2008). On the French Revolution, André Corvol, *La Nature en Révolution*, (Paris, 1993) and Mary Ashburn Miller, "Mountain, become a volcano! The Image of the Volcano in the Rhetoric of the French Revolution", *French Historical Studies*, vol. 32, no.4, Fall 2009, pp. 555-585.

[8] Aimé-Henri Paulian, *Dictionnaire des novellas découvertes faites en physique*, (Paris, 1787), pp. 207ff. Paulian authored numerous works, which shared material…

idea of a benevolent deity. Clearly Nature itself could be malevolent or at least, like God, if he existed, indifferent to man. For Maillet, in *Telliamed* (1748), the Earth's four billion years, for Buffon its age in millions, suggested not only age, but ruin and decrepitude, with all life to be extinguished either by burning or freezing. Man's hold on "his" God-given world was precarious.[9]

It was above all mountains, the "archives of the world" – and especially their fossils, "medals" testifying to antiquity – from which one might wrest a history of the world, <u>forcing</u> nature to reveal her secrets. For the Earth's fractured surface is "a succession of documents which prove a succession of revolutions on this planet".[10] Sometimes the evidence was disconcerting. For a materialist (prudently calling himself N) nothing on Earth was regular. "No form is exact on Earth". None of the processes or events which had scarred the earth (earthquakes, the collapse and emergence of continents, the rise and fall of mountains) had obeyed a "fixed rule". There was no rest for matter. Enormous masses moved immense distances: mountains changed places, "One might almost say they took walks across the globe". Naturally a world of mountains was also a world of dangerous abysses.[11]

The notion of "primitive mountains", notably of granite, was widespread among natural philosophers: these, above all, would tell the Earth's whole history, whether of 6000 or 4 billion years. But N denied that any "original constitution" could be discovered: history was broken, whether that of man or his world. What was certain was that cataclysms had not ended, as the Lisbon earthquake of 1755 testified. So mountains challenged philosophical optimism (*Candide*) as well as religious conviction. If "our globe is now only a pile of debris, collapsed inwards or propelled outwards", the small areas that man had civilised appeared derisory. Man deluded himself in thinking he was formed expressly to inhabit the best and most important of all possible worlds. N suggested that few would be brave or honest enough fully to face this fact.

Buffon was among many who saw society, and religion, as arising from the fear produced by natural catastrophes, especially volcanoes. This was hardly religious orthodoxy. *Telliamed* had man emerging from the sea, first as extremely primitive form(s) of life: and many others saw him (and her) as establishing themselves on mountain tops as the universal sea receded. But how, then, could

[9] Benoît de Maillet, *Telliamed*, (Amsterdam, 1748). Translated and edited by Albert V Carozzi, (Urbana, 1968) - the earliest editor altered the work to fit Christian cosmology.

[10] F.X. Burtin, *Réponse à la question…sur les révolutions générales qu'a subies la surface de la terre*, (Haarlem, 1790), pp.5-6. BL, Ac942/2.

[11] Le Comte de N***, *Essai sur les montagnes*, (Amsterdam, 1785), pp.7ff, 234, 241ff, 496. BL, 990g16/17.

such isolated islands produce a mankind with Adam its common ancestor?

If Biblical history was, for some, unconvincing, human history was limited. In "the incommensurable past", the disjuncture between the world's history and man's was unbridgeable. At best man might grasp only the short span involving him (and her). Origins constantly receded into a Derridean "always already". However, the memory of cataclysmic struggles was preserved in myth and fable. Poets were the earliest historians, the battles sung by Homer were between natural forces. The awe-inspiring qualities of nature, related especially to mountains, made them places of profound religious value: but, around their summits, gods were often malevolent and vindictive. But wasn't Jehovah this too?

The awful sacredness of mountains was connected with an intense interest in mythology (neglected by most recent accounts of the Enlightenment) but also with an anthropology of religion: for the sacredness of mountains was, it seemed, universal, with Christianity a late, appropriating arrival, with no special claim to truth.[12]

All religions were based on man's weakness and fear. For Valmont-Bomare, the earliest mountains were of a horror "to terrify the coolest imaginations".[13] For Golitsuin, even thinking about their age "frightens the imagination". Volcanoes of "inconceivable fury" had rent the Earth asunder.[14] The invocation of "imagination" was frequent. Even "scientists", some of whom declined to "penetrate" the remoter recesses of Nature, often had recourse to imagination, sometimes contrasted with the reason, and observation, usually seen as the basis of science. The grandeur but especially the diversity of nature, baffled mere reason. To create a "system" was widely seen as hazardous. To penetrate nature, one had to traverse "immense piles of ruins and debris which seem to bar the profane from entering this sacred place".[15]

Clerics writing treatises on physics could fall back on revelation, or miracles suspending natural laws, stressing the dangers of an overweening Reason. Feller rebuked man's "dangerous curiosity", which from Adam to Buffon showed him

---

[12] Most works on mountains , with or without a theory of the Earth, dealt with the emergence of religion(s) and the import of mythology - some derided past attempts to relate "real" to mythological history: others made strenuous attempts to reconcile these. Of course, some saw no difference between religious and mythological accounts. A comprehensive survey, *Encyclopédie méthodique*, 5 vols, *Antiquités, mythologie*, (1788-1794) and J.P. Rabaut de St Etienne, *Lettres sur l'histoire primitive de la Grèce*, (Paris, 1787).

[13] Jacques-Christophe de Valmont-Bomare, *Dictionnaire raisonné universel d'histoire naturelle*, 15 vols, (Lyon, 1791).

[14] Prince DA Golitsuin, *Lettres sur quelques objects de minéralogie*, (The Hague, 1789), pp. 10ff.

[15] Picot de La Peirouse, *Traité sur les mines de fer et les forges du Comté de Foix*, (Toulouse, 1786), pp. 334-6. Extremely good on ways of life, knowledge, language of miners and forge workers.

striving to share God's power and knowledge.[16] Attempts to reconcile Biblical orthodoxy and contemporary physics, by the Swede Wallerius for example, led into numerous aporias, resolved by invoking the creator's omnipotence. Though God had prescribed immutable laws for the universe he could change them at will.[17]

Science, however defined, had its own pitfalls. While moderate imagination might aid science, excessive imagination harmed it. Buffon's works were often described as novels. Moreover, an over-systematic mentality was as crippling as a literal Biblical one. National bias distorted research, Italian researchers, understandably, seeing volcanoes as the key to Earth's history. There was no secure foundation to knowledge – unless one believed with Paulian that "All good physics is founded on the existence of a God", it being presumably obvious which one.[18]

The abbé Barruel posited polemically a direct clash between religious and scientific viewpoints, earth-theorists being generally "anti-Moses, anti-Religion". It was an abuse of reason to attribute to physical causes what "Holy Scripture clearly attributes to the immediate miraculous operation of the Divinity". Those who described a world destined to burn, freeze or liquefy deprived man of free-will. But another abbé, Soulavie, attacked theologians who condemned "peaceable naturalists" who "criss-cross our Pyrenees, our Cévennes, our Alps, traverse their precipices, suffer the inclemency of the seasons to discover yet more traces, identifying the epochs these represent". The new idea of "a history of the successive ages of nature" would be basically mineralogical since "Each class of minerals represents a particular epoch of nature" and these epochs stretched back into a remote past. A "passing Flood" could not split mountains, tear out their "entrails", carve out deep valleys... The scientist, following Gassendi, Descartes, Mallebranche, and Fontenelle, to mention only the French, had the right to philosophise on the earliest state of the physical world. But Barruel accused Soulavie of materialism, of seeing minerals as active and eternal, denying Creation

---

[16] F.X. de Feller, *Examen impartial des Epoques de la Nature*, (Maastricht, 1792), pp. 206-7.

[17] J.B.D. Wallerius, *De l'Origine du monde et de la terre en particular,* (trans. Warsaw, 1780).

[18] Paulian, *op. cit.*, p. 88.

and the spiritual soul.[19]

Certainly there is much physical determinism in Soulavie. His work on the extinct volcanoes of the Vivarais showed them to have "preceded by an infinity of centuries all the known ages of our history". Erosion had been long at work and would, eventually, make Earth one vast plain. (A colleague calculated that the Pyrenees, declining 10 inches a century, would disappear in a million years). Just as plants were determined by soil or rock, and altitude, so were men: those in the mountains of the Auvergne were, certainly, "determined" towards liberty of a sort, having long resisted the centralising monarchy – but they had also escaped enlightenment. Soulavie proposed a map of France superimposing vegetal and human life on a mineralogical base.

A fellow-Languedocian, Gensanne, had certainly spoken of the "growth", "maturity", decay and death of minerals. Nature, he explained, employs in the formation of bodies in the mineral reign roughly the same processes as in the two other reigns. Others collapsed the boundaries between the reigns, threatening all order. Moreover, implacable forces, even if "orderly", reduced man's autonomy: and if strata were seemingly laid down gently over "the infinite *durée* of the past", the fact that lighter rock was often found above heavier, indicated that "convulsions" had periodically "tormented" the Earth.[20]

This picture was not invariably discouraging. If some, crossing hills made by millions of once-living creatures, thought gloomily of their own mortality, for N, the idea that millions of years had preceded Man, was a perspective which liberated man's mind and raised his spirit, opening up vast vistas for the pursuit of truth.[21] Faujas felt that contemplating the world's "inexpressible upheavals" "prodigiously enlarged man's ideas". While, in the Velay, travellers might be depressed by the aridity and confusion of the rocky landscape, the "exercised eye" discerned "antique and mysterious monuments, a series of hieroglyphic characters which it alone can unravel". Mountains were texts which "the naturalist, as a

---

[19] Jean-Louis Giraud-Soulavie, *Les classes naturelles...des minéraux et les époques de la Nature correspondantes à chaque classe*, (Academy of Saint Petersburg, 1786), p.3, deriding sedentary theologians: BL, B343. His superb magnum opus: *Histoire naturelle de la France méridionale*, 8 vols, (Nîmes/Paris, 1780-84) - vol. 5, p.238, on scientists. For information on Barruel vs. Soulavie, *Pièces relatives à l'Histoire naturelle de la France méridionale*, (Paris, 1784), BL, FR 451(9) and Jacques Godard, *Suite des pièces...* (Paris, 1785), BL, F1024(15). Soulavie had shown part of his forthcoming work to Barruel, as a fellow Languedocian and churchman but, treacherously, Barruel showed it to the authorities... causing Soulavie ennuis with the Academy of Sciences.

[20] Gensanne, *Histoire naturelle de la province de Languedoc*, 5 vols., (Montpellier, 1776-1779). On an official mission for the provincial Estates, Gensanne vividly documents the wretchedness of many highland communities, too demoralised to "improve".

[21] Comte de N***, *op. cit., passim*, especially pp. 378ff.

reward for his exertions, has the right to read".[22]

Such exertions were sometimes dangerous, if mountain dwellers took a botanist for a sorcerer, a mineralogist for a gold-prospector or Soulavie for a tax-inspector. Nature herself was hostile. To Pasumot, the Pyrenees "look as if they are approaching their end, ready to collapse". The Gavarnie offered a prospect of chaos.[23] If some suspected a melodramatic exaggeration, an outbidding to make one's narrative more saleable, Valmont-Bomare appreciated "the strong and vivid expression which enlivens their narrations and makes them frightening". Complete truthfulness came from successfully conveying to "the soul of the reader the feeling he himself experienced".[24]

The experience and expansion of the soul was often invoked in a mountain literature which, addressed to the general reader, has little for thrills and spills to envy that of the next century (especially given the lack of equipment). Certainly, utilitarian considerations were not absent, medical for botany; mining for mineralogy... Likewise the advancement of science, the establishment of disciplines...[25] But the immediacy of the aesthetic and spiritual experience of the peaks invariably impresses. Soulavie sketching the first draft of a chapter on a summit while exulting in the view suggests the intimate relationship between science and the soul. Climbing in the snows of the Pyrenees, dodging avalanches and rock falls, sheltering from violent electrical storms, was exhilarating and enjoyed as such but the baggage, as it were, of the climber was naturally "scientific": no one, except smugglers or hunters, went that high without a few experiments in mind.[26] A test for the individual and companions, sometimes an ordeal, the spiritual dimension had perhaps changed little since Petrarch's ascent of Mont Ventoux in 1336. Even in as potentially a "boring" compilation as a

---

[22] Barthélemi Faujas de Saint-Fond, *Recherches sur les volcans éteints du Vivarais et du Velay*, (Grenoble, 1778), pp. 347ff.

[23] François Pasumot, *Voyages physiques dans les Pyrénées en 1788 et 1789*, (Paris, 1797), p.191.

[24] Valmont-Bomare, *op. cit.*, vol. 15, p.120.

[25] Being "philosophical", many writers on mountains were concerned not only with the advancement of science, but with the mapping and naming of different branches of knowledge, inventing compound names ("minéralogie géographique", etc) - with chemistry being frequently combined, or linked, with other branches. We may add here that many of the French works cited come from the library of Joseph Banks. Antoine-Grimoald Monnet, *Nouveau système de minéralogie*, (Bouillon, 1779) was especially pushy in his claims...

[26] Ramond de Carbonnières wrote splendidly in such works as *Observations faites dans les Pyrénées*, (Paris, 1789), fully appreciated in the studies of Claire-Elaine Engel cited above. See Cuthbert Morton Girdlestone, *Poésie, Politique, Pyrénées: Louis-François Ramond (1755-1827)*, (Paris, 1968). If I allow myself a personal opinion: the writings on the Pyrenees are much more exciting and challenging than those on the Alps, while those on the Auvergne are outstanding on all aspects of *la vie montagnarde*.

dictionary, Valmont-Bompare wished to "communicate a certain freedom of spirit, a noble boldness of thought which is the seed of philosophy".[27]

This, then, was a world of constant creation and destruction, action and reaction: "Everything acts on everything else. One matter attacks another, subjugates it... Enormous mountains, whose mass terrifies, and which appear beyond all attack, nevertheless experience the power of the years, imperceptible deteriorations, but sometimes very sudden ones. Their summits either fall in stages or collapse on their own base".[28]

The Revolution was pictured as erupting like a volcano. Revolutions as convulsions was a familiar notion to some. However the imagery now became pervasive, not least among those hostile to or fearful of the Revolution. Analogies, whether facile or far-fetched, between political structures and processes and geological-cum-topographical ones proliferated. So much that had been politically (and spiritually) elevated was seen to have long been eroded or undermined, now to come crashing down (the notion that the old regime collapsed on its own base is now historiographically orthodox). However, images of ascension and elevation sustained and inspired the revolutionary élan and *essor*. The timeless tradition of seeking laws from mountaintops, amidst thunder and lighting, in an atmosphere of secret terror, was re-enacted as Robespierre, leader of la Montagne ascended an artificial summit to sacralise the Constitution and proclaim the Republic's belief in the Supreme Being and immortality of the soul (an experience felt by many real mountaineers). Such sublimity sought to crush all that was low – those of the Plaine or Marsh, those creatures, toads or reptiles, who crawled and grovelled in the mud of a base politics.[29] Robespierre denounced "materialism". But this was a complex phenomenon. Some naturalists had held that all beings, all materials, aspired upwards. If what was viscuous seems the exception, minerals were certainly spiritualised (and sexualised) by popular or populist "scientists".[30] A rather strange "mystical materialism" emerged politically in the "cultural revolution" of the Year II, perhaps expressing the fusion of the spiritual and material needs, desires, aspirations of the "lower classes". (See

---

[27] Valmont-Bomare, *op. cit.*, vol.1, pp. vi-vii.

[28] Dom Ulloa, *Mémoires philosophiques, historiques et physiques concernant la découverte de l'Amérique*, 2 vols., (Paris, 1787), vol.1, pp. 356-7.

[29] For a harrowing description of the abjection of marsh-dwellers, J.A. Baudin, *Du dessèchement des marais*, (Paris, 1792). The film *Ridicule* begins with scenes of marsh life and ends with a tribute to the engineers of the Revolution for their efforts to eradicate such degrading (and unhealthy) conditions. Both film and revolutionary writers stress the social inequalities which had aggravated and perpetuated them.

[30] Charles Pougens, *Essais sur divers sujets de physique, de botanique et de minéralogie...* (Paris, 1793).

Sylvain Maréchal).[31]

Certainly bourgeois revolutionaries like Robespierre wished to "elevate the people", raise them from abasement and abjection. In mythology or mythologised history (whether with Ossian or William Tell) – and of course with Rousseau – mountain peoples were natural friends of liberty and equality, of simple republican virtues. However, revolutionary reality was proving otherwise. Those, aristocrats, bourgeois and clerics with experience of mountain areas – and Robespierre's Arras could hardly be flatter – had ambivalent views regarding their inhabitants (a subject in its own right). Suspicion gave way to sympathy at their often dire plight but also exasperation at their acceptance of it. Could reading the works of "mountaineers" have prepared idealist or illusionist revolutionaries for the fact that mountain areas, seen as the natural refuge of oppressed liberty, had become fastnesses of superstition, obscurantism and counter-revolution? Or were mountains mainly "of the mind", and the bourgeois mind at that? Were their uplifting qualities wasted on those who had to live there? Certainly some mountaineers, notably Ramond and Picqué, of the Pyrenees, Soulavie of the Auvergne, did embrace the ideals of the Revolution, partly fuelled by indignation at clerical and feudal exploitation. And Soulavie's opponent Barruel became a virulent counter-revolutionary.

The Revolution's attempted identification with a Nature itself so recalcitrant yet irredeemably inconstant was extremely fraught.

***

The very concept of nature was, of course, ambivalent: no one agreed on its definition, even were one to be hazarded. One might say the same about the Revolution. Any identification of one with the other was risky and readily derided by the Revolution's enemies. When the human element is foregrounded, in "politics", complexities become formidable. Did mountain-dwellers live particularly "close to nature?" Were they, as such, noble savages? Sturdy descendants of peoples who had withdrawn into the mountains to avoid conquest and enslavement, perhaps preserving a spirit of independence – or had they degenerated to become mere remnants? How did they relate to their environment – with indifference, curiosity, pride?... How did outsiders see them: to be envied

---

[31] Pierre Sylvain Maréchal, *Dieu et les prêtres. Fragments d'une poème philosophique*, (Paris, 1781 - enlarged Year II, ie 1793-4). Best known for his play *Le jugement dernier des rois*, (An II) where European monarchs, deported to a tropical island, perish in the eruption a vengeful volcano.

or pitied, their situation to be safeguarded, protected, improved?

Some "notions of nature" may first be noted. To say that "All that is in nature is true: all that is true is in nature" is rather trite.[32] But many, in 1789 thought a reconciliation of nature and religion, in a new regime of truth, was possible in a total "regeneration", as both political tyranny and religious intolerance were overthrown. Despotism had been "an outrage against nature", the Revolution was "a resuscitation of nature", a "second Creation" fulfilling the promise of the first.[33] The Declaration of the Rights of Man and the Citizen, sponsored, as it were, by the Supreme Being, consecrated the lessons of the Gospels. Natural laws, on which the new French Constitution was based, were derived from a *Genesis* not necessarily taken literally. Nature had been "buried in the night of arbitrary power", of human abjection and political chaos. Once stripped of the Church's temporal power and pretensions, a more spiritual religion was also more in tune with nature, including human nature – a nature tending to be pastoral and orderly. God was frequently thanked for this harmony in open-air ceremonies uniting the religious and the political, and men and women of all classes. Nature was not "a blind destiny, nor an inanimate mechanism, but God alone, creator and dispenser of the natural order".[34] An enthusiastic priest announced: "Nature speaks God to the whole Earth". The Revolution was to be "as beautiful as nature, as regular as the stars, as enduring as time".[35]

This unity owed much to emotion and wishful thinking. Notions of the nobility of the high and the baseness of the low did not evaporate. For the former, the Third Estate or people were purely material, bent to the ground, ground down by manual labour: or, in Bakhtinian terms, they were the belly of the body politic. Labour, a result of the Fall, shrank and dragged down the soul.[36] But it was the Church hierarchy which was the most intransigent. For the Archbishop of Lyon, France had been gripped by vertigo: "the earth is in consternation, the universe is collapsing", overwhelmed by a flood of irreligious productions... The "physical calamities" presaging and accompanying this general catastrophe included volcanoes.[37] For the bishop of Evreux, to venture beyond the line set by the Church, was to "wander aimlessly, from abyss to abyss,

[32] Jean-Jacques de Barrett, *De la loi naturelle*, (Paris, 1790).

[33] Toussaint Castan, *Aux âmes pieuses de la France*, (Béziers, 1790). BL, R352(3).

[34] *La question du divorce...* (Paris, 1790). BL, F535(9).

[35] *Mémoire pour la ville de Morlaas*, in the Béarn, (1790?). BL, R579(24).

[36] *Lettre de Junius*, (Paris, 1790). BL, R206(2) and *Déclaration de Madame Noblesse*, (Paris, 1789). BL, F407(3).

[37] Archbishop of Lyon, *Les malheurs actuels prédits par le prophète Isaïe*, (Paris, 1789). BL, F178(12). *de*

precipice to precipice".[38] For many churchmen, nature was still depraved: what the philosophes called nature was "pure animality and the instinct of the passions; reason is one's particular feeling – not usually a very respectable authority. Nature, taken as matter, or as an abstract being, does not wish anything, prescribe anything or give birth to anything".[39] Moreover, "The word Nature is philosophy's secret. It is constantly pronounced but never defined" – this a pronouncement of one for whom "Every citizen should be Catholic".[40] For the abbé Bonneval, nature gives no rights, only needs and, sparingly, means to satisfy them – therefore any idea of equality was futile as well as pernicious.[41] Pronouncements to the effect that nature, without religion, provided no moral compass were legion. And God's punishments – bad harvests, volcanoes, floods – were also legion. It was easy to see the Revolution itself as "a destructive volcano". And the terms used of revolutions of the Earth ("bouleversement", "ébranlement", "convulsions") were, anyway, time-honoured items in the ecclesiastical vocabulary.

Since, for some, "nature knows no brusque transitions", a warning: "Do not take tempests as models".[42] So, a rather plaintive call: "Why can't we make political revolutions proceed like those of Nature? These are always a long time in preparation and all the changes they operate, however large they appear, make themselves imperceptibly". If governments had the people's happiness at heart, they would give affairs "the same impulsion" and "one would then avoid those terrible revolutions", which usually bring "an infinity of misfortunes".[43]

In fact, nature (and reason) were frail reeds: unlike "rock" they hardly formed a firm base for the constitution (but most nobles lived on, or were named after, rocks, hence their "insensibilité"). As the Revolution rushed onwards like a torrent knocking down all before it, rhetoric became more fevered and language, though a major preoccupation, hardly became more precise. The doctrine of the sovereignty of the people, obviously anathema to "le papisme", was "the God of Spinoza. In this monstrous system, each portion of matter was a portion of the Divinity".[44] An émigré ecclesiastic fulminating from Burgos saw the attribution of sovereignty of the people to nature as inviting "a return to barbarism and savagery". Religious toleration, extended by the Revolution to Protestants and

---

[38] (Ex-) bishop of Evreux, *Lettre de Monseigneur*, at Rome, (Paris, 1792). BL, F160(5).

[39] *Observations sur le divorce*, (Paris, 1790). BL, FR207(9).

[40] Charles de Moy, *Le petit moy pour rire*, (Paris, 1792). BL, F140(3).

[41] *Lettres de M. l'abbé Bonneval*, (Paris, 1791). BL, F163(4). *Correspondance d'un habitant de Paris*, (Paris, 1791). BL, F1310.

[42] *Réponse d'un habitant de Paris*, (1789). BL, FR18(12).

[43] F.X. Lanthenas, *Adresse présentée à l'Assemblée nationale* [on] *égalité des partages…* (Paris, 1790).

[44] *Opinion de Louis-Sébastien Mercier sur les Capet*, (Paris, 1793). BL, F919(12).

Jews, was the "work of darkness". Revolutionary violence had burned for two centuries before erupting: the Revolution was "the theory of impiety realised and the morality of the philosophers in action". The Revolution was an almost irresistible force: "Everything serves it, even chance; if chance is not Providence which hides itself to mortals". Seemingly as fatalistic as the damned materialists, the bishop stated that "the Revolution's centre is everywhere".[45] But clearly the more cataclysmic and, in secular terms, inexplicable, the catastrophe the more effective God's punishment.

But if the Revolution was a force of nature, so too was religion. A History of Religions pointed out, in 1791, that almost all religions were derived from "the various systems which men have formed regarding the physics of the globe and the pious dreamings that they have peddled to explain often inexplicable phenomena", whereas, with recent discoveries regarding electricity, one need not fear gods launching lightning bolts from Olympus. Religious men deified matter, more easy to adore than define. The Creation was an allegorical account of physical revolutions. This work followed the tradition of tracing religion back to fear of natural catastrophes, with Christianity no different from other, allegedly inferior, cults.[46] As superstition, we add, it flourished particularly in the mountains. But with Catholics and royalists now persecuted, they now took refuge in the hills – in the camp of Jalès in the Vivarais, whose mountains "seem the last shelter for expiring liberty".[47] Their enemies could now scoff: "The French aristocrats [like the Hebrews] go to await their Messiah till the end of the world. They ceaselessly look to see if he'll descend from the Alps or the Pyrenees".[48]

With the abolition of censorship, "We can now speak of nature and politics with the boldness they inspire". So La Vicomterie invoked the millions of years in which human life had repeatedly flourished, died and reappeared, as the axis of the earth changed, with the poles and deserts changing places, as it were. (The same "combinations" would be repeated *ad infinitum*). One local revolution had seen the volcanoes of the Vivarais doused by the onrushing sea. The millions of heavenly bodies proclaimed that "all are sovereign", especially since Man was part of "le Grand Tout", ie God. From this emerged a sort of heroism, suggesting, in no very "rational" terms, that Man could survive any catastrophe: "A sort of courage is needed to grasp man struggling, overwhelmed in this chaos, only

---

[45] *Instruction aux Catholiques sur les causes de la Révolution française* - from Burgos, March 1792. BL, F960(10).

[46] F.H.S. de L'Aulnaye, *Histoire générale et particulière des religions*, (Paris,1791).

[47] *Manifeste et protestation de cinquante mille Français fidèles*, (Jalès, Oct. 1790). BL, F886(9).

[48] J.A.J. Cérutti, *Bréviaire philosophique*, (Paris, 1791). BL, FR139(34).

resurfacing from time to time, carried off by the almost invincible force of the torrent engulfing him". In some future, man might emerge on "a plateau torn apart by volcanoes, an elevated or deep site, surrounded by forests, marshes, lakes". Having lost all existing religious and political systems, he would have to embrace new ones, closer to nature. Since the late eighteenth century was experiencing the greatest upheaval ("secousse") in ages, perhaps this eventuality was nigh.[49] Little wonder that one publicist in 1790 – the "peaceful" year of the Revolution – confessed that he was torn apart by conflicting feelings of hope and terror. He thought that a better knowledge of the laws of physics, already showing more marvels than credulity conjured up, might provide more reliable bearings.

But besides the religious, stressing the limits of reason, the indispensability of revelation, the need for mysteries and the ultimate impenetrability of nature, committed revolutionaries expressed bewilderment. A pamphleteer lamented that "the nature of man is entirely unknown to us. Everything on this earth is for him conditional, relative, apparent and without absolute reality. Man here below is like a sleep walker not knowing whence, nor when or how he fell into this state, nor what the issue will be". For this writer, as for many others, "the abyss", rather than the lofty peaks, beckoned.[50]

What is also intriguing is that the naturalisation of politics was also a politicisation of nature, though rarely made as explicit as by the writer who claimed that the physical revolutions of the globe were allegories of "révolutions populaires". If this had not been hidden by the priests of every religion, would not "the people" have refused to accept its inferior position as "natural"?[51]

What was "popular" was hardly without menace, even in the eyes of "bourgeois" revolutionaries. The eruption of the people onto the scene of history was profoundly unsettling. Charles Villette, fearing war, noted that this would be "une guerre populaire" not "une guerre royale". Rather than the geometric patterns of the learned general, war would be a "choc" of men "en masse" – part, no doubt, of the massive "secousse" noted above. As war would now be "nation against nation", Etna would fight Vesuvius and universal disorder would result.[52] After the "popular" insurrection that led to the overthrow of the monarch (10 August 1792) and the September Massacres, Garat, deputy of the Convention, discussed the "right of insurrection". Could this be regulated – arguably, be

[49] L.T.H. de La Vicomterie, *République sans impôts*, (Paris, 1792). BL, F186(1).

[50] *Correspondance d'un habitant de Paris*, (1791). BL, F1310.

[51] Lamaignère, *Discours ...dans le temple de la Raison, 20 ventôse II*. BL, R337(16).

[52] Charles Villette, *Lettres choisies*, (Paris, 1792). BL, F840(1).

severely limited? "Nature's tempests have laws, why should not social tempests and crises not have laws too?" Then chance, and obviously violence, would have a minimal role in human affairs.[53] Another intellectual politician, Condorcet, produced a draft constitution that suggested the regulation of the exercise of the people's natural right of resistance to oppression. This was attacked by a deputy, Bacon, who stated that when nature produced a great upheaval, like an earthquake, "it will tell you that the different inflammable materials gather imperceptibly, pile up over time, and when the fermentation attains its highest degree, the explosion immediately bursts out". So, when an insurrection becomes necessary, it is because of "the accumulation of abuses and oppression raised to the highest degree".[54]

A lot was being carried away, destroyed, but what remained was stated to have its basis on Nature, just as the "fundamental nature" of man was revealed in revolutions. To sample the rhetoric: "The Revolution advancing, its political oscillations, in their accelerated movement, have prepared and brought about the fall of everything which did not have its foundation in Nature".[55] Or: "The waters of the revolutionary flood have swept away the muddy mire and the impure remnants of the regime under which a debased France has, for thirteen centuries, been sunk".[56]

Clearly, the Mountain – even for purposes of alliteration – was not founded on mud. This was hardly an aspect of nature to be claimed by the Terror (except to drown priests and royalists in the muddy water of the estuary of the Loire, the notorious "noyades" of Nantes, soon repudiated as shameful). If religion was based on Fear, on "religious terror", could the Revolution, always aspiring to elevation, risk the same degrading identification? But the relationship between terror and Fear, between the Terror and fear is too complex, and no doubt too profound, to be explored here. Clearly the trial and execution of Louis XVI did not seek to elicit mere fear, in any vulgar sense. Striking down the pinnacle of society, God-backed guarantor of a transcendental (but also daily) order, a majesty – a "terrible majesty" also seen in nature's peaks – was intended to arouse awe. On 22 September 1793, the representative Fouché organised three executions in the Nièvre *département* – at dawn, so that, "by terror, [justice] has prepared souls to feel more keenly the sweet emotions of nature and of holy fraternity". But the accompanying fete inaugurating the statue of Brutus sought an effect opposite to

---

[53] Dominique-Joseph Garat, *Considérations sur la Révolution française*, (Paris, 1792). BL, F1289(4).
[54] P.J.J. Bacon, *Examen impartial*, (Paris, 1793). BL, R85(1).
[55] J.B.C. Mathieu-Mirampal, *Rapport fait à la Convention*, (Paris, 1793). BL, F494(10).
[56] Marc-Antoine Jullien, *Rapport sur Lorient*, (Lorient, 1793). BL, R237(23).

this "horror". Having, purely metaphorically, looked over the "frightful precipice of Etna", now the sight of a "smiling countryside", illuminated and no doubt warmed by the rising sun, produced "a gentle shivering which the soul feels (...), happy result of the shock of opposed and diverse sensations".[57] Strikingly, this "doux frémissement" was precisely what the guillotine had been advocated as producing, almost agreeably, on the victim's neck (as bitterly illustrated in Wajda's *Danton*).

That much of the Terror's terminology was religious has often been noted; that much also had an affinity with the "mountain vocabulary" of the old regime is also noteworthy. But it is precisely as an escape from that regime that it emerged, whether from the artificiality of Court or from the noisy, senseless bustle of the towns...or just from the deadening routine of a daily job. Such a release was often frankly avowed but resort to the mountains, absorption in nature, has sometimes had sinister, as well as "sublime", or pseudo-sublime, aspects, an element of inhumanity. (Perhaps not, we will suggest, for those willing and wishing to come to a genuinely sympathetic but realistic – unsentimental, unromantic – engagement with mountain-dwellers neither picturesque nor sublime).

The forces of nature to be deployed by the Terror, that is, power, had to tap into what many enlightened writers had often deplored as man's penchant for, addiction to, "the marvellous", "the extraordinary". Expressions of the would-be cosmic dimension of the Revolution drew on speculations, imaginings or longings pre-dating 1789 – the invocations of millions of worlds, millions of years – but were now given particularly vivid expression. That modern science, Revolution and "the marvellous" could co-operate could, however, be seen by all as aerostats soared into the sky: on 18 September 1791, one rose to 13,000 feet, through all that nature could throw at the intrepid balloonist, who toasted the new Constitution, copies of which he threw overboard, laws coming literally from aloft...[58]

If to control the seas was traditionally seen as the key to control of the land, to control the skies or at least the heights was perhaps an option for France. The present occupant, God, had to be displaced, that "invisible tyrant, the fantastic idea of whom brought desolation and delirium to the terrified heart of mortals". (The government, to the consternation of some, sent this diatribe to the popular

---

[57] Joseph Fouché, *Procès-verbal de la fête de l'inauguration du buste de Brutus*, (Moulins, 1793). BL, 936f7(7).

[58] *Procès-verbal du voyage aérien*, (Paris, 1791). BL, F1060(24).

clubs throughout France).[59] For another writer, God was an imaginary, more terrible executioner and all religions appalling. Thus the makers of religions had never been able to make their precepts as many and as severe as they would have liked: "They have enthusiastically outbid each other in severity". Unfortunately, here, nature operated only by destruction: all beings were at constant war with each other and the more civilised man became, the more he killed and the more cleverly he was able to disguise this. Fear could produce only slaves and despots: men rendered servile were inclined to submit to the first master who came along.[60] A "Jacobin priest", addressing an audience of *sans-culottes* of the Hautes-Alpes, rejoiced that the sun lit the tops of their mountains before the rest of France: "The sun of reason, in turn, will dissipate all theological vapours". The Alps kept at bay "all *ultramontain* exhalations". Luckily many of France's frontiers were indeed "natural".[61]

Those who lived at these extremities claimed to be uplifted by the mountains. Protesting at the divisive use of the terms Mountain and Plain, the revolutionaries of Valence in the Rhône valley said that they did not wish to spoil the gentle affections associated with these words: "At the foot of the Alps, our thoughts elevate themselves at the sight of these mountains" and the Plain was about to deliver a rich harvest. However internal divisions worsened and the war intensified.[62] Grenoble boasted that "for the first time in the immensity of centuries, a million men defend the cause of humanity", with weapons forged from the iron ore of the surrounding mountains. The archives document the strenuous efforts of scientists and workers to exploit the veins, combining theoretical and practical knowledge (some derived from published work on the mineralogy of Dauphiné). The noise from the mountain forges, the den of Cyclops, should reach to the Danube and Tiber, "to disturb the last moments of the tyrants".[63] Few petitions sent to Paris but reminded politicians that the Revolution was born, in 1788, amidst these mountains. But, deeper into the hills, resistance to the Revolution increased. Chambéry, capital of the new *département* of Mont-Blanc warned Cluses that "vermin" (priests) were obtaining shelter in peasant *cabanes*, threatening village municipalities with "the punishments of

---

[59] François Peyrard, *De la Nature et des Lois*, (Paris, 1793), BL, 8704eee13 and Jault, *Dictionnaire philosophique*, (Paris, 1794). BL, F515(6).

[60] A.J.E. Baconnière-Salverte, *Epître à une femme reasonable*, (Paris, 1793). BL, R391(10).

[61] Sunderson Bérard, *Entretien du citoyen SB, curé Jacobin, avec un maître d'école*, (Gap, 1794). BL, F176(5).

[62] *Les autorités constitués* [of *département* of Drôme], (Valence, 1793). BL, F16*(19).

[63] Departmental authorities, Isère, Grenoble, letter of 3 *frimaire* II/ 23 Nov. 1793, Archives départementales (AD), Isère, L110.

another world" if they carried out revolutionary policies.[64] Rewards were offered for the seizure of refractory priests, who were indeed referred to as "black game", to be hunted down by *chasseurs*.[65] One of the most contentious policies involved the "descent" of church bells, to be melted down for cannon. Villagers, especially women, often resisted this assault on their traditional culture – partly because bells were thought to ward off thunderstorms. Scoffing at such superstitious nonsense, the revolutionaries delighted in dragging the bells in the dirt, reducing them "to the rank of ordinary things".[66] The highest valleys were the least patriotic and sheltered not only priests but young men escaping call up. The day of the union of Chambéry to France, on 22 September 1792, was a year later declared to be "worthy of being engraved in ineffaceable characters in our hearts and on the summits of our mountains". Far from intimidating the patriots, the violent thunderstorm accompanying the celebration of union ("our political resurrection") was nature welcoming "the thunder of liberty" and soaking only the vile satellites of despotism (the reverberation of thunder in the mountains is, of course, often evoked by travellers). The flag of three colours should be placed proudly atop Mont Blanc.[67]

At Annecy the union was to have been commemorated by a painting of Mont Blanc but this for some reason, pictorial or otherwise, proved problematic. In the mountain valleys, crosses pulled down by the revolutionaries had been put up again and trees of liberty cut down. Such setbacks – which, after all, proved the superiority of the patriots – merely intensified a rhetoric in which some of our themes featured strongly. Lyricism was not lacking: the *montagnard* club of Bonneville informed the Convention: "Our hearts see in all the brilliance of its colour the red bonnet contrasting with the snow of the summits and the glaciers".[68] Annecy described the new Constitution as speeding from the Montagne "like thunder escaping from the clouds". The acclamations accompanying its reception had been carried by "the echoes of our mountains to the despot of Piedmont and to all his armies. Already these same echoes have brought back to us the tyrant's shaking in rage and despair as he topples from his

---

[64] Letter of Department of Mont-Blanc, to District of Cluses, 19 *nivôse* II/8 Jan. 1794. AD de la Savoie, Chambéry, L28.

[65] *Lettres diverses, copie de note*, 24 April 1793, AD Savoie, Chambéry, L377.

[66] Deliberation of Dept., Chambéry, 16 *brumaire* II/ 6 Nov. 1793, AD Savoie, L27.

[67] *Procès-verbal de la fête civique* at Chambéry, 22 Sept. 1793 (celebrating a year of union with France), AD Savoie, L25.

[68] Club of Bonneville, to Jacobin Club of Paris, 23 Dec. 1792, AD de la Haute-Savoie, Annecy, 1J696.

throne".[69] It was not that easy, however, even if defiance rather than despair asserted itself. Mountains were a barrier for a new Thermopylae : but "Let all the mountains be swept from the face of the earth before liberty disappears from the soil that bears me". Mountains, <u>our</u> mountains, opposed tyranny: "our rivers indicate the direction of our penchants", running towards France. "The order of nature would have been disturbed if our government was not the same".[70]

But such stirring pledges were not the only documentation reaching Paris. The search for resources, and statistics, revealed the crushing poverty, the abject "misère", moral and physical, of snow-bound provinces – "wretched countries abandoned by nature", in the words of the authorities of Gap, faced by famine. This was a country where "for three or four years nature has become a merciless stepmother" ("marâtre" – "unnatural mother").[71] To suggest that poverty was the guarantor of the virtue of the mountain peasant was derisory. At Briançon, the inhabitants lived, in the heat of their animals, buried for long months in snow. When asked to state its resources, one highland authority of Provence was reduced to citing its medicinal Alpine flowers and sending a book about them. (At least a lowland one was able to send the Convention some early potatoes).

The inhabitants of the Pyrenees "are *montagnards* by sentiment as well as by nature". The republicans of Foix asked the Convention: "Accustomed to struggling against bears, would our hearts be susceptible to the perfidious caresses of the enemies of the Revolution?" No! And could "the infected vapours of the Marsh rise up to us and corrupt the pure air which we breathe in our mountains?" Likewise a ringing No![72] A description of a festival of Reason shows, by comparison with our stormy Alpine examples, that the weather, whatever its moods, favoured the Revolution. At Foix, "A serene day, the mountains suspended above our heads and covered with snow; below, wide prairies, streams of transparent water, offered a picture of all the seasons. It seemed that the sky [heaven?] was celebrating its festival of reason". After a "truly Spartan" communal dinner, fraternity and equality (and propriety) presided over the evening's civic ball.[73] However, here, as in the Alps, and for many of the same

---

[69] *Conseil général* of Mont-Blanc dept., Annecy, 21 July 1793. AD Haute-Savoie, 1L24.

[70] *Conseil général*, Mont-Blanc dept., Annecy, *fête* of union with France, report of 9 *frimaire* II/29 Nov. 1793. AD Haute-Savoie, 1L24.

[71] Department to Four Districts, 6 *pluviôse* II/ 25 Jan. 1794; and to Commission des subsistances, 29 *nivôse* II/ 18 Jan. 1794. AD des Hautes-Alpes, Gap, L675. District of Briançon, to Serres, deputy in Convention, 14 May 1792. AD, Hautes-Alpes, Gap, L1082.

[72] Jacobin Club of Foix to Convention, 10 *frimaire* II/ 30 Nov. 1793. AD of Ariège (Pyrenees), 7L8.

[73] Jacobin Club of Foix, 12 *nivôse* II/ 1 Jan. 1794. AD Ariège, 7L7.

reasons, disputes were bitter. Resistance to the Revolution's policy towards the Catholic Church was strong. Clearly, revolutionaries had to refute accusations of atheism. Citizen Gahin told the club of Massat that while "the atheist conspirator tried by speeches and writings to cause upheaval in the great cities of the Republic, his impious voice respected our mountains' sacred refuge", protected by the Supreme Being.[74] Citizen Tartanac, a gendarme commander accused of sacrilegiously seizing the churches' sacred vessels, judiciously explained his principles to the *sans-culottes* of the club of Mazarès: "Although they tend somewhat towards philosophy, they pertain, with greater wisdom, to the divinity".[75] Clubs were aware of being islands of reason and philosophy in a sea of fanaticism and superstition: Montagnards were, as it were, light years ahead of *montagnards*. (One clubist boldly calculated the advance at 800 years). The higher one went in the mountains, the lower the level of revolutionary zeal. The people of Saint-Laurent were "naturally fierce and superstitious", ready to repulse republicans with fusillades in the narrow *défilés*. The clubs, which provided "philosophic sermons" for their members, sent "civic apostles" or "missionaries" to preach "l'Evangile civique" to the benighted country people. In vain.

In the mountains, the Revolution reached degree zero, often absorbed into age-old disputes between villages, acrimonious relationships between neighbours, struggles between classes for power, land, jobs: this was a deeply humiliating descent for revolutionaries high on principles. Often the Revolution was imposed from without: the new clergy were resisted as "devils", "demons" and, just as bad, "intruders". Sometimes the Mountain of Paris was seen as "launching its lava", destroying all indiscriminatingly. Its members, sent into the Jura, were bearers of monstrous, "volcanic" powers . But the local mountains stood firm... This was a titanic struggle which the revolutionaries might seem to be losing: "Stay united and cramponned [*sic*] to the summit of the Mountain!" urged Mallarmé, perhaps as much in desperation as in hope.[76] A few weeks later, on 9 *thermidor*, (27 July 1794), the Mountain came crashing down.

✳✳✳

Might the reading of "mountain literature" have made the revolutionaries better-informed, that is, forewarned, about mountain-dwellers? Should one even

---

[74] Gahin, *Discours prononcé le 20 prairial à Massat*, (8 June 1794). AD Ariège, 7L17.

[75] Tartanac, speech of 23 *nivôse* II/ 12 Jan. 1794. AD Ariège, 7L18.

[76] F.R.A. Mallarmé, *Discours prononcé à la Société populaire de Longuyon*, 28 *floréal* II/ 17 May 1794. BL, R650(33).

begin to enlighten them? And if so, how? Even those who had visited the hills lauded the peerless qualities of *montagnards* the world over, whether the "Ossianic Scots" or the "Spartan" inhabitants of the Pyrenees.

In fact, the "encounter" with these particular savages was as fraught as that with Iroquois or Hurons. If Soulavie seems to have had a very deterministic approach, aiming to contribute to "the natural or physiological history of man" through exploring "the medical geography of our provinces", and holding that character depends on "the different degrees of altitude of the climate where one lives", he, like many of his fellows, was much more nuanced in his actual descriptions. He observed: "There is a great store of natural spirit in the Vivarais. That spirit merely lacks means and a favourable opportunity to develop", the strong grip of "feudalism" and of an oppressive clergy being the main obstacles. So not all was due to altitude. Moreover, some "ferocity" had already been "softened". Perhaps the relationship between nature and civilisation was quite complex? For, if further enlightened, the appreciation by "our highlanders" of the "most magnificent tableaux of nature" in which they lived would be enhanced. Trade and industry, developed in some areas, had already had beneficial effects: should, then, communication with "the plain" be further encouraged? Certainly here, in the Auvergne, as in the Pyrenees and French Alps, many did encourage this: roads <u>were</u> being built. But communication and contamination were virtual synonyms – and Soulavie's condemnation of townspeople (effeminate, pusillanimous, a prey to illness…) was severe. Already "luxury" was corrupting some of the mountainfolk.

Was a "realistic" discourse on the highlander possible? For Faujas, because of cushing taxation and feudal dues, the peasant's diet was wretched, his hovel filthy, his language crude, his beliefs superstitious – any stranger was seen as a spy for tax collector or seigneur. Yet a gift of tobacco won him over, while any disdain was bitterly resented. And our visitors did stay in these hovels, shared the soup, and got beyond praising the hospitality of "primitive peoples". What emerges is an awareness of the ambiguities of "development": the roads which might bring out the produce of rural industry might well accelerate a rural exodus. So too might schooling. The "avidity" of highlanders for education was often noted approvingly, (the Swiss and Scots proving this) whereas avidity *tout court* was generally seen as the first sign of their corruption. Remoteness or backwardness had their virtues: to preserve the purity of a language, the liveliness of a sociability elsewhere degraded or a knowledge of traditional remedies elsewhere lost. Who can say whether peasant "suspicion" or "sullenness" was misplaced?

One might well need to proceed with caution. Only one simple, if crucial point can be elaborated now – one which is not intended to suggest the futility of the revolutionary effort... Warnings that change (whether we think it beneficial or not is irrelevant here) would be slow were frequent. In 1778, Pierre Poeydavant, a minor official in the Pyrenees, observed: "It is not by treating violently the inhabitants of a *pays* far from the centre of the kingdom, who hold by the manners, customs and prejudices transmitted by their fathers, that one will succeed in making them adopt the tastes, usages and methods which may be received in the rest of France". Time was needed to "correct the local imperfections and to bring about advantageous changes imperceptibly".[77] On the very eve of revolution, Jean-Pierre Picqué noted that the distinctive customs of the Pyrenees were more powerful than "the skilfully complicated codes of our modern legislators". As he was about to become one of these, he no doubt carried to Versailles the admonition: "It is not in the power of any legislator to destroy the national spirit, the political regime and habits of such peoples". Past centuries, with all their physical revolutions, had not changed the nature of the Bigorrais at all. Yet, Picqué described the very different characters of the peoples of different valleys, perhaps deriving from ancient races (and the Arab influence was marked) so though, in general, a northerner would be "as foreign here as in another world", complexities bequeathed by "3000 years of antiquity", were not to be ignored.[78] Nor would Soulavie – who wrote excellently on history-writing – be likely to ignore them. He published an open letter to Louis XVI recalling all the works of "longue durée" (his words) by which the Bourbons had dragged most of France from barbarism. Louis could add a positive chapter to the "géographie politique" of his kingdom by rescuing the Auvergne highlanders from their "extreme wretchedness".[79] Despite reservations noted above, to encourage trade and industry, given the hard-working nature of the people (except where utterly demoralised by poverty) would be to advance "civilisation" and Louis (and no doubt his successors) would rule over "a happy and enlightened people"... "Convulsions" were to prove otherwise.

---

[77] *Le Roussillon à la fin de l'Ancien Régime*, (Perpignan, 1987), pp.340-1.

[78] Jean-Pierre Picqué, *Voyage dans les Pyrénées*, (Paris, 1789), pp.158 and 287.

[79] Jean-Louis Giraud-Soulavie, *Histoire naturelle de la France méridionale*, (1780-84), vol. 3, pp.39ff.

A living picture of Hell:
the eloquence of violence in seventeenth-century New France

JAMES DARRIN RUSSELL
University of Aberdeen

Homo homini lupus; man becomes a wolf to other men, when he allows himself to be governed by Demons. – Barthélemy Vimont, S.J. (Thwaites 1896-1901 [1642]: 22:265)

Of all the early-modern ethnographic commentaries on the aboriginal peoples of the North American continent, the most detailed and comprehensive are the missionary reports of the Society of Jesus, the *Relations des Jésuites de la Nouvelle-France* (1632-1673). The Jesuits published a record of their missionary activity in order to stimulate interest in their mission and to secure financial aid from European benefactors, as well as providing the ethnographic evidence for the Society's theological position on post-lapsarian humanity (Healy 1958). To this end the Jesuits mobilised representations of aboriginal peoples as 'savages' as a powerful rhetorical technique. In particular, the Jesuits' descriptions of 'savagery' indicated a condition of disorder, in which, rather than exercising their faculty of reason to govern their passions, people were instead being governed by them (Russell n.d.). The most graphic and persuasive of these accounts of 'savagery' are those narratives describing Iroquoian torture rituals. However, if we read against the grain of these torture narratives we can see how the Jesuits' behaviour at these rituals was seen by Iroquoians as indicating that the Fathers were in fact dangerous and anti-social 'Others'.

As Francis Jennings argues, if 'savagery' is defined as ferocity, Europeans were equally as savage as Native Americans (Jennings 1975: 160). This begs the question: why did Europeans not perceive the institutional violence of Europe to be equally as savage as the practices of those whom they designated as 'savage'? Jennings (1975: 146-174) argues that the legitimate violence within Europe was not compared to that of the Americas, since institutional European violence was perceived to be structured and ordered. In contrast, the violence within and between aboriginal societies was considered 'savage', not because the actual acts of violence were necessarily more violent *per se*, but because the 'myth of the savage' suggested that they were necessarily disordered, and unrestrained. Albeit agreeing with Jennings that the violence of aboriginal peoples was interpreted through the 'myth of savagery', I stress that the supposed unrestrained violence

Explorations in Cultural History: Essays for Peter Gabriel McCaffery,
edd. David F. Smith & H. Philsooph (Aberdeen 2010)   ISBN 978-0-9567059-0-7

of 'savagery' was understood to be the result of people gratifying their passions, in contrast to the 'civilised' violence of Europe which was governed by reason.

In order to explore this further, and how the assumed violence of the savage 'Other' constituted eloquent and persuasive theme within the *Jesuit Relations*, I will consider the Fathers' descriptions of Iroquoian platform torture in light of European judicial torture and capital punishment. My intension is not to provide a direct comparison with how Iroquoians treated war captives with the treatment of criminals in Europe, but rather to consider how the Fathers judged similar violent acts as being either civilised or savage. There is as of yet no definitive study on Iroquoian torture rituals, and when torture does feature in the secondary literature it tends to appear as a supplementary issue to a larger study. The following is not intended to fill this gap; rather I wish to address a similar lacuna in regard to the Jesuits' interpretation of and participation in these rituals. In doing so, I shall contrast the Jesuits' participation in, and interpretation of these rituals with how Iroquoians would have understood the Jesuits' behaviour at these events. By participating in these rituals the Jesuits were not only attempting to minister to the torture victims, but they were also attempting to demonstrate Christian charity and brotherhood to a wider audience. However, from the Iroquoian point-of-view, the Jesuits' behaviour in this respect was the inversion of the reciprocity that was meant to exist between kin and allies.

A modern interpretation of judicial torture posits it as a barbaric and cruel custom, a holdover from a more violent and less 'enlightened' time. However, rather than a violation of the law that produced an unreliable truth, in seventeenth-century Europe torture served the judicial process by revealing a spontaneous truth that could not be faked (see Silverman 2001). Further, due to the emotive nature of the term *torture*, in the following discussion judicial torture should be read as: the dispassionate application of regulated and measured pain. As Foucault argues: 'Torture is a technique; it is not an extreme expression of lawless rage' (Foucault 1979: 33). This is not a matter of semantics; this distinction will have important consequences for understanding how the Fathers conceptualised the difference between Iroquoian institutional violence and that of Europe.

In Roman law countries like France, examination under torture was only permitted in the adjudication of those crimes that were deemed serious enough to require 'blood sanctions' (death or mutilation), such as murder, heresy, witchcraft, and treason. The 'law of proof' in early-modern Europe required two wholly unimpeachable eyewitnesses for a conviction in any case in which the accused contested the charge levelled against them. Due to the subjective nature of determining culpability from circumstantial evidence, even if overwhelming, such evidence was not considered sufficient proof to demonstrate guilt, unless the accused voluntarily confessed (Asad 1993: 92-95, Langbein 1978: 4-5, Mentzer Jr. 1984: 97, Ruff 2001: 92-96, Silverman 2001: 42-45). Therefore, due to the seriousness of both the crime and the punishment, questioning under torture was deemed necessary in order to satisfy beyond doubt the guilt of the accused.

However, there were strict rules to regulate the application of judicial torture. Torture was only permitted in cases where 'half proof' had been clearly demonstrated against the accused, such as one eyewitness or where there was sufficient circumstantial evidence. Further, torture was not permitted as a means of securing an unsubstantiated confession; whatever was confessed during torture had to be corroborated by factual details of the crime that only the perpetrator could know. The examiner was also prohibited from engaging in suggestive questioning by providing the accused with details of what he wanted to hear (Asad 1993: 94, Langbein 1978: 5-7, Mentzer Jr. 1984: 98-100, Silverman 2001: 42-45). Finally, judicial torture was only to be used as an instrument of investigation not as a means of punishment (Höpfl 2006: 220).

The Society of Jesus had no objections to judicial torture, or the death-penalty, being carried out under specific circumstances (Höpfl 2006: 220). As Höpfl notes:

Jesuit moralists like almost everyone else took it for granted that torture was a legitimate part of the ordinary judicial process, as it had been in Roman law. All that was contentious was which tortures might be used or threatened, under which conditions, and what degree of pain might legitimately be inflicted (Höpfl 2006: 294-295).

Consequently, 'Elaborate legal regulations were considered necessary so that the infliction of torture *would be purposeful and not merely represent individual barbarity*' (Knowles 1940: 151 My emphasis). It is important to keep the above in mind when considering the descriptions and value judgments given by Jesuit commentators regarding Iroquoian platform torture. As we shall see, at root it was not the acts themselves that the Jesuits objected to, but the reasons for which they were enacted.

In the seventeenth century, the Huron like other Iroquoians were primarily semi-sedentary slash and burn horticulturalists; though hunting and gathering, and especially fishing were also economically important (Richter 1992, Trigger 1976).[1] Though stateless societies, Iroquoian communities were far from the anarchic sites of licence suggested by the 'myth of the savage'. Iroquoian villages were

---

[1] For an ethnographic overview of the Huron and Iroquois, see Anderson (1991), Richter (1992), Snow (1996), and Trigger (1967).

politically based and organised around matrilineal clan segments. Though village headmen did possess considerable authority they lacked any means of physically coercing obedience (Trigger 1976, Trigger 1963). Unlike Europeans Iroquoians punished the crime not the criminal. Iroquoian law was normatively restitutive, and aimed through the payment of compensatory gifts from the transgressor's family to victim's family to re-establish normal relations. Only if the family of the transgressor refused to pay did the victim's relatives have the right to seek redress through violence. Though like Europeans Iroquoians recognised treason and witchcraft as two crimes that deserved a death sentence, executions were swift and discrete and bore no comparison to the public and often protracted spectacles of Europe (Trigger 1976: 59-62, Trigger 1969, see below).

By the time the Jesuits had established a mission in Huronia (1634), the trade of beaver pelts with Europeans for European trade goods had become an important part of both Huron and Iroquois economies (Richter 1992, Trigger 1976, Trigger 1963). The most popular and enduring explanation for the seventeenth-century warfare between the Huron and the Five Nations, the Beaver Wars hypothesis, is based upon this factor. The story goes that after contact with Europeans, the Iroquois became dependent on European trade goods for their own cultural survival. After depleting the beaver population within their own territory the Iroquois instigated the Beaver Wars with the Huron and other aboriginal peoples in order to gain new supplies of beaver pelts and secure the position of middlemen in the trade for European goods (see Hunt 1940, Trigger 1976). The major flaw with this hypothesis is that it ignores cultural differences by assuming the Iroquoians were essentially the same as Europeans; consequently, their motivations for engaging in warfare must have been the same (Brandão 1997, Keener 1999, Rich 1960). However, rather than economic, political or territorial gain, the primary objective of Iroquoian warfare was to acquire captives to either socially or symbolically fill the role of deceased individuals through adoption or platform torture respectively. Psychologically for the bereaved family and socially for the community as well as demographically for the population, war captives helped to fill the void that was created by the death of an individual (Brandão 1997, Richter 1983, see below).[2]

Upon the war party's arrival home, prisoners were given to those families

---

[2] The following is a generalised account which applies to both Huron and Iroquois warriors. Though women and children were also taken captive, they were far more likely to be adopted than men, and even if killed they do not appear to have been subjected to the extended ritual described below. For a more detailed survey, including the differences and similarities in Huron and Iroquois practices, see Anderson (1991: 162-191), Axtell (1975b), Brandão (1997: 36-44), Fenton (1978: 315-316), Knowles (1940), Richter (1983), Starna and Watkins (1991), Trigger (1976: 70-75).

who have recently lost someone. At this point, though all captives were symbolically adopted not all were socially adopted. If the prisoner pleased their adoptive family, they were given the name and role of the person they were replacing. It appears that as long as captives were willing participants in this process of assimilation, their adoptive family would make every effort to naturalise them within their new community.[3] This process of adoption seems to have been most effective with children. Nevertheless, that adoptions at any age could be genuinely felt by both sides is testified to by the fact that captives could rise to positions authority, and by the men who joined war parties against their former people (Axtell 1975b, Knowles 1940: 212-213, Lafitau 1974 [1724]: 2:171-172, Trigger 1976: 72).

However, if it was decided that the prisoner should die, the whole village was invited to a final farewell feast that was given in honour of the prisoner. During the feast, and for the remainder of the ordeal, which could last for several days, the condemned were treated with the utmost courtesy, and addressed as if they were kin. Moreover, throughout the 'prisoner was expected to display the primary virtues of a warrior: courage and the ability to suffer without complaining', whilst exhorting his captors to do their worst to him (Anderson 1991: 162-191, Trigger 1976: 72-75, Thwaites 1896-1901: 13:37-87).[4] In regard to the Jesuits' participation in these rituals it is worth stressing that although the prisoner was expected endure the ordeal, *failure* to break the prisoner by making them give in to the pain, and thus depart from the role of the consummate warrior by crying out, was interpreted as an ill omen for future warfare (Trigger 1976: 73). Though known as platform torture, it was only the finale of the ordeal that was conducted upon a raised platform, from which the ritual takes its name.

Though the enactment of this ritual appeared to the Jesuits as 'a living picture of hell' (Thwaites 1896-1901: 13:63), this was not unrestrained mob violence. Whether the ritual was to last one night or several days, it was important that the prisoner died upon the platform, in the open air and at sunrise. To this end everyone was expected to behave in a retrained and orderly fashion. The object of the ordeal was to torment the victim and to inflict the maximum amount of pain

---

[3] Failure to please the adopting family could result in the captive being given for torture or summarily executed (Brandão 1997: 31-44, Knowles 1940: 212).

[4] This popular participation, in which men, women, and children all took part, horrified the French (Trigger 1976), and was yet another indicator of the savagery of these events. In contrast to state sanctioned role of the executioner, we can infer that these events would have appeared as mob violence to the Fathers (see below).

possible without actually killing them.[5] Therefore, throughout the ordeal the prisoner would be given a brief respite and refreshment whenever they were upon the point of succumbing. Captives were finally executed by either being beheaded or having their head broken.

It has also been suggested that the coincidence of the ritual's finale with the sunrise may indicate a religious aspect to the ritual. The subsequent consumption of parts of the victims' body may have been a means of appropriating the strength and courage (personal power) of the victim through the consumption of their body (Anderson 1991: 162-191, Brandão 1997: 36-40, Richter 1992: 36, Thwaites 1896-1901: 13:37-87, Trigger 1976: 72-75), though all of this is far from certain.

One of the most detailed analyses of platform torture is provided by Karen Anderson. Building upon the work of Daniel Richter (1983), Anderson argues that for Iroquoians:

warfare was a socially sanctioned outlet for the expression of rage, grief and anger that was not permitted to be displayed in [Iroquoian] society in any other way (Anderson 1991: 170, cf. Trigger 1976: 48).

Moreover, she argues that by transforming the 'Other' into kin – through the ritual adoption of prisoners; the use of kinship terms, such as cousin, brother and uncle throughout; as well as the false familial concern for the wellbeing of the prisoner, such as describing the violence they inflicted upon the body as 'caresses' – meant that Iroquoians 'were able to mock all the constraints placed on them by a society in which they were never permitted to express anger [or violence] against anyone, no matter what the offence' (Anderson 1991: 177). However, although the Jesuits noticed that these rituals were a means of coping with grief (Thwaites 1896-1901: 9:299, 10:227), they interpreted this through the lens of 'savagery'. Platform torture was thus an expression of the inordinate need that the passion driven 'savage' had for revenge (Thwaites 1896-1901: 6:245).

Apart from Father Isaac Jogues' account of his own capture and captivity by the Iroquois (1642-1643) (Thwaites 1896-1901: 24:271-307, 25:43-73, 28:105-135, 33:55-77), the most detailed firsthand description concerning the ritual torture and adoption of captives comes from the Huron *Relation* for 1637. In this, Father François Joseph Le Mercier, S.J., devotes an entire chapter to the efforts made by Jean de Brébeuf, S.J., Charles Garnier, S.J., and himself towards the conversion of

---

[5] As Foucault argues in regard to tortuous deaths such as quartering, 'death-torture is the art of maintaining life in pain' (Foucault 1979: 33). As we shall see, although European torture rituals shared a similar concern with the regulation of pain, Europeans saw no similarities between torture rituals of Europe and New France.

an Iroquois prisoner of war (Thwaites 1896-1901: 13:37-83). Admittedly to the modern reader the lurid descriptions of the torture and subsequent execution of this prisoner are the most striking and dominant features of this chapter. However, in terms of what Le Mercier was attempting to convey to his readers, these are merely background details for the narrative of this warrior's eventual salvation.

Before proceeding to consider Le Mercier's account in more detail it is worthwhile pausing to consider the veracity of these torture narratives. For example, we should take into consideration Le Mercier's admission:

For me to describe in detail all he endured during the rest of the night, would be almost impossible; we suffered enough in forcing ourselves to see a part of it. Of the rest we judged from their talk; and the smoke issuing from his roasted flesh revealed to us something of which we could not have borne the sight (Thwaites 1896-1901: 13:65-67).

This admission suggests that some of the details of the torture narratives contained within the *Relations* may have been supplied by the 'myth of the savage' theme within Jesuits' own imaginations.

To contextualise this admission, it is worth noting as Trigger points out, that:

the ritual torture practiced by the Indians did not disgust most seventeenth-century Europeans to the extent we imagine it should have done. Mutilations and prolonged and brutal forms of execution were part of the hangman's art in all parts of Europe at this time; so that Europeans who came to the New World were generally familiar with the sort of cruelties that the Indians practiced (Trigger 1976: 254).

As we shall see, this disgust originated not from the acts themselves, but from the Jesuits' belief that indigenous institutional violence, unlike the institutional violence of Europe, was chaotic and disordered. Rather than being governed by reason and directed towards the public good, the ritual was interpreted as an expression of people revelling in their passions, and was thus simply cruelty.

Le Mercier describes how upon the arrival of a returning war party at the village of Onnentisati, Sa[o]uandanoncoua, an Iroquois warrior was given to a prominent Huron captain to replace a nephew who had been recently captured by the Iroquois (Thwaites 1896-1901: 13:37-39). Even though it was decided that Sa[o]uandanoncoua should die, Le Mercier emphasises that throughout the ordeal Sa[o]uandanoncoua was still addressed as though he was kin. Le Mercier wrote: 'I will say here that, up to the hour of his torment, we saw only acts of humanity exercised towards him' (Thwaites 1896-1901: 13:39). It was this 'charity' that the Jesuits' perceived to be the real horror of the process; it was not simply the violence of acts which Sa[o]uandanoncoua was made to endure, but that his captors 'treated him only as a brother and friend' (Thwaites 1896-1901: 13). All of which the Jesuits saw as means of inflicting even more pain upon the victim (Thwaites 1896-1901: 13:39). By emphasising platform torture as a process of inversion, and juxtaposing the ordeal of platform torture with the Fathers' efforts to baptise torture victims, salvation narratives implicitly express the ideals of Christian charity and of all humanity being related through Christ.

The Jesuits were not only shocked that Iroquoians called the tortures they inflicted 'caresses', but also that the family, rather than being the source of security, were instead transformed into the victim's persecutors (Thwaites 1896-1901: 25:237, 39:65). During Sa[o]uandanoncoua's farewell feast, Le Mercier wrote:

Meanwhile, a Captain, raising his voice to the same tone used by those who make some proclamation in the public places in France, addressed to him these words: 'My nephew, thou hast good reason to sing, for no one is doing thee any harm; behold thyself now among thy kindred and friends.' Good God, what a compliment! All those who surrounded him, *with their affected kindness and their fine words*, were so many butchers who showed him a smiling face only to treat him afterwards with more cruelty (Thwaites 1896-1901: 13:39-41 My emphasis).

Le Mercier explains that even the pronouncement of the death sentence was couched in the terms of familial kindness, as to put Sa[o]uandanoncoua out of his misery (Thwaites 1896-1901: 13:53-55). In describing the tortures that Sa[o]uandanoncoua was made to endure, Le Mercier emphasises the 'care' with which Sa[o]uandanoncoua was treated throughout this process, such as whenever he was on the point of collapse he was permitted a brief respite, and given food and water. The horror being that these 'kindnesses' were only done to him so that the process could then continue anew (Thwaites 1896-1901: 13:67).

It was the inversion of familial concern which the Jesuits found particularly abhorrent. The care and tenderness with which the Huron treated Sa[o]uandanoncoua belied the violence that was being inflicted upon his body. The Jesuits might have found this easier, if the behaviour of the Huron in this respect had conformed to the trope of 'ignoble savagery', and the violence inflicted upon Sa[o]uandanoncoua's body had been expressed in a frenzy of hate and contempt. This at least would have been recognisable. But to quote Le Mercier:

One thing, in my opinion, greatly increased his consciousness of suffering – that anger and rage did not appear upon the faces of those who were tormenting him, but rather gentleness and humanity, their words expressing only raillery or tokens of friendship and good will [...] and No one spared himself, and each one strove to surpass his companion in cruelty. But, as I have said, what was most calculated in all this to plunge him into despair, was their raillery, and the compliments they paid him when they approached to burn him (Thwaites 1896-1901: 13:67).

Le Mercier uses this chapter to contrast this apparent parody of familial concern with Brébeuf's active Christian charity.

He juxtaposes 'this affected kindness' and 'fine words' with the comfort the Fathers tried to provide Sa[o]uandanoncoua through their efforts to secure his salvation. Le Mercier describes how Brébeuf told Sa[o]uandanoncoua:

that he would in truth be miserable during the little of life that remained to him, but that, if he would listen to him and would believe what he had to tell him, he would assure him of an eternal happiness in Heaven after his death (Thwaites 1896-1901: 43).

In contrast to this charity and concern for Sa[o]uandanoncoua's salvation, Le Mercier depicts the torture of Sa[o]uandanoncoua as 'a living picture of Hell' (Thwaites 1896-1901: 13:63). Whereby:

The whole cabin appeared as if on fire; and, athwart the flames and the dense smoke that issued therefrom, these barbarians – crowding one upon the other, howling at the top of their voices, with firebrands in their hands, their eyes flashing with rage and fury – seemed like so many Demons who would give no respite to this poor wretch. They often stopped him at the other end of the cabin, some of them taking his hands and breaking the bones thereof by sheer force; others pierced his ears with sticks which they left in them; others bound his wrists with cords which they tied roughly, pulling at each end of the cord with all their might. Did he make the round and pause to take a little breath, he was made to repose upon hot ashes and burning coals. It is with horror that I describe all this to your Reverence, but verily we experienced unutterable pain while enduring the sight of it. I do not know what would have become of us had it not been for the consolation we had of considering him, no longer as a common Savage, but as a child of the Church, and as such, of asking God to give him patience, and the privilege of dying in his holy grace (Thwaites 1896-1901: 13:63).

The good death is a prominent feature of these torture narratives, whether it is the constancy and stoicism of converts, French captives, or the Jesuits themselves, these deaths were intended to inspire the piety of their audience back in France (Thwaites 1896-1901: 17:65, 22:261-263, 33:93-95, 46:53-63).

The Jesuits ultimately see Sa[o]uandanoncoua's ordeal as a blessing, since his suffering enabled him to achieve salvation. Though he experienced bodily pain now, his soul had escaped the everlasting pain of damnation (Thwaites 1896-1901: 13:45, 81). However, these rituals permitted the Jesuits to not only minister to the victims, but also to the whole village (Thwaites 1896-1901: 13:71-75). By participating in this ritual, the Jesuits were attempting to communicate through word and action not only Christian charity, but also the universality of humanity being related through Christ.

The Jesuits' behaviour towards Sa[o]uandanoncoua, though conforming to the ideal of Christian brotherhood, and especially the parable of the Good Samaritan, caused considerable consternation among the Huron. As mentioned above, Le Mercier describes how Brébeuf attempted to comfort

Sa[o]uandanoncoua by assuring him that what he was about to suffer was only temporary, and that through his baptism he was ensured salvation. However:

Those who were present there had very different thoughts. Some looked at us, and were astonished to see us so strongly attached to him, – following him everywhere, losing no occasion to speak to him, and to give him some word of consolation (Thwaites 1896-1901: 13:57-59).

This confusion is not surprising. The Jesuits were telling the Huron of their desire that the Huron and the French would become one people (Thwaites 1896-1901: 14:19, 42:101, 121, 44:31-33). However, by showing concern for the well being of an enemy, rather than expressing solidarity with the Huron, the Jesuits' behaviour would have seriously questioned this claim and communicated a troubling doubt as to their reliability as allies and kin.

Though the Jesuits behaviour conformed to reciprocity inherent within Christ's injunction to love thy neighbour, the Huron found this consideration for an Iroquois prisoner, an enemy of both the Huron and the French incomprehensible. Le Mercier wrote:

For when some one asked him [Brébeuf] if we felt compassion for the prisoner, he affirmed that we did, and that we greatly longed that he might be soon delivered from his sufferings and go to Heaven, there to be forever blest. This gave him occasion to speak of the joys of Paradise and the grievous afflictions of Hell, and to show them that if they were cruel to this poor wretch, the Devils were still more so to the condemned. He told them that what they made him endure was only a very rough picture of the torments suffered by lost souls in Hell, whether they considered the multitude of them, or their magnitude and the length of their duration; that our having baptized Sa[o]uandanoncoua was only to deliver him from those punishments, and to enable him to go to Heaven after his death. 'How now?' retorted some of them, 'he is one of our enemies; and it matters not if he go to Hell and if he be forever burned.' The Father replied very appropriately, that God was God of the Iroquois as well as of the Hurons, and of all men who are upon the earth; that he despised no one, even if he be ugly or poor; that what won the heart of God was not the beauty of the body, the graces of the mind, or the abundance of wealth, but, indeed, an exact observance of his holy Law; that the fires of Hell were lighted and burning only for sinners, whatever their nation might be (Thwaites 1896-1901: 13:71-73).

The Jesuits evidently believed that this occasion had provided them with an excellent opportunity to preach what being a Christian truly meant. However, they do not seem to have understood how perplexing and potentially threatening their actions would have been in this respect to the Huron. The Jesuits' lack of reciprocity in their refusal to take part in socially reaffirming rituals, such as eat-all feasts and healing ceremonies (Thwaites 1896-1901: 10:175, 17:169, 189-193, 33:209, 42:157-167), combined with their concern for an enemy, would have been extremely worrying to the Huron.

It is not unreasonable to surmise, that because aboriginal peoples understood the Jesuits to be powerful shamans (Morrison 2002, Richter 1985), the Jesuits' 'altruistic' behaviour during these rituals would have been interpreted as the Fathers using their own personal power, not for the benefit of the village, but for a hated enemy. In light of the object of breaking the prisoner, the Jesuits, in giving comfort to the victim, would have appeared to have been subverting this ritual, and putting the entire village in danger by attempting to give strength to the enemy. This also helps to explain why Iroquoians attempted to prevent the Jesuits baptising captives as well as the 'fury' they inflicted upon baptised prisoners (Thwaites 1896-1901: 17:65-69, 26:179-181, 39:79-81).[6]

In 1663 Father Jérôme Lalemant, S.J., noted similar sentiments:

The Hurons, although feeling less hatred toward the Iroquois [than the Algonquins], since they speak almost the same tongue, yet were so bitter against them at the time of first receiving our teachings that whenever they captured any of these foes, and we endeavoured to prepare the latter to receive the waters of salvation in the midst of the flames, they would exclaim: 'What, my brothers, would you have those people go with us to Paradise? How could we live there in peace? Do you imagine you can make the soul of a Huron agree with that of an Iroquois?' (Thwaites 1896-1901: 48:109).

Despite Lalemant's declaration that:

Poor ignorant creatures that they then were, not yet knowing that, according to St. Paul, God makes no distinction between Jew and Gentile, Iroquois and Huron, Algonquin and Frenchman. This lesson our victors have learned since then, and they put it in Practice respecting their prisoners (Thwaites 1896-1901: 48:109),

this example suggests that a quarter a century after Le Mercier's account, the Jesuits were still struggling to explain an alternative metaphor of kinship to the Huron, that of being related through Christ.

It is worthwhile considering why individuals such as Sa[o]uandanoncoua would agree to baptism under such conditions. Iroquoians believed that anyone who died a violent or unnatural death was excluded from the village of the dead. Captives therefore faced separation from family and friends both in this life and the next (Hewitt 1895, Richter 1992: 38). If we take into consideration that one of the principal reasons that aboriginal peoples gave for converting was to join relatives in the next life (Thwaites 1896-1901: 13:3), baptism may have offered a means of escaping the loneliness of this fate. It is also possible that these conversions were not only a means of escaping this horrifying fate, but also a

---

[6] Admittedly the Jesuits interpret this fury as being a specifically directed towards the Faith; however, there is nothing unique in this treatment of Christian prisoners. This 'fury' was the result of Iroquoians attempting to break any prisoners who was successfully enduring the ordeal (Thwaites 1896-1901: 10:227, 22:263-265)

means of snatching a semblance of a victory from defeat by snubbing their persecutors.

To return to Le Mercier's narrative; Brébeuf was asked:

'But thinkest thou,' […] 'that for what thou sayest here, and for what thou doest to this man, the Iroquois will treat thee better if they come some time to ravage our country?' 'That is not what concerns me,' replied the Father, 'all I think of now is to do what I ought; we have come here only to teach you the way to Heaven; as to the rest, and as to what regards our persons, we leave that entirely to the providence of God.' 'Why art thou sorry,' added someone, 'that we tormented him?' 'I do not disapprove of your killing him, but of your treating him in that way.' 'What then! how do you French people do? Do you not kill men?' '*Yes, indeed; we kill them, but not with this cruelty.*' 'What! do you never burn any?' 'Not often,' said the Father, 'and even then fire is only for enormous crimes, and there is only one person to whom this kind of execution belongs by right; and besides, they are not made to linger so long, – often they are first strangled, and generally they are thrown at once into the fire, where they are immediately smothered and consumed' (Thwaites 1896-1901: 13:73-75 My emphasis).[7]

Brébeuf is clearly distinguishing between those acts he believed were backed by law and reason and the passion driven disorder of savagery.[8] The Jesuits believed the purpose of aboriginal warfare was not for defence but rather to satisfy their taste for revenge by acquiring prisoners to torture to death (Thwaites 1896-1901: 10:227), thus platform torture had nothing to do with justice.

In an age where high treason was punished by being hanged, drawn and quartered, Brébeuf's claims may strike us as being disingenuous. However, by considering how 'cruelty' was intrinsic within the French conception of aboriginal violence, we can see that Brébeuf was being completely sincere.

In 1609 after the Battle of Lake Champlain, Samuel de Champlain made similar claims to the Huron in regard to French justice not being cruel. Before examining this incident more fully it is worth noting that Champlain, confident in his own cultural superiority, assumed that European tactics *etcetera* were necessarily superior to those of his allies. He believed that this 'gave him the natural right to lead them and to censure any conduct of which he did not approve' (Trigger 1971: 91). In regard to this belief, *his allies* should be read as *his subordinates* not as *his equals*. As far as Champlain was concerned they were *his* troops.

Champlain describes how his Algonquian and Huron allies:

---

[7] The stake was reserved for heresy, sodomy, and witchcraft. Though some victims were strangled prior to burning, it is not always clear why this was done. It may have been a form of clemency offered for cooperation or recantation and repentance (Nicholls 1988: 50, 64)

[8] For example, in 1636 Paul Le Jeune maintained that those who were most cruel and active in the torture of captives were those who had recently lost someone. He believed that it was the 'recollection of the death of their kindred that fills their hearts with this madness' (Thwaites 1896-1901: 9:299). Rather than being guided by reason, in their grief people were giving themselves over to their passions.

begged me repeatedly to take fire and do like them [to the prisoners]. *I pointed out to them that we did not commit such cruelties,* but that we killed people outright, and that if they wished me to shoot him with the arquebus, I should be glad to do so. They said no; for he would not feel any pain. *I went away from them as if angry at seeing them practice so much cruelty on his body.* When they saw that I was not pleased, they called me back and told me to give him a shot with the arquebus. I did so without his perceiving anything, and with one shot caused him to escape all the tortures he would have suffered rather than see him brutally treated (Champlain 1971 [1613]: 2:103 My emphasis).

Champlain apparently saw this as the Huron and Algonquin warriors accepting his authority. However, these entreaties were more likely his allies trying to cement the alliance between them more fully by incorporating Champlain into this ritual. Moreover, rather than capitulating to his demands, they would have been attempting to maintain their alliance with Champlain, a powerful but temperamental captain.

As Hirsch argues, Iroquoian warriors integrated torture into their code of honour though their ability to stoically endure torture. However, for Europeans, although torture was acceptable within the confines of European jurisprudence, 'martial tradition held it dishonourable in the nobler trial of arms' (Hirsch 1988: 1192). Further, as noted above, seventeenth-century Europeans did not share our cultural sensibilities in regard to corporal or capital punishment. In relation to this, Trigger argues, 'Chaplain's anger was less an emotional revulsion against cruelty than the result of his conviction that his allies were acting unfairly in so treating a prisoner of war', and 'It is doubtful that he would have objected to the torturing of someone who was guilty of treason, heresy, or sexual deviancy' (Trigger 1976: 254).

Though any interpretation of the reactions of the French to the torture of prisoners must be cognisant of Trigger's argument, I maintain that there is more to Champlain's reaction than what Trigger suggests.

Champlain's language implies that his response was feigned. He wrote that he walked away 'as if angry'. This suggests that he intended this as a lesson to *his* allies on how *he* expected them to behave in future towards captives. This was a lesson he attempted to make more explicit a few years later. In 1615 Champlain 'reprimanded' one of his allies for cutting the finger off a female captive's hand. We are told that Champlain:

represented to him that it was not the deed of a warrior, as he called himself, to behave cruelly towards women who have no other defence but tears, and whom by reason of their helplessness and weakness we should treat with humanity: but that this act, on the contrary, would be deemed to proceed from a base and brutal disposition, and that if he allowed any more cruelties, he would not encourage me to assist or aid them in their attack (Champlain 1971 [1619]: 3:64-65).

It could be argued that Champlain's reactions (as well as being a rhetorical presentation of himself as chivalrous chevalier) are as much to do with an attempt to assert his authority as they are with what his allies were actually doing.

It is also worth noting that despite the aforementioned developments in regard to the treatment of prisoners of war, neither Champlain nor Brébeuf appear to have had any qualms in regard to prisoners of war being executed. I would argue that what did shock them was the reasons (or lack of reason as the French would have seen it) that Iroquoians gave for platform torture. Albeit agreeing with Trigger that the French did not feel the revulsion that we would expect, I would further argue that Champlain and Brébeuf were complaining that the treatment of captives served no purpose other than the self-gratification of the torturers, and in this sense it was cruelty.

When considering French commentaries on Iroquoian torture we should remember that in the seventeenth century punishment was very much a public spectacle. French law recognised five separate forms of capital punishment: burning at the stake, drawing and quartering, hanging, breaking on the wheel, and decapitation (Grabowski 1996: 429) – all of which can be described as torturous deaths.[9] As with judicial torture, Europeans believed that in public executions, pain not only served a purpose, but its application was conceptualised as being regulated, impersonal and dispassionate (see Foucault 1979: 32-69).

For example, in 1663 Jérôme Lalemant recorded that a sieur de Beaulieu and one of his valets had burned to death in an accidental house fire. However, a few days later, Lalemant wrote:

It turned out that the fire which had caught in the house of sieur de Beaulieu had not occurred by accident but through the malice of a valet, after he had killed his master and another valet, his comrade. He was convicted and sentenced to have his hand cut off, and to be hanged and then burned. Monsieur the governor was contented that he should die upon the scaffold; after having been tormented thereon by the executioner, he was shot, on the 8th of June (Thwaites 1896-1901: 47:303-305).[10]

Lalemant's dispassionate account of the gruesome end of de Beaulieu's valet, like Foucault's (1979: 3) graphic account of Robert-François Damiens's execution in 1757 for the attempted regicide of Louis XV, demonstrates that French justice was no less 'savage' than that meted out by Iroquoians. However, within the *Relations* no Jesuit ever compared fate of those who went to the platform to that

---

[9] Though decapitation and hanging may appear quick when compared to the other choices, the trap door on the scaffold and the guillotine as techniques to avoid the slow deaths of the condemned were late eighteenth century innovations (Foucault 1979: 12-13).

[10] It was a common feature of early modern sentences to stipulate that the member which had committed the crime was to burned or cut off prior to execution (Ranum 1980: 71).

of the victims of French justice.

This lack of relativism in comparing the torture rituals of Europe to those New France was due to the Fathers not viewing the pain inflicted upon the body during these torturous expressions of French justice as unnecessary. Rather than being unnecessary, pain was considered to serve a very specific purpose, the common good. However, unlike platform torture, the pain inflicted during European torture rituals such as this were not considered 'cruel' because it was inflicted neither for pleasure nor for any personal gratification. This is what Brébeuf and Champlain were alluding to when they claimed that the French did not practise such cruelty. Indeed the highly ritualised public executions of criminals in the early modern period can be viewed as eloquent warnings, 'a form of morality play staged by magistrates for the edification of the populace' (Nicholls 1988: 49). Executions were not a brutal form of public entertainment, rather 'they were manifestations of the power of state and church', vehicles which demonstrated:

that crime did not pay, that the wages of sin was death, and that those guilty of serious crimes would live to regret their actions before becoming the sacrificial victims of social and cosmic order (Nicholls 1988: 49).

The acts inflicted upon the body may have been similar, but the Jesuits were not being hypocritical in seeing no cruelty in their own rituals. They believed one to be governed by reason and the other by the passions. For the Jesuits the gulf between the two was unbridgeable.

Moreover, as Jaenen notes:

All European nations, at one time or another, used torture against the Amerindians either to extract information or to punish refractory behaviour. But, in European eyes, the context was completely different from the Amerindian ritualistic use of stake and platform (Jaenen 1974: 139).

The following example offers us a profitable comparison with the aforementioned Iroquoian torture narratives.

In 1696 the Father Jacques de Lamberville, S.J., described how during a campaign conducted by the then governor of New France Louis de Buade, Comte de Frontenac against the Onondagas, the French captured a partially blind old man whom the French wished to execute. Lamberville describes how:

the Christian Iroquois asked that he be killed with a club or be Stabbed to death, instead of being burned. But the French peremptorily demanded that he be burned at a slow fire – which they themselves did with many – [in sight of his relatives,] who belonged to our party (Thwaites 1896-1901: 65:27-29).

However:

When this came to the Governor's knowledge, he had pity on him, [and would have granted him His life] after an hour's torture, had he not already been burned all over. On account of his condition, one among those who were present, touched with compassion, broke his head (Thwaites 1896-1901: 65:29).

What is significant here is that, although the roles of 'civil' and 'savage' appear to be reversed, the Jesuits still play the same role of facilitating this man's redemption through the sacrament of baptism (Thwaites 1896-1901: 65:27-29). Lamberville presents the compassion shown by the Christian Iroquois warriors as indicating a profound change in practice (outlook), thus indicating the progress the Jesuits have made in their mission. Admittedly, it does appear as if the French are the 'savages' in Lamberville's narrative. However, I would stress that in this incident it was the rabble who acted like 'savages', not Frontenac, who once he became aware of this incident re-established order by granting clemency of a sort.

We can compare the above to French judgements on secular riots of the late sixteenth century. For example, the grain-rioters of Lyon were described as 'the dregs of the populace, with no order, no rein, no leader [...] a beast of many heads [...] an insane rabble', and the Parisian mob as:

an ignorant multitude, collected from all nations [...] governed by the appetite of those who stir them up [to] extreme rage, just looking for the chance to carry out any kind of cruelty (Davis 1975: 154).

We can speculate that the Jesuits would have agreed with these assessments of European mob violence as being a breakdown of law and order.

In regard to behaviour of colonists being like that of the mob, Father Joseph-François Lafitau, S.J., argued that the ferocity by which the Iroquois waged war meant that 'the gentlest people are forced to put aside their natural gentleness when they see that it becomes a pretext for barbarous neighbours to become prouder and more intractable' (Lafitau 1974 [1724]: 2:162). He believed that this was the case with the French, and:

When, to avenge themselves on the Iroquois, they were permitted to treat their prisoners as the Indians treated ours, they did it with so much ferocity and zeal that they were, in no way, inferior to the barbarians but even surpassed them (Lafitau 1974 [1724]: 2:162).

He argued that this cruelty was necessary, since it was only by making the Iroquois fear the French that they were able to make peace with them (Lafitau 1974 [1724]: 2:162).

Though Lafitau's reasoning is an apology for the savagery of the supposedly civilised when fighting the savage 'Other', the idea of mob violence suggests that atrocities would inevitably occur when the lower orders temporarily managed to evade the boundaries provided by civil society. To return to Lafitau's argument concerning the French adopting Iroquois customs, Lafitau argued:

I shall add that, when the French and English become naturalized Indians, they adopt the bad in their customs and practices so vigorously [without taking the good] that they are even more wicked than [their models]. The Indians can very well reproach us with it. The fact is so well proven that we have no answer (Lafitau 1974: 2:162-163).

These adoptees were perceived to have degenerated into 'savages' by escaping the bounds prescribed by civil authority. From a European perspective these individuals could also be viewed as being worse than the 'savages', since unlike their new 'savage' kin these European 'savages' could make no appeal to not knowing better!

As we have seen, the 'myth of the savage' dominated Jesuit thought in regard to aboriginal institutional violence, and although as missionaries the Jesuits are noted for their sympathetic approach to cultural difference (Duignan 1958), in this respect the Fathers displayed no evidence of cultural relativism whatsoever. Iroquoian platform torture never prompted the Jesuits into a reflexive mode in regard to either the use of judicial torture or the torturous deaths of the European judicial system. As Jennings argues:

It seems reasonable to infer that comparably painful practices in the two societies were sharply distinguished in European minds by what was conceived as their relative lawfulness. Torture by commission of civil authority was merely execution of the law [...] but torture by a self-governing rabble was savagery (Jennings 1975: 161).

This belief was underpinned by the dichotomy of actions governed by reason versus passions. This is what Father Barthélemy Vimont, S.J., meant when he exclaimed: '*Homo homini lupus*; man becomes a wolf to other men, when he allows himself to be governed by Demons' (Thwaites 1896-1901: 22:265).

The 'myth of the savage' as a known fact thus enabled the Jesuits to present Iroquoian institutional violence to their readers as a persuasive argument for the need of their mission. As with the torturous deaths of Europe, the 'mania' of platform torture would have eloquently informed Europeans of the need for a hierarchically structured civil society. The Jesuits also believed that their participation in the rituals provided them with not only an excellent opportunity of emulating the apostles, but also one where they could eloquently demonstrate true Christian charity in contrast to the parody of altruism that they believed lay at the heart of these rituals. However, to the Iroquoian peoples the Fathers were attempting to establish these relationships with, the Jesuits' 'altruism' would have been read as a form of aggression, communicating that the Fathers were in fact dangerous anti-social 'Others'.

Bibliography

Asad, T. 1993. *Genealogies of religion.* Baltimore: The John Hopkins University Press.

Anderson, K. 1991. *Chain her by one foot: the subjugation of women in seventeenth-century New France.* London: Routledge.

Axtell, J. 1975. 'The white Indians of colonial America'. *The William and Mary Quarterly,* 32(1), pp. 55-88.

Brandão, J. A. 1997. '*Your fyre shall burn no more': Iroquois policy toward New France and its native allies to 1701.* Lincoln: University of Nebraska Press.

Champlain, S. de. 1971. *The works of Samuel de Champlain.* 6 vols. Toronto: The Champlain Society.

Duignan, P. 1958. 'Early Jesuit missionaries: a suggestion for further study'. *American Anthropologist,* 60(4), pp. 725-732.

Fenton, W. N., 1978. 'Northern Iroquoian culture patterns'. Pp. 296-321 in *The handbook of North American Indians: Northeast, Vol 15,* B. G. Trigger, ed. Washington: Smithsonian Institution.

Foucault, M. 1979. *Discipline and punish: the birth of the prison.* New York: Vintage Books.

Grabowski, J. 1996. 'French Criminal Justice and Indians in Montreal, 1670-1760' *Ethnohistory,* 43(3), pp. 405-429.

Healy, G. R. 1958. 'The French Jesuits and the idea of the noble savage'. *The William and Mary Quarterly,* 15(2), pp. 143-167.

Hewitt, J. N. B. 1895. 'The Iroquoian concept of the soul'. *The Journal of American Folklore,* 8(29), pp. 107-116.

Hirsch, A. J. 1988. 'The Collision of Military Cultures In Seventeenth-Century New England'. *The Journal of American History,* 74(4), pp. 1187-1212.

Höpfl, H. 2006. *Jesuit political thought: the Society of Jesus and the state, c. 1540-1630.* Cambridge: Cambridge University Press.

Hunt, G. T. 1940. *The wars of the Iroquois: a study in intertribal relations.* Madison: University of Wisconsin Press.

Jaenen, C. J. 1976. *Friend and foe: aspects of French-Amerindian cultural contact in the sixteenth and seventeenth centuries.* New York: Columbia University Press.

_____1974. 'Amerindian views of French culture'. *Canadian Historical Review,* 55(3), pp. 261-291.

Jennings, F. 1975. *The invasion of America: Indians, colonialism, and the cant of conquest.* Chapel Hill: University of North Carolina Press.

Keener, C. S. 1999. 'An ethnohistorical analysis of Iroquois assault tactics used against fortified settlements of the Northeast in the seventeenth century'. *Ethnohistory,* 46(4), pp. 777-807.

Knowles, N. 1940. 'The torture of captives by the Indians of Eastern North America'. *Proceedings of the American Philosophical Society,* 82(2), pp. 151-225.

Lafitau, J. F. 1974 [1724]. *Customs of the American Indians compared with the customs of primitive times.* 2 vols. Toronto: Champlain Society.

Langbein, J. H. 1978. 'Torture and plea bargaining'. *The University of Chicago Law Review,* 46(1), pp. 3-22.

Mentzer Jr., R. A. 1984. 'Heresy proceedings in Langudoc'. *Transactions of the American Philosophical Society, New Series,* 74(5), pp. 1-183.

Morrison, K. M. 2002. *The solidarity of kin: ethnohistory, religious studies, and the Algonkian-French religious encounter.* Albany: State University of New York Press.

Davis, N. Z. 1975. *Society and culture in early modern France: eight essays.* Stanford: Stanford University Press.

Nicholls, D. 1988. 'The theatre of martyrdom in the French Reformation'. *Past and Present,* 121(49), pp. 49-73.

Ranum, O. 1980. 'The French ritual of tyrannicide in the late sixteenth century'. *The Sixteenth Century Journal,* 11(1), pp. 63-82.

Rich, E. E. 1960. 'Trade habits and economic motivation among the Indians of North America'. *The Canadian Journal of Economics and Political Science,* 26(1), pp. 35-53.

Richter, D. K. 1992. *The ordeal of the longhouse: the peoples of the Iroquois League in the era of European colonization*. Chapel Hill: University of North Carolina Press.

_____1985. Iroquois versus Iroquois: Jesuit missions and Christianity in village politics. *Ethnohistory*, 32(1), pp. 1-16.

_____1983. 'War and culture: the Iroquois experience'. *The William and Mary Quarterly*, 40(4), pp. 528-559.

Snow, D. R. 1996. *The Iroquois*. Cambridge, MA: Blackwell Publishers.

Starna, W. A. and Watkins, R. 1991. 'Northern Iroquoian slavery'. *Ethnohistory*, 38(1), pp. 34-57.

Ruff, J. R. 2001. *Violence in early modern Europe, 1500-1800*. Cambridge: Cambridge University Press.

Russell, J. D. n.d. *Civility and savagery: becoming related in seventeenth-century New France*. Unpublished PhD thesis (under review). Aberdeen: University of Aberdeen.

Silverman, L. 2001. *Tortured subjects: pain, truth, and the body in early modern France*. Chicago: The University of Chicago.

Thwaites, R. G. ed. 1896-1901. *The Jesuit Relations and allied documents: travels and explorations of the Jesuit missionaries in New France: 1610-1791*. 73 vols. Cleveland: Burrows Brothers.

Trigger, B. G. 1976. *The children of Aataentsic: a history of the Huron people to 1660*. Kingston: McGill-Queen's University Press.

_____1971. 'Champlain judged by his Indian policy: a different view of early Canadian history'. *Anthropologica, n.s.*, 13(1/2), pp. 85-114.

_____1963. 'Order and freedom: Huron society'. *Anthropologica, n.s.*, 5(2), pp. 151-169.

'The glorious Empire of the Turkes, the present terrour of the world': Richard Knolles's *Generall Historie of the Turkes* (1603) and the background to an early modern commonplace

ANDERS INGRAM
Durham University

Richard Knolles's *Generall Historie of the Turks* (1603) was the first major original English account of the Ottoman Turks. This work was repeatedly republished, copied, and extended, and had an unparalleled influence on numerous seventeenth century authors as a source of information and authority on the Ottoman Turks.[1] Knolles' *Generall Historie* and, in particular, his famous opening line 'THE glorious Empire of the Turkes, the present terrour of the world' has received copious modern scholarly attention. This phrase, and the range of attitudes it supposedly encapsulates, have been presented as representative of wider English perceptions of the Ottoman Turks. From the first significant survey of early modern English literature on Islam, Samuel Chew's *The Crescent and the Rose* (1937), which contained a chapter introducing English accounts of the Ottoman Turks entitled 'The present terrour of the world',[2] to Aslı Çırakman's more recent *From the "terrour of the world" to the "sick man of Europe"*,[3] virtually every scholar studying such literature seems to have felt honour-bound to discuss this phrase. Matar, Vitkus, Dimmock, Barbour, Burton and MacLean are amongst the most recent and well known.[4]

The purpose of this essay is threefold. Firstly, I will seek to contextualise

---

[1] On the *Generall Historie*, see V.J. Parry, *Richard Knolles' History of the Turks* (Istanbul, 2004); Christine Woodhead, 'The History of an Historie: Richard Knolles' *General Historie of the Turkes*, 1603-1700' in *Journal of Turkish Studies*, edited by Şinasi Tekin (Cambridge, 2002), 349-57; Bodin, Jean, trs. Richard Knolles and ed. Kenneth D. McRae, *The Six Books of a Commonweale* (Cambridge, 1962).

[2] Samuel C. Chew, *The crescent and the rose: Islam and England during the Renaissance* (New York, 1937), pp. 100-49.

[3] Aslı Çırakman, *From the "Terror of the World" to the "Sick Man of Europe": European Images of Ottoman empire and society from the sixteenth century to the nineteenth* (New York, 2002).

[4] Nabil Matar, *Islam in Britain* (Cambridge, 1998), p. 12; Matthew Dimmock, *New Turkes* (Aldershot, 2005), p. 201; Daniel J. Vitkus, 'Early Modern Orientalism: representations of Islam in sixteenth and seventeenth-century Europe.' in *Western views of Islam in medieval and early modern Europe*, edited by M. Frassetto and D. Blanks (New York, 1999), p. 210. The other scholars mentioned will be cited when discussed.

Explorations in Cultural History: Essays for Peter Gabriel McCaffery,
edd. David F. Smith & H. Philsooph (Aberdeen 2010)   ISBN 978-0-9567059-0-7

Knolles' use of the phrase 'terror of the world'. I will survey usages which occur in Knolles' sources and late sixteenth century English writing prior to Knolles. In particular I will emphasise this expression's commonplace connection with the story of Timur Khan (d. 1405, Tammerlaine, Tammerlane or Tamburlaine in English accounts), founder of the Central Asian Timurid dynasty. I will then demonstrate that these contexts are consistent with Knolles' own usage of the phrase. Following from this, I will suggest that Knolles' deliberate choice of the commonplace 'terror of the world', as a description of the Ottoman Turks, is part of the rhetorical strategy through which Knolles conceives of Ottoman history and presents it within the framework of a grand moralising meta-narrative, ultimately illustrating the working of divine providence.

Secondly, I will reflect upon modern critical readings of Knolles' *Generall Historie*, and particularly the phrase 'terror of the world', as part of a wider discourse of English and European perceptions and depictions of the 'East'. I will compare and contrast my survey of usages of the expression 'terror of the world' to these readings, and argue that this approach risks significantly underplaying important contemporary contexts and discourses in which the *Generall Historie* engaged. As an alternative I will discuss Skinner's and Pocock's notions of discourse, and the questions they raise for a critical reading of Knolles' *Generall Historie*, and his usage of 'terror of the world'.

Thirdly and finally, I will develop a reading of Knolles as a historian. In other words I will examine Knolles' the *Generall Historie* as a work engaged in a discourse on the dynastic history of the Ottoman Turks, through the conventions and language of 'History'. By 'History', I mean contemporary concepts and understandings of written history, and the role and responsibilities of the historian. I will emphasise the methodology that Knolles makes explicit, his sources and his attitude to them, the models which he drew upon, and the context of sixteenth century English historical writing. I will also discuss Knolles' motivations for writing this work, patronage, and the Ottoman-Hapsburg 'Long War' of 1593-1606, which prompted a significant number of other contemporary English authors to produce substantial English works on the Ottoman Turks. My central argument is that an approach to the *Generall Historie* which relates it to chronicle histories of the Ottomans, and contemporary notions of 'History', produces a more nuanced and historical reading, than an approach which treats it as a node within a larger network of European discourse of the 'East', without such specific contextualisation.

'THE GLORIOUS EMPIRE OF THE TURKES, THE PRESENT TERROUR OF THE WORLD'

THE glorious Empire of the Turkes, the present terrour of the world, hath amongst other things nothing in it more wonderfull or strange, than the poore beginning of itselfe ...

Richard Knolles, The Generall Historie of the Turkes (1603)[5]

THe *Turke* is admired for nothing more, then his sodaine aduancement to so great an Empire ...which is become now a terrour to the whole world.

John Speed, A Prospect of the most famous parts of the World (1631)[6]

IT is neither agreed on by the best writers, nor well known to the *Turks* themselves, from whence the Empire of this barbarous Nation, the worlds present terrour, first took its small & obscure beginning.

Andrew Moore, A Compendious history of the Turks (1659)[7]

The above sentences all introduce seventeenth-century English accounts of the Ottoman Turks. They draw upon the same convention, describing the Ottomans as 'the terrour of the world'. The first opens Knolles' voluminous *Generall Historie* (1603). The second introduces a brief two-page description of 'the Turkish Empire' in Speed's *Prospect of the most famous parts of the World*, an atlas containing various maps with potted geographical and historical descriptions on the reverse. The last begins the main text of Moore's *A Compendious History of the Turks*, a book largely cribbed from Knolles' earlier work.[8] Speed and Moore's use of this expression was directly drawn from Knolles, virtually repeating his sentence. However, by the mid-seventeenth century the use of this phrase to describe the Ottoman Turks became ubiquitous to the point of cliché.[9]

It is possible that Knolles was the first to apply the phrase 'terror of the world' to the Ottomans; though he certainly did not coin it. The expression appears in a number of mid to late sixteenth century sources, notably continental chronicles. This phrase was often applied to Timur Khan (Tammerlaine). Paulo Giovio's *Elogia Virorum Bellica Virtute Illustrium* (1551) says of Timur, that he was called 'orbis terror & clades Orientis' ('terror of the world and scourge of the

---

[5] Richard Knolles, *Generall Historie London*, (London, 1603), p. 1.

[6] John Speed, *A Prospect of the Most Famous Parts of the World* (London, 1631), p. 35.

[7] Andrew Moore, *A Compendious History of the Turks* (London, 1660), p. 1.

[8] Moore claims a number of sources and does not mention Knolles explicitly. However, vast sections of text are recognisable as clumsily edited from the *Generall Historie*. Examples are too numerous to list. e.g. compare Moore (1660), pp. 366-7, 735-6 to Richard Knolles, *Generall Historie* (London, 1638), pp. 337-8, 763-4.

[9] For a longer survey of sixteenth and seventeenth century usages of 'terror of the world' see Anders Ingram, *Sixteenth and seventeenth century English Literature on the Ottoman Turks*, unpublished PhD (University of Durham, 2009), appendix 1.

east').[10] John Foxe's *Acts and Monuments* (1583) says 'Seb. Munsterus writing of this Tammerlanes recordeth that he ... was called terror orbis, the terror of the world'.[11] Nor was this description limited to chroniclers such as Foxe, Münster or Giovio. The most famous uses of this phrase come in Christopher Marlowe's *Tamburlaine the Great* (1590), where it occurs no fewer than eight times.[12] Giovio and Münster are of particular significance here as they are both among the authors whom Knolles lists explicitly as his main sources for the *Generall Historie*.[13]

By the sixteenth century Timur had become a historical staple. Godshalk notes that the semi-mythical story of 'Tammerlane' and 'Baiazet' appears 'in as many as one hundred Renaissance sources'.[14] The essential elements of this story were Timur's rise from humble origins, as a shepherd or minor noble, his rapid conquest of a vast empire, and defeat and humiliation of the proud and tyrannical Ottoman sultan Bayezid I at the battle of Ankara (1402). Thomas and Tydeman comment

... for Renaissance authors the cataclysmic phenomenon which was Tamburlaine supplied a graphic case-history through which to validate the legitimacy of relentless aspiration, deplore the vagaries of Fortune's favours, or regret the ruthlessness inseparable from outstanding martial prowess.[15]

They add that the events and details of this story were probably widely known in England before Marlowe's plays.

In addition to referring to Timur, the phrase 'terror of the world' (and similar variants such as 'terror to the world'), also appears in a number of other late sixteenth century usages. These tend to show substantial thematic overlap with the association with Timur. The first of these themes is the phrase's use to describe peoples viewed as barbarian invaders who serve as the instrument of divine punishment upon the wicked. The so called 'Bishop's Bible', sponsored by Archbishop Mathew Parker, gives an explanatory note to Ezekiel which says of 'elam', a fallen kingdom listed with Assyria, Meshech, Tubal and Edom, 'They which being a lyue were a terrour to the worlde'.[16] Similarly, Thomas Lodge's *The famous, true and historicall life of Robert second Duke of Normandy* (1591) applies this expression to the Babylonians. Later, seventeenth century examples apply the

---

[10]Pauli Iouii, *Elogia Virorum Bellica Virtute Illustrium* (Florence, 1551), p. 93.

[11] John Foxe, *Actes and Monuments* (London, 1583), vol. 1, p. 739.

[12] Christopher Marlowe, *Tamburlaine the Great* (London, 1590), pp. 7, 31, 83, 83, 83, 123, 124, 125.

[13] Knolles, (1603), sig. Avi^v.

[14] William Leigh Godshalk, *The Marlovian world picture* (The Hague, 1974), p. 103.

[15] Vivian Thomas and William Tydeman, *Christopher Marlowe* (London, 1994), p. 70.

[16] *The Holie Bible* (London, 1568), Ezechiel 32:24 marginal note, sig. Uv^v.

phrase to Attila the Hun and the Scythians.[17] A second theme common in usages of this expression is powerful monarchs, often eastern, or regarded as tyrants, and associated with rapid conquest or military success. Loys le Roy's *Aristotles Politiques* refers to 'Xerxes King of Persia, who had ben the terror of the world'.[18] Similarly, *England, or historicall map of the same Island* (1586) applies this phrase to Rome.[19] A third, and final, theme is the downfall of great men through hubris, such as Xerxes and Brutus, who *The lamentable tragedie of Locrine* (1595) introduces as 'So valient *Brute* the terror of the world'.[20] All three of these themes are of course present in the story of Timur, the barbarian conqueror, and instrument of divine wrath, who rapidly conquers a vast empire and humbles the proud tyrant Bayezid I.

In the late sixteenth century, the expression 'terror of the world' was a recognizable commonplace with several related thematic associations. These centre upon the story of Timur and the moral lessons his story was often taken to illustrate; divine punishment of hubris and tyranny, the transience of worldly glory and wealth, and the working of providence. Knolles' usage of the 'terror of the world' is entirely consistent with this picture. Knolles uses this phrase no fewer than ten times in the *Generall Historie*.[21] Three of these in fact refer to 'Tammerlane', who Knolles describes as '*The wrath of God*, and *Terrour of the World*'.[22] Knolles' retelling of the Timur story, reflects his sources, sixteenth century chronicles and lives such as Giovio and Münster, but also his wider understanding of Ottoman dynastic history. He uses it as a vehicle for pithy reflections with which to illustrate great moral lessons. Following 'Tammerlanes' imprisonment of 'Baiazet' Knolles has him declare, 'Behold a proud and cruell man, he deserueth to be chastised accordingly, and bee made an example vnto all the proud and cruell of the world'.[23] Tamerlane does not stop there but parades Bayezid around his kingdom using him as a footstool when mounting his horse and inflicting various other humiliations: 'all of which *Tamerlane* did, not so much for the hatred of the man, as to manifest the just judgement of God against the arrogant follie of the proud'.[24] Having lingered on the fall of the proud tyrant for

---

[17] Ingram (2009), appendix 1.

[18] Loys le Roy, *Aristotles Politiques* (London, 1598), p. 323.

[19] *Albions England, or historicall map of the same Island* (London, 1586), p. 66.

[20] W.S. *The lamentable tragedie of Locrine* (London, 1595), sig. A3ᵛ.

[21] Knolles (1603) in fact uses this expression ten times (with variant spellings 'terror' and 'terrour'), pp. Sig. Aivᵛ, 1, 3, 113, 176, 211, 220, 273, 391, 918. Seven of these usages refer to the Ottoman Turks.

[22] *Ibid.* (1603), p. 211.

[23] *Ibid.* (1603), p. 220.

[24] *Ibid.*

some time, Knolles reflects on the transitory nature of worldly power, commenting sagely, 'By this one daies event, is plainly to be seen the vncertantie of worldly things, and what small assurance euen the greatest haue in them'.[25] As we shall see in the third section of this article, these themes are intimately related to Knolles' wider presentation of Ottoman history throughout the *Generall Historie*.

This brief survey illustrates three key points. Firstly, it highlights the character of Knolles' key sources, continental Chronicles and Lives such as those of Giovio and Münster. Secondly, it suggests that Knolles not only drew incidents and events from these sources, but also images, language, concepts and models through which he interpreted the meaning of Ottoman history. Thirdly, it raises the question of why Knolles would use this expression as the opening line for his *Generall Historie*. The widespread contemporary examples of the phrase 'terror of the world', suggest it was a commonplace expression with strong associations. Many of Knolles' contemporaries, including at least two of his sources apply this phrase to Timur, and Knolles himself follows this usage. Further, Knolles' narration of the Timur story as an example of God's judgment upon pride and tyranny, reflect similar moralistic narratives common in his sources. Given the substantial synchronicities between Knolles' usage of this phrase, and those of his contemporaries, it does not seem far fetched to suggest that Knolles applied this expression to the Ottomans for deliberate rhetorical effect, to illustrate the moral themes central to his history.

CRITICAL READINGS

Much of the modern scholarly attention directed at Knolles has addressed, or directly focussed upon, the expression 'the terror of the world'. This phrase has often been read as a convenient epithet for early modern English perceptions of the Ottoman Turks, reflecting English reactions to the rapid military expansion of the Ottoman Empire in the early to mid sixteenth century, as well as its fearfully alien religious and cultural character.

Castigating images of violent and lascivious Turks abound in English texts of the early modern period. Famous among these is Richard Knolles's 1603 assessment of the Turks as the "present terror of the world" (1), a raging threat to Christian welfare and morality. This is the figure derived from a century of Ottoman military victories in Europe, including the capture of Belgrade, Rhodes, and most of Hungary in the 1520s, and the later campaigns in Vienna, Southern Italy and Corfu, Western Italy, Malta and Poland, and capturing Cyprus. This is the figure looming offstage in the opening moments of both Marlowe's *Jew of Malta*

---

[25] *Ibid.*

and Shakespeare's *Othello* when the action is interrupted and redirected by the threat of Turkish invasion. And this is the figure humbling European armies in plays like *II Tamburlaine*, *Soliman and Perseda*, and *The Corageous Turk*.[26]

Burton makes 'the terror of the world' a cipher for the pejorative images which 'abound' in early modern English texts, alien and in stark opposition to Christendom. These images are a direct response to Ottoman military advances into Europe (Burton does not mention Ottoman conquests in Egypt, North Africa and the Holy Lands). Vitkus treats this phrase in a similar light. Contextualising a discussion of Marlowe's *Tamburlaine* he comments

Clearly, the *Tamburlaine* plays were meant to provide pleasure in the spectacle of Tamburlaine defeating the imperial power that Knolles calls the "the present terror of the earth," the Turk, and in subduing other Islamic potentiates such as the Persian emperor and the sultan of Egypt. Anxieties about the Turks' growing dominion find relief in the fantasy of Turkish defeat and humiliation.[27]

Interestingly, while Vitkus allows Knolles' use of 'terror of the world' to stand as representative of English views of the Ottomans, he does not discuss Marlowe's earlier usage.

Another major theme in critical evaluations of English depictions of the Ottoman Turks is an emphasis on their characteristic ambiguity and ambivalence. Englishmen viewed the Ottomans with not only fear, but also fascination. Again the 'terror of the world' has been taken, by critics, as representative of wider English views. MacLean introduces the term 'Imperial Envy' to describe this phenomenon.

Envy- that ambivalent and complex structure of feeling that blends malicious hatred with admiration of another's excellence – in this imperial form had inherited a traditional enemy in the Ottoman Empire: the 'present terrour of the world' as Richard Knolles and others once thought.[28]

Barbour captures the balance of these conflicting imperatives through the metaphor of a mobile.

The book's opening words- "The glorious Empire of the Turkes, the present terrour of the world" (1) – set a characteristic pattern of ambivalence. The parallel phrases span alternate views … Knolles' periodic sentences, like weighty mobiles, lift incompatible claims into restless balance.[29]

---

[26] Jonathan Burton, *Traffic and Turning: Islam and English Drama, 1579-1624*, (Cranbury, 2005) p. 37.

[27] Daniel J. Vitkus, *Turning Turk: English theater and the multicultural Mediterranean, 1570*-1630 (New York, 2003), p. 50.

[28] Gerald MacLean, *Looking East: English writing and the Ottoman empire before 1800* (Basingstoke, 2007), p. 208.

[29] Richmond Barbour, *Before Orientalism* (Cambridge, 2003), pp. 17-18.

This 'characteristic pattern of ambivalence' is supported by my earlier survey of contemporary usages of the 'terror of the world'. Usage of this phrase was not confined to a pejorative sense, to refer to objects of terror and fear. With its overtones of unstoppable military might, rapid conquest and imperial might this expression was often also applied to widely admired figures such as Caesar, Alexander the Great, and of course Timur.[30] Thus, Knolles' use of 'terror of the world' to describe the Ottomans can be read in context as an attempt to portray them, not only as a terrifying and alien threat to Christendom, but also as a mighty and glorious imperial power, to be admired as well as feared.

In treating Knolles' usage of the 'terror of the world' as symptomatic of early modern English views of the Ottomans at large, the above readings situate this phrase within, and indeed central to, a discourse of English phrases, images and associations, through which the Ottomans (and perhaps also Islam and the 'East') might be depicted and conceived. However, my attempts to contextualise Knolles' use of the 'terror of the world', also questions the critical readings advanced above. My reading suggests that Knolles did not simply reflect wider English views of the Ottomans with a carefully crafted and memorable turn of phrase. Rather, I have suggested that Knolles drew on a widely used commonplace, and was pursuing a specific rhetorical agenda in choosing to apply this phrase, and its associations with divine punishment, tyranny, hubris and providence, to the Ottomans.

The issue at stake here is fundamentally one of discourse. A critical reading of Knolles' use of 'terror of the world' is dependent upon the context in which this phrase is situated by the critic. The figure of Edward Said looms large over theoretical approaches to English writing on the Ottomans, Islam and 'East'. Several of the authors mentioned above, notably Matar, propound significant critiques of Said's *Orientalism* thesis. However, Said's summary of his topic as 'that collection of dreams, images, and vocabularies available to anyone who has tried to talk about what lies east of the dividing line',[31] remains an apt characterisation of the field, even if his precise formulation of it can be questioned on many levels.

In response to the weaknesses of 'Orientalism' as a model for understanding early modern English perceptions of the Ottomans, alternatives have been sought, notably the notion of the Islamic or Turkish 'Other'. The nuanced and

---

[30] In the seventeenth century usage of this phrase became broader still and I have found it applied in numerous contexts including Attlia the Hun, Gustavus Adolphus (King of Sweden), the Spanish Armada, France, England and even God, see Ingram (2009), appendix 1.

[31] Edward W. Said, *Orientalism* (London, 1978), p.73.

subtle refinements of this conceptual construct forwarded by critics such as Vitkus and Birchwood provide a schema through which one might well interpret elements of the *Generall Historie* and relate them coherently (perhaps too coherently) to contemporary English depictions of the Ottoman Empire and the 'East'.[32] However, while these models have their strengths, my earlier discussion suggests that contemporary English discourse on the Ottoman Turks, Islam and the 'East', alone, does not provide a specific enough context to allow a critical reading of Knolles' *Generall Historie,* and his usage of the 'terror of the world'. The question becomes how we can best theorise a description such as the 'terror of the world' in a way which allows us to contextualise it in a meaningfully historical way.

In theorising his notion of discourse Skinner comments, 'any act of communication will always constitute the taking up of some determinate position in relation to some pre-existing conversation or argument'.[33] He continues '[t]he appropriate context for understanding the point of such writers' utterances will always be whatever context enables us to appreciate the nature of the intervention constituted by their utterances'.[34] In other words, the contexts the historian needs to examine most urgently are those which help to explain what the author was 'doing' in making certain 'utterances', and fundamentally, what the nature and mode of those 'utterances' was.

Pocock makes a similar point, he defines discourse as

a sequence of speech acts performed by agents within a context furnished ultimately by social practices and historical situations, but also- and in some ways more immediately- by the political languages by means of which the acts are to be performed.[35]

This definition is substantially denser and more technical than Skinner's summary of his position. However, it drives towards a fundamentally similar set of questions. The contexts in which we must read a discourse are not only historical and social, but also, and often more immediately, the 'political languages' through which the debate is conducted. Pocock defines such a 'political language' as

a distinctive mode of utterance: a 'language' or 'rhetoric', therefore, possessing its own terminology, style and conventions, and revealing as we come to know it the implications and assumptions on which it rests and from which it regularly proceeds towards conclusions...[36]

---

[32] Vitkus (2003), pp. 1-12; Matthew Birchwood, *Staging Islam in England: drama and culture, 1640-1685* (Cambridge, 2007), pp. 4-14.

[33] Quentin Skinner, Visions of Politics (Cambridge, 2002), vol. 1, p. 115.

[34] *Ibid.,* p. 116.

[35] J.G.A. Pocock, Political Thought and History, (Cambridge, 2009). p. 67.

[36] *Ibid.,* p. 76-77.

Applying these models of discourse to Knolles' *Generall Historie* raises new questions.

What arguments and discourses was Knolles' work engaged in? What distinctive 'modes of utterance', and 'terminology, style and conventions', did Knolles draw upon? What 'implications and assumptions' did they rest upon? What is the appropriate context for understanding this work and the utterances it contains? Knolles' *Generall Historie* is a long and complex work, and a short essay has limited scope to examine issues such as these. Nonetheless the next section of this essay will address these questions through a, necessarily brief, examination of Knolles' methodology and sources, and the wider context of late sixteenth century English historical writing.

KNOLLES THE HISTORIAN

Richard Knolles was the school master of Roger Manwood's Free School at Sandwich. He wrote the *Generall Historie* at the behest of his original patron's son Peter Manwood, whom Knolles describes as 'the first moouer of me to take this great Worke in hand, and my continuall and onely comfort and helper therein'.[37] Manwood's motivations in encouraging this work remain somewhat obscure. It seems unlikely that the inception and expansion of the English Levant trade from 1580 acted as a stimulus, as the *Generall Historie* (1603) at no point mentions or alludes to the English trade. A more likely motivation is the Ottoman-Hapsburg 'Long War' of 1593-1606. Not only does Knolles describe this conflict in detail, but several contemporaries who translated lengthy continental chronicles on the Ottomans into English present this as their motivation. Examples include Ralph Carr's *Mahumetane or Turkish history* (1600), Abraham Hartwell's translation of Minadoi's *The History of the Warres betweene the Turkes and the Persians* and the anonymous author of *The Policy of the Turkish Empire* (1597).[38] In Pocock's terms, the social practices and historical situations which form the context to the *Generall Historie* are the 'encouragement' of Knolles' patron Manwood, to whom he owed his livelihood, and the English response to the vivid threat of continued Ottoman military expansion into continental Europe.

Peter Manwood provided Knolles not only with motivation, and livelihood, but also the scholarly resources necessary for an undertaking such as the *Generall Historie*. In 1617 Peter Manwood was listed as one of the surviving members of

---

[37] Knolles (1603), sig. Aiii[r].

[38] Uberto Foglietta, trs. Ralf Carr, *The Mahumetane or Turkish Historie* (London, 1600), sig. B2[v]; Giovanni Tommaso Minadoi, trs. Abraham Hartwell, *History of the Warres Betvveene the Turkes and the Persians* (London, 1595), sigs. A3[v]-A4[r]; *The Policy of the Turkish Empire* (London, 1597), sig. Aiii[v].

the, by then defunct, Society of Antiquaries. Parry links Manwood's connections to the Society of Antiquaries, and prominent members such as Robert Cotton, William Camden, John Stow, Abraham Hartwell and Archbishop Whitgift, to the sources which Knolles drew upon while writing his history.[39] Knolles' 'indvction' helpfully includes a list containing 'the names of the Authors whom we especially used in the collecting and writing of the *Historie of the Turkes*'.[40] These sources are for the most part Latin chronicles. Amongst them are several translated into Latin from Greek and even some from Turkish, notably from 'Leunclavius' (who worked from Italian and Greek manuscripts deriving from Ottoman originals as well as some Ottoman texts).[41] The majority are, however, simply continental Latin chronicles, many of which we have already encountered. In particular, Knolles mentions Giovio and Minadoi (whom Hartwell translated into English). In addition, Knolles mentions some general works, not specifically on the Ottomans, which he presumably employed for reference. These include the famous geographical works of Abraham Ortelius, Sebastian Münster and the copious historical and geographical writings of Æneas Sylvius (Pope Pius II).

By examining what Knolles says about his sources and comparing and contrasting the work he produced to theirs we can begin to answer the kinds of questions Skinner and Pocock's models of discourse suggest. Notably, what preexisting debates and conversations did Knolles draw upon and what was his stance in relation to these? What conventions, terminology and assumptions did he draw from these? What discourse was he contributing to?

Knolles describes his task with a rhetorical question.

to make proofe if out of the dispersed workes of many right worthie men, I could set downe one orderly and continuat Historie of this so mightie and Empire … and as it were vnder one view and at one shew, to lay open vnto the Christian reader, what I was glad to seeke for out of the defused labours of so many. [42]

Knolles' criteria for selecting material out of this 'varietie, or more truly to say, contrarietie' gave priority to 'such as were themselues present and as it were eyc-witnesses'. Following which he 'gathered so much as [he]could of that remained, out of the works of such, as being themselues men of great place, and well acquainted with the great and worthie personages of their time, might from their mouths as from certain Oracles report the undoubted truth'. Finally he was forced to rely on 'other learned and credible authors'. There are two main points

---

[39] Parry (2004), p. 7.
[40] For a general treatment of Knolles' sources, see Parry (2004), appendix III, pp. 111-45.
[41] *Ibid.*, pp. 119, 137 n. 62.
[42] Knolles (1603), sig. Av[v].

here. Firstly, Knolles aimed to gather his material out of diverse sources and work it into one coherent narrative, rather than simply repeating sections of his source material, as the translators and compliers of chronicles had done. Secondly, all of his sources for the edition of 1603 are textual, and none are English.[43] Despite Knolles' pretension to the ideal of the humanist historian, as the man at or near the centre of events who records them, such as 'Ceasar' or 'Iouious' (Giovio), his sources are essentially books, largely chronicles and chronicle compilations.

The contrasts and comparisons between Knolles' work and his sources are revealing. For example, the *Chronicorum Turcicorum* (1578), a chronicle compilation set into Latin by Phillip Lonicer, was drawn on heavily by Knolles.[44] This chronicle is made up of works by several authors and including Marin Barleti, Antonio Menavino, 'Antoniuos Sabellicus and 'Jacobus Fontanus', all of which are sources mentioned by Knolles. Consulting compilations such as Lonicer's was probably one of the ways in which Knolles was able to gain access to such a large number of sources. There are other indications that Lonicer was a major source for Knolles. The structure of the first section of Lonicer's work, *Turcorum Origio, Principes, Imperatores, usque ad Selimum II*, is very similar to that of Knolles' *Generall Historie*. Each begins with a short account of the origins of the Turks, followed by an account of the crusades, which then leads on to a reign by reign account of the lives of the Ottoman sultans. Indeed, the similarity does not end there. Each individual 'life' begins with an engraving of the sultan in question, underneath which appears an epigraphic poem, drawing together moralistic themes; a format Knolles copied. This is confirmed by the images themselves. The Lawrence Johnson engravings from *Generall Historie* (1603) include some which are clearly copied from the Joost Aman engravings that appeared in Lonicer's work. Further, some of the epigraphic poems are cited as 'Phi Lonicer. Hist. Tur. Li. I.'.[45]These similarities are striking enough to suggest that Knolles used Lonicer's summary of Ottoman history as a model for his own account.

The contrasts between the *Generall Historie* and *Chronicorum Turcicorum* are even more revealing. The first of these contrasts is the level of detail and stylistic

---

[43] The second edition of 1610 contains a small amount of material from first hand accounts. Later editions were supplemented by disparate 'continuations' by various authors.

[44] Phillip Lonicer, *Chronicorum* (Frankfurt, 1578). Lonicer's work is a Latinised version of the *Türkische Chronica* (Frankfurt, 1577), translated and complied by one Heinrich Müller, published the previous year by the same publisher (Sigmund Feyerabend).

[45] John H. Astington, 'The "unrecorded portrait" of Edward Alleyn.' *Shakespeare quarterly*, 44, no. 1 (1993), pp. 73-86. Astington misidentifies Knolles' source for the engravings as Müller's *Türkische Chronica*, which contains the same Joost Aman engravings. Astington identifies other sources for Johnston's engravings as Boissard's *Vitae et Icones Sultanorum* and Giovio's *De Rebus et Vitis Imperatorum Turcarum*.

assimilation to which Knolles aspires. While Lonicer's lives of the sultans are brief affairs, comprising only the first third of the first of his three tomes, Knolles' lives are exhaustive. On a more fundamental level, however, the greatest contrast is that while Lonicer's work remains a somewhat *ad hoc* collection of translated chronicle excerpts, several of which overlap, Knolles is much more ambitious and systematic. Although Knolles draws on many such chronicle sources, and the classic chronicle format of lives and years, he assimilates these sources into one stylistically coherent and definitive account. His aspiration to produce a definitive, comprehensive and edifying History of the Ottoman Empire was far more ambitious than either his English contemporaries or most of his sources. The *Generall Historie* is a different *kind* of book than the *Chronicorum Turcicorum*.

It seems appropriate to place Knolles' *Generall Historie* into what Woolf has characterised as 'the borderland between history and chronicle in Renaissance England [from Vergil to Stow] … a final humanist-influenced stage in the transition of English historiography from the chronicle into the various forms that developed in the late sixteenth and seventeenth centuries'.[46] Woolf characterises these 'borderline' works as more detailed and drawing on a greater variety of sources than earlier chronicles (which often merely replicated their source) but still essentially in the same genre. Such a description might certainly stretch to Knolles. However, Woolf's attribution of a 'dry and abrupt narrative style' would not. This is no mere quibble as historiographical arguments regarding contemporary definitions such as 'historian', 'antiquary', and indeed 'chronicler', have emphasised the role of eloquence and style as central to the early modern English ideal of the historian.[47]

The importance of formal characteristics, such as style and coherence to Knolles' conception of 'History' is evident in his attitude to his 'Turkish' sources, primarily the translations of Leunclavius.[48]

[Y]ea the Turkish Histories and Chronicles themselues (from whom the greatest light for the continuation of the Historie was in reason to haue beene expected) being in the declaration of their owne affaires (according to their barbarous manner) so sparing and short, as that they may of right be accounted rather short rude notes than iust Histories, rather pointing things out, than declaring the same; and that with such obscuritie, by changing the auntient and vsuall names as well of whole kingdomes, countries and prouinces, as of cities, townes, riuers, mountaines, and other places, yea, oftentimes of men themselues, into other strange and barbarous names of their own deuising, in such sort, as might well stay an intentiue reader,

---

[46] D.R. Woolf, 'Genre into artifact: the decline of the English chronicle in the sixteenth century.' *Sixteenth century journal* 19, no. 3 (1988), p. 329.

[47] D. R. Woolf, *The idea of history in early Stuart England: erudition, ideology, and 'the light of truth' from the accession of James I to the civil war* (Toronto, 1990).

[48] On Leunclavius' 'Turkish' sources see Parry (2004), appendix III pp. 113-118.

and depriue him of the pleasure together with the profit he might otherwise expect by the reading thereof; whereunto to giue order, perspicuitie, and light, would require no small trauell and paine. Not to speake in the meane time of the diuersitie of the reports in the course of the whole Historie, such as is oftentimes most hard, if not altogether impossible to reconcile.[49]

The modern reader may smile at the irony of Knolles' exasperation with 'strange and barbarous names of their own deuising', given that he himself intended to write a 'Sarasin Historie', and note that Knolles assumes the fault lies with the 'Turkish' chronicle rather than the translator. However, this passage also reveals much of Knolles' attitudes to the purpose of history and the historian's purpose. These attitudes apply beyond Leunclavius' chronicles, to the 'sea and world of matter' from which Knolles drew his information. Fundamentally, the task of the historian is to bring 'order, perspicuitie, and light', and to rescue the reader from the 'obscure' and 'reconcile' conflicting accounts. As Woolf puts it 'the task facing the Elizabethan author was … not the discovery of new facts, or the reweaving of the old into new cloth, but the harmonizing of conflicting accounts'.[50]

Knolles' task as the first major English historian of the Turks was not to reassess the Ottomans and their place in history, or to discover new information about them. Rather Knolles sought to harmonise existing accounts and points of consensus regarding the Ottomans and shape them into a stylistically coherent account which elevated the topic and gave it meaning through a clear and moralistic framework. In this regard Knolles was singularly successful and it is difficult not to admire the remarkable consistency of style that the *Generall Historie* displays, even given its length and the diversity of sources from which Knolles drew. Knolles' scorn of the 'Turkish Histories and Chronicles' stems not only from their 'rude' and 'barbarous manner' (i.e. their lack of polished rhetorical style), but also their 'obscure' deviation from the details of his other sources. However, it is Knolles' comment that these accounts are not true histories, 'rather pointing things out than declaring the same', that is most revealing. The implication is that Knolles regarded the role of the historian as far more than merely recounting facts, instead resting fundamentally on his ability to give them meaning by harmonising and presenting them within a wider moral, and indeed scriptural, framework.

RHETORIC AND HISTORY

Knolles' great achievement was bringing coherence and order to this source

---

[49] Knolles (1603), sig. Av^v.
[50] Woolf (1990), p. 34.

material through the use of a grand moralising narrative and steady rhetorical style. By 'rhetoric' I mean the language, imagery, allusions and themes through which Knolles structured the episodes of his *Generall Historie*, and through which he directed his reader to consider the role and meaning of the Ottoman dynasty in 'History'. This rhetoric is nowhere sharper and clearer than the opening paragraph of the 'Authors indvction to the Christian Reader'.

THE long and still declining state of the Christian commonweale, with the vtter ruine and subuersion of the Empire of the East, and many other most glorious kingdomes and prouinces of the Christians; neuer to be sufficiently lamented, might with the due consideration thereof worthily mooue euen a right stonie heart to ruth: but therewith also to call to remembrance the dishonour done vnto the blessed name of our Sauiour Christ Iesus, the desolation of his Church here millitant vpon earth, the dreadfull danger daily threatened vnto the poore remainder thereof, the millions of soules cast headlong into eternall destruction, the infinit numbers of wofull Christians (whose grieuous gronings under the heauie yoke of infidelitie, no tongue is able to expresse) with the carelesnesse of the great for the redresse thereof, might giue iust cause vnto any good Christian to sit downe, and with the heauie Prophet to say as he did of *Hierusalem*: O how hath the Lord darkened the daughter of Sion in his wrath ? and cast downe from heauen vnto the earth the beautie of Israel, and remembered not his footstoole in the day of his wrath?

lament.
Hieremie, cap. Secundo. [51]

The most significant feature of this passage is the biblical quotation with which it ends. The quotation is taken from the Old Testament book of Lamentations, which describes the aftermath of the destruction of Jerusalem and Judah by the Babylonians, who took the Israelites into exile and captivity. Chapter I describes the desolation of Jerusalem, while Chapter II, from which the quote is taken, explains these events as God's punishment of a sinful Israel, and presents the Babylonians as the rod of God's wrath.[52] However, the passage does not merely end with a quotation from the Book of Lamentations but is highly reminiscent of its themes and style throughout. Although, in general, Knolles tends to use sentences of an unwieldy length to a modern eye, this passage seems to push this tendency to its limits and resembles nothing so much as a dense block of printed verse, or indeed a monotonous litany or dirge. This similarity combined with the repetitive dwelling on imagery of loss, despair, desolation, destruction and sorrow, culminating in the explicit reference, suggests Knolles intended the entire passage as an allusion to Lamentations.

Through his appropriation of this biblical text, Knolles is placing his account of the history of the Turks, Ottoman and pre-Ottoman, within the frame of

---

[51] Knolles (1603), sig. Aiv^r.
[52] 'I am the man that thorowe the rodde of his wrath have experience of miserie' Lam. III.1. *The Holie Bible conteynyng the olde testament and the new* (London, 1568), sig. Si^r.

Biblical history. The biblical nation of Israel is elided with 'the Christian Commonweale', in which Knolles includes both Latin and Eastern Christians. Thus the Babylonian captivity of Israel, which forms the context of Lamentations, although not explicitly mentioned, can be understood as an allegory of the status of Christians suffering under the Ottoman 'yoke'. Knolles' formulation uses a biblical allegory to suggest that as the Babylonians were God's chastisement of a sinful 'Israel', so the Ottoman Turks fulfil a similar role towards the 'Christian commonweale'.

Knolles' use of Lamentations, with which he begins his 'indvction', serves similar rhetorical purposes to his use of the commonplace, 'terror of the world'. Knolles' reference to Lamentations alludes to the scriptural Babylonians, and the phrase 'terror of the world' was applied to the Babylonians by several late sixteenth century Englishmen. Further, the crux of both Lamentations and the Timur story, with which this phrase was so heavily associated, are God's use of barbarian conquerors as agents of divine retribution. Just as the Babylonians are the rod of God's wrath, Knolles refers to Timur as 'the wrath of God'. Knolles uses the references to both Lamentations and the 'terror of the world' to frame the events of Ottoman History as the workings of providence and scriptural history, specifically divine punishment. However, a detailed reading of Knolles' rhetoric is only possible after examining the contexts which illustrate the 'mode' of these utterances; the sources from which he drew not only the incidents of his *Generall Historie* but much of its assumptions, style and conventions. Ideally, this would also include a detailed discussion of other concepts central to Knolles' understanding of 'History'. Such concepts include the cyclical nature of history (particularly in relation to the rise and fall of Empires), prophecy, and most importantly, eschatology. However, detailed discussion of these is beyond the scope of this present essay.

CONCLUSIONS

This essay has argued that Knolles' *Generall Historie* drew upon, and to a large extent might be read within, a continental discourse of Latin chronicles of Ottoman dynastic history. By both comparing and contrasting some of Knolles' terminology, imagery, format and style to that of his sources I have sought to illustrate Knolles' conception of 'History', and argued that this was central to the meanings and moral values he attributed to the events of Ottoman history. In Pocock's terms I have argued that to produce a critical reading of the *Generall Historie* we first need to situate this work in relation to an established continental 'discourse' of Ottoman dynastic history, and the contemporary 'language' of historical writing, or, 'History'.

I have contrasted this reading of the *Generall Historie* to the treatment it has received from modern scholars, which have situated this work primarily in the context of early modern English discourse on the Ottomans (and even Islam and the 'East'). I have sought to illustrate the contrast in these two approaches by a detailed examination of Knolles' famous expression the 'terror of the world'. Numerous modern scholars have treated this phrase as representative of wider early modern English views of the Ottomans. They have read into it either the fear of a powerful non-Christian, non-European 'Other', that nonetheless had to be confronted, or the ambiguity which also seems to characterise English depictions of the Ottomans. My reading situates Knolles' use of the 'terror of the world' within the context of its use by his sources, and also this phrase's widespread contemporary usage and associations as a commonplace. I have then argued that Knolles' highly visible and deliberate use of this phrase as the first line of the *Generall Historie* pursues a cogent agenda, which is consistent with his rhetoric and understanding of 'History' throughout this work. Relating Knolles' usage of the 'terror of the world' to contemporary and later English depictions of the Ottoman Turks is not wrong, per se. However, to do so without examining the context of this expression, and therefore missing the point that it is fundamentally a commonplace expression which Knolles utilised, rather than a striking phrase of his own creation, is a substantial misreading.

It should be emphasised that I am not seeking to provide a detailed critique of the work of the scholars examined above and their models, or the field at large. In particular, I am not attempting to critique, or discard, the notion of the 'Other' as a conceptual construct. Rather, I am presenting an alternative model, which, I have argued, provides substantial advantages when reading a text such as Knolles' *Generall Historie*. It is worth reflecting that Skinner and Pocock's models of discourse developed from debates within Political History and the History of Ideas. They are, therefore, particularly suited to contextualising a lengthy scholarly work such as the *Generall Historie*. This approach is perhaps less well suited to shorter sources such as pamphlet literature and ballads, where authorship is uncertain, or plays, in which specific textual contexts and sources are often much harder to establish (certainly in contrast to Knolles' convenient list of main sources). It is notable that Vitkus, Birchwood, Dimmock, Barbour and Burton are all primarily, though far from exclusively, concerned with drama. Further, I do not wish to deny that Knolles' *Generall Historie*, in some sense, engaged in a discourse of English depictions and views of the Ottoman Turks. It is certainly the case that a very large body of seventeenth century authors, far beyond those writing historical works, drew information from the *Generall Historie*, cited Knolles as an authority on the Ottoman Turks and alluded to his work. However, they are again beyond the scope of the current essay.

Bibliography

Albions England, or historicall map of the same Island (London, 1586: STC 25082A), in Early English Books Online, http://gateway.proquest.com/openurl?ctx_ver=Z39. 88-2003&res_id=xri:eebo&rft_id =xri:eebo:citation:99854796

Annotations upon the Holy Bible, being a continuation of Mr. Pools work (London, 1685: Wing P2823), in Early English Books Online, http://gateway.proquest.com/ openurl?ctx_ver=Z39.88-2003&res_id =xri:eebo&rft_id=xri:eebo:citation:12601746

Astington, John H., 'The "unrecorded portrait" of Edward Alleyn.' *Shakespeare quarterly*, 44, no. 1 (1993), 73-86.

Barbour, Richmond, *Before Orientalism* (Cambridge, 2003).

Birchwood, Matthew, *Staging Islam in England: drama and culture, 1640-1685* (Cambridge, 2007).

Bodin, Jean, trs. Richard Knolles and ed. Kenneth D. McRae, *The Six Books of a Commonweale* (Cambridge, 1962).

Burton, Jonathan, *Traffic and Turning: Islam and English Drama, 1579-1624* (Cranbury, 2005).

Chew, Samuel C., *The crescent and the rose: Islam and England during the Renaissance* (New York, 1937).

Çirakman, Asli, *From the "Terror of the World" to the "Sick Man of Europe": European images of Ottoman empire and society from the sixteenth century to the nineteenth* (New York, 2002).

Dimmock, Matthew, *New Turkes* (Aldershot, 2005).

Foglietta, Uberto, trs. Ralf Carr, *The Mahumetane or Turkish Historie* (London, 1600: STC 17997).

Foxe, John, *Actes and Monuments* (London, 1583: STC 11225).

Godshalk, William Leigh, *The Marlovian world picture* (The Hague, 1974).

The Holie Bible (London, 1568: STC 2099), in Early English Books Online, available at http://gateway.proquest.com/openurl?ctx_ver=Z39.88-2003&res_id=xri:eebo&rft_id=xri:eebo:citation: 99857223

Ingram, Anders. *Sixteenth and Seventeenth English literature on the Ottoman Turks*, unpublished PhD (University of Durham, 2009).

Iouii, Pauli, *Elogia Virorum Bellica Virtute Illustrium* (Florence, 1551).

Knolles, Richard, *The Generall Historie of the Turkes* (London, 1603: STC 15051).

Knolles, Richard, *The Generall Historie of the Turkes* (London, 1610: STC 15052).

Le Roy, Loys, *Aristotles Politiques* (London, 1598: STC 760), in Early English Books Online, http://gateway.proquest.com/openurl?ctx_ver=Z39.88-2003&res_id=xri:eebo&rft_id=xri:eebo:citation: 99842553

Lonicer, Phillip, *Chronicorum Turcicorum* (Frankfurt am Main, 1578).

Marlowe, Christopher, *Tamburlaine the Great* (London, 1590: STC 17425), in Early English Books Online, http://gateway.proquest.com/openurl?ctx_ver=Z39.88-2003&res_id=xri:eebo&rft_id=xri:eebo:citation: 99857253

Matar, N. I., *Islam in Britain, 1558-1685* (Cambridge, 1998).

Matar, N. I., *Turks, Moors and Englishmen* (New York, 1999).

MacLean, Gerald, *Looking East: English writing and the Ottoman empire before 1800* (Basingstoke, 2007).

Minadoi, Giovanni Tommaso, trs. Abraham Hartwell, *History of the Warres Betweene the Turkes and the Persians* (London, 1595: STC 17943), in Early English Books Online, http://gateway.proquest.com/ openurl?ctx_ver=Z39.88-2003&res_id=xri:eebo&rft_id=xri:eebo:image:23114

Moore, Andrew, *A Compendious History of the Turks* (London, 1660: Wing M2530), in Early English Books Online, http://gateway.proquest.com/ openurl?ctx_ver=Z39.88-2003&res_id=xri:eebo&rft_ id =xri:eebo:citation:12254782

Müller, Heinrich, *Türkische Chronica* (Frankfurt am Main, 1577).

Parry, V. J., *Richard Knolles' History of the Turks* (Istanbul, 2004).

The Policy of the Turkish Empire (London, 1597: STC 24335), in Early English Books Online, http://gateway.proquest.com/openurl?ctx_ver=Z39.88-2003&res_id=xri:eebo&rft_id=xri:eebo: image:19306

S., W., *The lamentable tragedie of Locrine* (London, 1595: STC 21528), in Early English Books Online, http://gateway.proquest.com/openurl?ctx_ver=Z39.88-2003&res_id=xri:eebo&rft_id =xri:eebo:citation:99842019

Said, Edward W., *Orientalism* (London, 1978).

Skinner, Quentin, *Visions of Politics*, vol. 1 (Cambridge, 2002).

Speed, John, *A Prospect of the Most Famous Parts of the Vvorld* (London, 1646: Wing S4882A), in Early English Books Online, http://gateway.proquest.com/ openurl?ctx_ver=Z39.88-2003&res_id =xri:eebo&rft_ id=xri:eebo:citation:99830357

Thomas, Vivien, and William Tydeman, *Christopher Marlowe: the plays and their sources* (London, 1994).

Vitkus, Daniel J., 'Early modern Orientalism: representations of Islam in sixteenth and seventeenth-century Europe.' in *Western views of Islam in medieval and early modern Europe*, eds. M. Frassetto and D. Blanks (New York, 1999), 207-30.

Vitkus, Daniel J., *Turning Turk: English theater and the multicultural Mediterranean, 1570-1630* (New York, 2003).

Woodhead, Christine, 'The History of an Historie: Richard Knolles' *General Historie of the Turkes*, 1603-1700.' in *Journal of Turkish Studies*, ed. Şinasi Tekin. (Cambridge, 2002), 349-57.

Woolf, D. R., 'Genre into artifact: the decline of the English chronicle in the sixteenth century.' *Sixteenth century journal* 19, no. 3 (1988), 321-54.

Woolf, D.R., *The idea of history in early Stuart England: erudition, ideology, and 'the light of truth' from the accession of James I to the civil war* (Toronto, 1990).

Solitude and silence:
some early modern English 'landscapes'

ALASTAIR BAIN
Independent Researcher

INTRODUCTION

Using three specific examples, this essay considers some cultural-historical aspects of solitude and silence in England in the three centuries from 1500 to 1800. It attempts to establish the extent to which people, under certain conditions, sought and reacted to solitude and whether silence was assumed to be an inevitable adjunct. Further objectives are to explore these points alongside ideas of privacy in early modern *mentalités* and to consider whether feelings of wistful recall for the past (or what we would now term as 'nostalgia') were in any way significant.

In academic studies the phenomenological approach, especially in the case of silence, has been characteristic of disciplines such as philosophy, linguistics and semiotics. On the other hand, a cultural-historical perspective on areas such as family dynamics, illness and debility, justice and retribution, and enthusiasm or indifference towards religion affords a more specific understanding of beliefs, practices and attitudes relating to solitude and silence. The above points have been considered elsewhere to varying degrees.[1] For present purposes, however, I wish to set out some thoughts against a background of three early modern 'landscapes' of solitude and silence – town and country; gardens; and the Christian discourse of 'wilderness'. Interwoven with these 'landscapes' are some references to power, misfortune, obedience and social anxieties. Questions of status intrude and while my sources are inclined to focus on the upper and middling ranks of society, the voices of others are included whenever possible.

The term 'solitude' and its cognates inevitably imply a sense of apartness, seclusion and loneliness. These meanings are all confirmed by the *Oxford English Dictionary*, quoting examples from not later than 1800; there are few indications of positive or negative associations, and silence is not taken to be an inevitable accompaniment to solitude. Understandably, dictionaries aim for semantic precision, but my theme throughout rests on the premise that solitude and silence are not absolute conditions. For example, while silence in early modern society

---

[1] Alastair Bain, 'A Cultural History of Silence in England, 1500–1800' (unpublished PhD thesis, University of Aberdeen, 2008).

Explorations in Cultural History: Essays for Peter Gabriel McCaffery,
edd. David F. Smith & H. Philsooph (Aberdeen 2010)   ISBN 978-0-9567059-0-7

may have been partly distinguished by modulations in speech, it did not necessarily rely for its expression on language, or indeed on any discernible sounds. In some situations silence was figured in such behaviour, gesture and demeanour as were usually, but not invariably, appropriate to the canons of the time. Two examples are submission and forbearance – fundamental aspects of a godly life which were expected to be made evident through non-verbal means just as much as through modification of speech. Similarly, solitude is capable of a wider range of expression. In *Shakespeare and the Solitary Man*, Janette Dillon suggests a definition which refers to Elizabethan times but, in my view, holds good for the longer early modern period:

Solitude … is a relative term, varying according to context. It can suggest the country life, the contemplative life, the melancholy humour, the refusal of public office, the studious disposition. It can be classified, as it was by contemporaries, as referring to time, place or the mind. It can be voluntary or involuntary, … an expression of self-love, love of the community, or love of God.[2]

Roger Chartier acknowledges that changes in attitude to solitude are useful markers of socio-cultural change during the early modern period. He suggests, for example, that in the sixteenth century, at the high point of the culture of civility, an incompatibility between civility and intimacy gave rise to the need for a personal space that was nevertheless public, within which the requirements of civility could be satisfied. A degree of 'public solitude' was therefore effected through the distancing of the body and the avoidance of any touches or glances which might be construed as intimate.[3] This would have been further enhanced in an environment of relative silence, partly achievable by not speaking. Private solitude was considered to be appropriate only for prayer[4] or any expression of personal feelings within an intimate relationship with God, whether these were silent or spoken aloud or *sotto voce*.

Chartier's distinction between civility and intimacy highlights the further consequence that acts of friendship or love were best suited to private space which had been created for that purpose. Such space, usually in the home, was also reserved for the writing of intimate thoughts in letters, diaries and poetry and Chartier suggests that it was through writing that privacy became public, with the resulting subordination of civility to intimacy.[5] This introduces the consideration that writing – an act of intimacy frequently conducted silently in private space –

[2] Janette Dillon, *Shakespeare and the Solitary Man* (London, 1981) p. 34.
[3] Roger Chartier (ed.) *A History of Private Life*, III (Cambridge, Mass., 1989) pp. 163–5.
[4] *Ibid.*, p. 5.
[5] *Ibid.*, pp. 163–5.

required, if it was to be understood, to be read. Reading aloud, if it was done for the benefit of those who could not read was often, perforce, carried out in space that was communal and public. In these circumstances the boundaries between public and private became increasingly blurred. Chartier's thesis leads one to conclude that social status was the main criterion governing the timing and the nature of variations in parameters of civility and intimacy, privacy and solitude. Inevitably, therefore, changes in the cultural significance of solitude (with or without silence) must be viewed in relation to education, housing, family economies, health and perceptions of personal well-being.

One might assume from Chartier's argument that the changing attitudes to solitude would have tended to present the purported characteristics of the solitary person, such as integrity, godliness and high intellect, in a positive light. That is close to the view taken by Keith Thomas who notes that in the Elizabethan age solitude was considered to be a pleasurable experience and that in the century following the Reformation 'the desirability of periodically being alone was urged by many Protestant divines'.[6] And for most circumstances confirming the positive connotation, Dillon draws on references from the early seventeenth century to chart the transition of the solitary individual from firstly someone who was to be ridiculed, secondly to a person of contemplative bent marked by intellectual superiority, and finally to someone whose superiority was displayed in a sincere but disdainful aloofness.[7] These forms of solitariness had come a long way from the sixteenth-century conventions of civility noted by Chartier. Apart from being an occasional subject for the lampooners, solitude and the solitary life came to be generally regarded as respectable objectives.

The respectability was further enhanced with the evolution of private space in houses and gardens and the perceived association of private study with the achievement of scholarly excellence. Montaigne's *Essays*, available in English translation from 1603, included 'On Solitude' which was written as early as 1571 when he had found peace on his own estates. His preferred solitude was one which could be 'enjoyed in towns and in kings' courts, but more conveniently apart'[8] and his only reference to silence immediately links it to solitude and the intellectual fulfilment which he was seeking:

Tacitum sylvas inter reptare salubres,

---

[6] Keith Thomas, *Man and the Natural World: Changing Attitudes in England 1500–1800* (London, 1984) p. 268.

[7] Dillon, pp. 25–26.

[8] Michel de Montaigne, 'On Solitude' in M.A. Screech (ed.) *The Complete Essays* (Harmondsworth, 1993) pp. 268–9.

Curantem quidquid dignum sapiente bonoque est.
(Walking in silence through the healthy woods,
pondering questions worthy of the wise and good.)[9]

A century later, *A Moral Essay preferring solitude to Publick Employment and all its appanages*, written in 1665 by George Mackenzie, Lord Advocate in Edinburgh elicited a response from John Evelyn in 1667 in the form of *Publick employment and an active life prefer'd to solitude and all its appanages, such as fame*. Both publications were typical of the philosophical debates which re-evaluated the merits and demerits of the solitary life and moral aspects of the conflict between public and private needs.

There was nothing unusual, however, in experiencing solitude in the company of others – even the disconcerting solitude which stemmed from 'being alone in a crowd'. In 1622 Francis Bacon wrote: 'But little do men perceive what solitude is, and how far it extendeth. For a crowd is not company, and faces are but a gallery of pictures, and talk but a tinkling cymbal, where there is no love.'[10] In some circumstances such solitude included silences which emphasised the separation from comforting familiarity. These, combined with distrust, contributed to Catherine of Aragon's unhappiness during her early life in England. Some of her letters suggest that she considered silence to be the only option if other people could not be trusted, even if it increased her sense of separation.[11] And enforced separation, often leading to abandonment, was employed as quarantine against plague, as in James Thomson's graphic description of

the doom'd House, where matchless Horror reigns,
Shut up by barbarous Fear, the smitten Wretch,
With Frenzy wild, breaks loose; and, loud to Heaven
Screaming, the dreadful Policy arraigns,
Inhuman and unwise[12]

In these terrifying conditions silence may also have been the first indication that victims had not survived. In day-to-day domestic life worries about absent family and friends created a form of solitude exacerbated by the silence of not knowing. One anxious parent, the seventeenth-century diarist Oliver Heywood, was so frantic when his sons were away from home that he dreamt one of them had

[9] *Ibid.*, p. 276; Horace, *Epistles*, I, iv, 45–5.

[10] Brian Vickers (ed.) 'Of Friendship' in *Francis Bacon: The Essays or Counsels, Civil and Moral* (Oxford, 1999) p. 59.

[11] Anne Crawford (ed.) *Letters of the Queens of England, 1100-1547* (Bath, 1994) pp. 167–8.

[12] James Thomson, 1730, ed. by James Sambrook, *The Seasons* (Oxford, 1981) Summer, 1074–8; Nathaniel Hodge, 1665, 'Loimologia: or, an Historical Account of the Plague in London in 1665' in Andrew Browning (ed.) *English Historical Documents*, VIII, 1660–1714 (London, 1953).

'fallen to the study of magic or the black art.'[13]

In other circumstances religious orders engaged in a communal solitude which was also governed by rules of silence, the bereaved may have shared the comfort of mutual solitude, and lovers and conspirators sought the privacy of their own company. Clearly, communal solitude did not preclude communication but John Donne and companion appear to have had the best of all worlds, sitting on a 'pregnant bank, swelled up to rest the violet's reclining head', and being so taken up with each other that no words passed between them:

And whilst our souls negotiate there,
We like sepulchral statues lay;
All day, the same our postures were,
And we said nothing, all the day.[14]

Intellectual creativity, such as diary writing, is often a solitary activity. But creativity can also derive from a state of communal solitude, as in the case of monastic scriptoria or in the example of John Locke who reckoned that the origins of *An Essay Concerning Human Understanding* lay in the intellectual exchanges of 'five or six friends meeting at my chamber'. And David Hume, in admitting that his *Treatise of Human Nature* was 'defined by his relation to [friends] who meet not in his chamber but in the course of his Treatise' was even acknowledging that imaginary company, combined with solitude, might generate intellectual fruits.[15]

I have suggested so far that, in cultural-historical context, silence and solitude have been imprecise concepts, despite attempts to render them more explicit. Silence, for example, rests somewhere between what we may perceive as 'utterly lacking in sound' and 'fairly quiet', and also in varieties of bodily comportment. Likewise, solitude merely implies a state of relative separation from others. But it does seem that in the early modern period there was a symbiotic relationship between silence and solitude which influenced prevailing perceptions of civility, manners, progress, intellectual achievement and morality. I now wish to test that proposition in greater detail with reference to the three 'landscapes' of solitude and silence mentioned above.

TOWN AND COUNTRY: SOLITUDE AND SILENT SPACES

'A very handsome apartment' was the term used by John Evelyn in 1641 to

---

[13] Ralph Houlbrooke (ed.) *English Family Life, 1576–1716: An Anthology from Diaries* (Oxford, 1988) Item 61.

[14] John Donne, 'The Ecstacy', lines 2-3 & 18–20, in T.G.S. Cain (ed.), *Jacobean and Caroline Poetry: an Anthology* (London, 1981) pp. 32–3.

[15] John Sitter, *Literary Loneliness in Mid-Eighteenth-Century England* (London, 1982) p. 22.

describe his new lodgings.[16] A few years later Sir George Pratt, a Berkshire gentleman, commissioned the building of a new house at Coleshill in which each bedroom and withdrawing chamber had at least one 'closet' to afford the necessary solitude and silence for diligent study, writing or prayer.[17] These were early examples of how house design responded to a growing desire for privacy although it was usually only those of wealth and status who could respond to such opportunities. Generally, living quarters were cramped and shared with servants and lodgers, and quiet neighbours may have been the exception rather than the rule. John Heywood's 1556 poem, *A Quiet Neighbour*, congratulated his neighbour on ten years without the sounds of impertinent servants, the dog and cat, whispering and kitchen activities.[18] In Southwark in 1654 Ellenor Goodwin's problem lay not with neighbours, but with her husband Wessel, an enthusiastic but incompetent musician. From her sick-bed Ellenor begged her husband to stop practising on his 'lute and other sorts of fiddles'. Wessel, however, 'went out in discontent and so fel to his musicke againe.' His wife died three days later.[19] Samuel Johnson, valuing the silence of his own company, wrote in 1751 that 'a garret [is remoter] from the outer door, which is often observed to be infested with visitants, who talk incessantly [and] raise their voices in time from mournful murmurs to raging vociferations.'[20] Even allowing for relative silence at night and in parks, gardens and churchyards it can hardly be suggested that towns were in any way quiet places.

In the late 1530s and early 1540s John Leland, on a commission from Henry VIII to survey the contents of monastic libraries,[21] had little time for descriptions of rural or urban sounds. Exceptionally, however, he was moved to record the great peace which he found at a fifteenth-century chapel near Warwick, where he seems to have been connecting the pleasures of contemplation and inspiration and imagining the sacred grove of Tacita, the so-called tenth Muse, the Muse of Silence.

It is ... a house fit for the muses. Silence may be found there, a charming wood, caves in the living rock, the happy sound of the river rolling across the stones, little shady groves, ... a

---

[16] *Oxford English Dictionary.*

[17] Mark Girouard, *Life in the English Country House* (London, 1978) pp. 122–3.

[18] John Heywood, 'A Quiet Neighbour' in Emrys Jones (ed.) *The New Oxford Book of Sixteenth-Century Verse* (Oxford, 1991) pp. 126–7.

[19] Anon., *A Brief Relation of the Strange and Unnatural Practices of Wessel Goodwin, Mehetabell Jones and Elizabeth Pigeon* (London, 1654) pp. 1, 2.

[20] 'The Advantages of Living in a Garret', *Rambler*, 30 April, 1751, in *The Works of Samuel Johnson*, IV, Yale Edition (New Haven, 1969) p. 261.

[21] John Chandler (ed.) *John Leland's Itinerary: Travels in Tudor England* (Stroud, 1993).

solitary place as well, enjoying silence, which of all things the muses love best.[22]

Observers were more inclined, however, to record their irritation with urban crowds and noise. At Wells in 1634, for example, Justices of the Peace staying at an inn were forced from their beds by 'Disorderly Drinkinge, quarrellinge and hoopinge', only to be 'affronted with very contemptious and uncivill speeches.'[23] In 1686 a complaint was lodged against a Hereford barber that 'on the Lord's Day, in time of divine service and sermon' his customers were involved in 'brawling, cursing and swearing, musick and danceing, singing and roaringe.'[24] In the early 1700s a Saxon physician observed that in England there was 'such a Concourse of People, that no body can avoid the Crowd that Walks a Foot; to say nothing of the eminent Danger from the perpetual hurry of their publick Coaches'.[25] By 1750 London had become the largest city in Europe and the street sounds of insults, bells and dog-fights which in Elizabethan times so intrigued the eponymous Caius in Everard Guilpin's *Skialetheia*[26] had intensified into Bruce Smith's raucous reconstructed soundscape of bells, cannon, musical instruments, street traders, metal-working, horses and the all-pervading sound of human speech.[27] The physician and botanist, William Maton, passing through the West Country in the 1790s, even concluded that noisy behaviour was worse in the manufacturing towns, whereas it was 'in villages only that we must look for temperance and its concomitant health and quietude'.[28] He was resigned to accepting that someone who was always busy in life might not be able to feel the 'refined sensations' of nature but admitted wistfully that 'it is not to be wondered at if [the contemplative man] should often look back with emotions of regret and tenderness to the serenity of nature'.[29]

But Maton was writing at the dawn of the Industrial Revolution when no-one would have expected factories to be places of silence or solitude. For example, in 1719 the silk mill in Derby had two hundred workers and one water-wheel

---

[22] *Ibid.*, p. 465.

[23] Joan Parkes, *Travel in England in the Seventeenth Century* (London, 1925) pp. 138–41.

[24] *Hereford Records*, BG/11/7/5/72.

[25] Christian Heinrich Erndtel, *The Relation of a Journey into England and Holland in the Years 1706 and 1707*, trans. (London, 1711) p. 26.

[26] Dillon, p. 24, quoting Guilpin, 1598, 'Satyra Quinta' in *Skialetheia*, Shakespeare Association Facsimiles, 2 (London, 1931).

[27] Bruce Smith, *The Acoustic World of Early Modern England* (London, 1999) pp. 49-95, esp. pp. 52–71; Peter Ackroyd, *London: the Biography* (London, 2000) pp. 71–80.

[28] William Maton, *Observations ... of the Western Counties of England made in the years 1794 and 1796*, 2 (Salisbury, 1797) p. 39.

[29] *Ibid.*, 2, p. 96.

ultimately driving 97,746 separate movements.[30] Visits to factories might nevertheless elicit an acceptance of turmoil, and in an Enlightenment vision of progress, a 1757 poem celebrated a 'noisy fulling mill':

Where tumbling waters turn enormous wheels,
Where hammers, rising and descending, learn
To imitate the industry of man.[31]

Fear was also commonplace. In 1784 a French geologist venturing into Scotland to observe the manufacture of cannon and cannonballs at the Carron Ironworks, noted 'the shrill creaking of pullies, the continued noise of hammers, the activity of those arms which give the impulse to so many machines'. The air pumps produced 'a sharp whistling noise, and so violent a tremor, that one could hardly avoid a feeling of terror'.[32] Another visitor to the same foundry thought that 'the Bellows made such a Noise that I durst hardly Come near them, the sound conveyed such an idea of their bursting with excessive heat, that fear kept me from looking into them.'[33] And a description of the engine at a Cornish tin mine, warned that 'the noise and the horrible appearance of the rod when lifted up ... occasions the most uneasy sensations imaginable'. Belief in the reality of hell might have encouraged the thought that unstoppable industrial progress with its terrifying flames, heat, continuous noise and monstrous machinery was the very work of the devil. Indeed, in 1769, the poet Thomas Gray, awe-struck by an iron-forge in the Lake District, reported that he 'saw the dæmons at work by the light of their own fires'. Whether he considered that 'the dæmons' were the workers or the machines, or both, is not clear.[34]

These travellers also had deeper reasons for feeling disconcerted. They were living in times of international unrest and change in the economic and social fabric of the country. In England and continental Europe revolution, war, and religious nonconformism, were already threatening the perceived security of the quieter life and the pleasures of solitary scholarly contemplation. Visits to factories provided observers with ample opportunity to ponder the social

[30] Herbert Heaton, 1920, *The Yorkshire Woollen and Worsted Industries from the Earliest Times up to the Industrial Revolution* (Oxford, 1920) pp. 353–4.

[31] John Dyer, *The Fleece*, 1757, quoted in Heaton, p. 342.

[32] Barthélemy Faujas de Saint Fond, 1797, *A Journey Through England and Scotland to the Hebrides in 1784*, 1, trans. 1799 (Glasgow, 1907) pp. 179, 181.

[33] Matthew Culley, 1794, *Diary*, quoted in Robin Gard (ed.) *The Observant Traveller* (London, 1989) p. 53.

[34] Thomas Gray, 1778, *Journal of a Tour of the Lakes*, quoted in Humphrey Jennings (ed. Mary-Lou Jennings and Charles Madge), *Pandæmonium: The Coming of the Machine as Seen by Contemporary Observers* (London, 1987) p. 64

consequences of divisions between themselves, the observers, and the observed. The observers could escape from the unpleasant images, terrifying noises and potential dangers, but it is questionable whether retreat to a quieter or more solitary life would have allayed their other anxieties. In those respects they differed directly from the people they were observing. These, the observed, had scant opportunity to seek silence or solitude at work or at home. On the other hand, the exigencies of everyday survival left little time or inclination to dwell on wider concerns.

Keith Thomas notes that irritation with urban noise was one reason why 'town-dwellers came to pine for the imagined delights of rural life',[35] and his caveat about the illusory nature of the delights is significant. Moreover, even if rural solitude and silence were readily accessible it does not follow that people who regularly experienced them necessarily ascribed some intrinsic value to them. A hankering for the countryside does not in itself indicate a longing for silence. It might just as readily imply a longing for countryside sights and smells, and sounds. The poets realised these distinctions well before the years of the European Romantic Movement. Shakespeare's King Henry VI, soliloquising over the uncomplicated attractions of a shepherd's life as an alternative to the trials of kingship, was longing for the simple peace and solitude that life in the countryside might offer:

O God! methinks it were a happy life,
To be no better than a homely swain;
To sit upon a hill, as I do now, ...
Gives not the hawthorn-bush a sweeter shade
To shepherds looking on their silly sheep,
Than doth a rich embroidered canopy
To kings that fear their subjects' treachery?[36]

Hildebrand Jacob, in 1734, addressing the goddess of silence, celebrated the combination of solitude and silence in nature and at night:

thee, at the still Noon of Night
When all is hush'd, delighted, I adore
Thus well attended, bless our Solitude!
There nothing shall suspend thy gentle Reign,
Save the low Murmur of a distant stream,
Except by chance sweet Philomel complains,
Or Cloë tunes her melting Voice and Lyre.[37]

[35] Thomas, p. 245.
[36] *The Complete Works of Shakespeare*, ed. by David Bevington, (New York, 1997) *King Henry VI, Part 3*, ll. 5. 21–23 and 42–45.
[37] Hildebrand Jacob, *Hymn to the Goddess of Silence* (London, 1734) lines 14–15; 65–69.

And in James Thomson's *The Seasons*, just like the shepherd leaving his 'mossy cottage', so also:

will not Man awake;
And, springing from the Bed of Sloth, enjoy
The cool, the fragrant and the silent Hour,
To Meditation due, and sacred Song?[38]

Writing specifically about the English Romantic Movement, Odell Shephard noted that motives for solitude included religion and the promotion of intellectual effort as well as a desire to experience silence in lonely places.[39] These wishes could doubtless be satisfied in the imagination by reading the romantic poets but they were just as likely to be ingrained in another form in those of more modest aspiration who lived and worked in the country and who were more likely to have appreciated the realities unembellished by the burgeoning gloss of European romanticism and undistracted by the romantics' characteristic, but appealing, quest for the unattainable.

Many eighteenth-century poets revealed their nostalgia for solitude and country life with a respectful glance at the agrarian tradition in classical poetry, such as Virgil's *Georgics* and *Eclogues*. Alexander Pope's *Ode on Solitude*, for instance, based on the second epode of Horace, and one of many examples of the *beatus ille* genre,[40] typifying the poems of rural retreat, gives a picture of uncomplicated peace and contentment, although Raymond Williams notes the irony that Horace was not writing from the countryside; he was merely imagining it[41]:

Happy the man whose wish and care
A few paternal acres bound,
Content to breathe his native air,
In his own ground.[42]

In similar vein to Pope, James Thomson also wrote of rural retreat, but in a companionable solitude:

Oh knew he but his Happiness, of Men
The happiest he! who far from public Rage,
Deep in the Vale, with a choice Few retir'd,
Drinks the pure pleasures of the rural life.

---

[38] Thomson, Summer, lines 67–70.

[39] Odell Shephard, *Solitude as a Phase of the English Romantic Movement with Some Consideration of Foreign Literatures* (Unpublished PhD thesis, Harvard University, 1916) pp. 81–113.

[40] Horace, *Second Epode*, line 1: *Beatus ille, qui procul negotiis* ... (Happy is the man who, far from the world of business ...).

[41] Raymond Williams, *The Country and the City* (St Albans, 1975) p. 29.

[42] 'Ode on Solitude', in *Alexander Pope, Selected Poems*, Bloomsbury Poetry Classics (London, 1994) p. 1.

Here too dwells ...
Calm Contemplation, and poetic Ease.[43]

Pope's 'paternal acres' and Thomson's 'Vale' are surely examples of Arcadia, or at least one of its successive re-inventions ranging, in Simon Schama's description, from the brutishness of a pre-selenic age through classical mythology and the imaginary landscapes of late-Renaissance painting to an idealised setting for peace and contemplation.[44] But the essence of Arcadia is that it is highly stylised and, inevitably, imagined. Arcadia, nevertheless, can readily be conventionalised as English and as an ideal where intellectual pursuits combine with gentle sensual pleasures, although such pleasures, as I will suggest later with reference to solitude and gardens, may at times give way to a more forthright eroticism.

In the early modern period the growing popularity of recreational walking as a substitute for the noisy and intrusive pastime of hunting[45] seems to suggest that, in some forms, exploitation of the countryside destroyed silence, although passive enjoyment of nature did not. Notwithstanding, noise and disturbance in the ever-spreading urban areas, combined with the growth of heavier industry, formed part of the impetus behind the formation of a cult which celebrated the real or imaginary peace and solitude which the countryside offered. One might expect that gardens – an intended microcosm of tranquillity, not only in the countryside, but also in the towns where they fulfilled a *rus in urbe* function – would have presented a range of opportunities to experience solitude and silence. But that was not invariably so.

GARDENS: SOLITUDE, POWER AND INFLUENCE

Alluding to the biblical Eden, Francis Bacon celebrated the quiet enjoyment of nature and the changing seasons that could be derived from gardens: 'God Almighty first planted a garden. And indeed it is the purest of human pleasures.'[46] Jane Brown, writing on the history of gardens takes issue with Bacon's 'purest of human pleasures', claiming that 'no garden of pleasure has ever been entirely pure [it] is rather more robust, it is sensual, physical, sexual'.[47] Brown is partly correct. Gardens offered a variety of pleasures apart from silence or private contemplation. For instance, the so-called pleasure gardens which flourished in

---

[43] Thomson, Autumn, lines 1235–39 & 1277.

[44] Simon Schama, *Landscape and Memory* (Bath, 1996) pp. 526–38, passim.

[45] Donna Landry, *The Invention of the Countryside: Hunting, Walking and Ecology in English Literature, 1671–1831* (Basingstoke, 2001) p. 22.

[46] Bacon, 'Of Gardens' in Vickers, p. 137.

[47] Jane Brown, *The Pursuit of Paradise. A Social History of Gardens and Gardening* (London, 1999) p. 28.

the eighteenth century were places of mass entertainment and commercial enterprise where one might find anonymity and excitement, but not peace. Taking another view, William Mason, eighteenth-century garden designer and author of *The English Garden*, appears to have valued pragmatism and toil more highly than any disposition to intellectual pursuits. He implied that it was natural for man to be productive through the harnessing of nature:

… In the waste
Place there that man with his primaeval arms
His plough-share, and his spade, nor shalt thou long
Impatient wait a change; the waste shall smile
With yellow harvests; what was barren heath
Shall soon be verdant meads.[48]

A triumph of industry, perhaps, over the supposed self-indulgence of private contemplation. Mason's view supported the utilitarian function of plant production for food, flavouring and medicine which applied to rural and urban gardens. Beyond this, however, gardens were also for relaxing, contemplating, and quietly communing with nature. On that level, the poet Andrew Marvell, enjoying a garden rather than being in 'busy companies of men', found 'Fair Quiet ... and Innocence, thy sister dear!'[49]

Nevertheless, the active creation of gardens for solitude and silence was usually a self-conscious, culturally constituted, act which was more likely to be within the grasp of those of sufficient means. It was therefore status-related. The fashion for a more informal approach to garden design was also exploitative, and in the eighteenth century grander gardens and the houses to which they were attached, continued to present metaphors of patrician influence, wealth, power and English expansionism. Informality still called for the manipulation of nature, and the vogue for the large-scale and costly creation of landscaped parks often involved, in addition, the manipulation of people's lives. Villages were eliminated from the landscape in favour of parkland and the sights and sounds of nature. West Sheen was demolished in Lancelot Brown's creation of Richmond Park and in Oxfordshire in 1761 the depopulation of Nuneham Courtenay goaded Oliver Goldsmith to write *The Deserted Village*.[50] In Goldsmith's synecdoche '[t]he man of

---

[48] William Mason, *The English Garden* (London, 1772–82) p. 6.
[49] 'The Garden', lines 9–10, in Elizabeth Donno (ed.) *Andrew Marvel, The Complete Poems* (Harmondsworth, 1996) p. 100.
[50] Mavis Batey, 'Oliver Goldsmith. An indictment of landscape gardening' in Peter Willis (ed.), *Furor Hortensis* (Edinburgh, 1974) pp. 57–71, passim.

wealth and pride takes up a space that many poor supplied'[51] and stands proxy for England's imperialism in relentless pursuit of commercial enterprise and the furtherance of the symbols and practices of English culture. This somewhat melodramatic view presents villagers as being condemned, in the name of progress, to the solitude of exile from family and friends, and landowners may, indeed, have been hoping to manage their estates to better effect for hunting and agriculture. But that does not wholly account for the destruction of evidence of human habitation.

Some of the answer may lie in the desire to remove any distractions that could interfere with the image of Enlightenment Man as thinker and philosopher in his own world courting intellectual inspiration through silence, solitude and nature. The image of the solitary thinker also rested on opportunities afforded by literacy, liberal education, the loosening of censorship, and in due course the encouragement given to rational enquiry. Heroic reconstruction of the landscape was consistent with achieving the grandeur symbolising the fruition of these intellectual pursuits. There is also a suggestion that some individuals professed a sense of melancholy because it was fashionable[52] and perceived to be connected with intellectual superiority and a love of solitude. That is partly the sentiment in Milton's *Il Penseroso*, an address to the goddess, Melancholy, that she should bring 'the Cherub Contemplation, and the mute Silence hist along' so that the poet may finally

Find out the peacefull hermitage,
The Hairy Gown and Mossy Cell[53]

In the years of the English Enlightenment, even if the combination of silence and solitude in pursuit of a greater knowledge of God may have seemed to decline in spiritual significance, the interdependency of social esteem and religious propriety nevertheless remained important, and for some who were developing their own gardens and estates one form of religious solitude presented itself as evidence of a connection between faith, wealth and intellect. Building hermitages and 'employing' hermits to be suitably melancholy, silent and contemplative on one's behalf was not unlike the fashion for commissioning swagger portraits as silent evidence of the subject's eclectic and scholarly interests. But perhaps the

---

[51] 'The Deserted Village', lines 91–2, in David Masson (ed.), *The Miscellaneous Works of Oliver Goldsmith* (London, 1895) pp. 580–9.

[52] Michael MacDonald, *Mystical Bedlam. Madness, Anxiety and Healing in Seventeenth-Century England.* (Cambridge, 1981) pp. 150–1.

[53] 'Il Penseroso', lines 54–5, 168–9, in H C Beeching (ed.) *The Poetical Works of John Milton* (London, 1904) pp. 24–8.

motives were more complex. Having a hermit in the garden praying for one's welfare and ultimate repose must have engendered a certain sense of comfort, and even served as a defiant symbol of Catholic piety for those who regretted the more distant passing of chantries and memorial obits. Some gardens also had grottoes specially built for silent contemplation. Alexander Pope had one at Twickenham although Dr Johnson thought, witheringly, that Pope's motives were false and that the grotto had been dignified 'as a place of silence and retreat from which [Pope] endeavoured to persuade himself and his friends that all cares and passions could be excluded.'[54]

The silence of a garden might occasionally be regarded as a metaphor of political desolation, as in Abraham Cowley's *On the Queen's Repairing Somerset House*. The poem, describing a house and garden rescued from ruin, is a thinly disguised reference to an England which, in a biblical sense, had been 'brought to silence' during the years of the Republic, only to be redeemed by the restoration of the monarchy:

The Pillars sunk, the Roofs above me wept,
No sign of Spring, or Joy, my Garden kept,
Nothing was seen which could content the Eye,
Till Dead the impious Tyrant Here did lye.[55]

In an era of ever-expanding scientific enquiry the transmutation of silent desuetude to flourishing optimism, albeit of a political nature, is an appropriate analogy. But in other contexts silence and a sense of apartness are also prominent measures of the nostalgia implicit in the desire to replicate what was imagined to be a past, enduring, and typically English, landscape.

This objective finds some correspondence with Steven Gores' suggestion that history, representing 'the precedents by which one determines one's relationship to culture', constitutes a 'cultural "space"' on which identity is partly established, and that in the eighteenth century the fascination for ruins provided a cultural and psychosocial link between the past and the 'realisation of mortality'.[56] In my view his final point unduly stretches the argument, although some wealthier landowners did, indeed, include ruins and follies in artificial or ornamental landscapes. At Lilford in Northamptonshire, for example, a new village church was built outwith the park, with the old building deliberately left in ruins as an ornamental feature

[54]Peter France, *Hermits: The Insights of Solitude* (London, 1997) p. 88.
[55]'On the Queen's Repairing Somerset House', in A.R. Waller (ed.), *Abraham Cowley: Poems* (Cambridge, 1905) pp. 433-5.
[56] Steven Gores, *Psychosocial Spaces: Verbal and Visual Readings of British Culture 1750–1820* (Detroit, 2000) pp. 95–7.

occupying a symbolic position on the outer limits of the estate.[57] But for landowners and their families instant 'pseudo-ruins', along with examples of imaginary landscapes in early modern painting, were more likely, I suggest, to be public statements of personal aspiration and identity rather than the ostentatious and introspective focus on mortality such as one might have found associated with intramural burials or family mausolea. Ruins provided an immediate visual link with the past and in terms of ambient sounds and silences the link was possibly also aural. Contemplation of ruins fulfilled an opportunity in which the solitary and silent observer could attempt to understand the past and ponder his or her respect for it.

The Gardener's Dictionary of 1731 alluded to opportunities for solitude and an escape into silence when it advocated the planning of 'smaller Serpentine Walks where Persons may retire for Privacy'.[58] Nevertheless, privacy was not always an objective for the solitary person. It could also have been useful for conspiratorial or romantic assignations. In Shakespeare's *Twelfth Night*, for example, the privacy of Olivia's garden had satisfied both extremes – on the one hand the abuse which characterised the unpleasant plot against Malvolio, and on the other, the innocence of the unfolding relationship between Olivia, Viola and Sebastian.[59] Equally, a quiet garden could have been the setting for sheer lust. To most appearances, the carefully designed wilderness area in large gardens was a far cry from the rampancy of the erotic landscape in Jacopo Sannazaro's 1485 *Arcadia* which had been laid out on the body of the nymph Amaranth 'between whose budding breasts a path ... descended towards deep and shady groves'.[60] Nor was it fully intended to recall the wilderness in *Paradise Lost*, encountered by Satan in his attempt to conquer the threshold where 'delicious Paradise'

Now nearer, crowns with her enclosure green,
As with a rural mound, the champaign[61] head
Of a steep wilderness, whose hairy sides
With thicket overgrown, grotesque and wild,
Access denied.[62]

Yet, if one interprets these as fantasies of the simultaneously desirable and forbidden, one may readily speculate on how the garden wilderness could have been exploited by those wishing to enjoy its privacy alone, unseen and unheard.

[57] Batey, p. 60.
[58] Philip Miller, 'Wilderness' in *The Gardener's Dictionary*, 1 (London, 1731).
[59] Bevington (ed.), *Twelfth Night*, in particular III. 1 & 4 and IV. 3.
[60] Schama, p. 531.
[61] flat country.
[62] John Milton, 1667, *Paradise Lost*, Book IV, lines 132-6 (Harmondsworth, 1996).

Gardens provided physical and spiritual sustenance as well as the simple pleasures of solitude, silence and contemplation. And particularly in Enlightenment England they alluded ambiguously to a respect for nature and to human triumph over it. For Christians, these allusions were also reminders of two special gardens, Eden and Gethsemane. The first, a setting of peaceful perfection ruined by mankind and resolving into pain and toil; a symbol of companionable solitude riven by Satan and human weakness. The second, an epitome of fear, betrayal, stark endurance and of silent loneliness, but leading ultimately to apotheosis and paradise, where it had all begun. But, like some gardens, the Christian condition, framed immutably by Eden and Gethsemane, also encompassed its own wilderness.

THE CHRISTIAN DISCOURSE OF WILDERNESS: SOLITUDE AND FORBEARANCE

In early modern religious discourse exhortations to pursue a Christian path employed the idea of 'wilderness', either as a physical, barren place, or as a desolate condition of the mind or spirit. The concept illustrated the perceived cathartic value of silence and solitude in confronting suffering with Christian compliance and forbearance. Some commentators went further and suggested that 'wilderness' and virtuous silence, albeit less welcome and less easy to accept, were ultimately more worthy, because they were deeply personal (perhaps even deeply deserved) and had to be experienced alone.

The usual biblical portrayal was as a deserted, unpopulated, unproductive place where silence and personal solitude were either sought or imposed, but where hardship eventually resolved, through determination, into triumph. For example, the silent wilderness of personal ruination was compared with the abandoned place of nettles, brambles, dragons, owls and vultures which had been created, in Isaiah's account, after the destruction of all nations by the vengeance of God.[63] But in due course, triumph was assured along with a rejection of silence and solitude: 'the desert shall rejoice ... even with joy and singing [and] the ears of the deaf shall be unstopped.'[64] St Matthew's Gospel records John the Baptist as declaiming that his is the voice 'crying in the wilderness, Prepare ye the way of the Lord, make his paths straight.'[65] John's reference is to Isaiah's Old Testament prophecy,[66] and the Gospel account can be interpreted as implying that the hardship of wilderness conditions is a necessary precursor to understanding and

---

[63] Isaiah 34. 13–15.
[64] Isaiah 35. 1–2, 5–6.
[65] Matthew 3. 3.
[66] Isaiah 40. 3.

following God's way. That is one of the justifications for the metaphoric approach to 'wilderness' employed by some of the early modern commentators. Equally, however, the Matthew account suggests a clear conflation of wilderness with physical desert. John the Baptist, sustained only by locusts and wild honey, was speaking from a barren place and from a wilderness life which became a precedent for the early Christian saints. Their quests for knowledge of God through solitary and silent asceticism and rejection of temptation and the material world, were chronicled in hagiographic works and in general histories by authors such as William Turner[67] and Nathaniel Wanley.[68] John the Silent, for example, one of the 'celebrated Saints of the oriental Desarts', was reputed to have spent years at any one time in silence.[69] And St Anthony's wilderness was a place for solitude with God and for temptation by Satan and devils.[70] In England, especially in the pre-Reformation years, the nearest equivalents to the desert saints were religious recluses, ranging in degree of withdrawal from ordinary members of religious orders to those who spent years alone in an anchoritic lifestyle, all of whom were following the example of the Augustinian monk, Thomas à Kempis, who had urged in 1418: 'No Man deserves inward and heavenly Comforts, who does not diligently examine, and willingly afflict himself. To be qualify'd for this Solitude, it is absolutely needful to "Commune with your own Heart in your Chamber, and be still."'[71]

Physical wildernesses, whether they were deserts or monastic cells, were barren places associated with personal withdrawal into solitude and silence. They were also considered as a natural setting for God to reveal his sustaining power through which patience, forbearance and faith would produce worthy lives. But for Christians a more credible day-to-day concept was that 'wilderness' suggested the figurative approach to which I have referred. As such, it represented the spiritual or moral desert of personal trials endured alone and with silent resignation, unsupported by much of the familiarity of social convention. In homiletic works 'wilderness' comparisons of that type were used to describe the deprivation, despair and hardship which some considered to be necessary precursors to discerning God's will and to an exemplary life and eventual salvation. Accounts of fortitude gave encouragement and from the Bible one of

---

67 William Turner, *A Compleat History of the Most Remarkable Providences both of Judgement and Mercy, which have Hap'ned in this Present Age* (London, 1697)

68 Nathaniel Wanley, *The Wonders of the Little or Moral World* (London, c.1790).

69 R. Challoner, *The Wonders of God in the Wilderness* (London, 1755).

70 *Ibid.*, p. 19.

71 Thomas à Kempis, *Of the Imitation of Jesus Christ*, trans. Stanhope (London, 1714) p. 46. Text from Psalm 4.4.

the most obvious examples was the description of Christ's temptations in the wilderness, an account which portrays Christ, weakened by fasting and subjected to temptation.[72] The implication is that this episode took place in desert conditions, in solitude and in a silence broken only by the taunts of Satan and by Christ's rejection of them. These conditions made it even more difficult to resist temptation and Sir Thomas Browne, reflecting on the sense of apartness implicit in Christ's trials, emphasised the dangers when he warned in 1635 that 'in a Wilderness, a man is never alone, not only because he is with himself and his own thoughts, but because he is with the Devil, who ever consorts with our solitude'.[73]

John Lougher, in a 1685 sermon, dealt with 'wilderness' as a metaphor for loneliness, solitude, terror, deprivation and errant behaviour,[74] all of these being natural and necessary conditions for the Christian. According to Lougher, God would always care for his people in the wilderness, but he required them to be there so that he could humble them and so that they would be 'so bewildered ... that they are brought to loathe themselves for sin.'[75] The wilderness, therefore, had to be a place for proving one's loyalty to God and for experiencing healing.[76] This was also the view of Samuel Shaw, a Leicestershire minister, facing an outbreak of plague in his household in 1664. Shaw survived, but three out of eight people in the house died. He wrote a series of discourses as gratitude to God for sparing him and the others, and for being able to endure the tragedies patiently. He was tormented by thoughts that the troubles had been brought on by his own sin and by over-indulgence to his children but in his desolation he concluded that Christian resolve can benefit and flourish from such trials.[77]

Ambiguity in some interpretations of 'wilderness' was often reflected by stressing further antithetical characteristics. Thus, like the human condition, the wilderness was beset with dangers but also offered the means of spiritual safety; for the suffering Christian it was barren, yet productive; it was a place of solitude and silence, yet the voice of God was ever-present, encouraging the Christian to ignore the voice of Satan. 'Wilderness' was an almost formless arena in which doubts were confronted and hardships endured. And as befitted a Christian society, it also promoted hope and it was from the wilderness that a new order was proclaimed. Experience of the wilderness was, therefore, spiritually cleansing. Silence and loneliness were part of the tribulations, but the new order dawned

---

[72] Matthew 4. 1–11.
[73] Sir Thomas Browne, 1635, *Religio Medici*, Everyman (London, 1965) p. 82.
[74] John Lougher, 'Wilderness-Provision' in *Sermons on Several Subjects* (London, 1685) pp. 95–136.
[75] *Ibid.*, pp. 105, 106.
[76] *Ibid.*, pp. 107–8, 110.
[77] Samuel Shaw, 1667, *The voice of One Crying in a Wilderness* (Edinburgh, 1751) pp. iii–vii, xii.

with the sounds of rejoicing in an outpouring of relief.

These, at least, were the established positions. Nevertheless, it could be argued that 'wilderness' might have had a liberating effect through its disassociation from convention, and among the ranks of those who were enthusiastic about religion some – even including those of unconventional antinomian tendency – envisaged a return to the innocence of what had originally been the benign wilderness of prelapsarian Eden. But the objectives of social order and the necessary maintenance of a godly society were more likely to be achieved by increasing the pressures for conformity. 'Wilderness' and its reputed cathartic effect had socio-political as well as religious and personal dimensions.

CONCLUSION

In the examples which I have discussed, solitude and silence were generally regarded as respectable objectives but there is no evidence to suggest that silence was considered to be a *sine qua non* wherever solitude prevailed. Therefore, a more useful approach is to regard the two conditions as complementary. More significantly, the pursuit of solitude, with or without the accompaniment of silence, represented some general aims such as the achievement of privacy or the fulfilment of a sense of respect and nostalgia for the past. These are manifest, along with other aims, in the three 'landscapes' which I have discussed.

Firstly, as a reaction to urban noise and overcrowding the desire for solitude gave rise to a romanticised version of a vanished age – one which looked back to images of peaceful rurality and also looked forward to opportunities for tranquil contemplation in the sole companionship of nature, bringing at least the impression of spiritual and intellectual benefits. Perhaps it is of little consequence that the wistful gestation of these ideas would most often have occurred in an urban setting, since it was only the very wealthy who had the means to bring them to impressive fruition in the countryside. These were instances of solitude imagined. Secondly, in a practical and symbolic sense gardens represented progress, order, cultivation and self-discipline. But if they were conventionally used for the simple pleasures of friendship, relaxation and appreciating nature they were also capable of fulfilling aspirations of conspiracy, power and intellectual prowess. Even at a modest level, and most certainly on the grandest scale when reconstruction of the countryside was involved, these were instances of solitude created and manipulated. Thirdly, unless it was associated with the benefits of prayer, solitude (either physical or metaphoric) was considered by many to be an inevitable, albeit unwelcome, part of the Christian experience. With God's help, the solitude of 'wilderness' trials formed an essential arena for resolving personal inadequacies, for acknowledging remorse and for proving oneself as a true Christian, well established on the road to a godly life and eventual salvation. These were instances of solitude divinely ordained.

It may well have been argued that all of these desires and objectives were fully justified and potentially an essential part of the development of an orderly and agreeable society. Solitude, increasingly linked to ideas of personal privacy, was usually seen as a virtue and a means of moral self-improvement. But in considering the above examples, I suggest that fashionable solitude (and perhaps silence as an accompaniment) masked a further dimension in the cultural and social life of early modern England. Considering that for some people the apparent respectability of these conditions endorsed a certain exclusion of sound, speech and the company of others, one is also tempted to draw attention to inherent connections with ideas of personal exclusivity such as were evident in distinctions of wealth, status and religious propriety. These, although possibly illusory in conception and less altruistic in intent, may have been just as much a part of the aspirations and experiences evident in the three 'landscapes'.

Roderick Murchison and the Urals

PAUL DUKES

University of Aberdeen

Cultural history encourages lateral thinking. In this way, I came to realise that the career of an eminent geologist unturns other stones.

Roderick Impey Murchison was born on 19 February 1792 at Tarradale, on the Black Isle, Ross-shire, Scotland. Although he remained proud of his old Scottish lineage throughout his life, and revisited his homeland on many occasions, one of his first recollections was leaving Scotland at the age of four on account of his father's ill health, and he spoke with an English accent. The father soon died, and the mother moved back to Edinburgh where she remarried. At the age of six, Roderick was sent to grammar school in Durham, where he remained for six years before embarking on a military career. After serving in the Peninsular War, he retired from the army with the arrival of peace in 1815. Living the life of a country gentleman for some years, he then embarked on a second, scientific career, with an emphasis on geology.

Murchison was already well-established and widely travelled when he first visited Russia in 1840. Having just published *The Silurian System* in two volumes in 1839, his aim was to find evidence among undisturbed rocks to support the order of sequence – Carboniferous, Devonian and Silurian – established in Britain in regions deeply affected by what he called 'convulsions of nature'. Briefed on the way by Prussian colleagues, Murchison and a French colleague Edouard de Verneuil were welcomed on their arrival in St. Petersburg by the chief customs officer. Thus, Murchison wrote, 'we had the advantage of having our things passed and sealed up with the Imperial arms, so that I might have smuggled a mammoth'. (Geikie, I, 295.) Accompanied by Russian colleagues, the two Western geologists went north for their first research expedition before heading home.

In the spring of 1841, Murchison and Verneuil returned to St. Petersburg, where again they were well entertained. They were received on several occasions by the Emperor Nicholas I himself, who asked Murchison about what he had already seen and what he was going to see. The Scotsman explained 'how dearly I was interested in the structure of a country the whole northern region of which was made up of strata which I had spent so many years in classifying and arranging in other parts of Europe; how their vast scale in Russia had surprised me, and how they offered evidences which were wanting in the western countries.'

Explorations in Cultural History: Essays for Peter Gabriel McCaffery,
edd. David F. Smith & H. Philsooph (Aberdeen 2010)   ISBN 978-0-9567059-0-7

(Geikie, I, 319) Murchison then explained why coal was not to be looked for in the north, but in the south. After further social engagements and a visit to the School of Mines, the Scottish and French geologists set off on an expedition aimed ultimately for the Urals in the company of the Baltic German Count Alexander von Keyserling, Lieutenant Koksharov and other Russians.

Rocks were the chief concern of Murchison's diary, but, passing a gang of manacled prisoners marching to exile in Siberia, he noted: 'Thank God in England we have the sea for our high-road to banishment; for such scenes are very harassing.' (On another occasion, he observed more generally: 'The Russ is certainly best land colonist in the world. By sea we flatter ourselves that we are.' Quoted in Stafford, p. 14) After the shock of the convicts, the disapppointment of the mountains. 'Though the Ural had been a chain in my imagination', he confessed, 'we were really going over it at a gallop.' He found the low watershed of Europe and Asia monotonous. (Geikie, I, 329)

Two difficulties ensued, one natural, one human. First, in the absence of 'convulsions of nature', the rock strata were so little disturbed that they lay in horizontal sheets like a series of sheets of cloth laid on a table. Secondly, as Murchison himself complained, 'Were I Emperor of Russia, I would make verily at least one thousand of my lazy officers work for their laced coats, and produce me a good map, or they could study physical geography in Eastern Siberia.' No proper map had been found in NizhniiNovgorod, nor in Kostroma. 'If such be the case in the heart of Russia, how are we to expect that the best-informed natives here in the Urals should have any idea of their broken and diversified region?', he asked. 'Russia must produce geographers before she can expect to have geologists.' (Geikie, I, 330–1)

In July, after great difficulties in making their way through the boggy forests that flanked the Ural, the members of the international expedition reached what Murchison called 'a true mountain', at the Katchkanar. From the peak, to the west they looked out on a rolling sea of dark pine, with an occasional snowy summit rising out of it like an island, to the east – over the vast Siberian plain, another sea, boundless and featureless. Murchison said that he taught the Russian members of the expedition to sing the new national anthem rather than 'our old "God save the King", which they had sung since the time of Peter the Great.' He hummed the new anthem, and 'this music of Levoff was thus first given out in the western borders of Siberia.' (Geikie, I, 335).

The members of the expedition went on to what Murchison considered to be their most exciting and instructive work on the exploration of some of the river-courses that had been manipulated for mining purposes. Helped by the local authorities and people, the travellers managed to descend several streams and cross more difficult terrain carrying out scientific observations, for example in deep gorges of Devonian and Carboniferous limestone, as they did so. As the party worked its way down a river, the boatmen sang as they abused the proprietors and *ispravniki* who had allegedly sold them bad vodka. Murchison's account continues as follows:

Other songs were gentle, plaintive love-ditties, so unlike what our [English] coarse country fellows would sing. With no stimulants, getting but black bread, and working in wet clothes, for they were continually in the river shoving the boat on, they sang in rhymes, one of which as translated by Koksharov was:-

> 'My love she lives on the banks of a rapid stream,
> And when she goes to the garden to pull a rose, she thinks of me.'
> Another of these ditties began – 'Mary, come back from the bower.'

A third was a comic song, quizzing a soldier who got into a house when tipsy. A fourth was a jollification of peasants in a drinking-shop, to beat the maker of bad brandy, with a famous loud refrain in which all the boatmen joined heartily. (Geikie, I, 340)

In Ekaterinburg, there was a dinner in honour of the expedition, with many delicacies and costly wines, with all the glasses thrown out of the building after a final bumper of champagne. In his speech of thanks, Murchison asked for a top and bottom of the broken glasses so that he could join them together with a silver plateback in England, and inscribe his gratitude. (Geikie, I, 340–1)

Having been to the flat middle and the mountainous north of the Ural, the travellers now encountered the southern grassy steppe, in places bare, barren and bad, with dried dung used instead of wood, and Kirgiz and Kalmyk faces in military uniforms in poor villages. Local Bashkirs were not happy with the digging of the geologists, saying 'Take our gold if you will, but leave us, for God's sake, the bones of our ancestors!' Yet, Murchison noted, the locals were so hospitable that 'they allowed us to grope for teaspoons and bread in the cupboards in which their bank-notes and roubles were lying loose!' In fact, less tea was drunk than koumiss. (Geikie, I, 342–3)

Laden with notebooks and samples, indicating Silurian, Devonian and Carboniferous strata, the expedition finally left the Ural after a final traverse south of Orenburg. It visited the shores of the Caspian, some chernozem and the coalfields of the Donets before returning to Moscow and then St. Petersburg. Murchison was awarded Second Class St. Anne in diamonds and Verneuil – a plain cross. Emperor Nicholas showed great curiosity about coal, gold and other resources in a farewell audience. (Geikie, I, 352)

To sum up, the expedition lasting seven months gave Murchison the same reputation in the geology of Russia that Pallas had achieved in its botany. (Geikie, I, 355) Along with his companions, he had extended the area of the Silurian system and defined the Permian system. To consolidate his reputation, the Scotsman laboured hard with his French colleague Edouard de Verneuil and his Baltic German colleague Alexander von Keyserling to complete their magnificent two-volume work, *The Geology of Russia in Europe and the Ural Mountains*. This enterprise involved further travel and fieldwork on the continent. During this period, he received a great vase of Siberian aventurine inscribed with the thanks of the Emperor in Latin standing on a steel plate with an inscription in Russian expressing the esteem of the Ministry of Mines. In general, Murchison loved such presents and honours, and rather liked a friend addressing him as 'Dear and most illustrious Count Silurowski Ouralowski.' (Geikie, II, 1, 13, 210. The vase has been returned to the Hermitage in St. Petersburg from the Museum of Geology in London. A bejewelled snuff box presented to Murchison by Nicholas I may still be found in the Museum of Geology's Vault.)

In the summer of 1844, Murchison travelled via the Baltic and Finland to consult with Keyserling and to present a gold medal to the Emperor in honour of the His Majesty's recent visit to Britain. Murchison offered to try to explain Russian policy towards Poland on his return home. (Geikie, II, 32, 37) In 1845, Murchison went again to St. Petersburg, this time with Verneuil so that they could present the two-volume work that they had completed with Keyserling to the Emperor. Nicholas took time off from his own labours on reform of the penal code, observing that he was responsible to God alone, and would never change in order to respond to the tirades of journalists whom he dismissed as *canaille*, adding 'No, I will never govern as a king of France or a king of England; the respective conditions of our peoples are entirely different, and what goes well with you would lead us to ruin.' Again, Murchison offered to serve the Emperor in extending science or lowering his enemies. The Emperor thanked him and kissed him on both cheeks. (Geikie, II, 43–5.)

Murchison may have been flattered by the tsar's attention and by the honours accorded him. But it is worth recording that he and his collaborators included in the Preface of *The Geology of Russia in Europe* the following tribute to what they called 'the hearty hospitality and generous support of all classes of Russians':

Recurring to that distinctive trait of national Moscovite character – a will which admits of no obstacle – they are bound to record, that their own impatient 'forward' was ever cheerfully responded to by the *mojno* of the natives.[1] With this talismanic word the Russia has, indeed, raised monuments on the Moskva and the Neva, that rival the greatest efforts of ancient and modern times.

Amidst such a people, no real difficulty could be experienced. If a bridge were broken, it seemed rebuilt by magic. Though a river-bed was dry, the travellers beheld it converted, as if miraculously, into a navigable stream. Was the water too shallow, then did the athletic peasants cheerfully lift the boats over rocks, enlivening their progress with a merry carol. Wet or dry, hot or cold, no murmur escaped these resolute men, and *mojno* was their only cry.

The Preface concludes: 'To the illustrious Monarch, then, of the wide realms whose structure they attempt to subscribe, and to all His loyal subjects with whom they held communication, the authors beg once more to express their sincere attachment and lasting gratitude' (xvi, including the footnote).

This paper has barely scratched the surface of its subject. Deeper penetration may be found in several archives in London, Edinburgh and elsewhere.

Bibliography

N.P. Arkhipova and E.V. Iastrebov, *Kak byli otkryty Ural'skie gory* by N.P. Arkhipova and E.V. Iastrebov, Perm, 1971.

Roger Bartlett, 'Graf Alexander Keyserlings Beziehungen zum russischen Kaiserhof', Michael Schwidtal, Jaan Undusk, eds., *Baltisches Welterlebnis: Die kulturgeschichtliche Bedeutung von Alexander, Eduard und Hermann Graf Keyserling*, Heidelberg, 2007, pp. 25–40.

Archibald Geikie, *Life of Sir Roderick I. Murchison*, 2 vols., London, 1875.

Roderick I. Murchison, Edouard de Verneuil and Alexander Keyserling, *The Geology of Russia in Europe and the Ural Mountains*, vol. 1, London, 1845; *Géologie de la Russie d'Europe et des Montagnes d'Oural*, vol. 2, Paris, 1845.

N.S. Shatskii, *R. I. Murchison*, Moskva, 1941.

Robert A. Stafford, *Scientist of empire: Sir Roderick Murchison, scientific exploration and Victorian imperialism*, London, 1989.

Note: I have not yet been able to consult M. Collie and J. Diemer, eds, *Murchison's Wanderings in Russia*, published by the British Geological Survey in 2004.

---

[1] 'The word *mojno,* the literal translation of which is, "It is possible", may be rendered into English by the colloquial sailors' phrase, "Ay, ay, sir".'

Section Three:
History and Sociology of Medicine, and Global Citizenship

From 'simples' to scientific innovation:
Healthcare in the Scottish Highlands, *ca*1620 – *ca*1820[1]

ALEX SUTHERLAND
University of Aberdeen

INTRODUCTION

For a long period from until about the middle of the seventeenth century, medical attention from a recognised practitioner was hard to come by in the Scottish Highlands and this was especially so for the poorer sections of the population and more isolated communities. Traditional explanations of illness and death in terms of the transgression of social norms or taboos, the actions of evil spirits, the evil eye or witchcraft lived on. Likewise, cures were to be found in the wearing of amulets, visits to sacred sites such as springs and wells, prayers to the gods or the relics of long dead saints, or the recitation of charms. There was also a thriving practical folk wisdom as to healthy lifestyle and medical treatment, as Martin Martin recorded in 1695 in his account of his visit to the Western Isles. Despite labouring 'under the want of knowledge of letters and other useful arts and sciences,' the inhabitants of the Western Isles were 'able to preserve their health above what the generality of mankind enjoys merely by temperance and the prudent use of simples taken from plants, roots, stones and animals.'[2] They also engaged in repeated experimentation until such time as 'they were able to remove the most stubborn distempers, where the best prepared medicines have frequently no success.' Only with the advent of university educated doctors did the remedies employed in the treatment of illness change from the use of 'simples' drawn from indigenous flora and fauna to more sophisticated drugs containing foreign ingredients.

This is not to suggest that the use of drugs entirely supplanted the use of 'simples'. The latter continued to be used by sections of the community but their effectiveness in healing was understood to be derived from natural, rather than supernatural, properties. By the time Doctor John Macculloch traversed the Highlands in the early decades of the nineteenth century he was able to report

---

[1] I am grateful to David Smith for his helpful comments on an earlier draft. A note on spelling conventions with regard to quotations: all English words with irregular spellings and capitalisations have been rendered in Standard English. Ampersands have been replaced with the word 'and'. Any archaic or Scots words not now in common use have been preserved.

[2] Martin Martin, *A Description of the Western Islands of Scotland circa 1695 (1994)*, pp. 63 & 238.

Explorations in Cultural History: Essays for Peter Gabriel McCaffery,
edd. David F. Smith & H. Philsooph (Aberdeen 2010)   ISBN 978-0-9567059-0-7

that 'there are very few of the ancient superstitious remedies remaining, and still fewer of the diseases to which superstitious or imaginary causes are assigned. The herbs, once supposed to be endued with supernatural virtues and signatures, seem now to have sank to their true level of natural remedies; and they are administered, as far as I have seen, without the ancient forms that partook of incantation.'[3]

In the art of healing, however, the professional physician had held a privileged position under the clan system from as far back as the twelfth century. A corpus of Gaelic manuscripts dating from medieval times bears testimony to a classical medical tradition with well known families such as the Beatons passing down their knowledge, based on Greek, Roman and Arabic texts, from father to son. At least one text shows an awareness of the different schools of medicine that existed in the ancient world; although the definition of the three main schools is clearly influenced by the preferences of the unknown writer.[4] The Empirics, we are told, used charms and specifics to cure diseases rather than working from experience which is our usual understanding of the school's doctrine; the Methodists put faith in omens and emphasised the treatment of diseases rather than the history of the individual; and according to the ancient text the Rationalists discovered the noble sciences of mathematics and physics.[5] The Gaelic physicians followed the methods of Hippocrates and used reason to acquaint themselves with the hidden causes of diseases, as well as the more evident causes. However, while recognizing the authority of the ancients, Gaelic physicians did not follow the texts blindly when their own experiences showed them to be wrong; one opines that 'it does not become us to contradict the dicta of the Doctors, but to bury them with honour.'[6] This classical tradition began to decline with the breakdown of the clan system in the seventeenth century and the emergence of a university taught medical profession. Changes to the medical profession were not unique to Scotland, the scientific revolution brought changes across Europe as the authority of ancient texts began to be questioned and medical practices and education were transformed in the light of new discoveries. Andreus Vesalius' anatomy dissections at Padua in the 1540s and William Harvey's discovery of the circulation of the blood in the 1620s were two notable milestones in a new understanding of the internal workings of the human body.

---

[3] John Macculloch, *The Highlands and Western Isles of Scotland, containing a description of their scenery and antiquities...* (1824) Vol. IV, p. 38.

[4] D. Mackinnon, *A Descriptive Catalogue of Gaelic Manuscripts in the Advocates' Library Edinburgh* (1912), p. 30.

[5] *Ibid.*, p. 29.

[6] *Ibid.*, p. 53.

John Beaton, a younger contemporary of Harvey, demonstrates his understanding of medical advances by citing Harvey's work in his own studies of sterility and obstetrics.[7]

The tripartite system of physician, who very rarely got his hands dirty but dispensed advice; the apothecary who made up and dispensed prescriptions; and the surgeon, who did the cutting, scraping and bone-setting, was maintained in Lowland Scotland, although the divisions were not so jealously guarded as elsewhere, such as in London. The Royal College of Physicians of Edinburgh were granted a royal charter by Charles II in 1681, but the Faculty of Physicians and Surgeons of Glasgow, founded in 1599, included physicians and surgeons in the same organisation.[8] When the barbers and surgeons of Edinburgh's Barbers and Surgeons Guild (formed in 1505) effectively parted company in 1648, the surgeons were joined by apothecaries and shared a 'Physic Garden' where their apprentices were trained in recognising the medicinal herbs and plants that constituted the *materia medica* of the time.[9] In 1778 the Edinburgh Corporation of Surgeons was given a royal charter, becoming the Royal College of Surgeons of Edinburgh. Medical men in the Highlands seem by necessity to have embraced the skills of more than one designated profession and the three terms of 'physician', 'surgeon' and 'apothecary' appear to have been often used interchangeably.

MEDICAL CARE OF THE HIGHLAND ELITE

We have Rev. James Fraser from the parish of Wardlaw near Beauly to thank for recording the movements of some of the few medical men who did exist in the Scottish Highlands in the seventeenth century. He recorded the minutiae of the world about him with particular reference to the Fraser family and he provides us with an insight into the medical practices of the time, including causes of disease, diagnosis, cures and doctor-patient relations.[10] Fraser notes for September 1622 that the Beatons appear to be no longer practicing medicine and had been replaced by a Doctor Lovell from Perth who had his 'fears of spells.' Lovell attended Sir Simon Fraser when he was confined to his chamber 'under physic for half a year, still decaying; and relapsing again and again ... so this brave spirit was

---

[7] J. Bannerman, *The Beatons: a medical kindred in the classical Gaelic tradition* (1986), p. 115.

[8] *Ibid.*, p. 126.

[9] The Royal College of Surgeons of Edinburgh http://www.rcsed.ac.uk/site/345/default.aspx (accessed 28/10/10)

[10] J. Fraser, *Chronicles of the Frasers: The Wardlaw Manuscript entitled 'Polochronicon Deu Policratica Temporum'* ... (1905), p. 246. Fraser wrote his Chronicles between 1666 and 1699.

in the end given over, put under a milk diet, yet died most perfectly in senses and intellectuals as ordinarily hectic persons do.'[11]

Fraser had further reason to lament the lack of medical expertise when in March 1633 Lord Lovat died from a swollen spleen following months of pain. Doctor John Philip from Dundee could do his lordship no good, 'for he said he came too late.'[12] Fraser was more condemnatory when Lady Lovat succumbed to illness in 1636:

for doctors and persons of skill we had not then in the North, a few common chirurgeons, and travelling charlatans out of Ireland. There was one Mr John Sholes, an Irish man vulgarly termed Doctor Sholes, that had past some experience in the country ... after his long stay in the family and using potions and topical applications [Lady Fraser] grew worse and worse. The good Lady's curious colour and complexion altered to dim yellow like a jaundice, which I judge might be her malady, but the poor fellow had no skill by proper evacuations to expel the morbisick matter. Drugs and foreign medicines could not be had, nor none of skill to consult so much as her constitution. Yet by God's blessing, with simples she might be recovered; yet the vile varlet, mistaking and misapplying what was administered, she was perfectly poisoned, her body after death spotted.[13]

Fraser does go on to show that medical skill of another kind must have been available because 'her body [was] dissected and embalmed, coffined and laid in a vault until, her friends at south were acquainted.'[14] Such invasive surgery was not confined to the dead; Fraser records that in September 1639 'William, Lord Lovat's fourth son sickened, and being cut of the stone, died of a malignant fever ... he was about thirteen years of age.'[15] The surgical skill of lithotomy was much prized and seems to have been peculiar to surgeons of Highland descent; a succession of 'stone cutters' with Gaelic names was appointed by the city of Glasgow from 1661 until after 1688 to 'exercise the cutting of the stone within

---

[11] *Ibid.*, p. 246. Fraser's reporting of the demise of the Beatons seems premature; a Donald Beaton signed a medical certificate for Sir Donald MacDonald of Sleat on 22 September 1716 and he may have been a physician of the traditional school. Bannerman, *The Beatons*, p.121. One Beaton, Neil, whom Martin met in 1695 and whose expertise was highly thought of, may not have been classically schooled. Martin describes him as an 'illiterate empiric' who did not become a 'physician' until the age of forty and then 'without the advantage of education. He treats Riverius's *Lilium Medicinæ*, and some other practical pieces that he has heard of, with contempt; since in several instances it appears that their method of curing has failed, where his has good success.' Martin, *A Description*, pp. 240/1.

[12] Fraser, *Chronicles*, p. 252.

[13] *Ibid.*, p. 258.

[14] *Ibid.*, p. 259.

[15] *Ibid.*, pp. 264/5. Fraser may be mistaken about the child's age – he may have been just three years old when he died – but an operation for the stone on one so young is feasible. Bladder stones, as distinct from kidney stones which develop over time and are caused by an over consumption of rich food and drink, were known by ancient Arab physicians to occur in 'thin' boys from infancy to adolescence. http://www.muslimheritage.com/uploads/urinarystone.pdf (accessed 20/ 8/10)

the bounds contained in their gift.'[16] The Fraser family seems to have been plagued by premature death; William's elder brother, Simon, took ill in the winter of 1639 from a 'hectic' thought to have been brought on by fatigue from too much travelling. 'Old Doctor Clerk, a Highland physician of singular skill attended him; yet nothing would do.' The patient appears to have exercised considerable control over his treatment; '[a] diet of cordials, milks and clarified whey, was his own prescripts.' He died in March 1640.[17]

Doctors came into the Highlands to treat patients who could afford their services. Some brought their medical expertise into the region when they chose to settle there. By the middle of the seventeenth century the inhabitants were becoming better served by an increase in medical men of all types. Rev. James Fraser was abroad in 1657/60 for what he called his 'Triennial Travels' and while in Pisa he met a Doctor William Forbes who subsequently returned to Scotland and settled in Inverness.[18] On Fraser's return he took ship from Gravesend to Inverness; among the passengers was a 'Mr Charles Mckullock, apothecary chirurgeon in Tain' who no doubt would have been familiar with the contents of a 'Chemist's Bill' found among the household accounts from Dunvegan for the year 1661.[19] It consists mainly of items prepared from ingredients such as syrup of violets, used for a variety of ills including coughs; cream of tartar, used as a diuretic or laxative; oil of almonds, an emollient; pectoral syrup, for coughs and congestion; and gentian root, used as a tonic.[20]

Alternatively, patients who could afford to do so travelled furth of the region to seek medical attention or effect some other form of cure. One such patient was Lady Lovat who in the summer of 1667 was indisposed and 'resolve[d] to try the Spa wells at York.'[21] She was accompanied by Dr George Mackenzie whom Fraser describes as a 'domestic' and 'a most knowing rational man.'[22] In all she was away for three months and on her return Fraser records waspishly that, '[a]ll the alteration I found on her was that her colour is more lively, and her stomach sharper; all that might be procured by her motion, travel, change of air, though drinking of water were not in the bargain at all.'[23] Lady Lovat had probably never

[16] Bannerman, *The Beatons,* pp. 93/4.

[17] Fraser, *Chronicles,* pp. 264–6.

[18] *Ibid.,* p. 454.

[19] *Ibid.,* p. 430.

[20] R.C. MacLeod (ed.), *The Book of Dunvegan: being documents from the muniment room at Dunvegan Castle* (1938) p. 185.

[21] Fraser, *Chronicles,* p. 473.

[22] *Ibid.,* p. 466.

[23] *Ibid.,* p. 473.

recovered from the birth of a son the year before. Dr Mackenzie had been in attendance then and was to look after Lady Lovat's 'chronic malady' for the remaining three years of her life.[24] As his own death approached in 1672, Hugh, Lord Lovat, often reflected on what Doctor Trial in Heidelberg had forewarned him of regarding his 'daily hectic decline,' consequently 'he refused any physic, but condescended to cordials, emulsions [and] ptisans,' – a drink of barley water and other ingredients such as herbs – administered by Dr Mackenzie who 'knew his constitution' and would 'tender him no medicine nor foreign drug, only simples and method of diet.'[25] Fraser's description suggests that medicines and foreign drugs were now available but that Dr Mackenzie, at the insistence of his patient, chose not to use them.

Some drugs with foreign ingredients were certainly available when Ann, Lady Tarbat, became ill, presumably at Castle Leod, Strathpeffer, in 1699. She was in her late sixties and had borne eight children. Her husband sought the advice of no less than five doctors in an effort to cure her. Among them was Archibald Pitcairn, then practicing in partnership in Edinburgh with a Dr Stevenson with whom he shared the same first name. They prescribed to Lady Tarbat (and her husband for his ailments) by letter. Although the doctors seemed to agree from 'information of some physicians with you' that 'her ladyship's trouble is plainly hysteric,' they differed about how best to treat her. Dr Stevenson seems more familiar with her condition, he is also seemingly unconcerned, prescribing the 'same pills' (they contained a small quantity of opium) and writing that 'if there be nothing else in her present colicks than was before, I am very hopeful will do well.'[26] He prescribes no strong purging but 'King Charles his famous drops which are of the volatile salt and spirit of raw silk', pills for the vapours and instructions to drink 'a posset' (hot milk curdled with ale, beer or wine, flavoured with spices, used as a remedy for colds) 'made of sack and double-sweet milk of a cow.'[27] When Stevenson is out of town, about a month later, Pitcairn writes instead, prescribing stronger remedies; Peruvian Bark for her stomach, and to prevent 'useless sweatings' a poultice for the sore parts, a 'pledget of flax pretty thick' covered in egg white 'soaked in Aqua vite or brandy, with two dram camphor and one dram spirits of hartshorn applied four or five times each twenty-four hours.' He adds, 'if the pain continues in one place make a poultice of cow's dung, milk

---

[24] *Ibid.*, pp. 466, 489/90 & 504.

[25] *Ibid.*, p. 504.

[26] Wm Fraser (ed.), *The Earls of Cromartie: Their Kindred, Country and Correspondence* 2 Vols. (1876) Vol. 1, pp. 139/40.

[27] *Ibid.*, p. 140.

and chamomile flowers and apply. Or cause bake a bannock … let it be pease or bean meal, and this apply warm to the places.'[28] Her ladyship's worsening situation and the contrary advice of a local Dr Pattisone – 'The King's Drops may be left off seeing they nauseate' – seem to have irritated Pitcairn who responded brusquely to what was presumably another anxious letter from Lord Tarbat; 'There needs no more be said in answer to it than that it is fit to give [Syrup of] Steel (it did well in the Lord President's case)' and he provides the prescription, namely, 'two ounces of steel filings to a quart of good white wine.'[29] Their patient died.

Archibald Pitcairn was considered to be one of the greatest physicians of his day and his engagement by the Tarbats illustrates the increasing use by wealthy Highland families of medical men recognised by the Lowland medical corporations. By far the most interesting remedy was King Charles' drops, prescribed by Dr Stevenson and seemingly endorsed by Pitcairn. Used for the treatment of fainting spells and apoplectic fits, they were made from 'hartshorn, ammonia, dried viper and oil distilled from the skull of a hanged man.'[30] Their creator was Jonathan Goddard, a member of the Royal College of Physicians and a councillor of the Royal Society. The local doctor whose intrusion seems to have irritated Pitcairn may have been the same Dr Alexander Patterson, described as a 'chyurgeon apothecary in Inverness' who attended Lady Rose of Kilravock in the early years of the eighteenth century. A bill for his services, running from 1712 to November 1714, consists chiefly of medicines. The importance of Paterson's remedies lies in their being drawn exclusively from herbal ingredients and as with the Chemist's Bill from Dunvegan half a century earlier they include plants not indigenous to the area. It would appear that Lady Rose suffered from what would then have been diagnosed as dropsy, for which white lily root was prescribed. In addition, the bill includes maiden hair, mouse ear and horse tail, all herbs used as diuretics; tussilago flowers (or coltsfoot) was primarily used as a cough suppressant, St Johns wort was also prescribed and had many uses including the treatment of mild depression. Penny royal and althea root could have helped with

[28] *Ibid.*, p. 141. Peruvian Bark from the Cinchona trees of South America was first exported to Europe in the 1640s. It contains quinine and was used to reduce fevers, calm the nerves and stimulate digestion. Its medical use was recorded in the *London Pharmacopeia* in 1677.

[29] *Ibid.*, p. 141 and M. Clough, 'A Research Note – material of medical interest in the Cromartie Papers', *The Scottish Society of the History of Medicine Report of Proceedings Session 1971–72*; 185–188. The prescription is taken by Clough from a manuscript in the Papers which include general remedies written in Scots, cod Latin or Greek. Some of these remedies appear to have been shared with other families.

[30] E.L. Furdell, 'Life and Work of Samuel Dodd Clippingdale, Medical Antiquarian,' *Journal of the Royal Society of Medicine*, Volume 82, December 1989, pp. 758–60, p. 759.

respiration and fenugreek seed was an aid to digestion.[31] Paterson, if indeed it was the same medical man, lost this patient too. His final service to her ladyship was to provide a 'large' waxed cerecloth for wrapping her corpse.

Some years later, Alexander Fraser, a surgeon who lived in Easter Ross, attended Simon, Lord Lovat. He submitted a lengthy account – which was to remain largely unpaid – covering the twenty months from 23 September 1742 until 24 May 1744, the bulk of which was for the supply of medicine.[32] Several of the remedies such as salt of hartshorn, syrup of violets, fine rhubarb and a pectoral electuary would have been familiar to 'the vulgar' of the region; others remedies perhaps less so. There are numerous entries for boxes of opium pills; a number for ipecacuanha vomits, whose use is self explanatory but the plants originate in Central and South America and so must have been a recent addition to the pharmacopeia; troches bechic, cough lozenges; mercury plaster and Peruvian bark are all prescribed. Frequent entries are for liquorice root and spermacæti lohoch. According to Culpeper's *Complete Herbal and English Physician* (1653) 'Lohoch' is an Arabic word – attesting to its classical origin – signifying 'a thing to be licked up … It is thicker than a syrup and not so thick as an electuary. Its use was against the roughness of the windpipe, diseases and inflammation of the lungs, difficulty in breathing, colds, coughs, etc. Its manner of reception is with a liquorice stick, bruised at the end, to take up some and retain it in the mouth, till it melt of its own accord.'[33]

These various accounts suggest that there had been a transition from providing remedies in the form of simples derived from indigenous natural resources to a more comprehensive *materia medica*, at least in the sickrooms of the upper reaches of Highland society.

THE HEALTH AND HEALTHCARE OF THE POOR

The health of the poorer Highlanders was more susceptible to the vagaries of the climate, congested and insanitary living conditions and the availability of food. Travellers provide conflicting reports about the general health of the inhabitants, but this is understandable when it is affected by the plenitude or otherwise of a healthy diet. On Mull in 1772, Thomas Pennant notes that they were 'much troubled with sore eyes, and in spring are afflicted with a costiveness that often proves fatal. At that season all their provisions are generally consumed; and they

---

[31] C. Innes (ed.), *A Genealogical Deduction of the Family of Rose of Kilravock* (1848), pp. 398/9.

[32] 'A Highland Medical Account of the Eighteenth Century, *Caledonian Medical Journal* Vol. XI, January 1921 No 10, pp. 250–6.

[33] Nicholas Culpeper, *The Complete Herbal and English Physician* (1653), pp. 312/3.

are forced to live on sheep's' milk boiled, to which the distemper is attributed.'[34] Macculloch bemoans the restricted diet of mutton and potatoes he was subjected to, even a lack of fish on the table in districts close to water, no fruit and vegetables to speak of other than the ubiquitous potato, the introduction of which he thinks is a 'great advantage' because 'the food of the people is less subject to casualties and failures than when it consisted of grain.'[35]

The basic diet before the introduction of sugars, white bread and tea was considered by many to contribute towards the longevity of some of the inhabitants; a disproportionate number of whom appeared to live to an advanced age.[36] Travellers frequently record the use of 'aquavitæ' as a 'catholicon' and Martin notes that children in Ferrintosh in Ross were taught to drink it from infancy.[37] He adds, perhaps unsurprisingly, that they 'are observed never [to] have any worms.' Travellers noted that the inhabitants 'are not much troubled with any diseases' but the harsh living conditions contributed to a high incidence of fevers, 'whereof they die commonly.'[38] The usual method of dealing with fevers involved a medical practice that featured prominently in ancient Gaelic manuscripts and continued to prevail in the Highlands. Phlebotomy – blood letting – was used for a wide variety of ailments, both therapeutically and prophylactically, but principally in the treatment of fevers, although the practice does not appear to have been universal.[39] While travelling in Argyll and Lorne in the winter of 1699 Edward Lhuyd noted that the people 'abhor physic and bloodletting and so they have few or no physicians.'[40] When Martin visited Jura he observed that 'blood-letting and purging are not used here.'[41] However, he notes while on Lewis and Harris that the common cure for removing fevers and pleurisies, is to 'let blood

---

[34] Pennant, *A Tour in Scotland and Voyage to the Hebrides 1772* (1998), p. 360.

[35] Macculloch , *The Highlands and Western Isles* Vol. III, pp. 332–48, p. 348.

[36] Martin, *A Description,* pp. 146, 237, 268/9, 373/4 & 377/8. *Statistical Account of Scotland 1791,* Vol. 14, p. 541.

[37] Edward Lhuyd, 'A Collection of Highland Rites and Customs', in Michael Hunter, *The Occult Laboratory,* (2001), p. 68. Martin in a Letter, 'Several Observations in the North Isles' to the Royal Society, 1695; RS Ref: cl.P/7i/52.

[38] Lhuyd in Hunter, *The Occult Laboratory,* p. 68 and Pennant, *A Tour 1772,* p. 273. Pennant had intended to visit Stornoway but was dissuaded on receiving news that 'a putrid fever raged there with great violence.' Pennant, *A Tour 1772,* p. 314.

[39] Mackinnon, *A Descriptive Catalogue,* p. 52.

[40] Lhuyd in Hunter, *The Occult Laboratory,* p. 68. This sentence is deleted from the original manuscript suggesting that Lhuyd had some reason to change his views, either about the practice of bloodletting or the dearth of physicians. Hunter suggests that the deletion was on the advice of John Beaton. Hunter, *The Occult Laboratory,* p. 218.

[41] Martin, *A Description,* p. 267.

plentifully.'[42] What seems clear is that despite these regional anomalies, blood letting as a cure for fevers and other ailments was widespread and a practice the Highlanders shared with mainstream medicine.

The practice seems to have been regularised on the island of Arran by the time Thomas Pennant visited in 1772. He reports that it was carried out twice every year 'with the utmost regularity at spring and fall. The Duke of Hamilton keeps a surgeon in pay; who at these seasons makes a tour of the island. On notice of his approach, the inhabitants of each farm assemble in the open air, extend their arms, and are bled in a hole made in the ground, the common receptacle of the vital fluid.'[43] Macculloch notes that it remained an acceptable medical practice and was not influenced by the vagaries of scientific opinion. 'Some one or other can bleed, in every community; and as this operation is here regulated and settled, while, in the scientific practice, the fashion of bleeding and of not bleeding revolves every ten years, or oftener, it comes precisely to the same thing, in the long run.'[44] Dr M. D. Macleod, writing in 1896, recalled that 'bleeding was much favoured for all diseases. I remember when lancets were a part of the equipment of the manse, and my father, till later years, bled his parishioners when he or they thought it beneficial.'[45]

As with all communities, especially rural ones, many remedies were administered by members of the family or non-medical practitioners. Mucculloch notes that 'many farmers, most of the lairds, or their wives, together with the schoolmasters and the clergymen, possess useful [medical] knowledge; and, what is not less valuable, active humanity.'[46] While medical knowledge continued to be disseminated by word of mouth it could also now be disseminated through the written word. Any transition from superstitious to scientific remedies and practices in the homes of the poorer sections of the community was influenced by what they could discover for themselves from the medical texts that were available. The very title of *The Poor Man's Physician, or, The Receipts of the famous John Moncrieff of Tippermalloch: Being a choice collection of simple and easy remedies for most distempers, very useful for all persons, especially those of a poorer condition* indicates that it was aimed at a popular audience. First published in 1712, it was widely read; a second edition appeared in 1716 and includes 'The Method of Curing the Small Pox and Scurvy by the Eminent Dr Archibald Pitcairn' first written in 1704 and

---

[42] *Ibid.*, pp. 93 & 144.

[43] Pennant, *A Tour 1772*, pp. 167/8.

[44] Macculloch, *The Highlands and Western Isles* Vol. IV, p. 37.

[45] M.D. Macleod, 'Popular Medicine and Surgery in the Highlands,' *Caledonian Medical Journal*, Vol. II No. 8, April 1896, pp. 288–290.

[46] Macculloch, *The Highlands and Western Isles* Vol. IV, p. 37.

published for the first time in 1715. A third edition of Moncrieff's work appeared in 1731 as it enjoyed continued popularity – it has been suggested that every manse and country mansion contained a copy – despite being largely a collection of folk beliefs and old wives tales.[47] A flavour of Moncrieff's medical skills can be gauged from his remedies for 'pissing the bed, or involuntary pissing, or not containing of urine.' He suggests; 'the brains and stones of a hare burnt and drunk; a snail burnt with its shell, given to drink; hare's dung; powder of burnt mice; the hoofs of a hog burnt; the ashes of date-stones; roasted hazel nuts; powder of egg shells. But above all, are commended the Powder of Agrimony and the inward skins of hens gizzards dried, given either by themselves, or mixed together with red wine.'[48] The only part of this remedy that would have been recognisable and acceptable to an eighteenth-century doctor versed in medical sciences would be the inclusion of the herb agrimony, its powers understood in ancient Chinese medicine and still used today to prevent urine loss.[49]

Through the medium of child healthcare, TC Smout compares Moncrieff's work with that of William Buchan's *Domestic Medicine* and suggests that turning from the one to the other was akin to turning 'from the world of witchcraft to the world of Dr Spock.'[50] Based on Buchan's medical experiences as surgeon and apothecary to the Foundling Hospital at Ackworth, Yorkshire, *Domestic Medicine* first appeared in 1769 and was still being printed in Britain until 1846.[51] It went through 22 revised editions in English, selling more than 80,000 copies in Buchan's lifetime, and was translated into all the main European languages.[52] The book was written in a common sense style that could be easily understood by the layman and in it Buchan emphasised the importance of paying attention to an infant's diet, clothing, need for fresh air and exercise. He also stressed the need for medicine as a liberal science to make its secrets known to as wide an audience as possible. It was, according to Buchan, 'never intended to supersede the use of a physician, but to supply his place where medical assistance could not easily be obtained.'[53] When the physician Alexander Morison emigrated from Skye to North Carolina in 1772 with three hundred of his neighbours he took a copy of

[47] http://www.canpub.co.uk/pmp/pmp1a.aspx (accessed 9/7/10).

[48] http://www.canpub.co.uk/pmp/pmp1a.aspx (accessed 9/7/10) page 41 of Moncrieff's book.

[49] http://www.herbalextractsplus.com/agrimony.cfm (accessed 9/7/10).

[50] T.C. Smout, *A History of the Scottish People, 1560-1830* (1969), p. 258.

[51] C.J. Lawrence, 'William Buchan: Medicine Laid Open' *Medical History*, Vol. 19, 1975, pp. 20–35. Lawrence makes a case for William Smellie, collaborator on the first *Encyclopaedia Britannica*, as being joint author of *Domestic Medicine*.

[52] P.M. Dunn, 'Perinatal lessons from the past, Dr William Buchan (1729–1805) and his Domestic Medicine', *Archives of Disease in Childhood*, Vol. 83 issue 1 (2000), pp. 71–73.

[53] William Buchan, *Domestic Medicine* (1799) 16th edition, pp. iii/iv.

Buchan's book with him.[54] He need not have bothered; it had been published in Philadelphia in 1771 and was last published in Boston in 1913.[55] Copies, many of them plagiarised, much to Buchan's annoyance, reached the furthest corners of the Canadian frontier.

Macculloch concurs with Buchan's views on the importance of an improved diet and general healthcare awareness but argues that better living conditions by themselves, unless fully understood, can have a detrimental effect on the health of the populace. 'Fevers, once so common and fatal in the Highlands, have become rare since famine has become less frequent,' he writes, before going on to argue that 'the chimney is a premature improvement in the Highland cottage' because previously the lack of a 'lumm' had meant that smoke could not escape and so suffumigated the cottage and everything in it. Fevers increased, he maintained, when chimneys were introduced because their introduction had not gone hand in hand with better personal hygiene. 'It is a good thing to make improvements,' he opined, 'but it is good also, to know how to begin at the right end.'[56]

Some Highland communities were so remote that their very remoteness protected them from many of the diseases that affected others. St Kilda was one such community; illnesses were so rare when Martin visited in 1697 that the inhabitants were 'ignorant of the virtues of [a range of healing] herbs [on the island]. They never had a potion of physic given them in their lives, nor know any thing of phlebotomy.'[57] When Macculloch called in 1815 the inhabitants did not recognise the medicinal benefits of eating green vegetables and they formed no part of their diet. This was in contrast to the people of Shetland and Orkney, for example, who cultivated small cabbage patches to supplement their diet.[58] Macculloch was informed that St Kildans rarely left the island and was mystified as to why the population did not increase in the same way as that of neighbouring islands. He was given two reasons. The inhabitants blamed the smallpox 'in former days,' which would suggest that the disease had been checked; and intriguingly 'it also appears that, from mismanagement of some kind, they lose an unusual proportion of children.'[59]

[54] Bannerman, *The Beatons*, pp. 123/4.
[55] Lawrence, 'William Buchan,' p. 20.
[56] Macculloch, *The Highlands and Western Isles* Vol. IV, pp 49/50.
[57] Martin, *A Description*, pp. 438/9.
[58] Macculloch, *The Highlands and Western Isles* Vol. II, p. 292.
[59] *Ibid.*, Vol. III, p. 190.

SMALLPOX AND ITS TREATMENT

The deadly disease of smallpox could ravage entire communities and yet in the Highlands it seems to have been rather less virulent than it was elsewhere. When in Harris, Martin records that 'it visits about once in seventeen years.'[60] Pennant writes that it visits Mull about once in twenty years and that in Rum there had been just one outbreak in thirty-four years when 'only two sickened, and both recovered.'[61] Martin notes that Lewis had 'not been troubled with epidemical diseases, except the small-pox, which comes but seldom, and then it sweeps away many young people.'[62] The young appeared to have been particularly susceptible although the region was not unique in this as 'very few adults [were] seen with it in Scotland as a whole.'[63] One method of trying to avoid the disease was to act in conciliatory fashion by speaking of it with reverence. A commentator, writing at the beginning of the twentieth century observes that 'to this day small-pox is alluded to in the outer islands as *bhean mhath* ("the good wife"), a form of euphemism the idea of which is that, in order to escape the ban of the disease, it should be spoken of respectfully.'[64]

More practical remedies were tried; Martin describes a cure which seemed to him to be effective for at least one of the Western Isles. 'When the small-pox is epidemical in the mainland over against Skie-Isle, the natives bathe their children in the infusion of Juniper Weed, and they generally escape; whereas those who neglect this precaution are observed often to die: of this I have seen several instances.'[65] Archibald Pitcairn, in his treatment of smallpox, recommends extensive bleeding in the initial stages and 'after the pox appears and fever is gone; steep a handful of sheep's purles [droppings] in a large mutchkin of hyssop water, then pour it off and sweeten it with a syrup of red poppies, and then drink it.'[66]

One Highland remedy which seems to have presaged scientific procedures was described by a Scots doctor, Peter Kennedy, a self styled 'Chirurgo-Medicus' who studied surgery, physic and anatomy in the university cities of the Low Countries, Germany and Italy before spending his final years in practice in

---

[60] Martin, *A Description*, p., 144.

[61] Pennant, *A Tour 1772,* pp. 273 & 280.

[62] Martin, *A Description*, p. 93.

[63] A. Monro, Senior, *An Account of the Inoculation of Small Pox in Scotland* (1765), p. 3.

[64] Mrs Robert Moodie, 'Highland Therapy' *Caledonian Medical Journal* Vol. V, October 1903. No. 8, pp. 320 - 341. p. 337.

[65] M. Martin, in a paper presented to the Royal Society on 12 November 1707; RS Ref cl.P/14/61.

[66] A. Pitcairn, *The Methods of Curing the Smallpox Written in the Year 1704: for the use of the noble family of March* (1715), p. 2.

London.[67] In 1713 Kennedy visited Constantinople where he describes the treatment of smallpox by variolation; the transference of a smallpox scale in powdered form through the nostril of the patient thus providing a mild case of the disease which conferred immunity. Sadly for Kennedy he missed an opportunity for immortality for he concludes his account by stating that 'my intention here is not with a design to introduce this practice into these parts, tho' the veracity of what I have advanced is not to be doubted; we in Britain probably being more timorous, and fearful of our lives in this case. My intention is to show how easily contagion may be communicated to the blood and this is more confirmed in some parts of the Highlands of Scotland, where they infect their children by rubbing them with a kindly pock, as they term it.'[68]

It was left to another far travelled Scot to introduce inoculation against smallpox into the country, doing so in 1726 in his native Aberdeenshire and then into the west of Scotland. He was Dr George Maitland, surgeon to the British embassy in Constantinople in 1716-18 during Sir Edward Worley Montagu's residency. While there, Sir Edward's wife, Lady Mary, who had survived the disease in London in 1715 arranged for Maitland to inoculate her five year old son and on return to London she persuaded him to inoculate her daughter during an epidemic in 1721.[69] Maitland's efforts in rural Aberdeenshire were not so successful, one of the six children he inoculated had a hydrocephalus which he was unaware of and when the child died the inoculation was thought to be the cause. This set back the practice in that area for some twenty years until reintroduced with some difficulty by Dr Rose, a physician from Aberdeen.[70]

In 1763/4 Alexander Monro, Senior, Fellow of the Royal College of Physicians and Professor of Medicine and Anatomy in the University of Edinburgh, carried out a survey into inoculation in Scotland in response to an enquiry from members of the Faculty of Medicine in Paris.[71] Monro sent a questionnaire to medical men across the country and doctors from Highland towns such as Thurso, Dornoch, and Inverness and from the islands of Skye, Orkney and Shetland replied with details of numbers inoculated against the

---

[67] P. Kennedy, *An Essay on External Remedies Wherein it is Considered, Whether all the Curable Distempers Incident to Human Bodies may not be Cured by Outward Means* ... (1715) np – preface.

[68] *Ibid.*, p. 156.

[69] C. Maitland, *Mr Maitland's Account of Inoculation the Smallpox* (1722), pp. 8–11.

[70] Munro, *An Account of the Inoculation*, p. 4.

[71] Inoculation had been introduced into France in 1755 by Theodore Tronchin, a doctor from Geneva, but French public and medical opinion was ambivalent. An epidemic of smallpox in Pars in 1762/3 was blamed on inoculation and the parlement banned the practice. It was reintroduced in 1774 following Louis XV's death from the disease. D.B. Hopkins, *Princes and Peasants: Smallpox in History* (1983) pp. 55, 62 & 70/1.

disease. Monro used the data to compare with parts of England and provided several explanations for the much better survival rates in the north including the observation that 'in some of the remote Highland parts, it has been an old practice of parents whose children have not had the small pox, to watch for an opportunity of any child of their neighbours being in good mild small pox, that they communicate the disease to their own children by making them bedfellows to those in it, and by worsted threads wet with the pocky matter round their wrists.'[72]

This method is similar to that described by Peter Kennedy and is a far cry from the one used by Charles Maitland whereby the patient was bled and purged, placed on a low diet and then had two deep incisions made below the skin into which the pocky matter was inserted. The preparation period could last as long as six weeks.[73] When Maitland inoculated the daughter of Lady Wortley he dispensed with the bleeding and purging on account of the child's state of good health but deep incisions remained standard procedure in parts of Britain, – contrary to the Turkish method – due to the belief that smallpox could only succeed through the issue of a poison from the seeds of the disease inherent within each of us – a belief that owed much to the humoral theory of medicine.[74] By the time Monro reported to his French colleagues he could state that blood letting and purging were now omitted in children and that 'a slight scratch is now generally made in the skin of one arm, into which a little piece of small thread passed through pocky matter is put, and kept there some days by a bandage.'[75] Claims have been made on behalf of several doctors, notably Robert Sutton in Suffolk and Lewis Williams in Kibworth near Leicester, as being the first to introduce inoculation without preparation into the country in the early 1760s but any astute Highland doctor observing and adopting local folk practice might be a candidate for this honour.[76] Dr Hew Sutherland, a 'worthy friend' of Monro's who died prior to his inquiry but who is credited with inoculating 600 in Orkney with the loss of only one patient, may be considered.[77] As indeed might a correspondent of Monro's; Mr Alex Mackenzie from Dornoch, who acted as Sutherland's assistant and inoculated 112 people in the northern isles. When Pennant travelled through Caithness in 1769 he appears to be making reference to this doctor when he notes that 'inoculation is much practiced by an ingenious physician (Dr Mackenzie, of Wick) in this country and also the Orkneys, with great success, *without any previous*

---

[72] Monro, *An Account of the Inoculation*, pp. 3/4.
[73] P. Razzell, *The Conquest of Smallpox* (1977), pp. 6 & 14.
[74] Maitland, *Mr Maitland's Account*, pp. 9–11; Razzell, *The Conquest of Smallpox*, p. 6.
[75] Monro, *An Account of the Inoculation*, pp. 18/9.
[76] Razzell, *The Conquest of Smallpox*, pp. 9 & 15.
[77] Monro. *An Account of the Inoculation*, p. 29.

preparation (emphasis added). The success was equally great at Sanda (Sanday), a poor isle ... in all these places the small pox is very fatal in the natural way.'[78] Pennant appears to be aware of the significance of inoculating without preparation and that it was an innovative procedure. However, its adoption was not universal.

Monro's statistics are far from complete and Highland parishes adopted inoculation with varying degrees of enthusiasm. The cost and availability of surgeons were to remain impediments to universal inoculation for some considerable time and with people too poor to pay the costs were often borne by estate owners or those running them on behalf of the crown. On 16 January 1780 Mr John Maclagan, surgeon in Taymouth wrote to William Barclay, Annexed Estates Office, Edinburgh to remind him that he had warned of the 'havoc the natural small pox was making in the neighbourhood of the king's lands of Rannoch ... that in a village where there were fourteen or fifteen children, eight or nine had died, while the survivors were much hurt in their eyesight, and that the disease would soon spread to Rannoch if not prevented by inoculation.'[79] Maclagan advised that the inhabitants would never consent to have their children inoculated unless it was done gratis. As there was no time to wait on a meeting of the board, he had proceeded – on Mr Barclay's responsibility – to inoculate '155 poor people's children (besides some of the better sort).' They all did well; but this caused the good doctor 'a vast deal of fatigue for many weeks, attending such a number, some of them being 20 miles distant from the other in such a country and with such roads. *Preparing them took up some time* (emphasis added).'[80] In November 1782 Mr Maclagan was asked by Robert Menzies, factor of the Annexed Estate of Strowan, to inoculate his son and thereafter appears to have inoculated sixty-five children of tenants and cottars in Strowan and Lochgarry.[81] Although the cost was borne by the estate we do not know what Mr Maclagan charged but when the factor needed the service again in February 1783 he saw fit to get a quotation from William Farquharson, surgeon in Dunkeld, who advised that, 'the common fee he charges the country people for inoculation is 5/- sterling a head, when there is a large number, for which he inoculates, affords medicines, and gives one or two visits when the children sicken.'[82] He continues that he 'has not looked upon it as part of his business to make money by, for since he settled

---

[78] T. Pennant, *A Tour in Scotland 1769* (2000), p. 121.
[79] A.H. Millar (ed.), *A Selection of Scottish Forfeited Estates Papers, 1715–1745* (1909) pp. 260/1.
[80] *Ibid.*
[81] *Ibid.*, p. 264.
[82] *Ibid.*, p. 260.

there he has inoculated above a hundred children for nothing.'[83]

One reason for the lack of uniform uptake was the religious views of the inhabitants. To many, the notion of deliberately introducing a disease into a healthy child was tempting God's providence.[84] This was the case in Urquhart and Glenmorriston and at Cromdale and Golspie, for example, and it was only the intervention of the clergy arguing a contrary view in public that enabled John Williamson, a Caithness country doctor, to inoculate some 645 people – a prodigious feat of which the good doctor was only too well aware – during an epidemic in Thurso in 1796. Williamson's experiences of contagious diseases as an army surgeon in the West Indies led him to the view that all children should be inoculated as a matter of routine at over four days old.[85] Although his views may appear to be innovative, he is writing some thirty years after Pennant's account of Dr Mackenzie's methods in Wick and is still recommending that some 'previous [unspecified] preparation is most commonly necessary.'[86] He thinks that 'domestic inoculation is dangerous' – Buchan was all for it – and would have been relieved had he known that in Forglen in upper Banffshire the people were by then reconciled to the practice and found it 'as good to let the doctor prepare them, and do it, as to let the children inoculate themselves at random.'[87]

MEDICINE AND WAR

Smallpox was just one of a number of contagious diseases that could wreak havoc on a population and the sudden influx of large numbers of outsiders bearing disease could have a devastating effect on the health of a community. Armies provide the most obvious example of foreign bodies invading a region and numerous armies have traversed the Highlands especially in periods of national unrest. James Fraser of Wardlaw was impressed by Commonwealth troops when they occupied Inverness during the Protectorate and laboured on building the Citadel there until its completion in 1655. 'They bought such stores of all wares and conveniences to Inverness …,' he observed. '[T]hey] set up an apothecary shop with drugs, Mr Miller their Chirurgion, and Doctor Andrew Monro their

---

[83] *Ibid.* This income contrasts with the sum paid to Charles Maitland who was commanded to visit Hanover in 1724 to inoculate the King's grandson, Prince Frederick, second in line to the throne. Maitland was awarded £1200 by a grateful king for his time and expenses without the need to render an account http://www.christies.com/Lotfinder/lot_details.aspx?intObjectID=4841130 (accessed 6/08/10).

[84] Monro, *An Account of the Inoculation*, pp. 5/6.

[85] *Statistical Account of Scotland 1791* Vol. 8, p. 253; Vol. 20. pp. 307 & 502–7; Vol. 21, p. 223.

[86] *Ibid.*, Vol. 20, p. 507.

[87] *Ibid.*, Vol. 14, p. 542; Vol. 20, p. 506.

physician. They not only civilised but enriched this place'.[88] Fraser's account suggests that the senior medical staff in the army interacted with the local population to the latter's benefit. In addition to the army having brought a physician, an apothecary and a hospital surgeon, a surgeon and his assistant was attached to each of the sixteen regiments and the artillery train stationed in Scotland.[89] To what extent their influence remained after their departure is a matter for conjecture but the civic authorities in Inverness clearly developed an understanding of the benefits of appointing a public medical officer. The burgh records show that on 22 November 1680 a Dr McKenzie was to be paid out of the public purse by the magistrates and council for 'attending and visiting the diseased persons of this burgh.'[90] This may be this same Dr Mackenzie, his tenure as 'domestic' physician at an end, who had cared for the Lovat family.

Armies may bring their doctors and surgeons but they also bring disease. When Edward Lhuyd visited Scotland he used the naturalist John Ray's *Dictionariolum Trilingue* to record words from Gaelic dialects and notes that in Argyle the term for 'the French-Pox' is 'Bòlgynach' and in Inverness it is 'Glanagorn,' a loan word from the Scots. Syphilis, as it came to be known is generally thought to have broken out for the first time in Europe in1494 among the inhabitants of Naples and the French troops besieging the city. Within three years this 'infirmity come out of France' or 'strange sickness of Naples' was widespread across Scotland and many towns and cites including Edinburgh and Glasgow had passed ordinances to try to check its spread. Aberdeen was the first to respond, a regulation dated 21 April 1497 instructs 'all licht women to desist from their venerie on pain of being branded on the cheek and banished from the town.'[91] Lhuyd makes no reference to the 'sivvens' a particularly virulent strain of venereal disease spread, according to Pennant, from the garrison at Inverlochy throughout the Highlands and Lowlands and borrowing its name via Lowland Scots from *Suibhean* the Gaelic word for raspberry and used to describe the raspberry like growths on the skin.[92] The garrison at Inverlochy was first established in the summer of 1654 when a thousand men from the English army in Ireland landed in Lochaber. The spread of the disease would have been compounded by the fact that Inverlochy was considered such an unpopular

[88] Fraser, *Chronicles*, pp. 415/6.

[89] C.H. Firth (ed.), *Scotland and the Protectorate 1654 -59: Letters and Papers, etc (1899)*, pp. 374/5.

[90] W. Mackay and G. Smith Laing (eds), *Records of Inverness* (1911) Vol. II, p. 288.

[91] J.D. Comrie, *History of Scottish Medicine to 1860* (1927) pp. 46/7.

[92] Pennant, *A Tour 1772*, pp. 414 & 767. W. P. MacArthur, '"The Sibbens," or "The Sivvens"? Correspondence to the Editor', *Transactions of the Royal Society of Tropical Medicine and Hygiene*, Vol. 47. No. 5 September, 1953, pp. 437/8.

posting because of its remoteness, lack of resources and difficulty in obtaining fuel that companies from each regiment of foot stationed in Scotland were sent there on six month rotation. They were chosen by lot to avoid charges of favouritism so that soldiers and their diseases were marching between garrison towns on a regular basis.[93] 'Sivvens', compared by medical men familiar with tropical diseases to *yaws* from West Africa, was treated like other venereal diseases by 'externals, bathing, sweating, unctions, etc before the use of mercury.'[94]

Sometimes more extreme remedies were required for treating 'the pox'. As a last resort the patient could be trepanned. Such an operation was performed by a kinsman of James Fraser, Alexander Fraser of Durris. Educated at Aberdeen, Leyden and Montpellier where he took his MD, he was physician in ordinary to Charles II and went under the name of the 'French Doctor' having practiced in France prior to taking up his royal appointment.[95] In February 1667 Dr Fraser was in charge when Prince Rupert of the Rhine, 'The Mad Cavalier,' was trepanned in an effort to relieve headaches caused by 'a clap of the pox' which he had acquired during a military campaign twelve years earlier and which was eating through his scull.[96] The operation, the second on the prince, was a success and contributed to the award of the doctor's knighthood prior to his retiring to Durris in upland Aberdeenshire in 1673.

Another military doctor who was to be knighted for his services was Dr John Pringle, a native of Stitchel in Roxburghshire. During the ill fated Jacobite Rebellion of 1745 he was physician general to the British forces in the Low Countries and accompanied the army when it was recalled to deal with the rising in the north. He served throughout the campaign, being present on the field at Culloden and afterwards having to deal with the sick and wounded government troops.

The military campaign in Scotland attracted several young surgeons from the London hospitals who answered the call for volunteers; the prospect of adding to their medical experience being one spur to joining up.[97] Some of the wounds from

---

[93] Firth, *Scotland and the Protectorate*, pp. xxxix & xl/xli.

[94] Pennant, *A Tour 1772*, p. 766. Kennedy, *An Essay on External Remedies …*, p. 148. J.S. McKenzie Pollock, 'Sibbens or Sivvens – The Scottish Yaws' *Transactions of the Royal Society of Tropical Medicine and Hygiene*, Vol. 47. No. 5 September, 1953, pp. 431–6.

[95] Fraser, *Chronicles*, pp. 32 & 427.

[96] http://www.pepysdiary.com/archive/1667/01/28/ & http://www.pepysdiary.com/archive/1667/02/02/ Diary of Samuel Pepys, (accessed 24/08/10). The operation took place in London; Pepys had the details from Dr Timothy Clarke who later became physician in ordinary to the king. J. Robertson (ed.), *Passages from the Diary of General Patrick Gordon of Auchleuchries AD1635–AD1699* (1859), p. 89n.

[97] Dr MacNaughton, 'Medical Heroes of the 'Forty-five' *Caledonian Medical Journal* Vol. IV, January 1900, No. 3, p. 113.

the battlefield which may have been familiar to a doctor working in the Highlands were new to the army medical staff. Pringle observed that, '[s]everal had cuts of the broad-sword, which till then had been uncommon wounds in our hospitals; as the openings were large in proportion to the depth, as they bled much at first, and as there were no contusions and eschars, as in gun shot wounds, to obstruct a good digestion.'[98]

Pringle, who arranged for two 'well-aired houses' to serve as a general military hospital, notes that the town of Inverness was overcrowded, the soldiers were encamped in and around the burgh, the jails were full of prisoners and measles and small pox were already 'prevalent' before the army arrived.[99] To alleviate the squalid conditions of prisoners, some were transferred to ships lying at anchor where they were supposed to be allowed on deck to get fresh air and some freedom of movement. This seemingly humane treatment is in stark contrast to accounts of conditions suffered by prisoners; in addition to being deprived of food and water for the first two days of their captivity, doctors who were among them had their lancets and other medical instruments confiscated to prevent them being used to alleviate the distress of their fellow prisoners.[100]

Although able to contain cases of illness throughout April and early May disaster struck at the end of that month with the arrival of a batch of thirty six Jacobite prisoners and army deserters who had been taken off a captured French vessel and had been transferred to Inverness to stand trial. They brought with them 'jail fever' which spread not only in the hospitals but among the inhabitants of the town. When the army moved south to Fort William on 3 June Pringle went with it, leaving behind about 600 sick in the charge of surgeon John Hawkins (also Hawkeens), an experienced army surgeon of middle years who had matriculated as a 'Chyrurgius' from Oxford University in February 1714.[101] He was on very good terms with, and sought the advice of, Charles Alston, Professor of Botany and *Materia Medica* in the University of Edinburgh. Alston, who had studied under Boerhaave in Leyden at the same time as Alexander Monro, Senior, started writing lectures on *materia medica* in 1720 and continued to deliver and

---

[98] Sir John Pringle, *Observations on the Diseases of the Army: in Camp and Garrison* (1752) p. 44.

[99] Pringle, *Observations*, p. 45.

[100] Accounts of the conditions of the prisoners in Inverness can be examined in *The Lyon in Mourning*, 3 Vols (1895) and *The Prisoners of the '45* Vol. I (1928).

[101] Welcome Trust MS. 2788. Hawkins also transferred to Scotland from the Low Countries and found time during his 'Scotch campaign' to obtain a 'Diploma for Doctor of Physick' from Marischall College, Aberdeen before returning to the continent in late 1746. The Diploma could be got on the recommendation of two well known and respected graduates and a fee (if any) of no less than £16. *Statistical Account of Scotland 1791*, Vol. 21, p. 126.

revise them for the next thirty-four years. He was sceptical of the use of simples when they were not studied scientifically by experiment. However, his experiments were at times rudimentary; and often involved mixing the simples with chemicals, but only after the senses, principally taste and smell, had been used to study various effects. Some claims, such as the virtues of burnt toad as a diuretic, he dismissed as 'founded on a fable.'[102] He examined the medical texts available at the time and notes the diminishing number of outlandish remedies such as *stercora* (excrements) listed in more recent editions; 'truly,' he observed, 'the *materia medica* may do without them.'[103] Alston's scientific approach and debunking of archaic remedies would have influenced an entire generation of medical students in Edinburgh.

On 28 June 1746 Hawkins wrote to Alston apologising that he had not be able to write sooner because he had 'much business ever since the Battle of Culloden; but now the wounded are either sent to Edinburgh, recovered or dead, and the present sickness which rages most is a terrible malignant fever that produces violent symptoms' which he goes on to describe and explain that at an early stage in the illness the patients are bled 'frequently and in large quantities' this being the 'greatest part of the cure for inflammatory diseases' employed by the army.[104] In addition to bleeding other remedies were tried; nitre, given to act as a cooler; had the effect of 'producing stools in plenty' but was not much use as a cure. Spermaceti was used to moisten tongues that had become dry and bled 'so bad I very seldom have seen.' Opiates, antimony, carbonate of ammonia and what Hawkins considered to be the best medicine, Virginia snake root, were all administered.[105] Before departing for Fort William, Pringle had left instructions with Hawkins to 'dissect all curious cases, and send him the history' which he unfailingly did. Most of the dissections were on the chest cavity to see the effects of fevers on the lungs but in one instance Hawkins opened the head of a man who had 'died quiet' to examine inflammation of the brain, being unable to explain the flux of watery matter issuing from his nose.[106]

In a postscript Hawkins notes that he wished he was leaving Inverness; 'for the town is become infectious by reason of sickness and dead bodies so that none of us desire to stay longer in it.'[107] When the camp at Fort William broke up in

---

[102] C. Alston, *Lectures on the Materia Medica* (1770), p. 499.

[103] *Ibid.*, pp. 550/1.

[104] A. Mitchell, 'After Culloden', correspondence to the *Caledonian Medical Journal* Vol. IV, (1901) July No.9 pp. 354–356 and Pringle, *Observations,* p. 76.

[105] A. Mitchell, 'After Culloden', pp. 354–356.

[106] *Ibid.*

[107] *Ibid.*, p. 356.

August between three and four hundred sick were carried to Inverness by which time Pringle noted that 'the hospital fever was frequent among the inhabitants of that town.'[108] However, it was 'milder than usual from the coolness of the weather and the openness of the place.' Despite the surgeons' success in alleviating symptoms, death from fever was generally inevitable. In all, from the middle of February 1746 when the army crossed the Forth until the end of the campaign, over two thousand men had been in hospital, of which nearly three hundred had died, most from contagious fever.[109] Pringle went on to write his *Observations on the Diseases of the Army: in Camp and Garrison* (1752). This opus earned him the sobriquet 'father of military medicine.' In it Pringle identifies hospitals as being the major cause of sickness and advocates cleaner accommodation, small numbers of patients and fresh air as preventatives to contagion. The numbers of townspeople infected by the fevers is impossible to quantify as is the extent to which the inhabitants of Inverness benefitted from the scientific experimentation and discoveries that were taking place in their midst. It is unlikely that they shared Rev. James Fraser's favourable opinion of the occupying forces of a near century earlier but it would appear that the environment, so often the cause of sickness and death, had helped alleviate their distress in this particular epidemic of contagious fever; a fact that had not gone unnoticed by Pringle.

CONCLUSION

The very nature of the Highlands, its inaccessibility, its ruggedness and inclement weather meant that getting medical attention from a qualified practitioner was no easy matter. It also meant that when qualified practitioners did venture into the region they were often required to have the expertise of more than a single medical profession and carried a designation such as 'surgeon-apothecary.' Initially their remedies were based on simples and were prescribed in conjunction with the patient. When, in an ever evolving *materia medica*, remedies changed over time the relationship between doctor and patient evolved into one in which doctors made the decision as to the best course of treatment even if doctors could not always agree among themselves. Treatment for the poorer sections of the community was usually managed by a member of the family, or the minister, or anyone who had some basic medical knowledge. Guidance on remedies, prescriptions, and medical matters was disseminated in books, some written in a style and printed at a cost that made them accessible to a popular audience. Simples continued to be

---

[108] Pringle, *Observations*, p. 52.
[109] *Ibid.*

administered but their healing properties came to be attributed to natural, rather than supernatural, causes. Bleeding for the alleviation of fevers and other illnesses had been practised for centuries. It continued to be practiced in mainstream medicine and among the population at large, many of whom, especially in the manse or country mansion, owned a lancet and acted as lay doctors.

In the case of smallpox, it seems that a form of inoculation was practiced by poorer sections of the community well before scientific inoculation was introduced. The uptake of inoculation against smallpox was not universal, although it was more readily accepted among the upper classes. Resistance was based on medical and religious grounds; often the sheer force of character of a parish minster would be enough to sway the decision for or against depending on his personal standpoint. The continued use of folk remedies, and old but accepted practices added to the complex mix of what was considered efficacious in the treatment of this and other diseases. When armies arrived they brought a range of medical men to care primarily for their own but they did impart medical knowledge to the local communities with whom they came into contact. They also brought their own diseases. New words entered the lexicon, new remedies and practices were developed to deal with the new diseases. Some of these practices appear to have been influenced by the distinctive Highland environment. Some medical practices evolved in the region, some incoming practices were adopted without change at the expense of existing practices, some were modified, and others were absorbed into the existing system. As the accounts of residents, travellers and visitors show, the Highlanders, across all sections of the community, looked after themselves by what they considered to be the most appropriate or accessible means and adapted to innovations and improvements in living standards and personal healthcare in their own way.

Dutch maternity care: lessons learnt

EDWIN R. VAN TEIJLINGEN
Bournemouth University

INTRODUCTION

Over the past ten years I have been involved in several studies related to childbirth, maternity care and maternal health care in various countries; this introduction is really the story of how it all began for me. It is common for general text books on health and medicine to start with a statement along the lines of "Pregnancy and childbirth are pivotal events in the lives of women and their families" or "Pregnancy and birth are not only the start of a new life, they are also the start of a new generation". Interestingly, pregnancy and childbirth were also events at the start of my academic career, not the actual physiological event in the lifecycle, but the social study of the organisation of maternity care. My PhD on the organisation of maternity care in Scotland and the Netherlands (van Teijlingen 1994) was supervised by Peter McCaffery in the Department of Sociology and Anthropology at the University of Aberdeen. I had been a visiting student from the Netherlands where I had completed three years in Economics, but in Aberdeen I had changed disciplines and had joined the third-year of the M.A. in Sociology for a one-year exchange. After considerable encouragement from several members of staff in the department, including Dr Peter McCaffery, Dr Mike Lyon, Dr Chris Wright and Dr Norman Stockman and, the then head of department, Professor Robert Moore, this one year became two years and I completed my undergraduate study in Sociology in 1986. After my graduation I started to prepare for my return to the Erasmus Universiteit Rotterdam in the Netherlands to finish my original undergraduate degree there in Economics.

Then one day in the early summer of 1986 Peter McCaffery, approached me to ask if I would be interested in conducting some interviews in the Netherlands with midwives, obstetricians, policy-makers and other stakeholders to finds out why the home birth rate was still so high in the Netherlands. Peter had just attended a Social Science Faculty Board meeting at King's College where it was announced that there was some end of year money left over which had to be allocated by the end of the week. Peter speaks and reads Dutch and completed his own PhD on Catholics in the Netherlands (McCaffery 1990), furthermore his wife Teresa is Dutch. I had a vague knowledge of medical sociology and a keen interest in cross-cultural studies and history so I told Peter: "Yes, that would be a

Explorations in Cultural History: Essays for Peter Gabriel McCaffery,
edd. David F. Smith & H. Philsooph (Aberdeen 2010)   ISBN 978-0-9567059-0-7

great opportunity." Peter wrote a short proposal and soon after received the research money to send me to do some fieldwork in the Netherlands. In those days before easy access to resources on the Internet we started the research with whatever Peter and I could locate in the library about Dutch maternity care, midwifery and health care. To cut a long story short, this short-term project was the starting point for my PhD research.

PhD supervision: Lessons learnt

This paper is not simply a paper on an academic topic Peter made me enthusiastic about many years ago, for me it is also about Peter as a supervisor. Peter McCaffery was my PhD supervisor in the good-old days when universities did not have graduate schools to dream up courses, paperwork and generally things to do for their graduate students. There were very few hurdles to climb, hoops to jump through and boxes to tick other than doing the actual research. In short, I learnt the art of doing a PhD 'on the job', with constant encouragement from Peter, and very little formal training. Peter was there to talk to about my work and me. Teresa had her first baby in a birthing pool in Aberdeen during my time as a PhD student, of course, which helped to strengthen our bond.

When I started to have my own PhD students I started to supervise them in the only way I really knew, the way Peter did it. 'When one of my PhD students wrote some kind words about my supervision style in the acknowledgements section of her thesis, I realized that I owed much of this to Peter's example. More importantly, the way Peter supervised me has now been passed on the next generation of PhD supervisors! The remainder of this chapter outlines some key sociological issues in the organisation of Dutch maternity care, starting with a short introduction of a sociological view of midwifery and maternity care.

What makes 'midwifery' so interesting for sociologists?

It is generally recognised that midwifery is one of the oldest professions in the world. In the words of the founder of the Frontier Nursing Service in Kentucky, Mary Breckinridge [1927:1147]: "The midwife's calling is so ancient that the medical and nursing professions, in even their earliest traditions, are parvenus beside it." If prostitution or sex work is really the 'oldest profession' then it not an unrealistic to claim that midwifery is likely to be the 'second oldest profession'. More recently, since the eighteenth century, midwifery has experienced 'competition' from doctors in giving care around birth. For many sociologists the medical profession is one of the most powerful professions ever (e.g. Freidson 1975; Turner 1987). Thus we can see why sociologists have been so interested in this field (e.g. Witz 1992; DeVries *et al.* 2001; Christiaens & van Teijlingen 2009).

At the same time, birth and death are among the most starkly physiological events in the human life cycle, but the way we organise maternity care, both socially and culturally varies widely across the world. Conception, pregnancy and birth are all biological and physiological events which are very much embedded in a social and cultural setting. The social construction of pregnancy and birth, the way women are supposed to behave, for example, the things women are supposed to do during pregnancy (or not supposed to do) are very much culturally defined. Thus sociologists and anthropologists have been keen to study birth as a social phenomenon, and to use it as an example to show how sociology can help society to understand the social construction of pregnancy and childbirth.

A third reason why this topic or field is so interesting for social scientists is that the organisation of maternity care is an exciting study area for organisational sociologists as different occupations interact in the care of pregnant women, these include midwives, obstetricians, general practitioners, anaesthetists, social workers, paediatricians and maternity care assistants (van Teijlingen & McCaffery 1987). Peter wrote about the pressure on the midwife attending home-birth, as she can be torn between delivering a women-centred service, being available 24/7, and the demands from friends and relatives (McCaffery 2004; DeVries 1993). Evidence from different countries, including the Netherlands and the UK suggests that midwives experience problems combining a private life with a job that requires total dedication and seven days a week and 24 hours a day continuous availability. No wonder Peter McCaffery concluded, in his introductory chapter to a section of academic papers on the politics of midwifery in our edited book '*Midwifery and the Medicalization of Childbirth: Comparative Perspectives*' (Figure 1), that midwifery was a 'greedy profession', i.e. a job which demanded great commitment, loyalty, time and energy, but where the rewards are great (McCaffery 2004).

Figure 1 Edited book on sociology of midwifery

DUTCH MATERNITY CARE AS SEEN ABROAD

This chapter starts with a short analysis of common views found in the English-language literature about Dutch maternity care and its midwives. Obstetric care in the Netherlands takes a more 'physiological' perspective on pregnancy and birth, than in many other industrialised countries, and it is widely cited as one of the better examples of how maternity services could be provided elsewhere. For example, in New Zealand (NZ) and Australia, Belton (1993) reminds us that Dutch midwifery is often held up as a guiding beacon to Australian midwives as the system of maternity care to strive for. Donley (1986 :153–4) pointed out that the Netherlands despite its "large rural population" manages good birth outcomes without having "a 'flying squad' of obstetrically equipped ambulances" like NZ has. In the United States of America (USA) we find arguments such as the following: "…aspects of the Netherlands' system could be used in the United States. For instance, nurses could investigate whether a maternity care helper program would help to lower the U.S. infant mortality rate" (Bradley & Bray, 1996). Whilst in the United Kingdom (UK): "The Dutch system of maternity care is occasionally held up as an example to be emulated by [its] health care providers" (Mander, 1995). Hilary Marland (1993: 21) in her history of midwifery in the Netherlands commented that many see:

"the Dutch system as a model to be followed. Because it gives the pregnant woman more choice of where, how, and with whom she will give birth, and the midwife a higher level of professional autonomy. Dutch obstetric services are seen as efficient and economic, and also maintain low rates of perinatal mortality."

Other Dutch researchers stated in their comments on industrialised countries in general: "The Dutch system of maternity care ... receives much attention from other industrialized countries, where home births are often depicted in a negative light" (Wiegers *et al.*, 1998). Wiegers (2009) more recently pointed out that: in the Netherlands almost 10% of women experienced medical induction of labour compared to 34% in the USA and 31% in England, at the same time only 27.5% of Dutch women received some form of pain relief compared to 86% in the USA 86% and 93% in England.

PAIN RELIEF AND CULTURE

The following study, conducted quite a few years ago now, is a good example, where cross-national research can help us gain insight into a sociological issue. Sport psychologists and educational researcher have shown us over the last four or five decades that if a person thinks she can do it, it is more likely that she actually achieves what she sets out to do and vice versa. The example I have selected here is a cross-country prospective comparative study conducted more than twenty years ago of pregnant women's expectations of pain in childbirth and their need for pain relief in two locations: Nijmegen (the Netherlands) and Iowa (USA). Pregnant women delivering in hospital were being asked how painful they thought their labour pain was going to be using some kind of pain scale. The first interesting finding the survey showed was that the women in the two countries prior to birth had different expectations of labour pain and different expectations of their ability to cope (Senden *et al.* 1988). Women were then asked after the birth their pain experience and their perceived need for pain relief. The link between these women's expectations and outcomes (pain experience and perceived need for pain relief) was remarkable. The authors highlighted: "Iowa women, in general, expected labour to be more painful than did Dutch patients, and further anticipated that they would receive medication for labour pain. In virtually the same proportion, Iowa women did receive pain medication. By contrast, women in the Nijmegen hospitals did not expect labour to be as painful, tended not to anticipate receiving analgesia, and usually did not receive any" (Senden *et al.* 1988: 542). This differences in pain were not due to differences in pregnancy complications as Senden and colleagues (1988: 543) noted in the Netherlands at the time: "... approximately 35% of births occur at home, whereas in Iowa, virtually all take place in a hospital. Thus, although the Dutch sample may be selected, any bias would be towards the abnormal and complicated labour, which should, if anything, underestimate any pre-existing differences in attitudes or expectations." The obvious difference to a sociologist is that there are cultural differences in notions of severity of pain, and more likely, notions of having the ability to cope.

DUTCH MATERNITY CARE AS AN 'EXAMPLE'

The enthusiasts who have used the Dutch as an example of more woman-centred maternity care, include obstetricians, midwives, student midwives, general practitioners, childbirth activists, researchers (in for example sociology, anthropology, medicine, midwifery and epidemiology), and consumer-groups, such as the Association for the Improvement in the Maternity Services. All have cited the way the Dutch organise midwifery and maternity care as a better way or even the ideal approach to providing maternity care for normal childbirth. Ray De Vries (2005: 23) distilled it clearly: "The peculiar obstetric habits of the Dutch often find their way into the professional literature as a foil for more ordinary (i.e., medical) maternity care practices, a way of promoting alternative approaches to birth."

As sociologists we do, of course, recognise the ideological foundations of some of the above claims. We also have to raise the question: "Why, if the Dutch maternity care system is so excellent, are the satisfaction levels among Dutch women about their maternity care lower than expected?" These lower than expected levels of user satisfaction have been highlighted by Baston and colleagues (2008) as well as sociologists from Belgium (Christiaens & Bracke 2009). Postpartum care is provided by midwives (or now very occasionally rural GPs) and maternity home care assistants at home. Hence the 'care path' in maternity care can be straight forward when pregnancy and birth are uncomplicated, but can become complicated if medical/obstetric complications occur (Wiegers 2009). When all goes well and women stay low risk they are likely to experience good continuity of care, but when women's status changes from low-risk to medium or high-risk during pregnancy or labour they are more likely to experience a break in continuity of care and most likely of carer. For example, Wiegers (2009) observed that most respondents in her study of 793 women in the Netherlands started antenatal care and finished postnatal care with a midwife in primary care, but just over half of them gave birth in a hospital, supervised by an obstetrician often assisted by a hospital-based obststric nurse. The different paths which were followed by one woman in three pregnancies in the Netherlands has been insigthfully described by Ireland (1999).

KEY ASPECTS OF DUTCH MATERNITY CARE

Key characteristics of the way the Dutch organise midwifery and maternity care include: (1) the role and position of midwives; (2) the high proportion of home births; (3) the support of obstetricians for a health system in which midwives do the risk selection; (4) the high up-take of maternity home care assistants; and (5) long-term government support for the current system with its home births. Of course, several of these characteristics can be found in other countries, for example in the UK risk selection is a very much part a midwife's task, and there is a growing number of maternity care assistants across the country. What differentiates the Dutch maternity services from nearly all other industrialised countries is the way these characteristics interact and have led to the unique organisation of maternity services in the Netherlands and the role and status of its practitioners. Each of these five key characteristics is detailed below, although their interaction makes the Dutch system what it is.

POSITION OF MIDWIVES

If the pregnancy is low risk and proceeds well, midwives based in the community (or occasionally general practitioners) are fully responsible for antenatal care, childbirth and postnatal care, whilst obstetricians attend the high-risk women. Thus there is a clear distinction between care providers' responsibility for pregnant women: physiology for the midwife and pathology for the obstetrician. In cases of imminent pathology, midwives can seek an obstetric opinion and change her care pathway to obstetric-led if necessary. When I was working on my PhD research twenty years ago I highlighted as a key difference between midwives in the Netherlands and the UK that UK midwives were generally trained as nurses first followed by a one-and-a-half-year specialisation in midwifery. Being trained as a nurse first would indoctrinate the future midwife into thinking that pregnancy and labour are potentially pathological events which would need medical interventions, rather than physiological events in which women need mainly psycho-social support and advice. Moreover, I argued in my thesis that this characteristic of midwifery training was one of the key differences between the two countries. Now I am not so sure about the relevance of this difference in training. In 2010 most UK midwives have been through direct-entry training, i.e. from day one of their midwifery education they are trained to become midwives. Although many of the midwives in charge will still have been trained as nurses first, I don't see much evidence of UK maternity services refocusing on physiological birth moving away from a pathological approach.

HOME BIRTHS

In a maternity care system which offers home birth as a genuine choice for low-risk pregnant women, women who opt for a home birth are less likely to be referred and have less obstetric interventions (van der Hulst *et al.* 2004). Midwives generally (a) prefer a non-technological birth; (b) have faith in the woman's ability to give birth normally; and (c) have a non-interventionist attitude (van der Hulst *et al.* 2007). And where better to let the woman labour naturally and avoid unnecessary obstetric interventions than at home? However, over the past thirty years the proportion of women in the Netherlands having a home birth has dropped to just over one-third of all deliveries, but the latest data put it at about 29% for the period 2005–2008 (CBS 2009). Most of these homebirths are attended by midwives.

SUPPORTIVE OBSTETRICIANS

Over the decades there have been obstetricians advocating the benefits of the Dutch midwifery system and the central role of the midwife therein. They have been particularly, but not solely, obstetricians affiliated with the Amsterdam Medical Centre (AMC), the academic hospital in the Dutch capital. The list of obstetricians supporting midwifery includes professors Kloosterman, Treffers, Bleker and Van der Post, the current chair in obstetrics at the AMC. These obstetricians support both home birth and midwife-led primary care, when there are other Dutch obstetricians who have a more American or British approach to obstetrics. Where else than in the Netherlands would one observe such phenomenon? De Vries (2005: 208) interpreted this apparent contradiction by distinguishing between two sciences of obstetrics in the Netherlands, he argued that: "For the Dutch, mainstream obstetric science supports a non-interventionist approach to birth; in other modern medical systems, mainstream research in obstetrics demonstrates the need for intervention."

MATERNITY CARE ASSISTANTS

For nearly a century the Dutch have had a provision of postpartum care at home by specially trained caregivers who have a variety of caring and supporting tasks (van Teijlingen 1990). The maternity home care assistants (in Dutch *kraamverzorgenden*) keep an eye on the condition of the new mother and her baby, offer advice on and instruction in baby care and feeding, do basic household chores such as cooking and shopping (van Teijlingen 2004). Expectant parents must register for these services early in the pregnancy; unfortunately, because of a shortage of *kraamverzorgenden* in recent years, the average number of hours of maternity care assistance spread over first eight days postpartum has been reduced from 64 to 44 hours after normal childbirth (DeVries *et al.* 2009). Having the support from *kraamverzorgenden* helps, for example, the midwife to focus on providing midwifery postnatal care at home. The midwife leaves much of the psycho-social support and health education to the *kraamverzorgende,* thus the latter is itself a factor which supports the autonomous position of the midwife (van Teijlingen & van der Hulst 1995: 182).

POLITICAL SUPPORT

Over the past half decade there has always been political support for the Dutch way of maternity care (De Vries 2005:93–137; van Teijlingen 2003). Partly due to this government support there is a noticeable lack of political activism in the Netherlands in the area of maternity care and midwifery, compared to countries such as the United Kingdom, where maternity consumer groups such as the NCT (National Childbirth Trust) and AIMS (Association for Improvements in the Maternity Services) and midwifery pressure groups (e.g. the Association for Radical Midwives) are active stakeholders.

SOCIOLOGY OF THE PROFESSIONS

Peter McCaffery stimulated my interest in looking at midwives, obstetricians and other occupations involved in delivering care to women in childbirth from the sociology of the professions' perspective. A cross-national analysis of maternity care can only be made when we also look at the health system in which these occupations exist and interact. The Netherlands has national health insurance system, within a welfare state with a Bismarck-style public provision of health services, whilst many of the health professionals practice privately (De Vries, 2005; van Teijlingen & McCaffery 1987). The 'Sick Funds' are fairly independent from Government control, but their existence has restricted the power of the profession of obstetrics vis-à-vis the that of midwifery. Consequently, in the Netherlands the balance of power does not lie in the hands of one particular group of practitioners, as is the case in other industrialised countries. The Dutch obstetric profession has not been able to claim the same jurisdiction in the field of normal childbirth as its counterpart in other industrialised countries. This 'failure' can partly be attributed to the accumulation of legislation supporting midwifery in the Netherlands. Legislation implies state intervention in inter-professional competition. Peter introduced me to *The System of Professions* (Abbott 1988), who offers a theoretical analysis of the professions and their development.

Chicago-based sociologist Andrew Abbott (1998:62) suggested that "Overall, legally established jurisdictions are extremely durable."

However, the status and role of these Sick Funds have changed over the past two decades to a more commercially-based system which has less control over the occupations working in the field, and consequently less protection for the midwifery profession. At the same time, midwifery in the Netherlands is involved in a professionalisation process which is part of midwives growing awareness of its own particular identity. For example, the first university chair of midwifery was recently appointed in the Netherlands.

Many have argued that maternity care in the Netherlands is less medicalised, or that "Dutch midwives, for their part, have taken a firm stand against the medicalisation of childbirth" (Smulders & Limburg 1988:235). Lower intervention rates as a consequence of this adherence to a more social model of childbirth has often been quoted as a consequence of the Dutch way of organising maternity care. Evers and colleagues (2010: 7) recently suggested that the role of the midwife in the Netherlands "is most likely one of the reasons that the rate of caesarean section is still the lowest in Europe." The independent midwifery profession, with its psycho-social approach, provides some competition in the 'market' for care of pregnant women. It can be said that Dutch obstetricians and hospitals have had to offer a more consumer/women-friendly service in order to 'attract' low-risk pregnant women into hospital for their deliveries.

FINAL REMARKS

The lessons touched up in this chapter are many fold. They centre on understanding the place of midwives and midwifery in the Dutch organisation of maternity care. These lessons include sociological theory concerning the professions and professionalisation as well as the medical model and medicalisation, but they also include personal lessons learnt about 'doing sociology' and being a PhD supervisor.

Acknowledgements

I am grateful for the very helpful comments on an earlier draft from Jillian Ireland, and my 'old' University of Aberdeen colleagues Norman Stockman and David Smith.

References

Abbott, A. (1998) The System of Professions: An Essay on the Division of Expert Labor, Chicago: The University of Chicago Press

Baston, H., Rijnders, M., Green, J., Buitendijk, S. (2008) Looking back on birth three years later: Factors associated with a negative appraisal in England and in the Netherlands. *Journal of Reproductive & Infant Psychology*, 26: 323–339.

Belton S. (1993) The Dutch model of maternity care, *Australian College of Midwives Incorporated* (Sept.): 13–15.

Breckinridge, M. (1927) The nurse-midwife–A pioneer, *American Journal of Public Health*, 17: 1147–51

Benoit, C., Davis-Floyd, R., van Teijlingen, E. Sandall, J., Miller, J. (2001) Designing Midwives: A Comparison of Educational Models, In: *Birth by Design*, R. DeVries, *et al.* (eds.). New York: Routledge: 139–165.

Bradley, P.J., Bray, K.H. (1996) The Netherlands' Maternal-Child Health Program: implications for the United States, *Journal of Obstetric, Gynecologic, & Neonatal Nursing*, 25: 471–475.

CBS (2009) *Minder Thuisbevallingen* (In Dutch: Fewer Home Births), http://www.cbs.nl/nl-NL/menu/themas/gezondheid-welzijn/publicaties/artikelen/archief/2009/2009-2696-wm.htm (accessed November 2010).

Christiaens, W., Bracke, P. (2009) Place of birth and satisfaction with childbirth in Belgium and the Netherlands. *Midwifery*, 25: e11–e19.

Christiaens, W., van Teijlingen E. (2009) Four meanings of medicalisation: childbirth as a case study. *Salute e Società* 8(2): 123–141.

Christiaens, W., Verhaeghe, H., Bracke, P. (2008) Childbirth expectations and experiences in Belgian and Dutch models of maternity care, *Journal of Reproductive & Infant Psychology*, 26 (4): 309–322.

DeVries, R.G. (1993) A cross-national view of the status of midwives. In: *Gender, work and Medicine: Women and the medical division of labour*. Riska, E. and Wegar, K. (eds.). London: Sage.

De Vries, R. (2005) *A Pleasing Birth. Midwives and Maternity Care in the Netherlands*. Philadelphia: Temple University Press.

DeVries, R., Benoit, C., Teijlingen van, E., Wrede, S. (eds.) (2001) *Birth by Design: Pregnancy, Midwifery Care and Midwifery in North America and Europe*, New York: Routledge.

De Vries, R., Wrede, S., van Teijlingen, E., Benoit, C., Declercq, E. (2004) Making maternity care. The consequences of culture for health care systems. In: *Comparing Cultures. Dimensions of Culture in a Comparative Perspective*. Vinken, H., Soeters, J. & Ester, P. (eds.) Leiden, the Netherlands: Brill.

DeVries, R., Wiegers, T., Smulders, B., van Teijlingen E. (2009) The Dutch Obstetrical System: Vanguard of the Future in Maternity Care. In: Davis-Floyd, R., Barclay, L., Tritten, L. & Daviss B.-A. (eds.) *Birth Models that Work*. Berkeley: University of California Press, 31–54.

Donley, J. (1986) *Save the Midwife*. Auckland: New Women's Press.

Evers, A.C.C., Brouwers, H.A.A., Hukkelhoven, C.W.P.M., Nikkels, P.G.J., Boon, J., van Egmond-Linden, A., Hillegersberg, J., Snuif, Y.S., Sterken-Hooisma, S., Bruinse, H.W., Kwee, A. (2010) Perinatal mortality and severe morbidity in low and high risk term pregnancies in the Netherlands: prospective cohort study *British Medical Journal*, 341:c5639 (accessed November 2010).

Freidson, E. (1975) *Profession of Medicine: A Study of the Sociology of Applied Knowledge*, Chicago: University of Chicago Press.

van der Hulst,, L.A.M., van Teijlingen, E.R., Bonsel, G.J., Eskes, M., Bleker, O.P. (2004) Does a pregnant woman's intended place of birth influence her attitudes towards and occurrence of obstetric interventions? *Birth* 31: 28–33.

van der Hulst, L.A.M., van Teijlingen, E.R., Bonsel, G.J., Eskes, M., Birnie, E., Bleker, O.P. (2007) Dutch women's decision-making in pregnancy and labour as seen through the eyes of their midwives, *Midwifery*, 23:279–286.

Ireland, J. (1999) One woman's three birth experiences in The Netherlands. *British Journal of Midwifery*. 7: 331–334.

Mander, R. (1995) The relevance of the Dutch system of maternity care to the United Kingdom, *Journal of Advanced Nursing*, 22: 1023–1026.

Marland, H. (1993) The Guardians of Normal Birth: The Debate on the Standard and Status of the Midwife in the Netherlands around 1900', In: Successful Home Birth & Midwifery The Dutch

Model, E. Abraham-van der Mark (ed.), Westport, Connecticut: Bergin & Garvey: 21–44.

McCaffery, P. (1990) The transition from unitary to pluralist Catholicism in the Netherlands 1920–1970. In: Hamnett, I. (ed.) *Religious Pluralism and Unbelief: Studies Critical and Comparative.* London: Routledge: 52–63.

McCaffery, P. (2004) The politics of midwifery: Introduction. In. Teijlingen van, E., Lowis, G., McCaffery, P., Porter, M. (eds.) *Midwifery and the Medicalization of Childbirth: Comparative Perspectives,* New York: Nova Science.

Senden, I.P.M. van der Wetering, M.D., Eskes, T.K.A.B., Bierkens, P.B., Laube, D.W., Pitkin, R.M. (1988) Labor Pain: A Comparison of Parturients in a Dutch and an American Teaching Hospital, *Obstetrics & Gynecology,* 71: 541–44.

Smulders, B., Limburg, A. (1988) Obstetrics and midwifery in the Netherlands, In: *The Midwife Challenge,* Kitzinger, S. (ed.), London: Pandora

van Teijlingen, E.R. (1990) The profession of maternity home care assistant and its significance for the Dutch midwifery profession', International Journal of Nursing Studies, 27 :355–366.

van Teijlingen, E.R. (1994) *A social or medical model of childbirth? Comparing the arguments in Grampian (Scotland) and the Netherlands* (Unpublished PhD thesis), Aberdeen: University of Aberdeen.

van Teijlingen E. (2003) Dutch midwives: the difference between image and reality. In: *Gender, Identity & Reproduction: social perspectives,* Earle S, Letherby G (eds.), London: Palgrave: 120–34.

van Teijlingen, E., McCaffery, P. (1987) The profession of midwife in the Netherlands, *Midwifery,* 3: 178–186.

van Teijlingen, E.R., van der Hulst, L. (1995) Midwifery in the Netherlands: More than a semi-profession?, In: G. Larkin, T. Johnson, and M. Saks, (eds.), Health Professions and the State in Europe, London: Routledge: 178–186.

Turner, B.S. (1987) *Medical Power and Social Knowledge,* London: Sage Publications Ltd

Wiegers, T.A. (2009) The quality of maternity care services as experienced by women in the Netherlands, *BMC Pregnancy & Childbirth* 2009, 9:18 [web address: www.biomedcentral.com/content/pdf/1471-2393-9-18.pdf]

Wiegers, T.A., van der Zee, J., Kerssens, J.J., Keirse, M.J.N.C. (1998) Home birth or short-stay hospital birth in a low risk population in the Netherlands, Social Science & Medicine, 46: 1505–11.

Witz, A.(1992) *Professions and Patriarchy,* London: Routledge

The rise and fall of multi-phasic screening as a public health service during the 1960s and the emergence of 'evidence based medicine'

DAVID F. SMITH
University of Aberdeen

INTRODUCTION

The phase 'evidence based medicine' has been popularised since 1992, when it was used in the title of a programmatic paper published by David Sackett's group of the department of Clinical Epidemiology and Biostatistics at McMaster University in Canada.[1] By 2005, when George Weiss published book on the history of quantification in medicine, some 3,400 papers with 'Evidence based medicine' in the title had been published.[2] But the key feature of the 'Evidence based medicine' programme, emphasis upon the importance of carrying out randomised controlled trials before introducing new treatments or services, had been present for some decades before 1992. Among the exponents of the randomised control trial in Britain during the 1960s were Archie Cochrane of the Medical Research Council Epidemiology Unit,[3] and Walter Holland, director of the Department of Social Medicine at St Thomas's Hospital, London,[4] and they are among the key actors in this paper. They were effectively arguing for 'evidence based medicine' although the phrase had yet to be born, hence the use of 'the emergence of' and inverted commas around the phrase 'evidence based medicine' in the title of this paper.

---

[1] Evidence-Based Medicine Working Group, 'Evidence-based medicine: a new approach to teaching the practice of medicine', *Journal of the American Medical Association*, 1992, **268**, pp. 2420–25.

[2] G. Weisz, 'From Clinical Counting to Evidence-Based Medicine', in G. Jorland, A. Opinel and G. Weisz, *Body Counts: Medical Quantification in Historical and Sociological Perspectives*, Montreal, McGill-Queen's University Press, 2005, pp. 377–93, on p. 382.

[3] For Cochrane's life and career see A.L. Cochrane, *One man's Medicine*, London, British Medical Journal, 1989. See also R. Doll, 'Cochrane, Archibald Leman (1909–1988)', rev., Oxford Dictionary of National Biography, Oxford University Press, 2004, internet: http://www.oxforddnb.com/view/article/40680, accessed 25 October 2010.

[4] Currently the best source for Holland's life and work are the transcripts of a series of interviews conducted by Dr Michael Ashley-Miller in 1996, available from the Medical Sciences Video Archive of the Royal College of Physicians and Oxford Brookes University. For details see: internet http://www.brookes.ac.uk/schools/lifesci/medical/, accessed 25 October 2010. See also, W.W. Holland, 'The jungle: an explorer's experiences of health services research', in A. Oliver, *Personal Histories in Health Research*, London, Nuffield Trust, 2005, pp. 101–20.

Explorations in Cultural History: Essays for Peter Gabriel McCaffery,
edd. David F. Smith & H. Philsooph (Aberdeen 2010)

ISBN 978-0-9567059-0-7

Health screening in Britain has recently been undergoing expansion to include a programme for colorectal cancer screening, following a series of carefully controlled trials and pilot exercises, as required by the strictures of 'evidence based medicine'. The new screening service involves the distribution of kits to the public for faecal sampling at home, which are returned for laboratory analysis.[5] Nearly fifty years ago, however, soon after the invention of the 'clinistix' test for the presence of sugar in urine, a similar approach was tried for diabetes testing. Raymond (or Paddy) Donaldson, medical officer of health for Rotherham (and father of Liam Donaldson, who retired recently as chief medical officer for England)[6] distributed envelopes containing a clinistix at the town's 1962 mass radiography exercise. Instructions were issued as to how to carry out the test, and to return the test strip to the Public Health Department in the event of a colour change.[7] Donaldson's project developed into an annual multi-phasic screening programme involving eleven different tests, as shown in Table 1, but the last screening clinic was held in 1967, when Donaldson was about to move to a post at Teesside. The Rotherham screening clinic received national and international interest from public health professionals and others, but also came under criticism from the advocates of randomised controlled trials. It is the Rotherham screening clinic experiment and its fate, as an episode in both the final chapter of medical officer of health-led local authority public health, and the emergence of 'evidence based medicine', which is the central focus of this paper.[8]

---

[5] See NHS Bowel Cancer Screening Programme: internet http://www.cancerscreening.nhs.uk /bowel/, accessed 25 October 2010.

[6] For Paddy Donaldson see S. Lee, 'Paddy Donaldson' (Obituary), *British Medical Journal*, 2005, **331**, p. 457.

[7] R.J. Donaldson and J. Connolly, 'The Detection of Diabetes as a Health Service', *Medical Officer*, 1963, **110**, pp. 85–8.

[8] The author's interest in this topic arose as a result of his involvement, as a supervisor, in a post-graduate project in which Donaldson was a key actor. S. McLaurin, 'Public Health Departments and Health Centres on Teesside', MPhil thesis, University of Teesside, 2000.

Table 1: Test offered at the Rotherham Screening Clinic 1962, 1964–7

Year	No of tests	Tests Available	Appointment system	Duration of clinic (days)	Total attendances
1962	3	Chest X ray, urinary sugar	Walk-in	12	6,7533
1964	5	As 1962 plus cervical smear, hearing, anaemia	Walk-in	6	3,753
1965	9	As 1964 plus breast cancer, glaucoma, lung function, visual acuity	Walk-in	9	5,522
1966	11	As 1965 plus cardiac function and mental health	Walk-in	9	5,763
1967	11	As 1966	Pre-arranged	10	2500

Sources: J L Girt, L A Hooper, and R A Abel, 'The Multiple Health Screening Clinic, Rotherham 1966: A Social and Economic Assessment', *Reports on Public Health and Medical Subjects*, 1969, no. 121, and R. J. Donaldson, 'Production-line Medical Screening', *New Scientist*, 1967, **36**, pp. 187–9.

DIABETES TESTING IN CONTEXT

In the 1960s the future of the medical officers of health and local authority public health were under question. In 1959, Ian MacQueen, Aberdeen's medical officer of health, argued that the medical officer of health should be the 'centre forward' of the health services team. This idea was picked up with approval by the chief medical officer of the Ministry of Health in his 1959 annual report, but this was the last annual report which included any extended discussion about the medical officer of health's role.[9] Soon, policy documents began to foresee and then implement the enhancement of general practitioners' roles in preventive medicine, at the expense of medical officers of health.[10] These policies culminated in the abolition of the medical officers of health in 1974, and the appointment of community medical specialists by the hospital authorities.[11]

The control of infectious diseases provided the rationale for the appointment of medical officers of health in the nineteenth century. As Jane Lewis has shown, during the twentieth century, they developed empires of bricks and mortar: infectious diseases hospitals, municipal general hospitals and nursing homes. By

[9] I.A.G. MacQueen, 'Teamwork and Leadership in Public Health', *Public Health*, 1960, **74**, pp. 244–52; J. Charles, *On the State of Public Health: Annual report of the Chief Medical Officer of the Ministry of Health for 1959*, London, HMSO, 1960, pp. 145–6.

[10] See, for example, Medical Services Review Committee, *A Review of the Medical Services in Great Britain*, London, Social Assay, 1962; Standing Medical Advisory Committee, *The field of work of the family doctor*, London, HMSO, 1963; British Medical Association, 'A new contract for GPs; a charter for the family doctor service', *British Medical Journal Supplement*, 1965, **3138**, pp. 89–91; H.K.M. Kindersley, *Seventh report of a Review Body on Doctors' and Dentists' Remuneration*, London, HMSO, 1966.

[11] J. Lewis, *What Price Community Medicine?: the philosophy, practice and politics of public health since 1919*, Brighton, Wheatsheaf, 1986.

the 1960s, however, infectious diseases were coming under control, in view of improved living standards and the availability of antibiotics, while local authority hospitals had been lost upon the establishment of the National Health Service.[12] Donaldson's autobiography, *Off the Cuff*, reflects the pessimism that was by that time prevalent among medical officers of health: '... by the 1960s in general, the belief was that the flickering flame of infectious diseases would soon be extinguished for good ... The public health service seemed somewhat less important, and many doctors had come to regard it as a dull and dreary discipline'.[13] Attempting to put new life into this 'dull and dreary discipline', Donaldson developed a screening programme in which he acted along the lines of MacQueen's 'centre forward' of the health service team. But screening was not an entirely new departure and could also be represented as an extension of a traditional role. School ·medical inspections, for example, were a form of screening,[14] while recently medical officers of health had been encouraged to become involved in phenylketouria screening.[15]

Donaldson's autobiography suggests that his venture into diabetes testing was inspired by a comment about undiagnosed diabetes made by Charles Best, one of the discoverers of insulin, during a trip to Britain to celebrate the fortieth anniversary of the discovery.[16] However, the diagnosis of diabetes was already an issue for wide debate and experimentation. In 1957, the College of General Practitioners appointed a working party which organised a survey covering some 19,000 people in Birmingham. One hundred and twenty-seven cases were discovered, including fifty-five 'florid' cases, the results being published in June 1962.[17] In the same issue of *British Medical Journal* there appeared a report of a survey carried out in Essex by the medical officer of health, funded by the British Diabetic Association. This covered 5,843 persons and revealed thirty-five new cases.[18] Also in 1962, the medical officer of health for Bedford found over a

[12] *Ibid.*

[13] R.J. Donaldson, *Off the cuff: reminiscences of my half century career in public health*, Richmond, Murray Print, 2000, p. 122.

[14] For the history of the School Medical Service see B. Harris, *The Health of the Schoolchild*, Buckingham, Open University Press, 1995.

[15] G. Godber, *On the State of Public Health: Annual report of the Chief Medical Officer of the Ministry of Health for 1962*, London, HMSO, 1963, pp. 89–91.

[16] Donaldson, *Off the Cuff*, p. 122.

[17] Research Committee, 'Diabetes detection drives', *Journal of the College of General* Practitioners, 1959, **2**, pp. 189–93; College of General Practitioners Working Party, 'A Diabetes Survey', *British Medical Journal*, 1962, **1**, pp. 1497–1503.

[18] J. Harkness, 'The prevalence of glycosura and diabetes mellitus', *British Medical Journal*, 1962, **1**, pp. 1503–7.

thousand high blood sugars among 26,000 people tested, of which 350 required treatment.[19] At the beginning of diabetes screening in Rotherham, there was therefore an element of joining a movement that was already established. However, there was no consensus regarding the appropriateness of moving from experiments to diabetes testing services. The Ministry of Health's key policy making committee, the Standing Medical Advisory Committee, decided against issuing a memorandum giving guidance on the development of diabetes testing, since there was 'little reliable evidence' that pre-symptomatic treatment was worthwhile.[20] Donaldson, however, explicitly regarded the Rotherham diabetes detection exercise as a step towards the development of a practical 'Diabetes Detection Service'. In view of this aim, as Donaldson and his assistant remarked in *Medical Officer*, economy of expenditure and manpower were desirable. They also explained that they had considered that a 'pilot study could well be attempted with the health conscious group such as person attending a Mass Radiography Campaign' and that this would 'provide a convenient limited period' for a trial.[21]

Donaldson and his colleague gave no hint that the value of mass mobile radiography was itself under question at this time. The mass radiography facilities were provided by regional hospital authorities, but the service was organised locally, and was associated with public health departments, some medical officers of health being particularly active in organising intensive mass radiography drives. Because of the decline in the incidence of tuberculosis, however, annual mass radiography was becoming less productive. Attendance was falling and it was noted by the chief medical officer that referrals from general practitioners produced far more positive findings than walk-in services. While more lung cancer cases were being detected, the treatments available for lung cancer were far less effective than those available for tuberculosis.[22] But in the report of Rotherham's 1962 screening exercise, defence of mass radiography did not appear to be a concern, although it was noted that having two tests available had increased attendance over the previous year. The emphasis was rather upon the co-operation achieved between the public health department, hospital authorities, and general practitioners, in planning, implementing and following-up the exercise. The role of the medical officer of health was that of leading innovation and co-ordinating the health services. Over

---

[19] 'Tests for Diabetes in Bedford', *British Medical Journal*, 1962, **1**, p. 1427; 'Bedford Diabetic Survey', *British Medical Journal*, 1962, **2**, p. 203; C.L.E.H. Sharp, 'Diabetes survey in Bedford', *Proceedings of the Royal Society of Medicine*, 1964, **57**, pp. 193–6.

[20] Central Health Services Council, 'Report for 1962', *Parliamentary Papers (Commons)*, 1962, **xix**, p. 18.

[21] Donaldson and Connolly, 'Detection of Diabetes', p. 85.

[22] G. Godber, *On the State of Public Health: Annual report of the Chief Medical Officer of the Ministry of Health for 1961*, London, HMSO, 1962, pp. 84–5.

twelve days some 17,000 test strips were handed to 6,700 people (as they could take strips for family members). In total, 246 persons reported positive results, and twenty-six were diagnosed as diabetic. Donaldson and his colleague suggested a range of future options. Self-test kits might be made available via hospital and local authority clinics, general practitioners, and industrial medical officers, or diabetes testing might take the form of a service along the lines of the mass radiography.[23]

In the report of the 1962 screening exercise no mention was made of the possibility of routinely combining diabetes testing with mass radiography and adding further tests to produce an annual multi-phasic testing service, but there were several precedents for such a development. In the United States of America multi-phasic screening had developed since the 1940s as a private health insurance-funded and public health exercise.[24] There were also a few British experiments, one being at Darbishire House, a health centre attached to Manchester medical school, financed by the Nuffield Trust and Rockefeller Foundation.[25] For Donaldson, the expansion of the screening operation provided an opportunity for him to press forward the policy he had adopted since arriving in Rotherham in 1955, of using his position not to compete with other sectors of the health services, but to lead and encourage co-operation.[26]

MULTI-PHASIC SCREENING

Besides diabetes testing, during the early 1960s cervical cytology was also under widespread consideration. Cervical cancer screening services were developing apace in North America, and British women's and labour organisations were demanding that Britain should follow suit. In this case there was some lead from the centre. The chief medical officer's report for 1961 concluded that 'The study of exfoliate cytology has now fully proved its worth as a screening technique'. Cervical screening was already available on a small scale as a hospital service, and the chief medical officer foresaw it developing along these lines, with 'more

---

[23] Donaldson and Connolly, 'Detection of Diabetes'.

[24] J.M.G. Wilson, 'The worth of screening', *Proceedings of the Royal College of Physicians of Edinburgh*, 1991, **21**, pp. 288–310, on p. 294; J.M.G. Wilson, 'Multiple Screening', *The Lancet*, 1963, **2**, pp. 51–4, on p. 51; J.M.G. Wilson, 'Medical screening: from beginnings to benefits: a retrospect', *Journal of Medical Screening*, 1994, **1**, pp. 121–3, on p. 121.

[25] M. Perry, 'Academic general practice in Manchester under the early National Health Service: A failed experiment in social medicine', *Social History of Medicine*, 2000, **13**, pp. 111–29. For some other early developments in North America and in Britain, see, W.W. Holland and S. Stewart, *Screening In Disease Prevention what works?*, Oxford, Radcliffe Publishing, 2005, pp. 1–2.

[26] Donaldson, *Off the Cuff*, p. 64.

gradual expansion into general practice'.[27] Max Wilson, Ministry of Health epidemiologist, visited North America in 1962 to study screening, and he published an article on his experiences in *The Lancet* where he remarked that the value of cervical cytology had been demonstrated 'beyond cavil'.[28]

In 1963, the Standing Medical Advisory Committee advised that laboratory and pathological services should be enhanced to allow the extension of cervical screening, in which 'reliance should be placed on GPs', but that the establishment of special local authority clinics would 'seldom be appropriate'.[29] However, when Donaldson decided to create a multi-phasic screening service in 1964, cervical cytology was included. The exercise was styled a 'Health Week' and the local press made much of the inclusion of cervical screening. Rotherham's mayor observed: 'Recently many women's organisations and also the Trade Union Congress have been pressing for a cervical smear prevention service, which was necessary as about 3,500 women died each year from cervical cancer'.[30] There was a strong element of municipal pride at work, for the mayor also remarked that 'Multiple screening had been carried out quite extensively in the USA during the past 10 years but as far as he was aware this was the first occasion in this country when anything on this scale as been attempted'.[31] The 1964 exercise was written up by Donaldson and J M Howell, his deputy, and was published in the *British Medical Journal* in October 1965. The results are summarised in table 2.

Table 2: Results from the 1964 Rotherham screening clinic

	No taking test	Results
Anaemia	2743	178 positive
Diabetes	5673	116 positive, 7 confirmed diabetic
Chest radiography	2824	3 active TB, 94 other abnormalities
Hearing	1184	251 failed, 30 referred to general practitioners
Cervical Cytology	1369	8 positive, which underwent treatment, 30 doubtful still under investigation, 85 other abnormalities referred to general practitioners

Source: R J Donaldson and J M Howell, 'A Multiple Screening Clinic', *BMJ*, 1965, **2**, pp. 1034–6.

[27] G. Godber, *On the State of Public Health: Annual report of the Chief Medical Officer of the Ministry of Health for 1961*, London, HMSO, 1962, p. 206–7. See also the Standing Medical Advisory Committee's position: Central Health Services Council, 'Report for 1962', *Parliamentary Papers (Commons)*, 1962, **xix**, p. 18. For an outline of the history of cytopathology more generally in the UK see O.A.N. Husain and E.B. Blanche Butler, 'Cytopathology in the United Kingdom: 1854 to the present', *Diagnostic Cytopathology*, 2000, **22**, pp. 203–6.

[28] Wilson, 'Multiple Screening', p. 51.

[29] Central Health Services Council, 'Report for 1963', *Parliamentary Papers (Commons)*, 1963–4, **xv**, pp. 14–15.

[30] *Rotherham Advertiser*, 7 November 1964.

[31] *Ibid.*

Donaldson and Howell's article emphasised the demand for cervical cytology:

Demand was so overwhelming that more staff had to be brought in, and by the end of the week four health visitors, five midwives, and four doctors ... were working almost full-time. Queues were extremely lengthy; yet a three-hour wait did not discourage some of the stalwarts who arrived at the busiest times ... Many women travelled long distances to take the test. Two elderly ladies came from Morecombe, 100 miles away; one of them had previously undergone a total hysterectomy.[32]

Publicity about the Rotherham clinic, however, was not only reaching one hundred miles from the town, but was circulating nationwide, and beyond. And from the start, Donaldson's screening activities also received political attention. In 1962, the Minister of Health, Enoch Powell, was asked in parliament about what thought was being given to combining radiography and diabetes testing. Powell merely replied that diabetes diagnosis could be accessed through general practitioners and claimed that combining the tests would reduce the response to radiography.[33] But by 1965, however, the Rotherham screening clinic was exposed to such publicity that Donaldson acquired a busy programme of talks to British Medical Association Divisions, at universities, and at other meetings. And soon the publicity would reach such a level that the new Minister of Health, Kenneth Robinson, would be unable to continue the simple dismissive strategy adopted by his predecessor.

THE SCREENING DEBATE

Donaldson later recorded in his autobiography that on the lecture circuit he generally found medical officers of health unenthusiastic about screening. Some visited Rotherham for more information, but few attempted to start their own screening services.[34] But he also came up against an explicitly hostile critic, Archie Cochrane, who was leading a Medical Research Council epidemiology group at Cardiff.[35] We have already seen that Donaldson seems to have begun the screening project because of professional anxieties concerning the future of local authority public health. Similarly, Cochrane's motivation for entering the field of screening arose from his own professional difficulties. Following the failure of several sociological projects he was experiencing problems in finding productive employment for his epidemiological team. But, as he explained in his

---

[32] R.J. Donaldson and J.M. Howell, 'A Multiple Screening Clinic', *British Medical Journal*, 1965, **2**, pp. 1034–6, on p. 1035.

[33] 'Diagnosis', *Parliamentary Debates (Commons)*, 1961–2, **668**, col. 942 (23 July 1962).

[34] Donaldson, *Off the Cuff*, pp. 126–7.

[35] Donaldson, *Off the Cuff*, p. 127.

autobiography:

Fortunately, while the doors of sociological projects seemed forever closing, another avenue of research came into view. Since setting up the unit I had been looking for the right kind of challenge for the team I led, preferably one connected with the delivery of health care, and like manna from heaven came the 1960s rash of enthusiasm for screening.[36]

It was subsequently largely through their critical studies of screening that Cochrane and his colleagues developed principles that cut away much of the rationale for Donaldson's screening programmes. They called for randomised controlled trials which demonstrated the validity of screening tests and the value of treatments, before screening programmes were implemented.[37] More generally applied, these principles would later become the major precepts of 'evidence based medicine'.

Besides face-to-face clashes between Donaldson and Cochrane at meetings, debate about screening was also played out in the medical journals. Among the issues at stake were the questions of, if screening was to be introduced, how rapidly should it be developed, and, under whose auspices should services be organised? In his 1963 *Lancet* article, Max Wilson of the Ministry of Health argued that the screening programmes in operation in America were inappropriate in Britain. In any case, since the natural history of most chronic disease was poorly understood, screening could not be recommended until 'the ground is first cleared by epidemiological studies'. However, he also remarked that in Britain 'it seems right that the early detection of diseases should naturally develop as an extension of family doctoring', and suggested that a trial in general practice be arranged.[38]

In 1963, R M Acheson, and a group of students from the London School of Hygiene and Tropical Medicine, published a paper entitled 'Thoughts on a service for the presymptomatic diagnosis of disease'. This argued that screening should be a local authority service.[39] Two years later, a seminar group of the School and the County Borough Group of the Society of Medical Officers of Health published similar views. But this article opposed the *blitzkrieg* approach of an annual screening exercise, implying that continuously open clinics were

---

[36] Cochrane, *One man's Medicine*, London, 1989, p. 194.

[37] See, for example P.C. Elwood, W.E. Waters, W.J.W. Greene, P. Sweetman and M.M. Wood, 'Symptoms and circulating haemoglobin level', *Journal of Chronic Disease*, 1969, **21**, pp. 615–21; A.I. Cochrane, P.A. Graham, J. Wallace, 'Glaucoma', in Nuffield Provincial Hospitals Trust, *Screening in Medical Care Reviewing the Evidence*, London, Oxford University Press, 1968, pp. 81–8.

[38] Wilson, 'Multiple Screening'.

[39] R.M. Acheson, 'Thoughts on a service for the presymptomatic diagnosis of disease', *Public Health*, 1963, **77**, pp. 261–73.

preferable.[40] In their *British Medical Journal* article, Donaldson and his deputy rejected this criticism, arguing that the 'centrepiece' of the screening clinic should be the Mass Radiography Unit, which was only available for a limited period each year. They emphasised the demand for their service, claimed that the expense was modest, and again celebrated the co-operation between the health services.[41]

While the implication of linking other screening tests to the annual mass radiography exercise was that screening would be co-ordinated by public health departments, elsewhere during 1965 Donaldson indicated that he was not adverse to general practitioners taking over screening. At a colloquium in Oxford on 'Surveillance and early diagnosis in general practice', Donaldson said that he thought that talk of 'who did what' was of little importance. In his view, the work was 'being done for the GP by someone else' but if 'he wants to do it himself, fair enough'. Donaldson added that 'One builds up a fund of goodwill over a number of years, and one draws on it at certain times'.[42] Here he was alluding to his long-term strategy towards general practitioners, a strategy quite different to that of many medical officers of health who continued the traditional antagonism between the two groups.[43] In his autobiography he describes how, as soon as he arrived in Rotherham, he sought to build bridges by leading the rejuvenation of the local British Medical Association branch and organising regular alcohol-fuelled social activities.[44] And, in writing up the 1964 screening clinic in his annual report, he emphasised the 'generous cooperation and assistance' of both general practitioners and consultants.[45] In his 1966 annual report, he declared that the time had come to explore the design of permanently available screening service operating in 'much closer association with general practice'.[46]

[40] C. Burns and M.D. Warren, 'The presymptomatic screening of disease', *Medical Officer*, 1965, **113**, pp. 133–5.

[41] Donaldson and Howell, 'Multiple Screening'.

[42] G. Teeling-Smith, *Surveillance and early diagnosis in general practice. Proceedings of colloquium held at Magdalen College, Oxford, Wednesday, 7th July, 1965*, London, Office of Health Economics, 1966, p. 41.

[43] S. McLaurin and D.F. Smith, 'Professional strategies of Medical Officers of Health in the post war period (2): 'progressive realism': the case of Dr R.J. Donaldson, medical officer of health for Teesside, 1968–1974', *Journal of Public Health Medicine*, 2002, **24**, pp. 130–5; H.L. Diack and D.F. Smith, 'Professional strategies of Medical Officers of Health in the post war period (1): 'innovative traditionalism': the case of Dr Ian MacQueen, medical officer of health for Aberdeen 1952–1974', *Journal of Public Health Medicine*, 2002, **24**, pp. 123–9.

[44] Donaldson, *Off the Cuff*, pp. 64–5.

[45] R.J. Donaldson, *The Health of Rotherham 1964*, Rotherham, 1965, p. 68.

[46] R.J. Donaldson, *The Health of Rotherham 1966*, Rotherham, 1967, p. 10.

'A RUNAWAY TRAIN'

The 1965 screening clinic opened for nine days to enable women who were menstruating to take the cervical smear test. The number of tests was increased, with the addition of breast cancer, lung function, visual acuity, and glaucoma tests.[47] As regards the latter, the clinic coincided with the advice of the Standing Medical Advisory Committee that, on the basis of work carried out by Cochrane's unit, mass screening for glaucoma was not justified.[48] The breast cancer test consisted of instruction on self-examination, followed by a clinical examination along the same lines. Some of the existing tests were refined. For those who failed the anaemia test, a sample of blood was taken for haematological analysis. The diabetes test kit now included some glucose to be taken before the test.[49]

The 1965 clinic was attended by 5,522 people but others were turned away, and this also occurred in 1966. On occasions, instead of closing at 7.00 pm as planned, the clinic was still working at 10 or 11 pm, and the police were called to control the queues. The media took much interest, and Donaldson reflects that 'the visually attractive scene of a functioning clinic … seemed to be an irresistible magnet to the TV crews'.[50]

In April 1966, the British Broadcaster Corporation's current affairs programme, *24 Hours*, included a discussion on screening featuring Donaldson and John Butterfield, Professor of Medicine at Guy's Hospital, who had been involved in following up the Bedford clinistix survey.[51] The programme was much in favour of screening and Rotherham's local press and Council were 'beside themselves with pleasure'. The Ministry of Health, however, was less impressed, and Donaldson was called to London to face, from a group of experts and officials, what he described as a 'a hostile barrage of verbal machine gun fire, all aimed at belittling the value of the project'. He reported this to the chair of Rotherham Council's Health Committee and the local British Medical Association, which, against Donaldson's wishes, led to questions in parliament.[52] The Minister,

---

[47] Donaldson and Howell, 'Multiple Screening'.

[48] Central Health Services Council, 'Report for 1965', *Parliamentary Papers (Commons)*, 1967–8, **xxxv**, pp. 10, 31.

[49] Donaldson and Howell, 'Multiple Screening'.

[50] Donaldson, *Off the Cuff*, p. 129.

[51] For Butterfield see H. Keen, 'Lord Butterfield of Stechford', *British Medical Journal*, 2000, **321**, p. 836. See also the transcripts of a series of interviews conducted by M. Blythe in 1991, available from the Medical Sciences Video Archive of the Royal College of Physicians and Oxford Brookes University. For details see: internet http://www.brookes.ac.uk/schools/lifesci/medical/, accessed 25 October 2010.

[52] Donaldson, *Off the Cuff*, pp. 129–30, 132–4.

Kenneth Robinson, provided a written answer to a question which enquired whether he would issue a circular urging other local authorities to emulate Rotherham's health weeks. His position was that the Ministry was interested in the scheme but its value had 'not yet been established', causing uproar in Rotherham.[53] As a result of Donaldson's encounters with the Ministry, it was arranged for the recently established Social Science Research Unit to conduct a study of the 1966 clinic. This was not to consider the scientific basis of the screening programme, but its social and economic dimensions, via questionnaires, interviews, and observation at the clinic.[54]

Donaldson gives the impression that he was embarrassed by the attention that he received and remarks that he felt as if he was riding a 'runaway train'. But it was a train that he was not yet prepared to abandon. And he introduced several further refinements to the clinic. In September 1966 he attended a conference in America and visited the Kaiser Permanante screening clinics in San Francisco and Oakland. The American tests were similar to those used in Rotherham, but the equipment was much more impressive and included a computer. One test he saw which he immediately incorporated into the Rotherham menu was a mental health questionnaire.[55] He was pleased with the results: of 1,853 people tested, the scores of 85 were sufficiently abnormal to justify referral to a psychiatrist. Of those referred, some eighty percent required treatment.[56]

During 1967 Donaldson continued to defend his screening programme and did so during at least two encounters with Cochrane. One, in March, was at a Society of Medical Officers of Health symposium on 'Emerging Patterns in Community Medicine'. In Cochrane's paper 'A medical scientist's view of screening', he defined the difference between the medical scientist's and the medical officer of health's approach. The former aimed to apply 'standardised tests to well defined populations in order to test hypotheses'. The aim of the latter, on the other hand, was 'case finding', and Cochrane thought this was only justified if there was 'evidence that one can alter the natural history of the disease in an appreciable number of those screened'. He emphasised this point, because the screener was in a different position to the ordinary practitioner. The screener's approach was 'evangelical' and he had a special responsibility to prove that he was

[53] 'Health Checks', *Parliamentary Debates (Commons)*, 1966–7, **728**, col. *174* (16 May 1966); Donaldson, *Off the Cuff*, pp. 132–3.

[54] Girt, Hooper and Abel, 'Rotherham 1966'.

[55] Donaldson, *Off the Cuff*, pp. 126, 139.

[56] R.J. Donaldson, 'Multiple Screening Clinics', *Public Health*, 1967, **81**, pp. 218–221, on p. 221; R.J. Donaldson, R.J. Kerry and R. Ormee, 'A community health screening procedure', *Acta psychiatrica Scandinavica*, 1969, **45**, pp. 198–204.

able to help the cases identified, before approaching the public.[57]

Cochrane examined several screening tests in more detail. As for palpation of the breast he remarked that there was no evidence 'that early diagnosis by palpation has ever altered the death rate'. Turning to cervical cytology, he bemoaned the fact that an opportunity was missed for a randomised controlled trial '15 or 20 years ago'. Now that cervical screening was already being introduced, the only acceptable evidence would be a fall in the death rate in areas where a high proportion of women were screened. However, no such evidence had yet been forthcoming and Cochrane thought that all-in-all there were real doubts about the value of cervical screening. As for anaemia testing, Cochrane explained that his colleague, Peter Elwood, had been unable to demonstrate any correlation between 'haemoglobin level and classical symptoms of anaemia' or any impact of iron therapy. Regarding glaucoma, Cochrane's colleagues had shown that ten per cent of the population had an intra-ocular tension high enough to warrant referral to an ophthalmologist. If this were to happen, chaos would ensue at out-patients' clinics. There was, in any case, no evidence that therapy could prevent visual field loss. In conclusion, Cochrane declared that it was randomised controlled trails that screeners ought to be doing. He was afraid that if screening was implemented before basic research, it might 'fall into disrepute'.[58]

Donaldson presented the Rotherham screening service as a consequence of a 'tide in public opinion, inspired by cervical cytology'. The first experiments had opened 'a door ... that could not be closed'. Local demand, backed by 'professional and lay opinion' had created 'irresistible momentum' towards a comprehensive service. He remarked that it was possible to rationalise the reasons for starting the service with 'altruistic notions about the new role of public health in meeting the challenge of the changing pattern of disease' but admitted that 'The real reason is a more primitive instinct of self-preservation, because I do not believe that the present public health service can survive if it continues in its present traditional role'.[59]

Donaldson acknowledged that the early detection of disease was complex but to him this seemed a 'poor excuse for inactivity'. As for the objection that screening had produced no effect on morbidity and mortality, he commented that it would be 'naïve to expect that the great cohorts advancing along the time scale

[57] A.L. Cochrane, 'A medical scientist's view of screening', *Public Health*, 1968, **81**, pp. 207–13, on p. 208.

[58] *Ibid.*, pp. 209, 210, 213.

[59] Donaldson, 'Multiple Screening', p. 219.

of disease development could be halted by the present measures'. On the other
hand, he felt that 'a beginning has got to be made' and concluded:

I genuinely and sincerely believe that the early detection of disease is a worthwhile
undertaking and although there are those who hold different ... opinion there is no definite
and conclusive evidence either way, but I think that the onus of proof lies with the other side.
So far as we are concerned in public health, I do not think we can afford to wait to see
because to stand still in a changing world is to retreat.[60]

Two months later Donaldson and Cochrane met at a symposium organised by the
Royal College of General Practitioners. On this occasion, before giving the results
for each test, Donaldson described the screening clinic, including the atmosphere,
emphasising that '... it has no morbid overtones, it is as if the people are having
an afternoon out and they shop around for whatever tests they want as they
would in a supermarket!'.[61] Besides Cochrane, the senior lecturer in General
Practice at the Welsh National School of Medicine also gave a paper. He foresaw
the future of screening in general practice, with no role for the medical officer of
health.[62] A paper by Max Wilson amounted to a further attack on Donaldson's
position. He favoured centralised decision making, so that if there was a case for
new services, they could made available universally. And if screening was to be
carried out, to ensure adequate follow up, he favoured it being located in general
practice. He described ten criteria which should be met before screening was
implemented, and used these to assess the cases for cervical cancer and glaucoma
testing. He expressed reservations as to whether cervical cytology met one
criterion – that the natural history of the disease should be well understood – but
was satisfied that it met the other criteria reasonably well. Since the national
cervical screening programme was now in place,[63] and since Wilson played a role
in policy formation, he could hardly cast stronger doubt on the validity of cervical
cancer screening than this. The test for glaucoma, however, failed to meet several
criteria. Finally, he mentioned a randomised controlled trail of screening in
general practice supervised by Walter Holland, director of the department of
social medicine at St Thomas's Hospital. The Ministry had a role in planning the

[60] *Ibid.*, p. 221.

[61] R.J. Donaldson, 'Screening procedures and the local authority', *Journal of the Royal College of General Practitioners*, 1968, **2**, Supp. No 2, pp. 37–41.

[62] R. Harvard Davis, 'Presymptomatic screening from the viewpoint of general practice', *Journal of the Royal College of General Practitioners*, 1968, **2**, Supp. No 2, pp. 42–7.

[63] Central Health Services Council, 'Report for 1966', *Parliamentary Papers (Commons)*, 1967–8, **xxiii,** pp. 10–11.

trial, which began at the end of 1967.[64]

In June 1967, Ministry of Health policy was spelt out in parliament, in response to a speech made by Joyce Butler, one of the leading campaigners for cervical screening. Butler quoted the results of the Rotherham clinics, and urged the Ministry to issue a circular to local authorities encouraging the creation of screening services. But, in reply, the Parliamentary Secretary merely repeated the Ministry's position: they were interested in the Rotherham scheme, were monitoring it, but were not convinced that it should be extended.[65] The Ministry's scepticism, however, did little to dampen media and public enthusiasm, and Donaldson continued to refine the clinic. *Tomorrow's World*, the British Broadcasting Corporation 'good news' science programme, had devoted an episode to the 1966 exercise, but if they had waited a year they could have shown images of an even more technologically advanced clinic. For the final clinic he organised in Rotherham before moving to Teesside, Donaldson arranged for the results to be analysed by computer, and introduced an array of sophisticated equipment.[66] There was a sense in which at least this aspect of the clinic was in line with central government policy, since exploring the potential for the automation of laboratory testing and data handling for research and health service administration, were part of both the Medical Research Council's and Ministry of Health's agendas.[67] The chief medical officer's reports encouraged these trends, and a discussion of screening in his 1965 report concluded that, 'With the development of the automatic laboratory and ... data handling techniques ... effective and economic mass screening ... becomes a real possibility for the future'.[68]

The Rotherham clinic showed that there was a 'high-tech' version of preventive, as well as hospital medicine: this was high-tech medicine for the benefit of the masses not just the few, and Donaldson explicitly compared the costs of screening with the costs of kidney dialysis. In December 1967 he

---

[64] J.M.G. Wilson, 'The evaluation of the worth of the early disease detection', *Journal of the Royal College of General Practitioners*, 1968, **2**, Supp. No 2, pp. 48–53; W. Holland, Commentary: A history of the South-East London Screening Study', *International Journal of Epidemiology*, 2001, **30**, pp. 940–2.

[65] 'Health Check Weeks', *Parliamentary Debates (Commons)*, 1966–7, vol. **748**, cols. 733–42 (14 June 1967).

[66] Donaldson, *Off the Cuff*, p. 129; R.J. Donaldson, 'Production-line Medical Screening', *New Scientist*, 1967, **36**, pp. 187–9.

[67] G. Godber, *On the State of Public Health: Annual report of the Chief Medical Officer of the Ministry of Health for 1963*, London, HMSO, 1964, pp. 159–6; G. Godber, *On the State of Public Health: Annual report of the Chief Medical Officer of the Ministry of Health for 1969*, London, HMSO, 1970, pp. 214–19.

[68] G. Godber, *On the State of Public Health: Annual report of the Chief Medical Officer of the Ministry of Health for 1965*, London, HMSO, 1966, pp. 217–25, on p. 225.

published an article in *New Scientist*, headed 'Production-line medical screening' which opened as follows:

In a temporary clinic set up in Rotherham last month, 2500 people were screened, at a rate of one per minute, for a wide variety of abnormalities. The information gathered was produced in machine-readable form to be processed by a computer, which even prints out letters addressed to those whom it finds clearly abnormal.[69]

He described the clinic and each of the tests. Probably because the Ministry's study had highlighted the high proportion of people attending who were from outside Rotherham, an appointments system had been introduced, enabling containers for urine samples to be distributed in advance. These were tested with a sophisticated 'dipstick' for glucose, acidity, protein, ketones and blood, and positive results were followed by further tests. Results were entered on a computer-readable card – one of a 'cheque-book' of cards issued to each user. The blood-testing station boasted a centrifuge, a haemoglobin measuring machine capable of taking forty samples at a time, and an auto-analyser which could 'perform automatically 12 complicated chemical analyses and record the results on graph paper', while producing punched paper computer tape. When all the data were processed the computer printed a 'health profile' for each patient. The computer divided abnormal results into two categories, and for those requiring immediate attention, printed a letter advising the patient. As for abnormalities not requiring immediate attention the decision as to whether further investigation was necessary was left to the general practitioner.

The Rotherham experience, Donaldson concluded, demonstrated the public demand for screening, but he admitted that medical opinion was divided:

There are … doctors who believe we should wait for absolute proof … of the need for presymptomatic treatment before wholesale screening schemes are launched. Yet it may take 20 or 30 years before such evidence becomes available, while enormous numbers of people continue to present themselves at doctors' surgeries with relatively advanced symptoms, having undergone irreversible steps in the disease process.

It may be that effective prevention or treatment of chronic disease is more a philosophy than an exact science, but it must strike most thinking people as a sound and acceptable philosophy. I regard the secondary prevention of the present widespread chronic diseases as a serious problem which should be tackled urgently and on a broad front. No part of the Health Service and no doctor can afford to be a passive partner.[70]

In his autobiography, Donaldson stated that as time went by he began to appreciate Cochrane's viewpoint and mentions the *New Scientist* article as showing

---

[69] Donaldson, 'Production-line', p. 187.
[70] *Ibid.*, p. 189.

his awareness of the flaws in Rotherham's screening system.[71] However, the above quote is a firm rejection of the epidemiologists' caution.

Donaldson's last annual report for his period at Rotherham does, however, suggest that by this time he was glad to be able to dismount the 'runaway train'. He acknowledged that his period of tenure was likely to be remembered for the screening clinic, but remarked that it had attracted an 'unwarranted amount of publicity which in a way masked the less dramatic, but probably more important, work that was carried out in the department over the period'.[72]

EVANGELISTS AND SNAILS

During 1968 a book appeared which supported the idea of local authority-led screening. *Screening for Health*, published by H P Ferrer, deputy medical officer of health for Lancaster, argued that '... screening procedures have always been present in embryo in community health services ... it is now possible that they may develop ... to become ... perhaps the whole *raison d'etre* of a comprehensive community health programme'.[73] Since other parts of the health services dealt with 'captive populations' and not the 'population as a whole', Ferrer declared that 'screening procedures are the special prerogative of the medical officer of health'. Donaldson, however, by now emphasised the need for an intimate relationship between screening and general practice, while central policy, such as it was, favoured screening in general practice.

Meanwhile, powerful voices urging caution were brought together by the Nuffield Trust, in a committee chaired by Thomas McKeown, Professor of Social Medicine at Birmingham University,[74] leading to a book, *Screening in Medical Care Reviewing the Evidence*, published in 1968, with contributions from Cochrane, Elwood, Wilson and others. The final chapter advocated a committee to 'establish the requirements of screening, to reveal deficiencies of knowledge ... and to indicate steps which should be taken to make good the deficiencies'.[75] The cautious line was likewise the key message of the World Health Organisation's publication, *Principles and Practice of Screening for Disease*, co-authored by Max Wilson

---

[71] Donaldson, *Off the Cuff*, p. 127.

[72] R.J. Donaldson, *The Health of Rotherham 1967*, Rotherham, 1968, p. 8.

[73] H.P. Ferrer, *Screening for Health*, London, Butterworths, 1968, p. 181.

[74] Nuffield, *Screening*. For McKeown, see E.G. Knox, 'McKeown, Thomas (1912–1988)', rev., *Oxford Dictionary of National Biography*, Oxford University Press, 2004, internet: http://www.oxforddnb.com/view/article/40074, accessed 25 October 2010.

[75] T. McKeown and E.G. Knox, 'The framework required for validation of prescriptive screening', in Nuffield, *Screening*, 159–73, on p. 172.

with G Jungner, a Swedish clinical biochemist,[76] the principles of which became known as the Wilson-Jungner criteria.[77] The sceptical line was especially explicit in a paper entitled 'Screening–the case against it', read by Cochrane and Elwood at the 1968 Royal Society of Health Congress. By this time serious doubts were being expressed about the validity of diabetes screening. John Butterfield had organised a randomised controlled trial in which patients exhibiting borderline blood sugars were either left untreated or treated for five years, the outcome suggesting that there was little value in early treatment. Cochrane and Elwood admitted that it may not be ethical to conduct a trial with a group exhibiting higher blood sugars, but suggested that the results of such a trial might be surprising.78

The report of the Social Science Research Unit's study of the 1966 Rotherham clinic appeared in 1969. The project had included time and motion studies, interviews with participating staff, and an analysis of the impact upon National Health Service costs. Before the 1966 'Health Week', data were collected on the awareness of the clinic among potential clients, and their health and other characteristics, which were compared with actual attenders..[79] The results showed that the attenders were untypical of Rotherham's population. One-third were from outside the borough, there were twice as many women as men, and an excess of middle-aged and higher-class people. Attenders were more worried about their health, were better informed than the general population, and consulted their general practitioners less. A significant proportion also had some worrying symptom, and so for them the clinic substituted for a normal consultation with a general practitioner. Over a third attended for specific tests, attenders taking, overall, 64 per cent of the tests for which they were eligible. Although the clinic disrupted normal routines, staff opinion favoured the annual walk-in clinic, while the majority of clients favoured an appointments system, and a third would be equally satisfied with workplace or general-practitioner screening.[80] As for the economic assessment, the impact of the clinic was described as 'proportionately very small' but a service in which everyone took

[76] J.M.G. Wilson and G. Jungner, *Principles and Practice of Screening for Disease*, Geneva, World Health Organisation, 1968.

[77] The enduring and widespread influence of Wilson and Jungner's publication, may be illustrated by the 19,800 'hits' obtained for a search on 'wilson jungner' using the 'Google' search engine (25 October 2010).

[78] A.I. Cochrane and P.C. Elwood, 'Screening – the case against it', *Medical Officer*, 1969, **121**, pp. 53–6.

[79] Girt, Hooper and Abel, 'Screening Clinic', pp. 5–6.

[80] *Ibid.*, pp. 45–6.

every test for which they were eligible would consume a major proportion of the health department budget. And the cost of following up cases would be 'a significant multiple of the screening costs'.[81]

The recommendations were about additional studies on motivations for attending clinics and the economic dimensions, but a foreword by Donaldson declared that that despite improvements in the final clinic, he had reached the conclusion that, 'the central pivot of the service must be the general practitioner with the Hospital and Public Health Services taking a supportive role'. He gave three reasons for this. Firstly, there was often no clear dividing line between health and disease, so that 'borderline' cases required 'long surveillance' which could only be provided by a general practitioner. Secondly, persons passing all the tests in a public health setting assumed they had a 'clean bill of health' whereas they ought to have an interview with a physician to discuss possible further investigations. Finally, screening via general practitioners would allow targeting of 'at risk' groups. But these conclusions did not mean that Donaldson had given up on screening, as he declared that it was his 'personal belief that early detection of chronic diseases should not be regarded as a concept for a distant and glittering future but should be tackled now with the, albeit imperfect, tools that are now available'.[82] After his move from Rotherham to Teesside in 1968, however, Donaldson concentrated upon developing local authority health centres as bases for group general practices. These had areas for local authority use which Donaldson hoped to use for screening services. But he made little progress in this connection.[83]

Enthusiasts for comprehensive screening services as a local authority public health function had effectively dissipated. In 1969 the Central Medical Advisory Committee and its Scottish counterpart established a Joint Standing Sub-Committee on Screening in Medical Care. This was chaired by McKeown with Cochrane and Holland among the members, and its remit included advising on the justification for screening, research, and resource implications.[84] The sceptical line, even on cervical screening, gained ground. In Cochrane's famous 1971 essay, *Effectiveness and Efficiency*, which is regarded as a landmark in the development of evidence based medicine, after a discussion of immunization, which he saw as setting the standard for preventive medicine, he remarked that apart from this the

---

[81] *Ibid.*

[82] *Ibid.*, p. vi.

[83] McLaurin, 'Public Health Departments, pp. 172–3.

[84] Central Health Services Council, 'Report for 1969', p. 21, *Parliamentary Papers (Commons)*, 1970–71, **ix**; Holland and Stewart, *Screening In Disease*, pp. 3–4.

record of the National Health Service was 'patchy', and continued:

There are sins of omission and commission. Of the latter the introduction of the programme
of cervical smears in the hope of preventing carcinoma of the cervix is the saddest. It
illustrates so clearly the consequences of assuming a hypothesis is correct and translating the
consequences into routine clinical practice before testing it with a RCT [Randomised
Controlled Trial].[85]

But if enthusiasts for public health screening had been silenced, official
encouragement had given birth to enthusiasm for screening in general practice,
represented by C R Hart's edited volume, *Screening in General Practice*, published in
1975.[86] Most of the twenty-nine contributors were general practitioners. To them,
however, the publication of Holland's study of screening in general practice,
published in 1977, must have been a great disappointment. Holland and his
colleagues found no significant differences in morbidity between their screened
and unscreened groups.[87]

In 1975, Holland, along with David Sackett had published a commentary in
The Lancet, 'Controversy in the detection of disease', which explored the ethical
issues surrounding screening, and categorised those involved as 'Evangelists' and
'Snails'.[88] Donaldson had clearly been an evangelist but by this time he had
successfully found a post-medical officer of health career at the London School
of Hygiene and Tropical Medicine, and had managed to shed his 'evangelical'
image.[89] In Sackett and Holland's footnote giving examples of 'evangelists', there
was no reference to Donaldson. The literature cited as examples were an article in
The Lancet on the prevention of coronary heart disease,[90] an American book on
preventive cardiology,[91] a chapter about the American Kaiser Permanante medical
group's screening clinics,[92] and a chapter by three Canadians on cytological

---

[85] A.L. Cochrane, *Effectiveness and efficiency Random reflections on health services*, London, Royal Society
of Medicine Press, 1999, pp. 26–7.

[86] C.R. Hart (ed.), *Screening in General Practice*, Edinburgh, Churchill Livingstone, 1975.

[87] South London Screening Study Group, 'A controlled trial of multi-phasic screening in middle-
age: results of the South-East London Screening Study', *International Journal of Epidemiology*, 2001, **6**,
pp. 357–63.

[88] D. Sackett and W.W. Holland, 'Controversy in the detection of disease', *The Lancet*, 1975, **2**, pp.
357–9.

[89] Donaldson's efforts, which attracted so much attention at the time have also been effectively
been written out of the history of screening. See, for example, Holland and Stewart, *Screening*, ch. 1.

[90] R. Turner and K. Ball, 'Prevention of Coronary Heart-Disease: a Counterblast to Present
Inactivity', *The Lancet*, 1974, **2**, pp. 1137–40.

[91] J. Stamler, *Lectures on Preventive Cardiology*, New York, Grune and Stratton, 1967.

[92] F. Collen, 'Automated Multiphasic Screening', in C.L.E.H. Sharp and H. Keen (eds), *Presymtomatic
Detection and Early Diagnosis A Critical Appraisal*, London, Pitman, 1968, pp. 25–66.

screening.[93] The 'snails', Sackett and Holland also referred to as the 'methodologists', among whom they counted themselves, as well as Cochrane, Elwood, McKeown, Wilson and others. They were obliged, when consulted, to offer tentative conclusions regarding screening proposals, but were entitled to change their minds as more evidence became available. Sackett and Holland admitted that they both had previously advocated prescriptive screening, but they had now seen the error of their ways.

CONCLUSIONS

This essay has sought to demonstrate that, during the 1960s, the formulation and rising influence of principles which became the foundation of what was later known as 'evidence based medicine', and the activities of the proponents of those principles, constrained some medical officers of health who sought creative solutions to their professional future. This is not to say that it was the epidemiologists' evidence that convinced and restrained the screening enthusiasts. Rather than engaging in debate over the results of Cochrane's studies and Donaldson's clinics, there was a tendency for these two men to 'talk past one another'. And, recognising that the evidence alone was not sufficient to convince their opponents, the sceptics sometimes turned to ethical arguments.

Man-of-action Donaldson argued that screening services, born of local initiative, public demand and professional collaboration, should be implemented without waiting for definitive evidence. But the development of public health screening was inhibited by the influences that epidemiologists, and the ideal of the randomised controlled trial, were achieving within the central health administration and policy making machinery. This same administration and policy making machinery was concurrently planning the enhancement of the role of general practice in preventive medicine, and the demise of the medical officer of health, and the creation of specialists in community medicine whose main claim to expertise would be in epidemiology.[94] It was the rise of epidemiology and the nascent evidence based medicine culture, within the context of the impending demise of the medical officer of health, rather then the evidence itself, which accounted for the disappearance of the vision of a future for public health based upon screening. Cochrane spoke of the screening debate as 'manna from heaven' – which helped to secure his professional future. The cautious approach of the nascent 'evidence based medicine' as a model of medical innovation, must also

---

[93] H.K. Fidler, D.A. Boyes and A.J. Worth, 'Screening for malignant disease by means of exfoliate cytology', in Sharp and Keen, *Presymtomatic Detection*, pp. 295–31.

[94] Lewis, *What Price?*, ch. 3.

have seemed like 'manna from heaven' for politicians and policy makers who, since the 1950s, had been grappling with the potentially runaway costs of the health services, for whom the possible development of expensive screening services threatened even greater financial pressure.[95]

This paper not only casts new light upon the fate of the medical officer of health, but also represents a contribution to the exploration of the rise and impact of 'evidence based medicine' during the late twentieth century. John Pickstone, in his introduction to *Medicine in the twentieth century*, regards trends towards what he calls 'consumerist medicine' as characteristic of this period, by which he means that the demands of patients had an increasing role in shaping medical services.[96] As we have seen, it was consumers' demands which, according to Cochrane, led to the creation of the cervical screening service, and according to Donaldson, led to the Rotherham screening clinic. But the rise of evidence base medicine principles has been a countervailing tendency, limiting the choices of consumers and providers, at least in terms of what is on offer within the state sector.

During the 1970s, the Joint Standing Sub-Committee on Screening in Medical Care effectively inhibited the development of further screening services, but it was disbanded in 1980, and, for a time during the 1980s the epidemiologists seemed to loose their grip on screening policy. In 1986, a Department of Health working group chaired by breast surgeon Sir Patrick Forrest recommended the development of a National Health Service breast screening service, which was accepted by the government a few weeks before the 1987 general election.[97] The implementation of a national breast cancer screening programme seems to have been largely the result of an alliance of professional and political interests. But compared to cervical cancer screening in the 1960s, the position of women's organisations has been less unanimously in favour of breast cancer screening. As with cervical screening, however, the value of the breast cancer screening has become controversial. Another breast surgeon, Michael Baum, played a central role in implementing the service. But he resigned from the Breast Cancer Screening Advisory Board in 1995 and subsequently regularly criticised breast

---

[95] C. Webster, *The health services since the war*, London, HMSO, 1988; George Weisz makes a similar point about the appeal of evidence based medicine in Britain. G. Weisz, 'From Clinical Counting' on pp. 382–3. See also S. Harrision, 'The politics of evidence-based medicine in the United Kingdom', *Policy and Politics*, 1998, **26**, pp. 15–32.

[96] J. Pickstone, 'Production, Community and Consumption: The Political Economy of Twentieth-Century Medicine' in R. Cooter and J.V. Pickstone (eds), *Medicine in the twentieth century*, Amsterdam, Harwood, 2000, ch. 1.

[97] P. Forrest, *Breast cancer screening. Report to Health Ministers of England, Wales, Scotland and Northern Ireland*, London, HMSO, 1987.

cancer screening, arguing that the service should cease.[98]

Since the mid-1990s the epidemiologists seem to have re-established their influence. The National Health Service screening programmes are now strictly controlled by a National Screening Committee established in 1996, which generates detailed and strict evidence based guidelines and carefully monitors the design and implementation of programmes.[99] The principles under which this machinery has developed were set out by chief medical officer Kenneth Calman, in a paper which appeared in the first number of *Journal of Medical Screening* in 1994.[100] But quite apart from National Health Service screening programmes, since the 1970s there has grown a thriving alternative commercial screening sector, offering tests ranging from, for example, postal hair analysis services, or home test kits, which generate reports detailing which dietary supplements one should consume to correct apparent nutritional deficiencies and combat environmental toxins,[101] to food intolerance and blood cholesterol testing operated by high street pharmacies,[102] to BUPA 'MOT' tests:[103] in these areas the key driving force is profit making and 'evidence based medicine' has little influence. These circumstances reinforce an important point that arises from this paper regarding how historians should approach the history of evidence based medicine. The proponents of 'evidence based medicine' regard it as the foundation upon rational health services must be built.[104] The example of the history of screening during and since the 1960s, however, suggests that exploring the actual impact of evidence based medicine, historians might view the phenomenon as a medical culture in competition with other medical cultures, which penetrates or fails to penetrate and exert influence in different settings, according to the historically contingent conditions in which services operate.

[98] M. Baum, 'Commentary: false premises, false promises and false positives–the case against mammographic screening for breast cancer', *International Journal of Epidemiology*, 2004, **33**, pp. 66–7.

[99] Holland and Stewart, *Screening In Disease*, p. 4.

[100] K. Calman, 'Developing screening in the NHS', *Journal of Medical Screening*, 1994, **1**, pp. 101–5.

[101] See, for example, 'A warm welcome from Integral Health': internet http://www.integralhealth.org/, and 'The 'Mineral Test Kit' - As used and recommended by the Diet Doctors': internet https://www.mineraltestkit.co.uk/, accessed 25 October 2010.

[102] 'New services in pharmacies: how much are patients prepared to pay?', *The Pharmaceutical Journal*, 2002, **268**, pp. 758–9.

[103] For a list of tests see 'BUPA Wellness': internet http://www.bupa.co.uk/wellness/asp/personal/health_assessments/best_choice/medical_tests/index.asp, accessed 25 October 2010.

[104] For a lead into web-based literature on evidence based medicine and its intended impact, see: The Cochrane Collaboration, 'Evidence based healthcare Reading & resources': internet http://www.cochrane.org/docs/ebm.htm, accessed 25 October 2010.

ACKNOWLEDGEMENTS

The author wishes to thank especially Susan McLaurin, whose research inspired this paper, as well as the organisers of and participants in the 'Health of Towns Conference' at the London School of Hygiene and Tropical Medicine, the Glasgow University Centre for the History of Medicine Seminar Series, and the Aberdeen University Cultural History Seminar Series, at which spoken versions of this paper were presented.

Development, peace, and global citizenship

NIGEL DOWER

University of Aberdeen

1. INTRODUCTION

In this paper I explore the three key ideas of development, peace and global citizenship and advocate certain ways of understanding their relationships. My key normative claim which may be called cosmopolitan pacificism is that we ought to accept as global citizens the cosmopolitan responsibility to promote the conditions of peace anywhere in the world.

I shall start with an examination of the empirical relations that development has to war and peace, and then look at the contested nature of development, arguing for a certain normative conception of it. Likewise the concept of peace is examined in which I advocate a conception of it as 'just durable peace'. The idea of pacificism is then elaborated. Finally an account of global citizenship is offered to reinforce the normative relevance of the preceding discussion for individuals.

An earlier version of this was given as the William E. Morgan Endowed Chair Lecture, Colorado State University, on 12th March, 2008. I have submitted this modified version for this book in honour of Peter McCaffery because the themes of this paper – peace, development and global citizenship – are all close to Peter's heart, and because my discussion, though very different in style to Peter's, I believe, complements Peter's approach to these issues– not least my summary of what an academic should be doing in the last paragraph.

2. DEVELOPMENT AND PEACE

It is commonly assumed these days, especially in United Nations documents, that peace and development go together in the sense that for development to occur there must be peace. Whilst I agree with the spirit of this judgment, it is certainly an overstatement and it is worth considering what is kernel and what is chaff in the statement.

Much actual development understood primarily as economic growth occurs in the context of various causal connections with war and violence. In tracing these connections I am not implicitly making a negative moral assessment of the phenomena, rather describing linkages. What the ethical significance is of these facts in another matter. First, much of the prosperity and economic development of richer countries like Britain depended on colonial empires held together partly by force of arms and on military dominance in the world generally; likewise in the modern world neo-colonial interests in controlling or installing friendly regimes in countries of the world rich in resources such as oil may occasionally underlie and, for some, justify military activities to secure them, which go well beyond the normal measures taken to secure global energy supplies. Second, in most countries there is a significant, if not large, presence of the military and a commitment to spend significant sums on arms and defense systems – as Eisenhower remarked, there is a powerful military-industrial complex in many countries – and this is seen as part of what a developed country ought to have, and also as contributing to the development of that country, both by directly stimulating economic activity and by maintaining a country's general geopolitical advantage in the world. (Defense is a conditional threat to resort to war under certain conditions (e.g. attack by another country), and as such shows a link between development and war, but one which for many is entirely justified, at least if the defence system is not excessive or likely to fuel arms races etc.) Third; in some countries a significant part of their prosperity depends on the manufacture of the weapons of war, often used through arms-sales to create the conditions of non-peace in other parts the world. Fourth, as is often remarked, it is in wartime – because there is a maximum effort, to use Clausevitz' famous phrase, to 'compel the enemy to do our will' (Clausevitz 1832: Bk 1 Ch. 1) – that some of the most rapid and dramatic developments in technology are made which then contribute to subsequent economic development.

All this has to be conceded. There is no *necessary* connection between development and peace. On the other hand there are also very strong empirical connections between development and peace as well – and here for the sake of argument I shall assume that development is taken to be what it is ordinarily understood to be – economic growth within a country, and peace is taken to be the absence of war or overt violence. As we shall see in a short while, neither conception of development and peace is in the least bit satisfactory or adequate. However, even on standard assumptions, the links are very strong.

For any person or group of people intent on pursuing their lives as they wish, it is important that they live in conditions of social stability, that they are free from attacks on themselves and their property, that the bases of their livelihood are not undermined and they can engage in economic activity in the confidence that contracts will be honoured and so forth. Conversely, for any individual the effects of war may be loss of life or limb for herself or for those she cares about, and it may mean, especially if the war comes to one's home territory, the loss of property and livelihood. As Hobbes wisely observed, the first law of nature for human beings is that it is rational that they seek peace (Hobbes 1651: Bk I, Ch. XIII). It is the precondition of almost all normal human activities and insofar as development enables people through greater prosperity to achieve greater capabilities to engage in such normal activities, development presupposes general peace.

Part of the reason why development is often thought to have causal links with manifestation of war is because two key further assumptions are made about the pursuit of development. The first assumption is that development is essentially economic growth or at least it is a process in which economic growth is essential for enabling people to have the basis for exercising effective choice, having control over their lives and generally exercising a full range of human power and capabilities. Second, the pursuit of development by a country is centred on *its own* development, and maybe done without regard to the impact it has on other countries. If arms sales cause or fuel conflict elsewhere, that is an externality that is justified, as would be military activities or threats of it in order to secure resources elsewhere or trade routes (which was partly why Britain tried to secure naval supremacy in the days of empire). These two assumptions need questioning.

3. DEVELOPMENT

You may have observed that I have started talking about the *pursuit* of development. This brings out a key point. Development is not merely something that happens, it is pursued. It is the object of public policy, by governments and other agencies. It is therefore necessarily normative, that is, it is premised on some set of values and norms which inform those who pursue it. As Aristotle remarked in the opening sentence of the *Nicomachean Ethics* 'every action and every pursuit aims at the good' (Aristotle, *Nicomachean Ethics*, c. 330 BCE, Bk. 1, Ch. 1). But this invites the question: are these the right values in development? If we had other values, we would pursue a form of development which was different. This leads me to my first critical move vis-à-vis the supposed connection between war and development: maybe development is linked sometimes to war because of the values which inform the pursuit of development. If we thought development should be informed by other values, then that link would be cut or at least diminished. Suppose we thought that development should not be centred on economic growth and/or we thought that the pursuit of development by any country or social unit should be done in such a way that it did not depend on or initiate what would impede or undermine development elsewhere, particularly through war-like destruction of development elsewhere, what then? The connection between development and peace would be more firmly established. And that is what I think we should accept.

One way of making the point I am making about development is to say that there may be a core idea or concept of development – as a process of directed socio-economic change for a social unit such as a nation-state – alongside numerous richer or thicker conceptions of development which are alternatives to each other partly because they are based on rival value and norms. In other words, as some writers like to put it, it is an essentially contested concept. And incidentally it is this contested field that provides the basis for the development of a new sub-discipline called development ethics which is the focus of the International Development Ethics Association.

One way of looking at development is to see it as a process of change in which human beings are increasingly enabled to lead full lives. This has been the thrust of current work by some philosophers, social scientists, economists and others, such as Amartya Sen, Onora O'Neill and Martha Nussbaum to develop a more ethically explicit account of development (e.g. Sen 1999; Nussbaum 2000; O'Neill 1986), as well as the motivation behind the United Nations Development Program's program of 'Human Development' as illustrated in their annual 'Human Development Reports' ever since 1991. Whilst it is generally recognised that economic growth plays a role in development, particularly for poor people and poor countries, what is stressed is the fact that there are many different dimensions to human flourishing, that we do not need so much material wealth as is often supposed in order to achieve flourishing, that we need firm commitment to principles of distribution to enable everyone in a society to achieve the basic necessary minimum for a decent life, not merely for a biologically continuing life. Influential amongst these normative conceptions has been the so called 'capabilities approach' as advocated by Sen and Nussbaum. Much important work has been done to promote this approach through the Human Development & Capabilities Association (HDCA). One dimension incidentally to the new conception of development is the idea of sustainability – itself open to many interpretations, which are partly dependent on just what values we want to sustain. One reason why many of us are critical of the centrality of the economic growth conception is precisely because it is universally unsustainable. The main reason why this is unsustainable is because it is damaging the environment, causing rapid loss of biodiversity, and undermining the quality of the life conditions for humans and non-humans, present and future – notably but not merely through our excessive carbon emissions.

Two features of this alternative paradigm of development are striking for the purposes of this paper. First, there is generally an interest in the *way* development is pursued, second there is a general commitment to a global ethic of some kind.

First, development is not merely about the pursuit of certain goals which are regarded as ethically appropriate; it is also about the rightness of certain means used to pursue it. As Denis Goulet – in many ways the father figure of development ethics who sadly died several years ago – put it, we need to see development as about the 'means of the means' or to incorporate an ethic of the means (e.g. Goulet 1995). Such 'means' values include procedural ones like the role of democracy, diplomacy, participation, transparency and procedural justice. I attended a seminar during a conference in Kampala in Uganda in 2006 in which postgraduates from all over Africa were debating development ethics and the one thing they all thought was the key impediment to development in Africa was 'corruption, corruption, corruption'. One of the points about these process values is that they are both about the ethically appropriate ways in which development should occur, but they also show that to the extent to which a society exhibited these values, then it is already achieving a dimension of development – that is, these things are part of what makes a society more developed.

Now it may not have escaped the reader's notice that the procedural values of democracy, dialogue and participation are themselves peaceful ways of making progress. These values are associated with peace. Now one can argue that the ways of peace – that is a general commitment to using peaceful ways of promoting one's interests and dealing with conflicts of various kinds – are indeed more generally ethically appropriate means of development and also that to the extent to which the ways of peace are embedded in the social life of people and the pursuit of development, we can say that society is more developed.

So we come to a significant conclusion: it is not merely that on the whole one needs peace to have development (or conversely – what is equally true – that in order to have peace you need certain forms of development). That would remain an empirical albeit an important empirical claim. It is that in a sense peace is internal to development or, to be more accurate, internal to an ethically adequate conception of development. A society's development is partly *constituted* by the peaceful manner of the social life in which its development is taking place and partly justified by the commitment to peace as the way of pursuing it. Given a certain conception of development, the connection with peace is internal or conceptual not merely empirical. For a philosopher at least that's a significant extra step!

The second key element of the paradigm of development that I am considering is the acceptance of a global ethic. A global ethic is an ethic with two key elements; an acceptance of certain universal values and of transboundary responsibility. It is an implication of much recent work on the ethical basis of development that we can give a universal account of human flourishing, albeit at a fairly abstract level. Development ethics is generally sensitive to the dangers of cultural imperialism and the need not to have a development paradigm that is rooted in values of one culture that are not necessarily appropriate to other cultures. So we need a universalism which is sensitive to pluralist interpretations and acknowledging the value of diversity – both of ways of living and of different worldviews which may support a widely shared global ethic (see Dower 1998: ch. 6). That human flourishing matters anywhere is the world however important for the second part of a global ethic, namely that we have responsibilities in principle to promote or at least not to impede the conditions of human flourishing anywhere in the world.

If, as cosmopolitans claim, all humans beings matter and matter equally, then we can no longer accept many common assumptions associated with theories of international relations or indeed with common assumptions associated with communitarian thought, namely that one has much more significant obligations to one's fellow compatriots than to people in the world generally. If we take this perspective seriously, then we can no longer countenance foreign policies that depend on things happening in other parts of the world which undermine development, such as war. So we should not start them, support them or supply arms for them. Indeed we should do much else that is more positive like giving effective aid – at least equal to or, I would argue, beyond the official commitment made in the UN to giving 0.7% of GNP. We can debate about exactly what effective aid is, but on the whole military aid does not help those who need our help most – the poor of poor countries. When I say 'we' should do these things, I do not mean just our governments, I mean ordinary people – but I come on to that in the last part of my paper.

4. PEACE

Although I have in a sense made the main point about development and peace, we can reach the same general conclusion by a different route, name by examining the idea of peace. Commonly a distinction is drawn between a negative conception – peace as absence of war – and a positive conception – peace as harmonious relationships.

Peace is defined negatively in terms of a relationship between countries (or other groups) which are not at war. If war is defined as Hedley Bull does in his seminal work *The Anarchical Society* (Bull 1977) as 'organised violence carried out by political units against each other', then two countries are at peace if they are not at war. This definition fits one common way of thinking of peace which is that, as Grotius put it, 'there is nothing in between (nihil medium) war and peace' (Grotius 1625: proleg., para 29): countries are either at war or they are in a state of peace. Only days before the outbreak of war in September 1939 Britain and Germany were still on this account at peace. This account is slightly more plausible than a wholly legalistic conception according to which countries are at war only if there has been a declaration of war: this formal account would have to treat the Falklands-Malvinas conflict between Argentina and Britain as not a war since there was no declaration of war.

Now this negative conception of peace is certainly not negative in an evaluative sense. It may be very valuable to be in this state. But if we ask what it is that makes this state of being at peace valuable we realise that more needs to be said than simply a negative claim that it is an absense of war. The trouble with thinking of it as an absense is that it seems simply to be state we are in, something that happens rather than something which is itself the object of activity – that is, active maintenance of it, if we have it, promotion of it, if there could be more of it or better forms of it, or pursuit of it, if we do not have it.

Two things make peace valuable: first, the quality of the peace we have which may involve many elements not necessarily present if we are simply not fighting; second, the fact that peace is not merely short-term but durable or, we might say these days, sustained. (I do not merely say this to be 'with it', but because in fact if we take sustainability seriously, peace is – or ought to be regarded as – as one the key things to be sustained.)

We can get a handle on the first idea from what may be seen as a curious quarter, namely Hobbes. For all his being associated with the realist school of international relations, Hobbes actually had some extremely perceptive things to say about peace. Hobbes defined war thus: 'War is not battle but a tract (i.e. period) of time in which there a known disposition to battle; all other time is peace' (Hobbes 1651: Bk I, Ch. XII). In other words, real peace depends on the lack of threats or on a known disposition not to hurl massive armaments at others, on mutual confidence etc. On Hobbes' analysis the cold war was rightly so called, since the quality of the peace that prevailed was hardly one that would fit Hobbes' definition. Although the cold war is supposedly over, the fact that major powers still have their 'weapons pointing at each other in the posture of gladiators', to use Hobbes' graphic phrase, and many other countries are working hard to join them – really should remind us that the conditions of the cold war really still exist – perhaps cooler since there is not so much distrust and mutual fear, but still there.

Peace as an absense of war is really only valuable too if it is sustained and has within it the dynamics that make it capable of being sustained. Iain Attack links what he calls the negative conception of peace with security (Atack 2005: 144) and argues that security requires a whole range of measures for it to be in place: real security does not depend on defensive postures which are based on the threat of win-lose scenarios, but on win-win measures of common security. We should recall that in the past certainly a number of thinkers such as notably Kant saw themselves as trying to work out what would be needed for us to have perpetual peace (Kant 1795). Whether or not we can be that optimistic – namely that we could eliminate war altogether from human affairs – we can at least acknowledge the impetus behind such projects, namely seeking ways in which peace can become more durable and war can be made less likely. What is required amongst other things is arguably the presence of justice – both procedural and distributive – in relations between groups (and individuals) – what Ian Atack calls a version of the positive conception of peace, as has the Quaker writer Adam Curle in his small but intriguing book *True Justice* (Curle 1981). Also needed is a general commitment, as I indicated earlier, to developing nonviolent ways of responding to conflict. (For a more extended discussion of this see Dower 2009.)

What emerges so far from this analysis is that peace – if it is to be really valuable and sustained – is not merely an absense but requires the active engagement of people, which involves most people just observing basic moral norms such as justice and others actively promoting the conditions of peace. This is an important result to have established: like development peace is something that only occurs if people *do* certain things and do them because they are committed to certain values. No doubt peace as temporary respite from actual war but still in conditions of threat and hostility is better than its absense. But if we ask what is really valuable about peace, it is a state of affairs which is durable, not based on threats of war and informed by core ethic values such as justice which are part of what makes it durable. This no longer the negative conception of peace, and lies, as we will see, somewhere between this and the so called positive conception.

In an article entitled 'The Conditions of Peace' Iredell Jenkins comes to much the same conclusion. He argues that we tend to focus a lot of attention on the wrong topic, namely war, and ignore peace which he characterises as a 'force, quality, mode of existence that is a real feature of the human world' (rather than a mere absence) (Jenkins 1973: 512) and gives the analogy of health and sickness: if we spend all our time on analysing sickness rather than health, we would be focusing on the pathological states not the normal states. Implicit in the approaches he discusses is the assumption that peace is an important subject for research. Although the causes of war are of course crucial areas to investigate and are studied in war studies, peace itself is a complex concept requiring analysis in peace studies.

What about the positive conception of peace? Some writers have wanted to argue against the negative conception (seen as the mere absence conception) for a conception of peace as one of harmonious relationships between individuals and groups. John Macquarrie, whose book *The Concept of Peace* (Macquarrie 1973) contributed significantly to this way of thinking, links the idea to that of 'shalom' in middle eastern thought and the idea of wholeness in social relationships, and he characterises peace as 'love socially transposed', and one can argue that this level of peace in social relationships can only really come from people who are themselves at peace with themselves or achieve inner peace or commit themselves to a life of nonviolence.

Is such a rich conception of positive peace (which goes far beyond what Attack had in mind in calling positive peace 'peace with justice') to be commended as preferable to negative peace, even as amended by our considerations earlier? There is no straightforward answer. The following three observations may help to clarify my approach. First, it is undoubtedly true that, *if* all human beings could achieve such a quality of personal peace in their lives, then the resultant character of social peace would be on a higher plane as it were than what is needed for durable peace. Second, since it is unrealistic to suppose that such a scenario could be achieved, in practical terms the main focus of practical endeavour by policy makers and by our leaders should be to focus on durable peace – that would be a real achievement itself. What really matters to most people, as people who benefit from others being at peace with them, is that we have a just durable peace not based on threat. Third, nevertheless the role of people who can achieve inner peace and the way of peace cannot be underestimated. This role includes but is not limited to those who take a personal pacifist stance. My point is that a society is generally more likely to be peace-sustaining (in the middle sense I have advanced) if there are those in their midst who live to a more idealist standard. They point to a better way and their lives provide a reminder of what is possible. Having said that, my own view is that there are a whole range of things we need to do to sustain, strengthen or achieve peace in the form I think that is practically most valuable. There is no single-track solution to the question 'what should we do to achieve peace?' such as 'if only everyone achieves inner peace'; 'if only everyone becomes a pacifist'; 'if only everyone becomes a Christian (or Muslim)'; 'if only everyone becomes a Marxist'; 'if only everyone becomes a libertarian', etc.

What I have been really arguing for is the practical importance of a conception of peace that falls somewhere in between the negative and positive conceptions:

Peace as (mere) absence of war	Peace as durable, justice-based, absent threat of non-peace	Peace as social harmony/wholeness

Thus far I have been arguing for a conception of peace that can apply both to the relations within a society and to relations between societies. It only remains to stress that given the cosmopolitan kind of ethic I have already indicated in connection with development, we need to make more explicit what our obligations and responsibilities are vis-à-vis peace so conceived. Given the central importance of such peace for almost all human goods and virtues (excepting the military virtues admired by militarists which are not really to be reckoned as unqualified virtues anyway), including as we have seen the pursuit of genuine development, we have not merely duties to maintain peace in *our* relationships to other countries and groups, but also to promote peace *anywhere* in the world.

If war and conflict undermine the flourishing of human beings anywhere in the world, then it is part of our cosmopolitan responsibility to see how to help others maintain peace elsewhere where they have it, and, where there is war, to help to stop it and build a durable just peace. This is in much the same way that we should accept a responsibility to give or support aid to relieve poverty and oppose economic practices that contribute to poverty elsewhere.

What I have just said is not intended to be a back-door way of insisting on pacifism. There may or may not be a 'ceteris paribus' clause inserted here. Maybe countries need to reserve the right to use force in certain limited circumstances, maybe not, both in respect to self-defence and in respect to intervening to stop human rights violations elsewhere (I would argue against the latter on another occasion). This does not affect the general responsibility both to maintain peace in our own relations and to promote it elsewhere. In terms of my current purposes, it is the second aspect that most concerns me: our responsibility to promote peace where possible anywhere, given its universal and central value.

5. PACIFICISM

I have in effect moved step by step into the approach I called at the beginning of the paper 'pacificism'. It is now time to unpack this idea further. Since pacificism and pacifism sound so similar – and indeed their etymology is identical – I need to clarify the distinction. I shall do this by using a semi-technical device. This is not to be found, so far as I know, in any standard textbooks on applied ethics. It is a Dowerism and the reader may conclude 'long may it remain just that'. We need to distinguish between two types of activity vis a vis any basic moral value 'x':

Acting x-ly)(promoting x

Take for instance another value first: justice. We can talk of someone acting justly and we can talk of someone promoting justice (or fighting injustice which is part of the latter). We can talk of someone respecting rights in his own behaviour and someone doing various things to protect human rights (or their observance) and opposing their violation by others. We can talk of someone committed to acting truthfully in her dealings with others, and someone who wish to campaign for truthfulness and integrity in business or public affairs. Likewise we can talk of someone acting peacefully or non-violently in terms of her own behaviour and someone promoting peace and non-violence. Now it will be apparent from a quick survey of human behaviour that people fall into three main categories.

Some people focus their moral lives on the first (acting x-ly in various ways), maybe with little or no interest in the wider promotion of such virtues. They might be called ethical quietists. What is important to them is that they keep their own moral house in order.

On the other hand there are those who devote a lot of their moral energy to promoting one or other kinds of values, but they may not be particularly attentive to making sure their behaviour fully or always expresses the values they advocate. They may just accept the familiar ethical doctrine of the end justifying the means: that is, we may have to promote peace sometimes by non-peaceful means; sometimes we have cut corners over justice and human rights in order to promote these grand goals more effectively. Those who defend ruthlessness in public life are taking sides on an issue like this.

And then there are those who take seriously both acting x-ly and promoting x, and try to live the values that they wish to see widely accepted. On this approach the end does not justify the means. The means has to be ethically assessed not just in terms of its efficacy in achieving an end. In this connection the idea of Gandhi's comes to mind: the means are the ends in the making (see e.g. Gruzalski 2001). This can be interpreted in at least two complementary ways: first, the means are already, as what you intend, part of the kinds of goals you really have; and normatively we ought to ensure that our means are value-consistent with the values in the ends that we pursue.

Whilst on another occasion I would argue for the third approach, my main purpose here is to distinguish two relationships one can have to a given value, reflected in the following two questions: 'Should we (always) act in accordance with the value?' 'Should we promote that value in various ways'?

We are now in a position to see that pacifism is an answer to one kind of question: should one act peacefully in responding to violence? And pacificism is as answer to another question: should we promote peace and if so in what ways and to what extent?

Pacificism may be characterised thus: a belief in the possibility of making peace more durable and robust feature in human relationships, both locally and globally, and in its ethical desirability.

A.J.P. Taylor coined the term to recapture an earlier set of concerns in previous centuries with a focus on trying to establish the conditions of peace (quoted in Ceadel 1987: 102). This is related to the agendas behind 'perpetual peace' projects. Pacifism had had this connotation but it became restricted to a more specific ethical position about the wrongness of fighting.

Martin Ceadel in his interesting and unusual book *Thinking about Peace and War* (Ceadel 1987) did much to promote the general approach (without endorsing it himself). His approach was to say that pacificism is premised on the non-inevitability of war and on the emergence of political institutions that had the capacity to make peace more likely.

His chapter focuses on the causal questions: what are the causes of war? what changes would cause the sustaining of peace? Many different competing theories are discussed. Three are regarded as 'marginal pacificisms': religious pacificism; disarmament pacificism; conflict resolution pacificism. Then he offers the major theoretical analyses: liberalism; radicalism; socialism; feminism; ecologism.

Ceadel presents pacificism as an alternative to what he calls defencism and pacifism. However it is not at all clear that this is the right way to conceptualise it. It would be right if the commitment to the thesis of the non-inevitability of war were taken as a very strong thesis that the pacificist know exactly what needs to be done to end all wars just like that. Historically in the inter-war period in fact many people were desperate to find a way of preventing a repetition of the war to end all wars and looked to the role of the new League of Nations, the development of international law and general disarmament agreements like the Kellogg-Briand Pact of 1928 claiming to provide the basis for the 'renunciation of war as an instrument of policy', to achieve this. When the rise of Hitler led to war, many gave up their pacificist stance.

But the pacificist approach need not be premised on such a strong thesis. All that is required is a belief that war can be made less likely and peace made stronger and more durable by various kinds of measures. This approach is compatible with both pacifism and just war theory. Ceadel also noted that pacificism is often used to mean 'anti-militaristic' (Ceadel 1987: 101) and here I believe lies the clue to what is significant about pacificism.

Two features of militarism (which is quite different from realism about war) are that war is in a sense inevitable and part of human nature or the human condition and that in any case it is not undesirable because it expresses certain human virtues. Pacificism rejects both these features. War is not inevitable and war is undesirable compared with peace. The strong thesis is that eventually we could eliminate war, the weak thesis is that we can significantly reduce its incidence. Thus, as I understand it, militarism and pacificism represent two alternative approaches to war and peace in a kind of spectrum of attitudes (with mixtures of attitudes in the middle) and as such cuts across the usual trichotomy of realism, just war and pacifism, in which there really is the basic choice: either all war is permitted, or some wars and ways of fighting are permitted or no wars are permitted (see Dower 2009).

There are many different answers – some complementary, some competing – to the question: 'how should we promote the conditions of peace in the world?' Some of these have already been mentioned in passing: the importance of justice; the role of pacifism and inner peace at least in some in a society; the development of international law and the idea of the rule of law globally and of international institutions like the United Nations. Others stress the role of peace education in people in general as well as the wider programme of cosmopolitan education of which it is a part (and to which I return shortly); the acquisition in some of mediation skills and the techniques of peacebuilding; the philosophy of nonviolence as a way of tackling social issues. Jonathan Schell for instance in *The Unconquerable World* (Schell 2003) documents what he sees as the upsurge in the modern world of interest in the techniques of nonviolence as a way of effecting social change.

Boutros Ghali's *Agenda for Peace* (Ghali 1992) made much of the idea of peace-building. As Atack says, there is a narrow conception which he put this way (Atack 2005: 141): 'the central aim of peacebuilding is to provide those countries emerging out of armed conflict with the skills and resources they require not only to rebuild but also to prevent the recurrence of political violence.' Peacebuilding is seen as a third stage of peacemaking (mediation; negotiation; diplomacy) and peacekeeping (interposition of neutral forces).

But, he says, there is a wider conception: 'armed conflict is preventable and conflict management can somehow replace or displace war and armed force as responses to political and social conflict'. (Atack 2005: 143). 'Peace' in peacebuilding is seen as an amalgam, as we noted earlier, of positive and negative peace – positive peace linked to justice (not idealistic harmony) and negative peace linked to security (in fact not merely an absence but involving appropriate measure to ensure sustained security). The wider conception clearly links it to the pacificist agenda.

6. GLOBAL CITIZENSHIP

The key question I now want to tackle is: what has all this got to do with ordinary citizens? Suppose we accept that in some general sort of way, development suitably defined is a good for everyone especially very poor people and that peace as I have defined it is essential too for their well-being, and that the international community ought – morally ought – to take measure to promote these things. What then?

Let me illustrate the challenge by recalling a conversation I had with Charles Beitz, a person for whom I have immense respect as a key player in putting international ethics on the map. He put forward a robust theory of international justice – liberal cosmopolitanism – which proposed radical redistribution of wealth from rich countries to poor countries with appropriate international institutions to achieve this (for his basic approach see Beitz 1979). In the course of the exposition he remarked as an aside that this proposal did not entail a commitment to world government or to world citizenship. The latter point about global citizenship puzzled me and I suggested that if a world based on such admirable redistributive policies were ever to be possible, it would require the active engagement of people exercising global responsibility as global citizens – in putting political pressure on governments to agree to set up such mechanisms, in being willing to live the values they advocate and be personally generous in helping to bring about a just global order, and, I now would add, in being willing publicly to welcome possible reductions of standards of living as a result of such redistribution. He dismissed this line of argument on the grounds that we had to 'insulate' the individual from too much pressure from the world. Here indeed is the challenge. My task is to strip away the insulation!

If the international community should do something about it, let us ask first what constitutes the international community? Now on a broad reading, it of course means everyone including you and me. But let us see what the implications are, if it means something more restricted – let us say, to those who are significant actors on the world stage. If we ask who these are, there are at least three categories of actors: (i) governments and their representatives plus inter-state institutions such as the World Trade Organisation, the United Nations and related bodies such as the International Monetary Fund, World Bank and so; (ii) powerful Multinational Corporations and the business sector; and (iii) non-governmental organisations (NGOs) and other organisations that make up what is loosely called global civil society. This third force is significant as a factor in what is now called global governance. Mary Robinson once said: there are two super powers in the world today: the USA and Global Civil Society!

Do we leave these matters to these decision-makers to get on with it and promote these agendas? Hardly. First, they may not have the right values and priorities; and second, what they do is partly a function of what we do or don't do, say or don't say. Let me explain. International institutions will reflect the priorities of their members – nation-states. Nation-states in their foreign policy will reflect what their citizens want them to do – at least in functioning democracies. Unless sufficient numbers of their citizens actually signal to them that they want their states to promote peace and development (ideally of course conceived the way we conceive them), it is unlikely they will do so. So it comes back to engaged citizens in their respective political communities.

What about NGOs in global civil society? Again they do not exist in isolation. They get their authority and effectiveness from the levels of support – through donations and membership – from ordinary people engaged as moral agents with ethical priorities for the world.

What about business companies? Formally they are beholden to their shareholders, but in fact they are responsive to consumer preferences. The ethical consumer / fair trade movement is testimony to the extent to which consumer preferences can change practices. Investors interested in contributing to change can either engage in alternative ethical investment or buy shares in standard companies and raise their voices at AGMs and so on. Either way, what type of society we have is shaped by the interests of sharcholders and consumers. That's ordinary people again and if enough of us took an interest in these matters, change is possible.

All these responses to government policies, to NGO activity or to the economic world are responses of people who see themselves as global citizens. Let me end by saying a little more about this important idea. It is customary to distinguish between an ethical component and an institutional component of global citizenship, or of its close equivalent – cosmopolitanism.

If someone says 'I am a global/world citizen' then at the very least she is saying something like: I accept that all human beings matter and that amongst other duties I have as an individual I have responsibilities that are trans-national. Such a person could merely be making such a claim about herself, but in all probability she is really making a general claim not just about herself but about human beings generally. That is, there are universal norms and values which either ought to be recognised by others generally or in fact are so recognised and that all people have in principle global responsibility towards one another. There are, as we noted earlier, two components to a global ethic – a claim about universal values and norms and a claim about trans-boundary obligations (see e.g. Dower 1998 & 2003).

Since I have already discussed the idea of a global ethic I will say no more about this now. I would only add to it the observation that Piet Hein the Danish poet, some forty years ago, pronounced at an international conference: 'we are global citizens with tribal souls' (quoted in Barnaby 1988: 192). He did not expand on the reasons, but in the context one can surmise that he was reflecting the fact that we hare a common humanity, that we are collectively responsible for global problems such as environment degradation and ought to take collective action, and that we do have transboundary obligations towards those who suffer in the world. But our lack of global souls means we are not aware of or at least sufficiently aware of these facts and dwell too much in more localised identities and concerns.

If we turn to the 'institutional' side of global citizenship, the side which captures what the 'citizenship' bit might mean, we can identify various factors.

If we turn to the more obvious institutional aspects of citizenship we can see three aspects of this – the legal, the political and the cultural. As T.H. Marshall made very clear is his citizenship studies, one part of citizenship is the bearing of legal rights (Marshall 1973). Whether these are political rights, civil rights or social rights, these rights are constitutive of citizenship. Transferred to the global sphere, we can see that international human rights law produces the international analogue of citizenship rights within the state. We all now have the status of being citizens under an international legal system. This may not be a lot, but it is actually quite significant.

Even if we are not formally citizens of a world state, there is still a sense in which we are world citizens in a political sense. If the active part to citizenship is about participation in the public decision-making processes that affect our lives, then there are various ways in which people can engage in what is generally called 'global governance'. In between the old internationalist model of Westphalian governance and a radically new form of governance in the form of world federalism lie various possibilities of governance. Tony McGrew (McGrew 2000:

407) has suggested for instance three models of global democracy – first, the internationalist model in which global civil society in the form of NGOs acts in a cooperative but also critically supportive role in relation to states in the international community (what may be called a neo-Westphalian model); second, NGOs and more informal networks operating in a more communitarian mode, almost bypassing the international system, in what Linklater has called a post-Westphalian world; and, third, the cosmopolitan democracy model of Held and Archibugi which advocates more formal representation of people at the global level (Archibugi & Held 1995).

Whilst the latter – cosmopolitan democracy – is like world government an idea not yet realised, there are grounds for seeing the other two models as currently emerging. Either way global civil society, certainly as manifested in the formal institutions of NGOs, constitutes an important factor in global governance.

Another part of the political aspects of global citizenship is shown in people operating through the political channels of one's own state – i.e. exercising one's ordinary citizenship with a view to global issues – campaigning to get UK foreign aid increased, for instance, or trying to stop the war in Iraq. This is how Bhikhu Parekh has characterised global citizenship – namely 'globally oriented citizenship' (Parekh 2003: 44). Certainly being a global citizenship need not be in conflict with being a citizen at all. They can complement one another and global citizenship can be expressed through citizenship. This is not to deny that in other contexts, global citizenship moral priorities may sometimes clash with citizenship priorities.

What I said illustrates the ways in which global citizenship can be expressed and shows how in several different ways we can all act to have an influence on governments, NGOs or businesses in respect to the pursuit of development and peace. My suggestion is that we all have responsibilities in principle to support these and other goals in one way or other. How we do it and to what extent we do it depend on many factors to do with aptitude, skills, spare time or money and the accident of where we are placed.

But I would not want to conclude without mentioning one other factor. I have been arguing that the big changes in the world will not come about without the little changes in all of us – whether we engage in changing laws, institutions or government decisions, working for NGOs and/or supporting them through donations, or influencing economic activity through our consumer life-styles. All this is premised on an optimism of which pacifism is just one expression – that if enough of us change what we do, then we can make a difference. Someone once described me after a talk I had given on the environment as a factual pessimist and a moral optimist. So be it. The global citizenship agenda is indeed premised on a realistic optimism.

7. CONCLUSION

In this chapter I have argued for four propositions:

(i)   Although there is no necessary connection between development and peace, a close connection can be show given an appropriate ethical interpretation of both concepts;

(ii) The connection between them can be made even more clear if we acknowledge that, if development and peace are both important goods, they are goods for all people everywhere and that, therefore, we have cosmopolitan duties to promote these goods anywhere;

(iii) The duty to promote peace is part of an approach which has been called pacificism which challenges the inevitability of war and regards the reduction of it as both feasible and desirable. Pacificism is not the same as pacifism which is a stance on the ethics of fighting; most pacifists are also pacificists but more importantly many who are not pacifists are also pacificists, so there is a reasonable expectation that a wide range of readers may come to see themselves as pacificists, though they may never have thought of themselves as this before;

(iv) If we accept that the promotion of peace and development in the world is ethically desirable, then the significant agents for this are not merely governments and international bodies, but also ordinary people; that is, part of the agenda of global citizenship is to make the case that we as individuals have responsibilities and this is partly because our governments will not really commit themselves to these goals unless sufficient numbers of us press them to do so.

What I have tried to do is combine a broad-ranging academic analysis with, if you like, a restrained moral passion. I do believe it is important that academics generally – not just philosophers – should be willing to tackle the big issues and leave their narrow specialisms. I also believe it is wholly appropriate for academics to engage with the real world and be quite explicit about what their ethical positions are – no academic enquiry is value neutral anyway. Whether I have succeeded in combining the two types of activity or I have rather fallen between two stools of saying nothing much in either, I leave for the reader to judge. But at least it is my offering – my pennyworth if you will – on what I regard as some of the most important challenges facing humanity today.

References

Archibugi, D. and D. Held (eds), *Cosmopolitan Democracy*, 1995, Cambridge: Polity Press.
Aristotle, *Nicomachean Ethics*, c. 330 BCE.
Atack, I., *Ethics of Peace and War*, 2005, Edinburgh: Edinburgh University Press.
Barnaby, F. (ed.), *The Gaia Peace Atlas*, 1988, London: Pan Books.
Beitz, C.R., *Political Theory and International Relations*, 1979, Princeton: Princeton University Press.
Boutros Ghali, B., *An Agenda for Peace*, 1992, New York: United Nations.
Bull, H., *The Anarchical Society*, 1977, London: Macmillan.
Ceadel, M., *Thinking about Peace and War*, 1987, Oxford: Oxford University Press.
Clausewitz, von, C., *On War*, 1832, in e.g. A. Rappoport, (ed.), 1968, Harmondsworth: Penguin Books.
Coates, M., *The Ethics of War*, 1997, Manchester: Manchester University Press.
Curle, A., *True Justice*, 1981, London: Quaker Home Service.
Dower, N., *An Introduction to Global Citizenship*, 2003, Edinburgh: Edinburgh University Press.
Dower, N., *World Ethics – the New Agenda*, 1998, Edinburgh: Edinburgh University Press.
Dower, N., *The Ethics of War and Peace: cosmopolitan and other perspectives*, 2009, Cambridge: Polity Press.
Goulet, D., *Development Ethics - Theory and Practice*, 1995, London: Zed Books.
Grotius, H., *De Iure Belli ac Pacis (On the Law of War and Peace)*, 1625, F.W. Kelsey, (tr.), 1925, Oxford: Clarendon Press.
Gruzalski, B., *Gandhi*, 2001, Belmont CA: Wadsworth.
Hobbes, Th., *Leviathan*, 1651, e.g. Tuck, R. (ed.), 1991, Cambridge: Cambridge University Press.
Jenkins, I., 'The conditions of peace', 1973, *The Monist*, vol. 57 no. 4.
Kant, I., *Perpetual Peace*, 1795, e.g. in H. Reiss, (tr.), 1970, *Kant's Political Writings*, Cambridge: Cambridge University Press.
Macquarrie, J., *The Concept of Peace*, 1973, London: S. C. M. Press.
McGrew, D., 'Democracy beyond borders', 2000, in D. Held & A. McGrew (eds), *The Global Transformations Reader*, 2000, Cambridge: Polity Press.
Marshall, T.H., *Class, Citizenship and Social Development*, 1973, Westport CN: Greenwood Press.
Nussbaum, M., 'Patriotism and Cosmopolitanism', in J. Cohen, (ed.), *For Love of Country – Debating the Limits of Patriotism*, 1996, Beacon Press.
Nussbaum, M., *Women and Development*, 2000, Cambridge: Cambridge University Press.
O'Neill, O., *Faces of Hunger*, 1986, London: Allen and Unwin.
Parehk, B., 'Cosmopolitanism and Global Citizenship', *Review of International Studies*, 2002, vol. 31, no. 2.
Schell, J., *The unconquerable world: power, nonviolence, and the will of the people*, 2003, New York: Metropolitan Books.
Sen, A., *Development as Freedom*, 1999, Oxford: Oxford University Press.